THE GOLDEN
HOME AND

THE GOLDEN HOME AND HIGH SCHOOL ENCYCLOPEDIA, while sufficiently comprehensive and detailed for family use, has been created principally for students at the high school level.

The aim of this reference work is twofold: first, to serve the student's immediate need for authoritative information on a wide range of subjects, and, second, to set forth and explain the many areas of knowledge, so that a student may explore them and thus more competently plan his educational future.

Arranged alphabetically in twenty volumes, here are thousands of full, accurate entries, written and reviewed by experts. The text is abundantly illustrated with full-color photographs and paintings.

Designed to complement the high school curriculum, this encyclopedia offers help with assignments and valuable guidance in the use of other reference tools —dictionaries, atlases, and various library materials. Extensive cross-references and a complete index direct the reader quickly to the information he seeks. A special feature of this work is the sound career information it offers in scores of job and professional fields.

Among the many subjects encompassed in these volumes are the newest developments in science, from microbiology to radioastronomy; fine arts and literature; history and government; religion and philosophy; the physical world, its plants and animals; the social sciences; invention and industry. Four-color maps and latest census figures contribute to an up-to-date view of the world, its continents, nations, and peoples.

Every care has been taken to make *The Golden Home and High School Encyclopedia* lively and stimulating, without sacrifice of accuracy. It is the hope of the editors that these volumes will be used with both advantage and pleasure.

VOLUME XV

HIGH SCHOOL ENCYCLOPEDIA

in 20 Volumes

*

Railroad • Scales, The, See Libra

GOLDEN PRESS • NEW YORK

FIRST PRINTING, 1961
Library of Congress Catalog Card Number: 61-13292

RAILROAD, a means of transportation in which people and goods are conveyed in cars or trains over a fixed track consisting of two rails. Railroads developed in Western industrial nations during the middle of the 19th century, but railroad development is still in its early stages in many nations today. Railroad equipment has been constantly improved.

EARLY DEVELOPMENT

Railroads with cars pulled by horses were used around mines and ironworks in England at the end of the 16th century. The first public railroad to use a steam locomotive was the Stockton to Darlington Railway, opened in England in 1825. The first locomotive to run on a standard railroad in the United States was tried out on a short wooden railroad in Pennsylvania in 1829. The first railroad in France was opened in 1832; in Russia, 1834; in Belgium and Germany, 1835; and in Austria, 1837. By the middle of the 19th century the transition to rail transportation had begun in Europe and in the United States.

In Asia, Africa, and Australia railroads began to develop in the second half of the 19th century. The first railroad in Asia (in India) was built in 1853; in Australia, in 1854; and in Africa (Egypt), in 1856. From 1890 to 1913 the network of railroads in Latin America, Asia, Africa, and Australia expanded to about 140,000 miles; in Europe, to about 76,000 miles; and in the United States, to about 89,000 miles.

RAILROADS TODAY

In the United States and Canada the period of railroad expansion has passed, and railroads are struggling today to survive against competition from other forms of transportation. However, in the Soviet Union, China, and other countries railroad development is underway today as a part of the general industrial development.

United States. About 29 percent of the world's rail mileage is located in the United States. In 1958, 221,826 miles of rails were open to traffic. About 99.6 percent of this mileage is standard 4-foot $8\frac{1}{2}$-inch gauge, and only about 1,772 miles of main lines were electrified as of 1958. At the end of 1958, 93.3 percent of all locomotives in service were diesel electric; 4.7 percent, steam; 1.9 percent, electric; and 0.1 percent, other. Diesel-electric locomotives handled 96 percent of freight traffic during 1958.

From a total of 30,626 miles of operated track in the United States in 1860, rail mileage steadily increased to 52,922 in 1870, to 93,267 in 1880, to 163,597 in 1890, and to 193,346 in 1900. The nation's railroad mileage reached its peak in 1916, with over 254,000 miles of owned track. Rail mileage has gradually decreased since 1916.

Freight traffic on the railroads in the United States is by far the most important factor in providing income for the lines. Although passenger service is important to many of the major railroads, a number of the Class I roads have discontinued passenger service since 1950 because of high expenditures. A number of railroads and trucking firms have agreements to ship trailer trucks by flat cars over long distances. This service is known as piggyback operation. It helps reduce trucking expenses and insures speedy delivery.

Canada. Almost all the railroad facilities in Canada are operated by two great transcontinental systems —the government-owned Canadian National Railways, which includes about half of the country's rail mileage, and the Canadian Pacific Railway Company, a joint stock corporation. In 1957, 59,097 miles of lines were open to traffic. The railroads are engaged in converting from steam to diesel traction; by the end of 1959 diesels were handling from 93 percent to 99 percent of all traffic. Piggyback service expanded 75 percent in 1959 over 1958.

Great Britain. The great boom of railroad building in Great Britain was from 1840 to 1875. Government intervention began in 1846, when Parliament passed a law prescribing a standard gauge of 4 feet $8\frac{1}{2}$ inches for new lines. All railroads were placed under government direction during World War I. They suffered from sharp competition and general industrial depression between World Wars I and II. The Transport Act of 1947 brought all railroads under public ownership.

In 1958 railroad mileage in Great Britain was 18,965. Only about 1,254 miles of main line were electrified. At the end of 1957, 95.1 percent of all locomotives in service were

This early locomotive was built in 1831 by Phineas Davis. Note the fuel chest and the barrels of water for the upright steam boiler.
Baltimore & Ohio R. R.

CHICAGO MILWAUKEE ST. PAUL AND PACIFIC

NEW YORK CENTRAL SYSTEM

GREAT NORTHERN RAILWAY

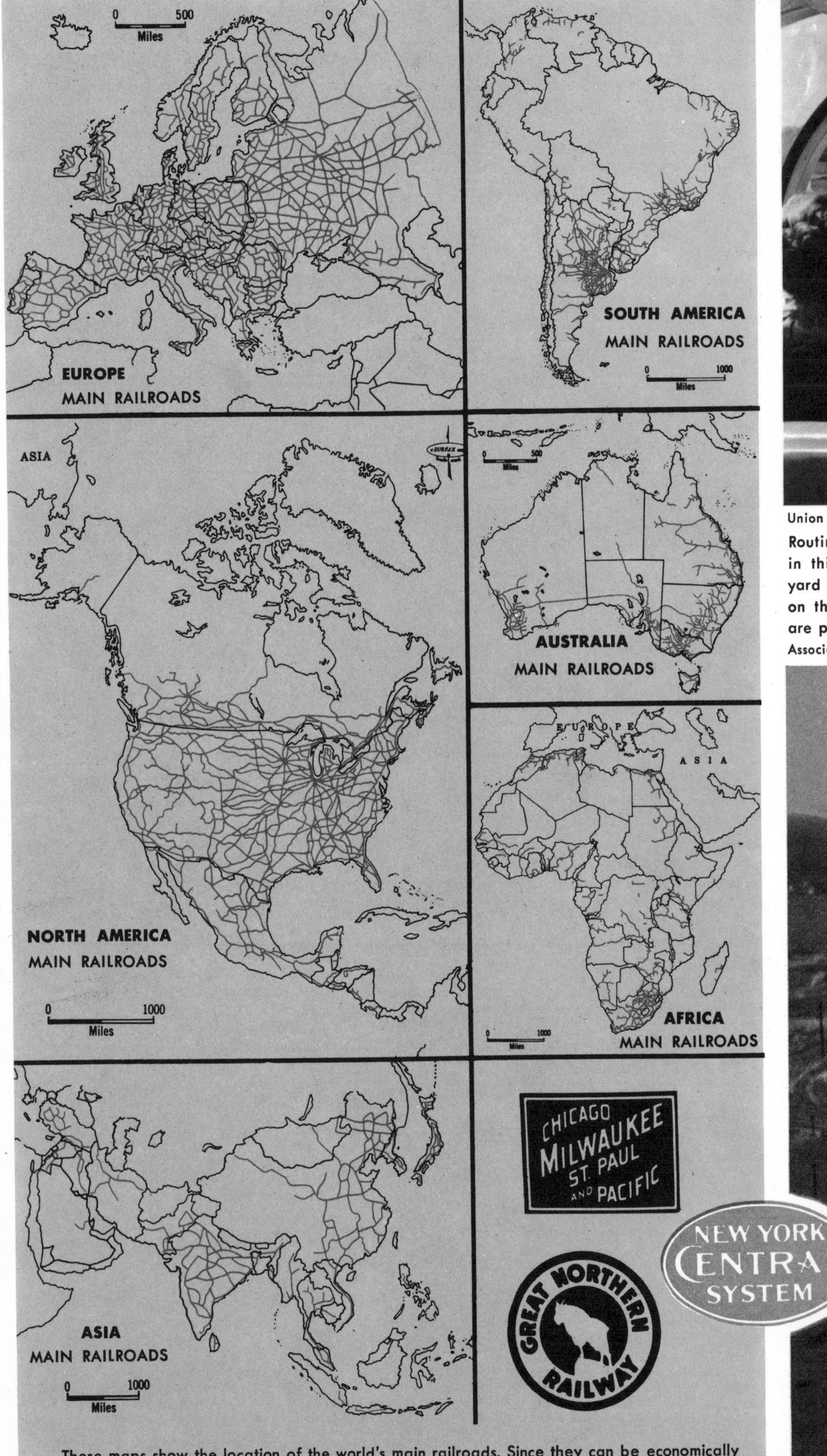

These maps show the location of the world's main railroads. Since they can be economically successful only where there is plenty of passenger and freight traffic, the railroads are concentrated in the world's most densely populated and most heavily industrialized areas. In many regions rugged terrain and a lack of traffic make the building and maintenance of a network of railroads both unnecessary and impractical.

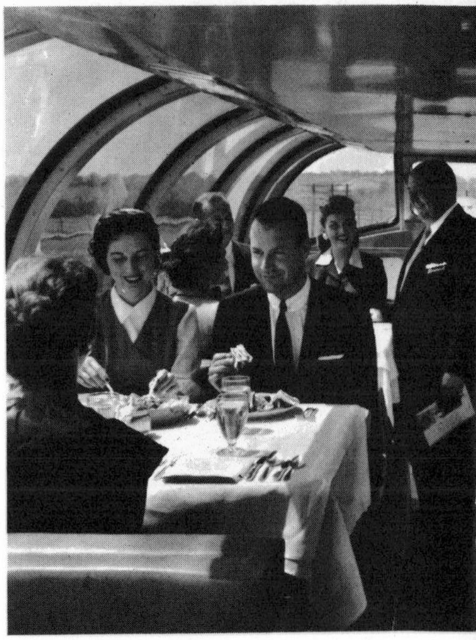

Union Pacific Railroad Photo

Routing of cars and assembling of trains in this automatically controlled freight yard (below) are determined by codes on the bottoms of the cars. The codes are picked up by electric eyes.

Association of American Railroads

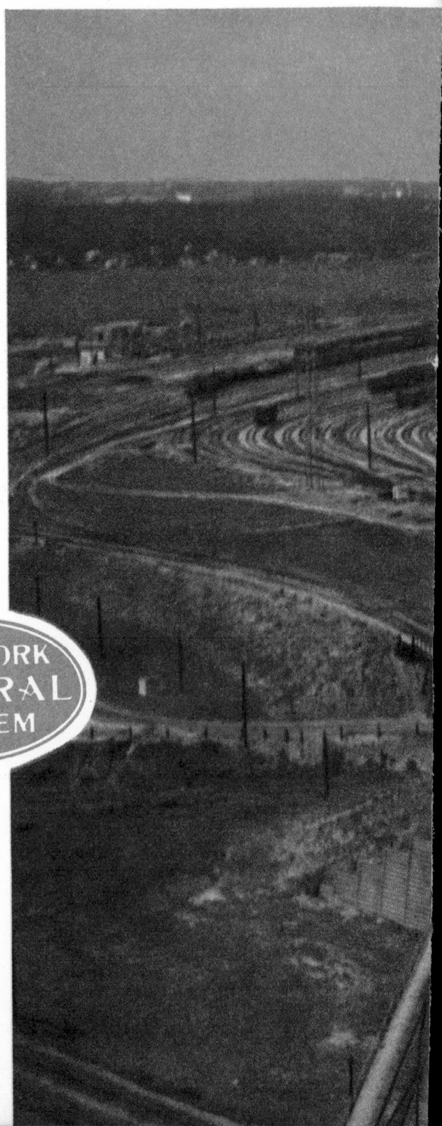

Passengers eat in the dining car (left) of a present-day passenger train. Large, panoramic windows permit them to watch the scenery while they eat. A waiter (white uniform) prepares to serve a table of diners. Chatting with the diners is the dining-car steward, who has charge of the entire dining car, kitchen as well as dining room. In the kitchen (right), a cook is preparing a steak. The kitchen is short, taking up only about one fourth of the dining car's length, and narrow, because a passageway for the passengers runs alongside it. In these compact quarters the cooks prepare hundreds of meals daily.

Union Pacific Railroad Photo

Union Pacific Railroad Photo

Switchmen in a yard in Council Bluffs, Iowa, (left) move a loaded refrigerator car into position. Using a diesel switching engine, they have picked up the freight car from a factory siding. In the yard the car will be incorporated into a train and sent toward its destination. In the yard's fueling station a workman is refueling a powerful diesel engine (below). At this time the motor and running gear will be inspected and cleaned, and any worn parts will be replaced or repaired. Keeping the engines and other rolling stock in top condition is a vital part of successful railroad operation.

Union Pacific Railroad Photo

steam powered; 3.7 percent, diesel electric; 0.8 percent, diesel; and 0.4 percent, electric. One gas-turbine electric locomotive was in use. Rail passenger services are very important in Britain, particularly in comparison with their importance in some other countries.

France. French railroads have been operated since 1938 by a nationalized company, in which the state controls 51 percent of the capital. The rail system was almost completely destroyed in World War II, and extensive modernization has been done during rebuilding. About 60 percent of all traffic is handled by electric traction, and diesel traction has been extensively substituted for steam. About 24,500 miles of track were open in 1959.

Soviet Union. Railroads today fill the major role in the Soviet transportation economy, although water transportation is still very important. In 1958, 81 percent of all goods and 77 percent of all passengers were conveyed over the approximately 76,200 miles of railroads. In 1913 the rail system included 36,300 miles of rails and carried 57 percent of goods and 91 percent of passenger traffic. Before 1917 only three main lines reached outlying areas; this internal rail system has been greatly expanded as part of the general industrialization program. Over 20 percent of main-line railroads had converted to electric and diesel traction by 1959.

China. In 1958 China had more than 19,220 miles of railroad track, not including special railroads serving factories and mines. In 1950 there were about 13,170 miles of track. The rail network has now been extended to all provinces and regions except Tibet. The new north-south and east-west trunk lines are in operation, the former shortening the distance to Moscow by about 620 miles. A total of about 1,430 miles of track, including some double tracking of old roads, was built in 1958.

Australia. Each state operates its own railroads, and the federal government operates the Commonwealth Railways in commonwealth territories and in Western Australia and South Australia. The federal government is providing financial assistance to the states for conversion of all interstate lines to a standard gauge. In 1958, 26,427 miles of rails were open to traffic.

Africa. Railroad development is generally still in its early stages in Africa. The government of the Republic of South Africa owns and operates a well-developed system of railroads. But many areas of the world, such as Somalia for example, have no railroads whatsoever. Although Cecil Rhodes's dream of a Cape-to-Cairo railroad was never realized, a complete east-west transcontinental rail route (except for steamer crossing of Lake Tanganyika) was finished in 1956.

South America. Physical obstacles to railroad building and lack of native fuels are major difficulties in the railroad development of South America. Argentina, with 27,000 miles of track operating in 1960, has the highest proportion of track to territory.

Other Areas. Several countries throughout the world have no railroads at all. In some cases railroads are unsuited to the country's needs. Thus Iceland has no railroads, but the island is served by an extensive system of highways in addition to sea transportation. In 1948 all rail service in Bermuda was discontinued, and a government-operated bus service was introduced.

In other cases lack of capital and ruggedness of terrain combine to discourage railroad building. Afghanistan, almost as big as Texas and having two million more people, has no railroads. (Texas had 15,212 miles of track in 1957, more than any other state of the United States.) Mountainous Laos, slightly smaller than Oregon but having a slightly greater population, also has no railroad. (Oregon had 3,212 miles of railroads in 1957.)

From his vantage point in the switchyard control tower the towerman controls the movements of the cars in the yard below.

Chicago & North Western Railway Co.

In many underdeveloped countries the small railroad mileage that exists is owned by, and operated principally for, outside interests. This is particularly true in the Caribbean area of North America. For example, most of the approximately 1,100 miles of track in the Dominican Republic is comprised of private lines on sugar estates and other large estates. In Costa Rica almost half of the 800 miles of railroads is owned by the United Fruit Company and is located on the company's plantations. Similarly, in Fiji in the South Pacific most of the 440 miles of light railway belong to the Colonial Sugar Refining Company.

Railroads, compared with other means of transporting mass quantities of freight, are low in cost. The movement of freight along rails requires ten times less hauling power than does such movement along roads. For this reason railroads will be of continuing importance in the economies of advanced coun-

OCCUPATION: Railroad Conductor

NATURE OF WORK: Seeing that railroad cars are moved according to train orders either on a run or in the yards

PERSONAL FACTORS—ABILITIES, SKILLS, APTITUDES: A pleasing manner and a neat appearance, the ability to lead and to work effectively with other people, and a sense of responsibility are needed.

EDUCATION AND SPECIAL TRAINING: Openings are filled on a seniority basis by promoting qualified brakemen who have several years' experience and who have passed qualifying examinations.

WORKING CONDITIONS:

1. **INCOME:**
   COMPARED WITH OTHER CAREERS WITH EQUAL TRAINING: Average
   COMPARED WITH MOST OTHER CAREERS: Average
2. **ENVIRONMENT:** Yard, freight, or passenger trains
3. **OTHER:** Forty-hour week at irregular hours; usual benefits; much travel; public contact; declining, limited opportunities; unionized

RELATED CAREERS: Brakeman

WHERE TO FIND MORE INFORMATION: Order of Railway Conductors and Brakemen, O.R.C.B. Building, Cedar Rapids, Iowa; Brotherhood of Railroad Trainmen, Standard Building, 1370 Ontario Street, Cleveland 13, Ohio; Switchmen's Union of North America, 3 Linwood Avenue, Buffalo 2, N.Y.

tries, despite the increase in automotive and aerial transportation. However, the modern railroad requires a heavy investment in capital equipment and particularly a heavy use of metal. This makes the cost of hauling freight for short distances many times more expensive than for long distances; for short hauls automotive transportation as a rule is less expensive.

RAILROAD EQUIPMENT

Along with their mileage extension, the railroads have also constantly improved and developed their physical properties. As contrasted with the 4-ton weight of an English locomotive of the 1830's, the average steam locomotive in the United States operated at a weight of about 128 tons when railroading had reached its peak. These locomotives were able to haul heavy passenger trains at speeds undreamed of in early days. Several important railroads incorporated electric locomotives into their systems, especially for commuter service in metropolitan areas and for hauling heavy loads over mountainous regions.

Early locomotives ran over rails made of wood, 20 to 30 feet in length, with iron straps protecting the running surface of the rails. The rails used today are generally made of steel. Originally, tracks had as many as 20 different widths between the rails. However, in the 1870's a standard gauge of 4 feet 8½ inches was adopted in the United States and is still in use. This standard originated in western Europe.

Early railroad freight cars were little more than wagons with flanged wheels, and the passenger cars were for the most part converted stagecoaches. These models were, of course, subject to various improvements, and at last cars were specially designed for individual functions. These cars include boxcars for general freight, flatcars, gondolas, refrigerator cars for perishable products, stock (cattle) cars, and air-conditioned passenger coaches of various types. The pullman sleeping car was a revolutionary development that followed the Civil War in the United States. There have been many other inventions and developments in railroad construction and operation during the past 100 years. These include the airbrake, automatic coupler for cars, automatic electric signal system, radiotelephone communication with moving trains, and many other devices that have improved service.

OCCUPATION: Locomotive Engineer

NATURE OF WORK: Running the locomotive safely and efficiently

PERSONAL FACTORS—ABILITIES, SKILLS, APTITUDES: Good physical condition, good eyesight and hearing, and an average intelligence are needed.

EDUCATION AND SPECIAL TRAINING: On-the-job training as a fireman who has advanced through the ranks is required. A fireman must pass a comprehensive examination on the operation of the engine.

WORKING CONDITIONS:

1. **INCOME:**
   COMPARED WITH OTHER CAREERS WITH EQUAL TRAINING: High
   COMPARED WITH MOST OTHER CAREERS: Average to high
2. **ENVIRONMENT:** Entirely outdoors; in rail yards and on the road
3. **OTHER:** Regular shift hours; much traveling; mileage-limitation restrictions on income; possible danger; unionized; declining, limited opportunities

RELATED CAREERS: Fireman

WHERE TO FIND MORE INFORMATION: Association of American Railroads, Transportation Building, Washington 6, D.C.; Brotherhood of Locomotive Engineers, 1112 Brotherhood of Locomotive Engineers Building, Cleveland 14, Ohio

RAILS, COOTS, GALLINULES, a family of 132 species of water birds found worldwide except in polar areas. Typically they inhabit marshy areas, but some live in fields, sandy areas, and tropical forests far from water. Their wings are short and rounded; the tail is short. All have thin bodies. This shape helps them in slipping through thick swamp vegetation and has given rise to the expression "thin as a rail." Rails are shy birds with secretive habits. When flushed they rise weakly, fly a short distance with legs dangling, and drop back into the marsh. Nevertheless, they make long migrations, flying mostly at night. Typical rails feed on seeds of water plants and on aquatic animal life; gallinules and coots also take underwater plants and other vegetation. The nest, built on swampy ground or anchored on vegetation above the water, usually contains from 6 to 12 eggs.

North America has six species of typical rails. The largest is the king rail, a brownish bird about 17 inches long, usually found in fresh water. The clapper rail, paler and grayish, is about 15 inches long; it breeds in salt-water marshes on both coasts. The Virginia rail resembles the king rail except that it is smaller and has gray cheeks; it prefers cattail or sedge marshes. The sora, the most abundant rail, is a plump, 9-inch bird, distinguished by its short yellow bill and its black face. It is closely related to the Old World corn crake. The yellow rail, about 7 inches long, is a bird of mystery, seldom seen although it nests widely in marshes and wet meadows. The black rail, even smaller, is another secretive bird. Since all young rails are black, they are often mistaken for adults of this species.

Gallinules and coots resemble ducks except that they have smaller heads and chicken-like bills. Gallinules have long toes, an aid in walking on swampy land and float-

The water birds below are members of the same family, and all are found in North America.

ing vegetation. North America has two species of gallinules, the purple and the common (or Florida). The purple gallinule is gaily garbed in green and purple plumage, with yellow legs, blue frontal plate, and red and yellow bill. It is often found in water-lily ponds of the southern states, where it steps daintily about on the floating plants. The common gallinule is dark with a red bill.

The American coot, sometimes called a mudhen, is a noisy, slate-gray bird with lobed toes and a white bill. It dives expertly and takes off from the surface with a great spattering of water.

RAILWAY EXPRESS AGENCY, now known as REA Express, a private business that transports shipments of all types and weights but is generally considered a small-shipment carrier. Nearly anything can be shipped by REA Express. The company operates on a third of a million miles of rail, air, and highway routes in the United States and Canada. It handles some 160 million crates and packages every year. It operates the Air Express Division, which serves directly more than 1,800 airport points by air and 21,000 off-airline communities.

William F. Harnden founded the express business on Mar. 4, 1839. His first shipments were carried in a carpetbag. The growth of Harnden's express business caused special baggage cars to be placed behind train engines. Competitors began to enter the field: Adams Express (1840), American Express (1850), and Wells, Fargo (1852). During World War I these companies were unified, and the new business was called the American Railway Express Company. In 1929 the railroads purchased the business and changed the name to Railway Express Agency, Inc.

On Nov. 7, 1910, the first air-express service was conceived. The first package ever shipped by air was carried by a Wright biplane from Dayton, Ohio, to Columbus, Ohio, a distance of 65 miles, in 66 minutes—a great speed in those days. However, regularly scheduled air-express service did not begin until 1927. Now it handles more than six million shipments yearly.

When the Railway Express driver picks up a package, he fills out an express receipt in several copies, the original of which he leaves with the shipper. On delivery, a receipt is obtained from the person to whom the package was sent. See PONY EXPRESS.

RAIN, precipitation that reaches the earth's surface as water droplets. Rain is of extreme importance in the hydrologic, or water, cycle. It is also necessary to agriculture, and the annual rainfall of an area may make it a desert or a steaming jungle. The study of rain has been one of the most challenging areas of modern meteorology. Weathermen began developing explanations of it about 1911, but they have not yet solved completely the question of rain formation.

The atmosphere contains water vapor. As portions of the atmosphere move upward, this water vapor condenses upon tiny particles (dust, smoke, salt) and forms clouds. However, the water droplets in a cloud are usually so tiny that it would take about two days for them to float to earth, by which time they would have evaporated. Somehow these droplets must grow so that they can become rain droplets. Just how this growth occurs is a problem.

It was once thought that water vapor simply continued to condense onto the water droplets in a cloud, causing them to become rain. Cloud physicists have shown that this is not the case. Only a "chosen few" among the cloud droplets grow to

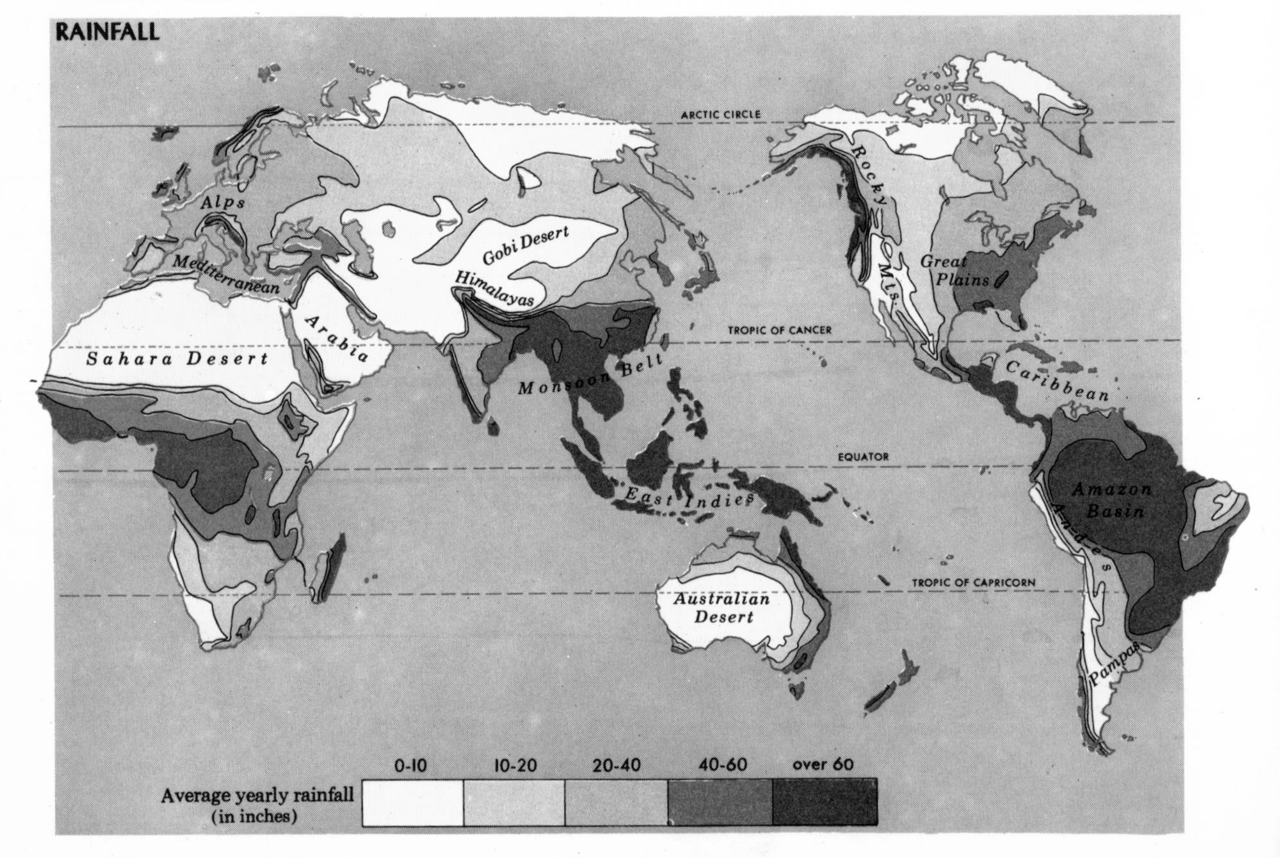

become rain droplets, which are about ten million times the size of the cloud droplets. A partial explanation of this fact was advanced by the ice-crystal theory of rain formation. This theory held that once ice crystals formed in clouds, they would continue to accumulate water and grow. According to Tor Bergeron the principal cause of growth is the vapor-pressure difference existing between liquid water and ice at subfreezing temperatures, which permits ice crystals to enlarge at the expense of supercooled water drops. Indeed, cirrus clouds reach high into the atmosphere, and their ice particles are probably very important in forming rain. However, in 1946 and 1947 a thunderstorm project was conducted by the U.S. Weather Bureau with the aid of the Air Force and the Navy. This project proved that rain is also formed in clouds too warm to contain ice particles. This complicated the situation.

Another explanation had to be advanced on rain formation in addition to the ice-crystal theory. Cloud physicists showed that some larger atmospheric dust particles collected water more rapidly and grew larger than did smaller particles. These water droplets formed on large particles tend to fall through the cloud, colliding with smaller particles that join the growing droplets. Soon these particles are so large that they fall from the cloud as rain. This "all-water rain mechanism" is especially important in forming rain from tropical clouds. See ATMOSPHERIC CONDENSATION; CLOUD; CLOUD SEEDING; HUMIDITY; PRECIPITATION; RAINFALL MEASUREMENT.

The two chief methods of rain formation and one other possible method are illustrated here. One of the chief methods (top left) operates when water droplets collect, often around dust particles, and tend to fall. As they fall, they collide with other droplets and thus grow large enough to fall as rain. Probably the most important kind of rain formation (left) occurs when tiny ice crystals and water droplets occur together in a cloud. Some water droplets evaporate and then collect on the crystals. The crystals grow and finally fall as snowflakes or ice pellets, which melt into raindrops as they pass through warm air. A possible method (above) involves lightning discharges. These produce oxides of nitrogen, which may attract moisture and become nuclei for raindrop formation.

RAINBOW, a colored arch formed opposite the sun on falling raindrops. It is seen whenever the necessary conditions of a passing shower on one side and a clear and not too high sun on the other side occur. Two bows are frequently seen, each exhibiting the full spectrum of colors from red to violet, but in the inner bow the red is the outer edge and violet the inner, while in the outer bow the order is reversed. The colors shade gradually into each other.

Rainbows have attracted speculation since the remote past. In the biblical story of the Deluge (Gen. 9:12-17) the rainbow is described as a symbol of the covenant between God and man. Aristotle thought, incorrectly, that the rainbow was the reflection of the sun's rays by the rain. Theodoric of Vriberg, a Dominican monk, was the first to indicate correctly the physical cause of rainbows. His essay, written in 1311, remained unknown until much later. On the basis of other scientific essays Descartes showed how the sun's rays were refracted by the rain. Isaac Newton finally explained the color display. A sunray strikes the raindrop and is refracted (bent) as it passes through the droplet. When it strikes the other side of the raindrop, the ray is reflected and rebounds to the front of the droplet again. On leaving the raindrop the ray is refracted once again. This is the geometrical explanation of the rainbow. The colors of the rainbow are the colors that compose the white sunlight. They are separated by the different refrangibilities (angles of bending, or refraction) of the colors that compose the sun's rays. The outer bow of the rainbow results when the line at which the ray touches the surface of the drop is crossed by the line at which the ray leaves the drop. This would place the violet colors at the outer edge, because their refrangibility is greater.

Rainbows, like eclipses, meteors, and auroras, have inspired much awe and superstition.

In a primary rainbow the red band is outside and the violet inside. This is because one sees only violet light from lower raindrops and only red from higher ones.

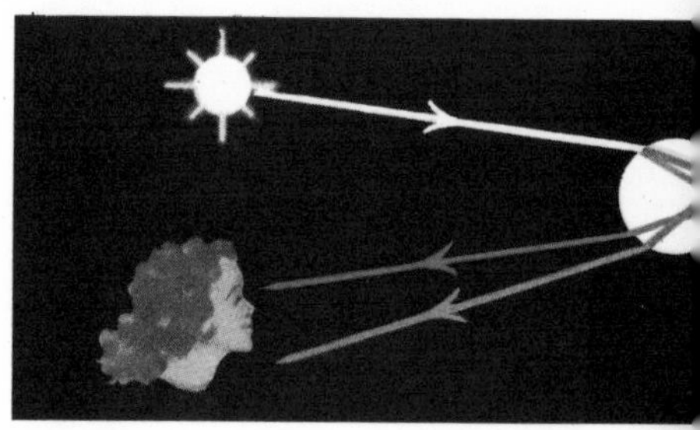

RAINFALL MEASUREMENT, the measurement of the vertical depth of rain. The measurement of the amount of rainfall each day or year might seem to provide interesting but somewhat useless knowledge. On the contrary, rainfall measurement provides valuable data about the weather. The amount of rainfall determines what kind of farming is suitable for a particular region. Together with other data about the weather, rainfall measurement helps the weatherman make his predictions.

The easiest way to measure rainfall would seem to be a large pan sunk in the ground. This is impracticable because of evaporation. Devices for measuring rainfall should be fairly accurate to the nearest hundredth of an inch.

The simplest rain gauge used by the Weather Bureau is the 8-inch gauge. The tipping-bucket gauge has a receiving funnel, which catches rain. The rainfall drips from the end of the funnel into one side of a delicately balanced bucket. This bucket is partitioned in the center and balanced upon a horizontal axis. The bucket tips over when 0.01 inch of rain has collected in it. The water falls into the bottom of the gauge, and the other half of the bucket automatically moves under the funnel spout. Each tip of the bucket is recorded electrically on a moving drum. When the rain ends, the amount collected in the bottom of the gauge may be drained off, measured and checked against the amount recorded.

Snowfall, however, cannot be measured in this simple rain gauge. The weighing-rain-and-snow gauge collects rain and snow in a receiving bucket, which may be balanced with weights or upon springs. Within the gauge is a drum, driven by clockwork, upon which a constant record of the accumulated precipitation is made.

The Weather Bureau is also interested in several other factors concerning the rain besides its amount. The reliability of rainfall is important. There is a great difference in agricultural possibilities between two areas receiving 30 inches of rainfall each year if one receives its precipitation only in the summertime and the other in equal quantities each month throughout the year. Evaporation is also vital to rainfall measurement. See ATMOMETER.

RAIN FOREST. See TROPICAL RAIN FOREST.

TIPPING BUCKET RAIN GAUGE

RECORDING RAIN GAUGE (housing removed)

RAINMAKING, the creation of rainfall by artificial means. Man has tried for many thousands of years to create rains when he needed them. Rain is very important to man. Compare, for example, a population map with a rainfall map of the same areas. In places such as Central Australia and the Sahara there is an extremely sparse population because of the fact that these areas have too little rain to support agriculture. Imagine the importance of rainfall to people living on the edge of such dry regions. Rain often means life or death.

Among the Bari tribe of the Upper Nile, the rainmakers are respected even more than the tribal chiefs. Among the peoples of Bechuanaland, who live by agriculture, droughts are major disasters, and the Bechuana rainmakers are highly revered. In Central Australia the process of making rain is very complicated and can only be performed with the aid of wizards. Tribesmen dig a hole and then erect a hut over it. The old men of the tribe gather in the hut, and the wizards make incisions in the arms of two members of the tribe. The blood from these minor wounds flows onto the old men. It represents rain. Handfuls of feathers are cast into the air. This symbolizes clouds. Finally, the men inside the hut push the structure down with their heads. This act signifies the breaking of the clouds. The fall of the hut represents the rain. This symbolic rainstorm is observed, according to the wizards, by the ancestral spirits, who send rain. Sometimes rain follows, although the scientific mind would consider this a coincidence. Among the Pueblo peoples of the American Southwest, rainmaking ceremonies were of the utmost importance. In one ceremony suds were made of a certain root and cast into the air to represent clouds, accompanied by an invocation to the Cloud People to bring rain.

In 19th-century America, professional rainmakers toured the country with cannon, drums, and explosives. The noise was supposed to create rain. One particularly successful rainmaker used to check the U.S. Weather Bureau to make certain that rain was on the way. Then he would visit a local community, set off his cannon, and wait to collect his fee. Modern rainmaking is done more scientifically. It is called cloud seeding. See CLOUD SEEDING.

Rainmaking has been a primitive hope, a 19th-century deception, and a 20th-century reality. The Hopi Indians (below, right) had special dances to induce rain. In the 19th century charlatans put on spectacular shows (below). The silver iodide generator (right) is a modern scientific rainmaking instrument.

RAISIN, a dried grape. Four tons of grapes are dried to make one ton of raisins. Eighty-five percent of the water in the grape is evaporated in the raisin-making process. Raisins are a highly concentrated energy food loaded with 460 calories per cup. Among the fruits only pitted dates, with 505 calories per cup, surpass raisins.

Eighty-three percent of the world's raisins are produced in the United States, Greece, Turkey, and Australia, in regions where the growing season is long and the sun hot. About one-third of the world's raisins are grown in the San Joaquin Valley of California. This valley is only 240 miles long and 50 miles wide. The valley was largely worthless desert until the gold-bearing streams of the surrounding mountains were piped in. Only during the gold-rush years following 1849 has California produced as much wealth in gold as its annual 50-million-dollar raisin crop.

In this valley of raisins 94 percent of the vines are Thompson Seedless grafted onto Muscat stock. The original Thompson Seedless cutting was brought from the hothouse of a nobleman in England by an observant horticulturist who migrated to California toward the end of the 19th century. The Thompson Seedless, a highly disease-resistant variety, produces a heavy crop of white thinskinned grapes that require a minimum of processing.

Golden raisins are both Muscats and Thompson Seedless dried in the presence of sulfur fumes. Seeded raisins are Muscats. They are also sold as cluster raisins. Sultanas, from Greece and Turkey, have a tart flavor and are used in cooking. Black Zante currants, a variety popular in Greece, are not currants at all. They are very small, dark raisins popular with bakers.

Thompson Seedless grapes, drying in the California sun, will be made into raisins.
Calif. Raisin Advisory Bd.

RALEIGH, SIR WALTER (1552?-1618), a famous English courtier and navigator, born at Hayes, Devonshire. He was one of the most gallant soldiers, most fearless sailors, most able authors, and most accomplished courtiers of the reigns of Elizabeth I and James I. Elizabeth invited him to court and gave him several honorable and profitable offices. Having obtained permission to colonize North America, Raleigh sent out two expeditions, both unsuccessful. Raleigh named the colony Virginia in honor of the maiden queen. The capital of North Carolina, Raleigh, still bears his name.

After the death of Elizabeth enemies poisoned the mind of the new king, James I, against Raleigh, and he was shorn of nearly all his honors and rewards. He was charged with having joined in a plot to place Lady Arabella Stuart on the throne and was brought to trial. For 13 years he languished in the gloomy Tower of London. He spent this time in making chemical experiments and in writing his *History of the World*. He was greatly admired by Prince Henry, the King's son. At last Raleigh was liberated by James and was sent with a fleet to the Orinoco River in search of a gold mine said to be on its banks. During this cruise he captured a Spanish settlement. The capture so enraged the King of Spain that he directed his ambassador in London to demand vengeance. James at that time was anxious to please the Spanish king, whose daughter he was hoping to get as a bride for his son Charles. James therefore arrested Raleigh on his landing in England and after a few months had him executed on the same old charges for which he had already suffered so much. Just before his execution it is said that Raleigh examined the ax and, passing his finger along the keen edge, said, "This is a sharp medicine, but it will cure all diseases." He died when about 66 years old.

The Bettman Archive

Elizabethan courtier Sir Walter Raleigh

RALEIGH is the capital of North Carolina and is a trade center for cotton, tobacco, and lumber. The city is located near the geographical center of the state. According to the 1960 census, it had a population of 93,931.

The industries include cottonseed, lumber and textile mills, printing and publishing plants, and foundries. Among the prominent government buildings are the granite Capitol and the governor's mansion. Pullen Park contains the house in which Andrew Johnson was born. North Carolina State College is here. Raleigh was selected as the state capital in 1788 and was founded in 1792. First known as Bloomsbury, the city was later renamed to honor Sir Walter Raleigh.

RAM, THE (constellation). See ARIES.

RANCH AND RANCHING. For purposes of this entry a ranch is a farm of extensive acreage that is rarely cultivated and on which only sheep and cattle graze. In the dry highlands of Montana each square mile of range can support only about 21 cows. One distinction between a ranch and an American Corn Belt farm is the lesser importance of machinery on the ranch. The sheep rancher, often with little more than his chuckwagon, his horses, and his dogs, grazes hundreds of sheep on rough pastures, meadowlands, hillsides, deserts, and even in forests without much attention to plowing, planting, and harvesting the grass or other kinds of forage. However, no sharp line between intensive cultivation and extensive grazing distinguishes farms from ranches.

On the great ranches of the Hawaiian Islands, which run up from the edge of the water to the mountain peaks, most of the grazing acreage has been laboriously dug out of the forest and must be constantly cut and plowed and replanted to maintain fertility and productivity. But on the 160 million acres of the Argentine pampas most of the soil is so rich and well watered that many of the huge ranches have been plowed up and converted into wheat farms.

Bob Taylor—FPG

Texas has long been famous for its cattle ranches. Above is a typical roundup scene on a ranch in the Lone Star State. Texas still raises more livestock than any other state.

Ranching began in the early colonial period in both South America and North America. A large part of Rhode Island colony was fenced off as a great ranch to raise the famous Narragansett pacers. The colony of Virginia tried to fence itself off from the Indians and to enclose its rapidly multiplying herds of horses, sheep, cattle, and hogs. At Cowpens in northwestern South Carolina, on Jan., 17, 1781, a band of frontiersmen beat a British army decisively. Cowpens was little more than a corral and a general store for the surrounding ranchers. From California half a century later, but long before the discovery of gold, ranchers were shipping loads of hides around Cape Horn to the New England shoe factories. Australia and New Zealand also started as ranching frontiers, where herds of cattle and sheep multiplied and grew fat on hundreds of thousands of acres of almost-free land. In Canada ranches, which are generally referred to as farms, have surpassed the grain producers as sources of national wealth.

For 25 years after the American Civil War farming and ranching competed west of the Mississippi River with the open-range country, which belonged to no one and across which millions of cattle were driven to the ends of the railroads as construction crept westward. These were the years of the romantic cowboy, who actually spent most of his working days in the saddle with now and then a week of wild celebration in a so-called cattle town. See CHISHOLM TRAIL.

But with the invention of barbed wire in 1874 and the near-extermination of the herds of semiwild cattle on the open range in the winter of 1886-1887, the rancher and the farmer took over, the farmer staying away from the regions of less than 15 inches of annual rainfall.

During recent years ranching has become more like farming as the result of scientific studies of the rates of growth of sheep and cattle. The modern rancher makes every effort to improve his rangelands by seeding and fertilizing and by eradicating gophers and mice. He provides ample feed and clean water nearby. The old Texas longhorn has been replaced by the massive Hereford with a scientifically developed personality so gentle that the range may be lightly and inexpensively fenced off to prevent its being overgrazed. In Louisiana and Florida, ranch managers have crossed native breeds with humpbacked cattle from India to produce heat-resistant and disease-resistant breeds.

The cowboy is still useful at the roundup, but the four-wheeled jeep is slowly displacing his horse in less rugged country. The soil of the entire American range country has been intensively mapped for locating areas of nutritional deficiencies in terms of cobalt, iron, copper, and calcium. Texas, Minnesota, North Dakota, and Montana soils lack phosphorus. The "Goiter Belt" extends across the northern states from California eastward as far as Pennsylvania. These nutritional deficiencies and some active soil poisons as well as poisonous plants weakened, stunted, and killed millions of cattle and sheep before ranchers understood the principles of nutrition, watering, and growth. But cowboys still ride. Carrying signal flags to mark the boundaries of each run, they team up with airplane pilots in the spraying of 1,000 acres a day with 2,4-D to control sagebrush, skunkbush, and many range weeds.

RANDOLPH PLAN. See VIRGINIA PLAN.

RAPALLO TREATIES, two treaties signed in 1920 and 1922 in Rapallo, Italy. The treaty of Nov. 12, 1920, signed by Italy and Yugoslavia, made the port city of Fiume (now Rijeka, Yugoslavia) a free city, independent of both Italy and Yugoslavia, and gave the city of Zara (now Zadar, Yugoslavia) and part of the Dalmatian coast to Italy. The Adriatic port of Porto Barros went to Yugoslavia. Fiume had been seized in Sept. 12, 1919, by a band of freelance soldiers from Italy led by the poet Gabriele D'Annunzio. He refused to give up the city, and his troops had to be driven out by the Italian army.

The Rapallo treaty of Apr. 16, 1922, was signed between Germany and the U.S.S.R., both at that time outcast powers. It provided for close diplomatic connections and economic cooperation between the two countries. Germany became the first European nation to recognize the Soviet Union.

RAPHAEL (1483-1520), in full Raffaello Santi, Italian painter, born in Urbino. About 1499, after studying with his father and perhaps with Timoteo Viti, Raphael became an assistant to Il Perugino, master of the Umbrian school. Raphael's first major work, "Coronation of the Virgin," as well as those that immediately followed, were painted in the master's manner. In 1504 Raphael established himself in Florence and soon came under the influence of the Florentine masters, especially Leonardo da Vinci and Michelangelo.

In 1508 Raphael was called to Rome to decorate the Vatican for Julius II. From that time on he enjoyed the patronage of the papacy. In this last period of his life Raphael freed himself from the traditions of his predecessors and developed his own style. Soon he was the master of what became known as the Roman school. This was a period of incredible artistic productivity. During the remainder of the reign of Julius II and during the reign of Leo X, Raphael produced such renowned paintings as "The Crucifixion," "The Transfiguration," "The Resurrection," "Coronation of the Virgin," "Marriage of the Virgin," and "Entombment." He also turned his talent to executing frescoes and designing tapestries. Highly regarded as an architect, he was appointed chief architect of St. Peter's in 1514. He was also guardian of antiquities and author of an archaeological work on Roman ruins.

RARE EARTHS, a group of 14 metallic elements of similar properties in Group III of the periodic table. They are also known as the lanthanide series. The rare earths include the elements of atomic numbers 58 through 71. The names of the rare-earth elements, in order of their atomic numbers, are cerium (Ce), praseodymium (Pr), neodymium (Nd), promethium (Pm), samarium (Sm), europium (Eu), gadolinium (Gd), terbium (Tb), dysprosium (Dy), holmium (Ho), erbium (Er), thulium (Tm), ytterbium (Yb), and lutetium (Lu). The rare earths are not actually rare. Cerium, the most abundant of the 14 elements, is commoner in the earth's crust than are copper, tin, zinc, or lead. Even the rarer of these elements are more abundant than gold or platinum. However, one rare-earth element, promethium, is found only as a product of uranium fission.

Only two minerals, monazite and bastnasite, are commercially important ores of the rare earths. Monazite is a rare-earth thorium phosphate. Placer deposits of monazite sand are found in Idaho, Florida, Brazil, India, and Australia. Pegmatite rocks containing monazite are found in the Republic of South Africa. Bastnasite, a rare-earth fluocarbonate, is found in California and New Mexico.

The rare-earth metals are silvery gray but tarnish quickly in air. Cerium is soft enough to be cut with a knife, but metals of higher atomic number are harder. The chemical properties of all the rare earths are very similar, so the elements are difficult to separate from each other. Rare earths are separated by fractional crystallization, ion exchange, or solvent extraction, of their compounds. The rare-earth elements are active reducing agents, that is, they give up electrons readily). They ignite in air at relatively low temperatures.

The rare-earth metals are available commercially as rare-earth materials (undifferentiated rare-earth metals), as cerium metal (which may contain several percent of other rare earths), as didymium materials (cerium-free rare earths), and as misch metal (a mixture, composed chiefly of cerium, neodymium, and praseodymium). Misch metal is used in the manufacture of lighter flints and in certain alloys. Rare-earth zirconium-magnesium alloys have outstanding high-temperature properties and are used for some jet-engine castings.

Rare-earth fluoride and rare-earth oxide are used in the cores of carbons for arc lighting in searchlights and motion picture projectors and for blueprinting, photography, and microscopy. Other rare-earth salts are used for coloring or decoloring glass during glass manufacture. Ceric and other rare-earth oxides are used in polishing spectacle lenses and other glass products.

Some of Raphael's finest paintings are of New Testament subjects. "The Adoration of the Kings" is one of the predella panels for his great altarpiece "Coronation of the Virgin." The "Coronation" was commissioned for the Church of San Francisco in Perugia, Italy, and it shows the influence of Raphael's great teacher Il Perugino.

Camera Clix

RASPBERRY, an edible berry that actually is a collection of individual tiny fruits grown together so compactly that they resemble a single fruit. The raspberry is termed an aggregate fruit and is formed by a single flower. Both black and red raspberries are native to North America, Europe, and parts of Asia. In North America they grow wild over large areas of the country. The red is commoner in the northernmost states, while the black is more abundant farther south.

Cultivated varieties of raspberries have been developed from wild ones. The former are usually larger than the latter. Purple raspberries are a cross between the red and black. There are also white and yellow varieties of black and red raspberry types.

Raspberry bushes are thorny and have five-petaled white flowers and compound leaves with three to seven leaflets. They are closely related to the other bramble fruits, the blackberries. Both are in the same genus of the rose family and have similar histories.

RASPUTIN, GRIGORI EFIMOVICH (1871-1916), a half-literate peasant who rose to become a major power in the Russian government. Rasputin was born Grigori Efimovich Novykh in Pokrovskoe, in Siberia. His epithet, "Rasputin," means, literally, "the dissolute." In 1903 or 1904 Rasputin became a holy wanderer, traveling from monastery to monastery in Russia, the Balkans, and Jerusalem and living on charity from the faithful. For a while he was associated with the Khlysty, or Flagellants, a religious sect that alternated orgies with fervent religious ceremonies. Rasputin was never a monk or a priest. In 1904 he was introduced into Moscow society. He was highly regarded by several influential churchmen, princesses, and a lady-in-waiting to the Czarina Alexandra. In 1905 he was introduced to the royal family.

The heir to the Russian throne, Alexis, was born in 1904. He was afflicted with hemophilia, a hereditary and incurable disease carried by the mother's genes. Rasputin, according to reputable accounts, was able on several occasions to control Alexis' bleeding, and the Czarina fell completely under the influence of the forceful and unscrupulous peasant.

From 1911 to 1914 Rasputin increased his power in the church and in Russian politics. He exercised great control over the appointments of Czar Nicholas II. In 1915 the Czar departed for the army, and Russia was dominated by Rasputin and the Czarina Alexandra. Even conservative supporters of the monarchy were vexed when the incapable Boris V. Sturmer was appointed prime minister, minister of the interior, and minister of foreign affairs.

Brown Brothers

Grigori Rasputin

A conspiracy, which included V. M. Purishkevich, the Czar's nephew, and Prince Felix Yusupov, murdered Rasputin on Dec. 17, 1916. Rasputin was buried and mourned by the royal family, but no serious reprisals were taken against the conspirators. Rasputin's role in creating the conditions leading to the Russian Revolution of 1917 is often exaggerated. He did contribute, however, to the monarchy's loss of prestige.

RAT, a rodent that is closely related to the mouse but usually is larger. The brown, or Norway, rat is now the most abundant species throughout the world. Its back and sides are dark grayish brown; its belly is ash gray. Its body is from 8 to 10 inches long; its tail is from 6 to 8 inches long. The Norway rat is most numerous in cities and near the seacoast. Its favorite haunts are sewers, cellars, wharves, and other filthy places. It also lives in the country around barns and corncribs, where it eats millions of dollars' worth of grain annually. It also eats meat, eggs, garbage, and refuse of all kinds.

The Norway rat did not originate in Norway. Its exact origin is unknown, but it has inhabited Europe for many centuries. It was carried as a stowaway on ships to seaports in every country of the world. After

The Norway rat invades barns and eats stored grains, fruits, and vegetables.

Norway Rat

The desert wood rat and the white-throated wood rat of southwestern North America are called pack rats because they build large nests of sticks and rubbish. The desert kangaroo rat of the same region is so named because it leaps along on its long hind legs as a kangaroo does.

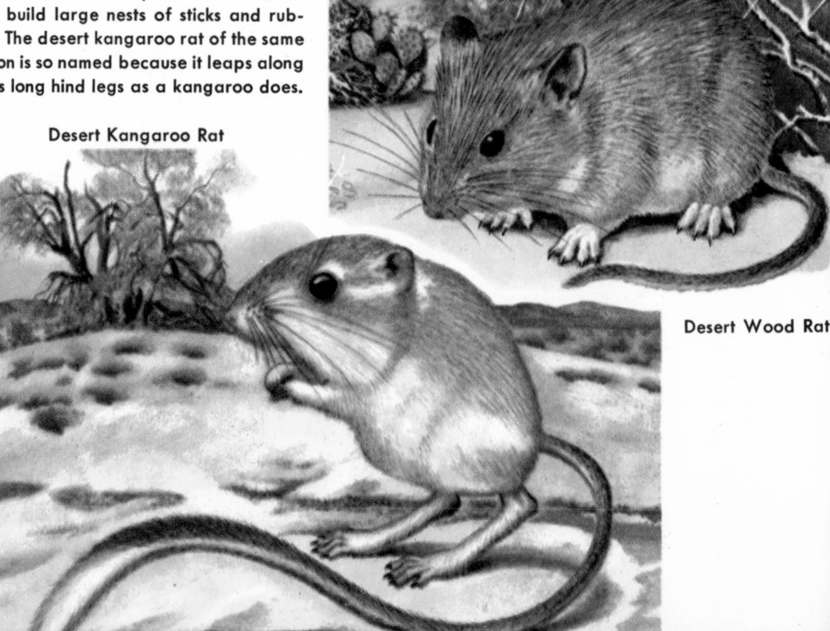

Desert Kangaroo Rat

Desert Wood Rat

arriving in the United States in 1775, the Norway rat almost completely exterminated the smaller black rat, which had come here from Europe about 200 years earlier.

Rats transmit diseases, including the dreaded bubonic plague, which killed a great many people during several widespread epidemics in Europe. Biting fleas carry the plague bacteria from the bloodstream of rats to the bloodstream of men. Rats multiply rapidly. During a single year a female will have from three to five litters, each containing from 10 to 15 young.

White rats are used extensively in medical and psychological research. In medical research new, untried drugs are given to them to ascertain whether the effects of the drugs are beneficial or harmful before they are given to human beings. In one type of psychological experiment rats are compelled to run several times through a maze to ascertain how quickly they can learn to run through it without error.

RATIO, the quotient of two quantities as an expression of their relative size.

The function of ratio can be seen from an example. To say merely that Adam can read 450 words per minute has little meaning. It means more when his rate is compared with 250, the average reading rate. How much faster than average can Adam read? This is expressed by the ratio of Adam's rate to the average rate, $\frac{450}{250}$ or $\frac{9}{5}$; Adam can read 9 words to the average man's 5, or $1\frac{4}{5}$ as fast.

A ratio must be a comparison of like quantities—words per minute to words per minute, quarts to quarts, men to men—and not of men to quarts, yards to pounds, and so on.

An equation in which the members are ratios is a proportion. A proportion may be written in three different ways:

$$18:27::2:3$$
$$18:27 = 2:3$$
or
$$\frac{18}{27} = \frac{2}{3}$$

The last two forms are preferred.

RATIONALISM, a philosophy that sets up human reason as the main source of knowledge. For example, rationalists felt that everything in theology had to be submitted to investigation, and if an idea could not be demonstrated from reason alone, apart from revelation, for example, it should be discarded. In the search for knowledge the rationalists considered human reason a tool superior to the senses.

Rationalism has historically been one point of view in the philosophic debate over which was the most important in the discovery of truths about the world—thought or observation. Can the mind derive certain fundamental truths without reliance on experience? Philosophers like Spinoza held the rationalist view that the mind can know things about the universe that are not observable. These are known as a priori truths. The empiricists denied that a priori principles existed, and some of them based all knowledge on experience, which "wrote" upon the human mind as upon a blank slate. John Locke tended to support the empiricist view. René Descartes, like Spinoza, supported rationalism. In his *Rules for the Direction of the Mind* he claimed that only two means of approach to truth were possible: intuition and deduction. Both Descartes and Spinoza thought that observation was important, but only as a way to illustrate what the mind could grasp by itself. It is not surprising that rationalists were very impressed by the lucidity and exactness of mathematics. Spinoza, in fact, wrote his philosophy (the *Ethics*) on the pattern of Euclid's *Elements*.

In theology rationalism enjoyed a vogue in the 18th and 19th centuries as an offshoot of the philosophical movement known as the Enlightenment. The logical outcome of rationalism was to reduce religion to an ethical system based on a few fundamental moral principles. However, rationalism continues to influence students of the Bible, and it has stimulated the search for historical knowledge pertinent to theology and the Bible.

Rationalism and empiricism harmonize in natural science. The rationalistic tendency allows the formulation of imaginative hypotheses and the application of mathematics and deductive reasoning. Empiricism demands the application of extensive experimental observation to these theories. Both approaches are necessary to the progress of scientific knowledge.

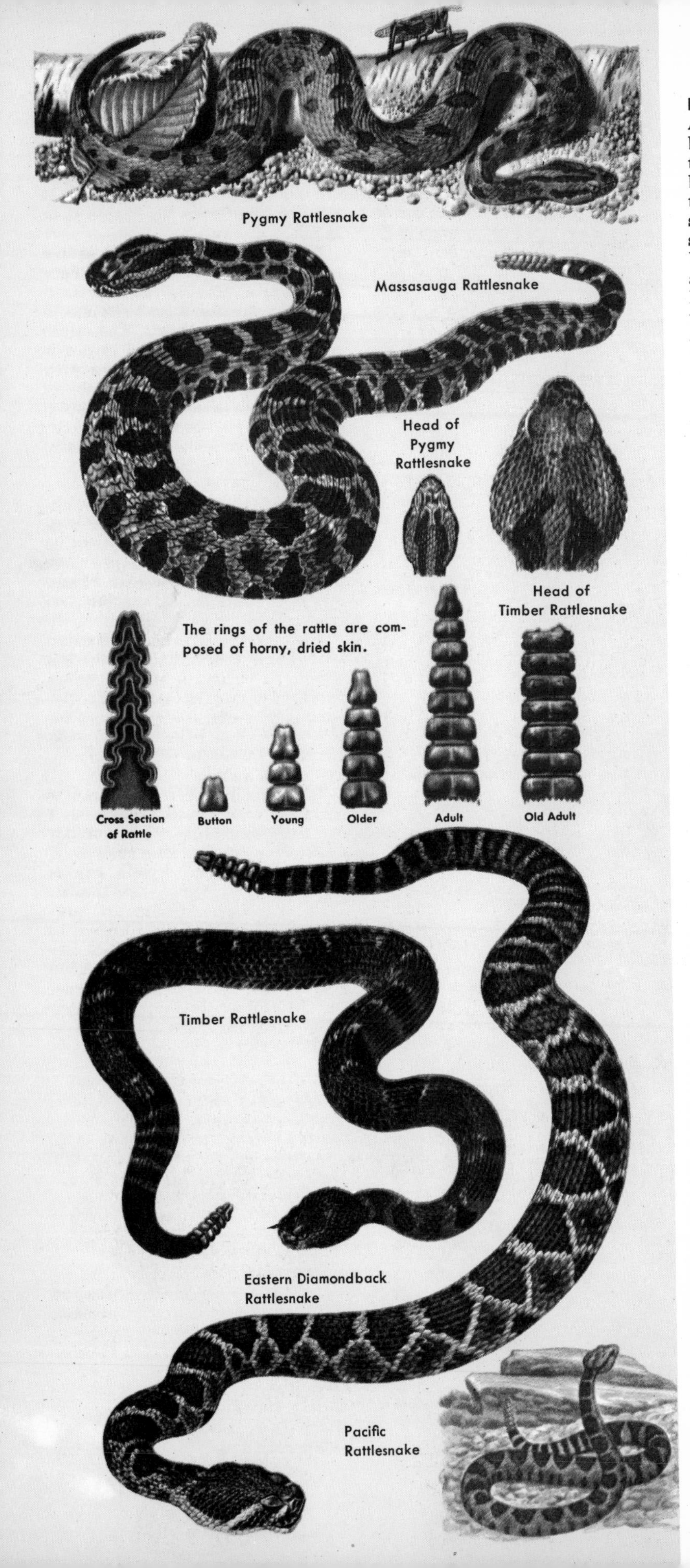

RATTLESNAKE, a large, poisonous American snake. It has a thick body, a slender neck, and a flat, triangular head with a deep pit between the eye and nostril. The tail terminates in a rattle that consists of a series of horny, cup-shaped, loosely attached rings. Whenever the snake molts its skin, a new ring is added to its rattle. However, since the skin is molted two or three times yearly, a snake's age can be ascertained only approximately by counting its rattles.

The rattlesnake has two poison fangs, one on each side of the upper jaw. The long, hollow, pointed fangs are modified teeth. The bottom of each fang is connected with a poison gland. When a fang pierces the flesh of man or animal, the poison is forced by muscular pressure through the fang into the wound. The bite of many rattlesnake species is dangerous and often fatal. Fortunately, when a snake is disturbed, it usually rattles audibly before striking.

Exactly 15 different species of rattlesnake are native to North America north of Mexico, most of them being found only in the West and South. The diamondback rattlesnake of these regions is 6 to 8 feet long when fully grown.

Rattlesnakes devour rats, mice, gophers, and rabbits by swallowing them whole. In colder regions they hibernate during winter by huddling together in rocky caves. Young rattlers are not hatched from eggs but are born alive during late spring, ten or more at once.

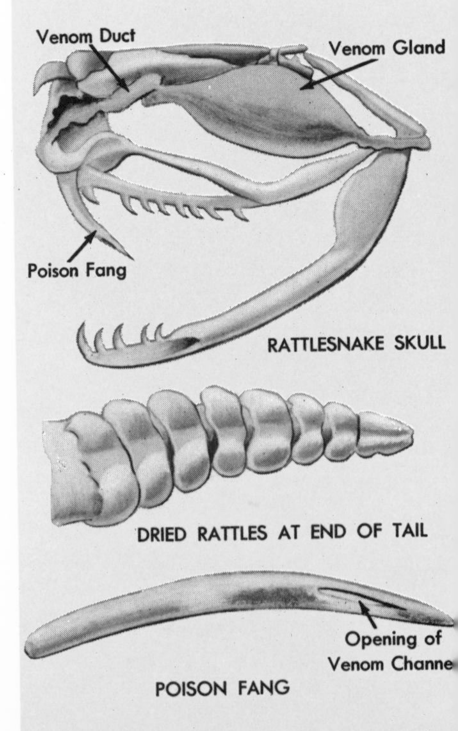

Brown Brothers

Maurice Ravel, French impressionist composer

RAVEL, MAURICE (1875-1937), a French impressionist composer, was born in Ciboure, but his family moved to Paris a few weeks after his birth. He began the study of the piano at an early age and in 1889 entered the Paris Conservatory. He made his public debut as a composer in 1898 with the composition *Sites auriculaires*. The following year he composed his *Schéhérazade* overture and his *Pavane pour une infante défunte*. During the years following he composed *Jeux d'eau* for piano, the String Quartet in F, and his song cycle *Schéhérazade*. Academically, he was unsuccessful in this period, competing four times for the Grand Prix de Rome and not winning once. His last failure, in which he failed to pass even the preliminaries, caused an uproar in French music circles and led to a change in the directorship of the conservatory.

Despite this, Ravel produced in the next few years some of his finest work, including: *Gaspard de la nuit*, a work for piano; *Histoires naturelles*, vocal music; and *Rhapsodie espagnole*, a work for orchestra. In 1909 he was commissioned by the impresario Sergei Diaghileff to compose the music for a ballet. As a result, Ravel composed his masterpiece *Daphnis et Chloé*. In 1911 Ravel's comic opera *L'Heure espagnole* was produced.

Other works of Ravel's middle period include: *Le Tombeau de Couperin* for piano, part of which was later orchestrated; *La Valse* for orchestra; *L'Enfant et les sortilèges*, an opera; and the famous *Boléro*.

In his last years Ravel composed two piano concertos. The first was the Concerto for Left Hand. This was written for the one-armed pianist Paul Wittgenstein, who introduced the work to the public in 1931. The second, Ravel's Concerto in G Major, was first played in 1932.

RAVEN. See JAYS, MAGPIES, CROWS, RAVENS.

RAWLINGS, MARJORIE KINNAN (1896-1953), an American novelist, is known for her stories of Florida life. After she was graduated from the University of Wisconsin, she became a journalist and worked on various magazines and newspapers. In 1928 she gave up newspaper work and devoted all her time to a writing career. Among her works are *Cross Creek* and *South Moon Under*. She received a Pulitzer prize in 1939 for *The Yearling*, the story of a boy's love for the pet fawn that his father is forced to kill when it ruins his crops.

Marjorie Kinnan Rawlings

UPI

RAY AND SKATE, flat-bodied marine fish that are related to the sharks. Rays and skates, like sharks, have cartilaginous skeletons, whereas most other fish have skeletons of bone. Rays and skates are much broader than other fish because of the great enlargement of their pectoral fins, one of which extends along each side of the body and head. These fish swim by the undulation of their very thin bodies. The tail is considerably smaller in diameter than fishtails usually are. The tail may be long and slender. It is much shorter in the skates than in the sting ray.

The flatness of rays and skates enables them to live along the floor of the ocean. Although most of them live near the shore, some range to a depth of 100 fathoms. The upper surface of most rays and skates is dark colored so that it blends with the ocean bottom when the fish are viewed from above. This enables them to escape detection by predators. The undersurface is usually lighter colored than the back.

Skates eat shrimp, crabs, lobsters, mollusks, and sometimes fish. All skates lay large eggs in leathery rectangular pods with curly tendrils at the four corners. These egg cases are often found at the seaside. Skates and rays have almost no value as human food.

The sting ray is so named because toward the base of its whiplike tail one or more sharp, barbed spines appear. These spines can inflict ugly, painful wounds on bathers. Contrary to popular belief, no poison is introduced into the wound made by the barbed spines.

The torpedo, or electric, ray is equipped with electric organs that can severely shock other animals and that are used to stun their prey, mainly fish. The torpedo ray is found on both sides of the Atlantic.

The devilfish, or manta, the largest of the rays, has been known to reach a width of more than 20 feet and a weight of more than 3,500 pounds. At the opposite extreme, the little skate is only 20 inches wide, while the barn-door skate is 5 to 6 feet wide.

Rays and skates, like sharks, are more primitive than most other fish and occupy a lower position on the evolutionary scale.

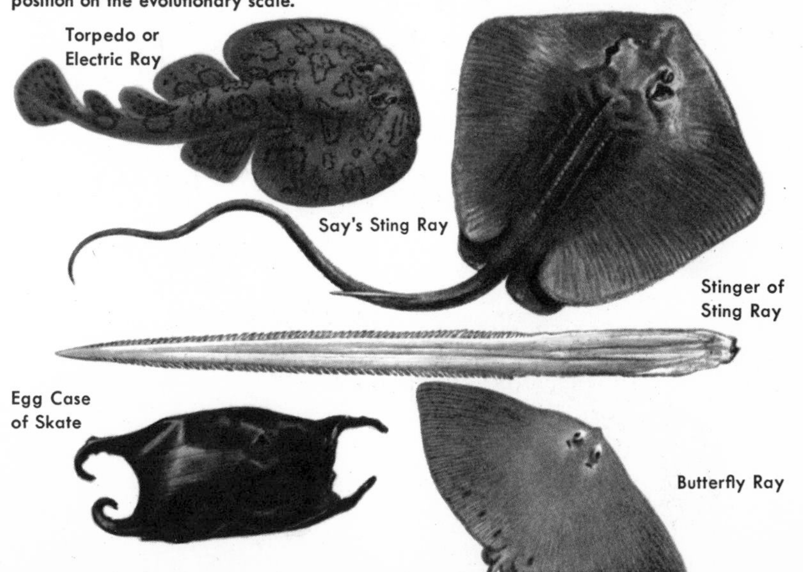

RAYLEIGH, JOHN WILLIAM STRUTT, 3D BARON (1842-1919), an English physicist who collaborated in discovering and isolating the inert gas argon. He was born at Witham, Essex, and studied science and mathematics at Trinity College, Cambridge. He served as professor of experimental physics at Cambridge from 1879 to 1884 and as professor of natural philosophy at the Royal Institution of Great Britain from 1887 to 1896.

While Rayleigh and the English physicist Sir William Ramsay were conducting research to ascertain the exact densities of oxygen and nitrogen, they discovered and isolated the inert atmospheric gas argon. In 1904 Rayleigh received the Nobel prize in physics for his discovery of argon and for his research into the densities of gases.

In 1908 Rayleigh was appointed chancellor of Cambridge University. He also determined the value of the ohm, the practical unit of electrical resistance, and conducted research on the resonance of sound.

RAYON, a man-made fiber from cellulose, or the solid part of plant cell walls. Liquid cellulose is forced from a spinneret and solidified, usually in an acid bath. Rayon has been produced and improved since 1891.

Along with cotton, flax, wool, and silk, rayon is considered one of the world's basic textile fibers. First used as a substitute for silk in the manufacture of hosiery and underwear, rayon is much used today mixed with other fibers. High-tenacity rayon is used for tire cord and for garments.

A bale of short lengths of rayon fiber called staple are being examined. The staple will be spun into "spun yarn."

Amer. Viscose Corp.

The cellulose used in making rayon is obtained from wood pulp or cotton linters. First the cellulose is chemically liquefied. Then the liquid is forced through holes in a nozzle, or spinneret, into an acid bath for regeneration. There the liquid hardens into fine strands of unbleached rayon fiber.

The first plant for producing rayon was built at Besançon France, in 1891. Not until 1911 was the first plant built in the United States, at Marcus Hook, Pa. After 1938 rayon was second only to cotton in terms of textile consumption in the United States.

RAZOR, an instrument for cutting or scraping off body or facial hair. Razors have been in use for at least 5,000 years, and razors and razor blades have been made in many shapes and of many materials.

The razors used in the 1800's were called straight razors. These modified sharp-edged knife blades with wooden handles are still often used. Such instruments were both difficult and dangerous to use. The sharpening of a blade was a tedious job and was accomplished by rubbing the knife edge along a thick strip of specially treated leather called a strop.

The razor in common use today is the safety razor. In the safety razor the plane of the blade is at right angles to the plane of the handle, and the blade has guards to prevent cutting the skin. King C. Gillette produced blades of the wafer type for safety razors in 1903. Wafer blades are inexpensive and can be thrown away when they become dull, so resharpening is eliminated. Wafer blades and safety razors are now mass produced.

Electric razors, or dry shavers, are being used increasingly. An electric razor has a motor inside to drive the cutting blades. The cutting blades are concealed by a perforated plate that is held next to the skin during shaving. Hairs pass through the perforated plate and are sheared off by the cutting blades inside the razor.

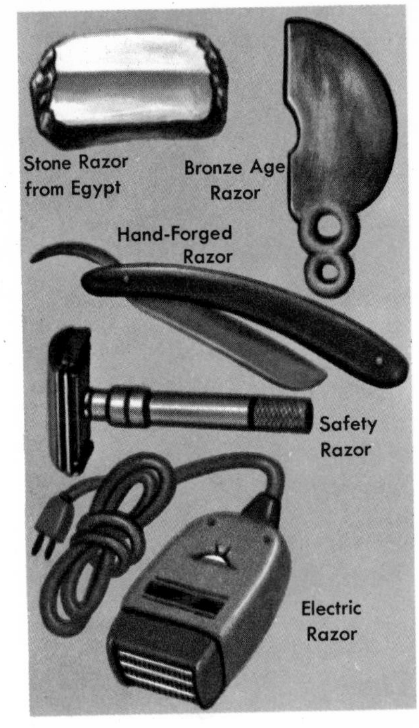

READING is the process by which a person comes to understand written or printed symbols. The symbols are usually words, but they may be music notes, Chinese ideograms, Egyptian hieroglyphics, or pictographs. The purpose of reading is to understand some message intended to be conveyed by the symbols.

Reading is important to civilization as the companion process to writing. Culture is preserved partly through written records, but such records are relatively worthless unless someone can read them. To the individual, reading is one of the most important means of education. Therefore the ability to read well is one of the primary requirements for becoming well educated.

HOW TO IMPROVE YOUR READING ABILITY

The first step toward improving your reading ability is to find out how well you can now read. Try to discover your specific weaknesses—any habits or skills that need improving. Then set up and follow a reading program designed to overcome these weaknesses.

To determine how well you read, compare your skills and habits with those of a good reader. Basically, a good reader reads rapidly and understands well what he has read. He has the habit of reading for a specific purpose and of evaluating what he has read. The good reader adjusts his reading rate according to the material he is reading, skimming some materials, reading others in great detail. He reads by thought units, not by single words. He avoids backtracking. Finally, he enjoys reading varied materials, and he develops his vocabulary through his reading—aided by a dictionary.

By measuring your own habits against these habits of the good reader, decide where your specific weaknesses lie. In addition, have your eyes and ears checked, and check the illumination and quietness of the place where you do your reading. Determine whether you read well aloud.

Now set up your own reading program. Make a list of books and other materials you want to read. Then set aside a definite time each day—at least 15 minutes—for reading. Concentrate both on increasing your reading speed and on improving your comprehension. To record your progress, time yourself regularly and make graphs of your reading rates in terms of words per minute. Most people find that their comprehension also improves whenever their reading speed improves.

REAL ESTATE is a term for landed property, including houses, trees, and other things that are part of the property.

The real estate business, which includes acting as an agency for owners and buyers of houses and other properties and renting and selling property one owns, has been especially important in the United States from the beginning of the nation. Many of the pioneers were attracted west by the advertisements of land companies. Later, the railroads continued this process in order to profit from their government-given land grants. Still later, real estate promoters contributed much to the growth of a number of cities, notably Los Angeles. Although the real estate business has not been as important in Europe as in the United States, real estate operators played a large role in the growth of Berlin during the 1890's.

In general, the real estate business has been more dependent on the state of the economy than have some other businesses. For example, the depression of 1929-1933 almost halved the number of people in the business in the United States.

Most real estate salesmen and brokers specialize in particular types of property. Some may sell farms and other land, others may concentrate on commercial property (such as hotels), and still others may specialize in houses. However, the real estate business has several specialties other than selling. These include the management of large apartment and office buildings for owners, valuation of property, property insurance, and building. Two types of building activity have become particularly important in the United States since the end of World War II—the construction of suburban housing developments and the government-aided replacement of deteriorating sections of cities with new housing.

Real estate practice is regulated to a certain extent in the United States by the code of ethics established by the National Association of Real Estate Boards, by state licensing requirements, and by city zoning and building rules.

The device pictured at the left is a Reading Accelerator. Used in schools, reading clinics, libraries, and the home, it is designed to help students increase their reading speed and their reading comprehension. The accelerator has a mechanically controlled shutter that moves down a page of reading material, covering it line by line, at a predetermined word-per-minute rate. The reader is forced to read as fast as the shutter moves, and with practice he learns to read phrases instead of one word at a time. A projector and screen are used for the same purpose when reading instruction is given in a classroom full of students (below).

Perpetual Development Lab.

REALISM, in art and literature, the depicting of things as they are, as opposed to things idealized, or as they should be. From modern philosophic realism realistic writers and artists accept the viewpoint that the objects perceived by man actually exist in the external world more or less as he senses them. Beyond this, however, the philosophic meaning of realism does not apply to realism as a literary and artistic movement.

The realist attempts to depict as honestly as possible actual settings and people. He generally tries to exclude his own subjective feelings and philosophic interpretations of the situations and people he describes. He presents a fullness of detail that allows the reader to share in the events and settings. As a general rule, a realistic novelist lets facts speak for themselves, although some realists, by the selection of settings and events, tend toward social criticism.

The realist avoids the portrayal of idealized and unreal beauty. He does not employ embellishments of literary style, and he does not depict the catastrophic tragedy and the violent passions that are such popular subjects with the romanticists. The realist, as a rule, does not portray heroes or other extraordinary people. Instead, he almost invariably describes such ordinary people as peasants, factory workers, or persons who belong to the lower middle class.

In the 19th century the French writer Honoré de Balzac was a forerunner of the conscious movement toward realism. Gustave Courbet, a painter, announced his intention of painting only contemporary and commonplace subjects. His paintings suggest realistic portrayal of a scene without resorting to the more photographic detail of naturalism. Realism was then adopted as a guiding principle by writers, many of whom were influenced by the literary criticism of Hippolyte Taine. The technique of realism was adopted wholly or partially by such writers as Gustave Flaubert, Maupassant, Tolstoi, Turgenev, Benito Peréz Galdós, William Dean Howells, Ernest Hemingway, and others. It is still a dominant tendency in literature, as evidenced by such novelists as Mikhail Sholokhov. See EXPRESSIONISM; NATURALISM.

RECALL (political science). See INITIATIVE, REFERENDUM, AND RECALL.

RECLAMATION, the process of improving desert, marshy, waste, or submerged land for cultivation or for other purposes. Methods of reclamation include drainage, irrigation, and the restoration of eroded land and cutover forest land. On a broader scale it includes related activities, such as financing projects, advising settlers, constructing dams and canals, and so forth. Since ancient times reclamation has been an important factor in promoting state or national welfare through increasing the land resources and thereby providing more economic opportunities.

If the land is too wet for cultivation, drainage improves the area. This method was used by the ancient Romans and is more often executed now as a large project or enterprise. In humid countries, such as France, Italy, England, and Germany, and in the Mississippi Valley, the Great Lakes region, and swamplands of the United States much land has been reclaimed through drainage.

Other improvements of land are made by drainage, washing, and soil correction of alkali areas of semiarid and arid sections. Unwatering, or the recovery of land from the sea, has been carried on notably in the Zuider Zee of The Netherlands and the fens of eastern England. Dikes and canals were built in the Zuider Zee to reclaim the ocean floor for farming. In order to protect areas from floods, programs involving reforestation and the construction of levees, reservoirs, and spillways have been successfully achieved. The clearing of cutover forest land has provided agricultural areas in the Pacific Northwest and in parts of the South and the northern lake states of the United States.

Of all the various types of reclamation, irrigation is the most extensive. It was used in ancient Egypt, Babylonia, China, and India. In the Western Hemisphere the Indian Cliff Dwellers of the southwestern United States, the Aztecs of Mexico, and the Incas of Peru changed stream courses for irrigation. In recent times reclamation has grown from a private or community enterprise to large-scale government programs. Laws have been passed to establish ownership of the water.

The Reclamation Act of 1902 was the first real start of irrigation work in the United States. The measure provided for irrigation projects in the arid and semiarid lands of the West. To administer the act the Reclamation Service, which later became the Bureau of Reclamation, was created. The objectives of the bureau are based upon the conservation, development, and utilization of the land-and-water resources of the West. Many of the federal dams are constructed and operated as units of basin-wide development, such as the Colorado River Storage Project and the Missouri River Basin Project. Supplemental income has come from hydroelectric power generated as a byproduct. Irrigation has been carried on to a large extent in Egypt, India, Australia, Italy, Mexico, and France.

USDA

Above is a picture, before reclamation, of an area included in the Meadow Lake drainage project in Washington. Left is a picture of the same area after completion of the project.

Reclamation has economic and social benefits and is important as a basic activity for governments and peoples of all nationalities. With government assistance national agricultural production is built up, private landowners are helped, and new land is opened for increasing population. See DRAINAGE; FLOOD AND FLOOD CONTROL.

RECONSTRUCTION PERIOD. During and following the American Civil War the process of reconstructing the governments and political structures of the Confederate states was begun. No legally recognized action took place during the war. However, in 1862 provisional military governors—such as Andrew Johnson in Tennessee—began under presidential authorization to reestablish loyal governments. In 1863 President Lincoln proposed a plan that included executive recognition of state governments when 10 percent of the 1860 electorates pledged loyalty to the federal government and when the states agreed to emancipate their slaves. This reconstruction plan was carried out in Arkansas and Louisiana; but, despite the fact that those states had followed the prescribed procedure, Congress refused to seat their representatives. Congress then challenged Lincoln with its own reconstruction plan, the Wade-Davis Bill. This plan would not readmit a state to the Union until a majority of its voters could swear that they had been, as well as that they would be, loyal to the Union. Lincoln killed the bill by a pocket veto, but congressional opposition to moderate reconstruction was to grow until it resulted in the impeachment of President Johnson.

Although Lincoln was assassinated shortly after the end of the war, his conciliatory policy was closely followed by President Andrew Johnson in his reconstruction proclamation of May, 1865. Johnson granted amnesty to most Confederates who took the oath of allegiance and organized provisional governments that quickly took the measures Johnson deemed necessary for admission to Congress. On Dec. 6, 1865, Johnson announced that the Union was ready to be restored.

This conciliatory policy was violently opposed by the radical wing of the Republican party, which was led by Thaddeus Stevens. Refusing to endorse Johnson's actions, those men claimed congressional rather than executive authority over the ex-Confederate states and refused to admit their elected representatives to Congress or to recognize their governments. In June, 1866, the radicals forced through Congress the 14th Amendment, which included Negroes in its definition of citizenship and which denied the right to hold public office to any rebel unless that right was approved by two-thirds of both houses. The amendment also forbade the questioning of the validity of the public debt and prohibited the payment of any debt or loss incurred by a person who participated in the Confederate cause. The 14th Amendment was passed partially because Southern enactment of Black Codes angered the North. Black Codes governed the rights of Negroes and usually bound them to the land. To prevent such subjugation, the Freedmen's Bureau was established in 1865. (See BLACK CODES; FREEDMEN'S BUREAU.) Other constitutional amendments associated with Reconstruction were the 13th, abolishing slavery, and the 15th, forbidding the states to deny the right to vote on grounds of race, color, or previous condition of servitude.

State ratification of the 14th Amendment was demanded by Congress before readmitting any of its former enemies to the Union. But only Tennessee ratified the amendment, for the other Southern states hoped that the radicals would be defeated in the 1866 elections. These hopes were not realized, and radical victory paved the way for the stern Reconstruction Acts.

The first of the Reconstruction Acts, all of which hindered Southern rehabilitation, was passed over Johnson's veto, Mar. 2, 1867. It divided the South, with the exception of Tennessee, into five military districts governed by military commanders. Moreover, since the former Confederate leaders were banned from office, state governments came under the domination of Northern exploiters, who were known as carpetbaggers, and Southern collaborators, known as scalawags.

Thus, under the political domination of profiteers, who were backed by federal troops, many Southerners lost the last vestiges of their property. However, the troops were usually withdrawn after the states had formed governments based on universal suffrage and these governments seemed secure. Graft increased most of the state debts more than fourfold between 1865 and 1875. Such corruption played a large role in undermining carpetbag rule, and eventually the federal troops, sent in again after the rise of the Ku-Klux, were withdrawn, and the South resumed direction of its own affairs.

By 1870, 11 states had been readmitted to the Union, and in 1872 the Amnesty Act returned officeholding privileges to all but about 500 ex-Confederates, thus turning out many carpetbaggers. In 1877 President Rutherford Birchard Hayes ordered the federal troops removed from South Carolina and Louisiana, the only states still under carpetbag control, and Reconstruction was ended.

RECORDER, an end-blown woodwind instrument, widely used in the 16th and 17th centuries both as a solo instrument and as a regular part of the orchestra. Recorders are today made in four sizes—soprano, alto, tenor, and bass. They are made of wood, have eight holes (three for the middle fingers of each hand, plus one for the thumb of one hand and one for the little finger of the other), and have a range of more than two octaves. The recent revival of the popularity of the recorder as a solo instrument has been in large part due to the increasing interest in 16th-century and 17th-century music.

The recorder probably originated in England, though its popularity rapidly spread throughout Europe. Frequent references are made to it in the works of Shakespeare, Milton, Pepys, and other writers of the time. It is reported that King Henry VIII of England, a recorder player, owned 76 recorders as well as an equal number of side-blown flutes. Arnold Dolmetsch in England and the Trapp family in America have been instrumental in bringing about the revival of interest in recorders both by making them and by giving recorder concerts.

The recorder is an easy instrument to play.

RECORD PLAYER, a device for playing phonograph records. It ordinarily consists of a turntable driven by an electric motor, a pickup arm with a crystal or other device for producing an electrical signal from the record, and an amplifier and loudspeaker to increase the volume of the sound to the desired level.

The modern phonograph was invented by Thomas A. Edison in 1877. His first machine consisted of a revolving cylinder covered with tinfoil and, pressing against this cylinder, a needle attached to a thin diaphragm. Sound waves striking the diaphragm caused it to vibrate, and the needle vibrated with it. As the cylinder turned, the needle impressed a groove in the tinfoil, and the shape of the groove represented the sound waves. A screw thread moved the cylinder lengthwise as it turned. The wavy groove could reproduce the original sound if the needle was made to follow the groove while the cylinder was turned again.

Edison's original machine reproduced sound very imperfectly. The tinfoil cylinders were quickly replaced by wax ones, and a more delicate mechanism was designed to improve the quality. In 1888 flat disc records were produced; and a method was developed for pressing many copies of a disc from a metal master mold, instead of making them individually.

Disc records that were 10 or 12 inches in diameter and rotated 78 revolutions per minute became standard during the 1890's. Early phonographs used spring-wound motors and the "morning-glory" horn, but around 1910 cabinet-type phonographs were developed, with the horn enclosed in the cabinet. Soon after 1920 came the development of electronic amplifiers and of techniques for recording with microphones and amplifiers instead of acoustical recording; these techniques provided enough power to cut better record grooves than was possible when only the energy of the sound waves could be conveyed to the recording stylus. The fidelity of recorded music was improved, but is was still limited by the quality of the shellac used for the final records. Records were later made of vinyl plastic but were still formed by heat and pressure; vinyl was much more uniform than shellac and produced less record scratch and surface noise. Since World War II practically all phonograph records have been made of vinyl.

The shellac record, operated at 78 revolutions per minute, had enough grooves on one side for only a few minutes of playing time. In the early phonographs the needle, the diaphragm to which it was fastened, and the air in the horn were vibrated by the waviness of the grooves of the record; all of the energy had to come from the record itself. For this reason the grooves had to be rather deep and widely spaced, and they wore rapidly. With electronic amplifiers the needle alone has to be vibrated by the record; the amplifiers provide most of the

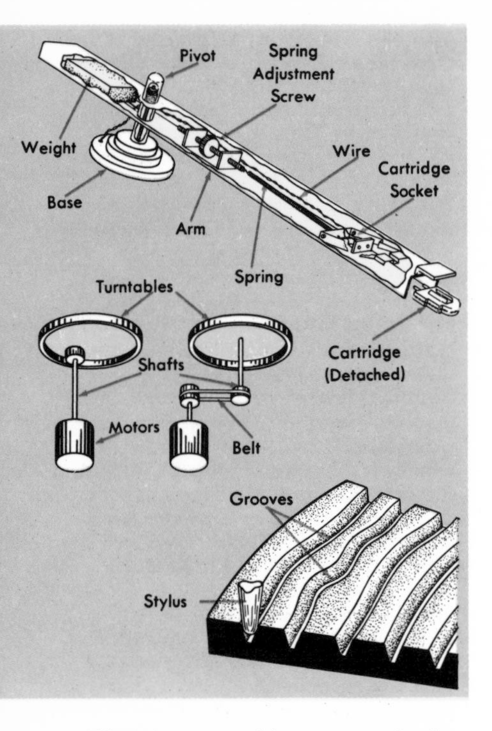

Shown here are a pickup arm, record surface with stylus, and two turntable mechanisms.

energy to produce the sound. It became possible to use much finer grooves, more closely spaced, and to turn the record at $33\frac{1}{3}$ revolutions per minute. The modern longplay record usually plays 25 to 35 minutes per side.

In the 1920's the demand for longer musical selections caused the development of automatic record-changing machines. These machines are still used. Coin-operated phonograph players, in which any one or any selected group can be played by inserting coins, are widely used; they often hold as many as 200 selections. Most of these machines use a disc record about 7 inches in diameter that is turned at 45 revolutions per minute; one side will play about 6 minutes.

The latest form of record is the stereo record, in which two patterns are cut in each groove, each at a 45-degree angle to the horizontal. When these two signals are played through two speaker systems, stereophonic reproduction results.

RECREATION, leisure activity engaged in simply for the enjoyment of the activity. It may consist of participating in or watching sports, of attending dances, parties, or the theater, of engaging in hobbies or other active occupations, or simply of reading, listening to music, or walking in the woods.

With the coming of industrialization and the concentration of population in large cities, the need to provide facilities for recreation became a serious one. It was discovered that recreation is essential to mental and physical health and to intellectual growth. Labor at mechanical, routine occupations in modern factories was found to lead to mental fatigue and tension. The congested condition of urban areas leaves little play space for city children. For these and other reasons, municipalities and private groups began in the 20th century to concern themselves with providing recreation facilities for the general population. During the 19th century the demand for recreation was met by commercial interests, which provided sports and entertainment for profit. Motion picture theaters, billiard and pool rooms, circuses, amusement parks, dance halls, night clubs, and baseball and football all grew into large-scale business enterprises with an investment and income of millions of dollars annually. The abuse of the public interest, which took the form of immorality and other undesirable qualities, led to a growing demand for public regulation of these enterprises. A growing realization of the importance of wholesome recreation led, in the early years of the 20th century, to the development in the United States of organized community recreation as a public responsibility. Private and philanthropic agencies were the first to promote this program. The YMCA, YWCA, social settlements, churches, and women's clubs gave support to the movement and began to urge local and state governmental participation in it. The movement was a great success. Today an extensive system of public recreational facilities is provided under local and sometimes state and national sponsorship. It includes parks and playgrounds, recreation centers, golf links, tennis courts, swimming pools, and facilities for dramatics, music festivals, and arts and crafts.

Commercial profitmaking recreation continues to provide citizens with many entertainment and play resources, but private and municipal facilities play a significant and growing role in the total recreation picture. In the 1950's the increase in juvenile delinquency aroused a more widespread interest in recreation as a public responsibility.

In Europe there was an increase of interest in recreation after World War I, with emphasis on recreation for workers. Trade unions and other labor organizations began setting up recreational programs for their members. After World War II a trend toward the adoption of American forms of recreation became apparent.

RED CROSS, an organization of mercy founded in 1864 at Geneva, Switzerland, to aid wounded soldiers and other victims of war. On June 24, 1859, Jean Henri Dunant, a practical humanitarian of Geneva, found himself among some 40,000 abandoned French and Austrian casualties of the battle at Solferina, Italy. Dunant gathered together a few Italian women and boys, some English tourists, an Italian priest, and three Austrian doctors to give, as volunteers, food, water, shelter, and medical aid to the helpless soldiers, without regard to their Austrian or French origins. He thereby laid down the fundamental principles of the Red Cross.

His account of these acts of mercy in *A Memory of Solferino* (published in 1859) so aroused humanitarians in other nations that four years later a conference on the relief of helpless sufferers of war, at which 14 governments were represented, was held in Geneva. Almost a year later, at a second conference, official representatives of 12 governments drew up the first Geneva Convention—the first of a series of agreements and treaties that have led to the establishment of Red Cross societies in over 80 nations. The recognized national Red Cross societies, together with representatives of the International Committee of the Red Cross, of the League of Red Cross Societies, and of governments that have signed the Geneva conventions, normally meet about every four years in the International Red Cross Conference, the highest deliberative assemblage of representatives of the International Red Cross movement. The League of Red Cross Societies, a federation of the recognized national societies, encourages the formation of new societies and promotes and coordinates the activities of its members. The International Committee of the Red Cross (ICRC), a body of 25 Swiss citizens having no national, religious, economic, or political commitments, intervenes during armed conflicts as a neutral intermediary to aid those in need of help by reason of war. The ICRC accepts money and supplies from individual donors and from the national Red Cross societies, as well as the loan

L.B. Prince

The American Red Cross headquarters is situated in Washington, D.C.

of personnel, but avoids emphasis upon the national origins of the aid.

National societies of the Red Cross are self-governing groups that subscribe to the Geneva conventions. These conventions provide for Red Cross activities in the impartial relief of suffering. In addition to activities agreed to under the Red Cross treaties the individual societies carry on many programs under charters procured from their governments. Most societies work closely with the armed forces, the civil-defense forces, and other relief agencies of the nations under which they operate. Under general-welfare clauses, such as are contained in the American Red Cross charter, they conduct blood programs and disaster preparedness and relief activities. Members of the Red Cross display a red cross on a white background. This symbol is generally regarded as a tribute to Switzerland (whose flag is a white cross on a red background), because the conferences at which the Red Cross movement began were held in Switzerland. In some Moslem countries the symbol is a red crescent; Iran uses a red lion and sun on a white field; the U.S.S.R. uses both the red cross and the red crescent.

Although the United States had two observers at the diplomatic conference of 1864, it had no Red Cross organization until the American Association of the Red Cross was incorporated in 1881. A year later the Geneva Convention of 1864 was ratified by the U.S. Senate.

During the next 20 years, under the leadership of Clara Barton, the American Red Cross aided the victims of river floods, organized the relief of Johnstown, Pa., after a dam broke, succored the survivors of a hurricane that devastated the Sea Islands and the coast of South Carolina, and aided United States and Cuban victims of the Spanish-American War. After the reorganization of 1904 the American Red Cross started training medical volunteers and nurses and began first-aid teaching, rural-health programs, and lifesaving and water-safety instruction. Between 1907 and 1917 the American Red Cross carried on famine-relief and drought-relief programs in China and sent relief expeditions abroad to assist in major disasters. But not until World War I did the American Red Cross become an institution for raising hundreds of millions of dollars to aid members of the U.S. armed forces, veterans, and their families.

Between the two World Wars the American Red Cross expanded its services so as to be able to move in at once when disaster struck in the form of fire, drought, flood, hurricane, and even economic depression. In the late 1930's chapters of the American Red Cross became active in blood programs. With the entrance of the United States into World War II in 1941 the American Red Cross greatly expanded its activities in this field and established the Red Cross Blood Donor Service to procure blood for the armed forces. During the war 2,200 local chapters collected 13 million pints of blood. In 1947 Red Cross blood services were reorganized, and a nationwide blood program was set up to meet needs of civilians as well as military personnel.

RED RIVER. Originating at the Texas–New Mexico border in the Llano Estacado, this river flows some 1,300 miles across the southern United States. It is the southernmost tributary of the Mississippi River. The river follows the Texas-Oklahoma line and flows through a corner of Arkansas. In Louisiana it passes Shreveport and Alexandria and reaches a point north of Baton Rouge. Here it forms two branches —one flowing into the Gulf of Mexico and one emptying into the Mississippi River.

River navigation is limited, but improvements have removed some obstacles. The multipurpose Denison Dam is the chief unit of the Red River basin project. The river received its name from the fertile red-clay farmlands in its semiarid upper basin.

RED RIVER REBELLION, a Canadian revolt of halfbreeds in 1869-1870, led by Louis Riel. The halfbreeds in the Red River region of what is now the province of Manitoba feared the loss of their land when the Hudson's Bay Company transferred its territory to the Canadian government in 1869. Stirred up by Riel, the rebels seized upper Fort Garry (now Winnipeg) without much opposition and set up a provisional government with Riel as president.

The new regime continued with little interference for six months, while negotiations were conducted with the Canadian government in Ottawa. The crisis came in March, 1870, when Thomas Scott, a young Canadian Protestant, was unjustly executed by the rebels, who were predominantly Roman Catholic. Great indignation was aroused, especially among the Orangemen of Ontario. The government sent an expedition under Colonel Garnet Wolseley, which dispersed the rebels without conflict and brought an end to the uprising. The Manitoba Act of 1870 guaranteed rights to the Red River settlers.

Red Cross volunteers fold bandages.
Ralph Pierson—Monkmeyer

Young disaster victims receive aid.
Courtesy The American National Red Cross

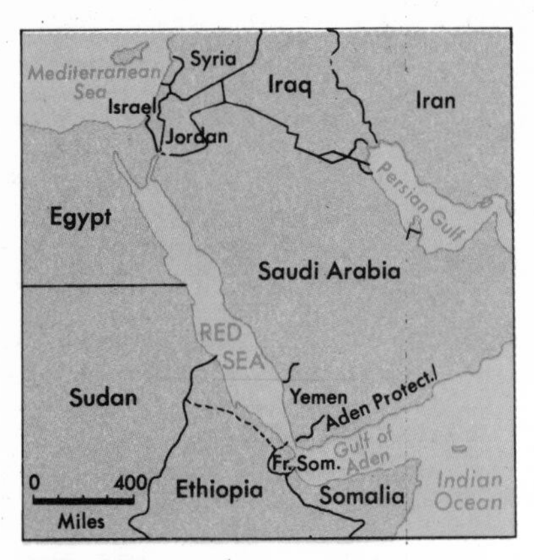

RED SEA, a long, narrow sea between northeastern Africa and the Arabian Peninsula of southwest Asia. It forms a part of the Great Rift Valley. Extending 1,400 miles, it has a maximum width of 220 miles but is much narrower in the far south and in the north. The sea's maximum depth is about 7,000 feet.

The Red Sea connects with the Gulf of Aden of the Arabian Sea through the narrow strait Bab el Mandeb. The north end branches into the Gulf of Suez on the west and the Gulf of Aqaba on the east. The Gulf of Suez is connected to the Mediterranean Sea through the Suez Canal. Chief islands are the Dahlak Archipelago, the Hanish Islands, and the Kamaran Islands.

The sea receives little rainfall and no rivers. The prevailing heat causes great evaporation, and the salinity of the water is high. The area is noted for its extremely hot, humid summers. There are many reefs and other coral formations. It is probable that the sea received its name from the red algae that float upon the surface.

The Red Sea has been used as a shipping lane since ancient times. After the discovery of the route around the Cape of Good Hope in the late-15th century the use of the Red Sea declined, but with the opening of the Suez Canal in 1869, it again became a major shipping route between Asia and Europe.

REDUCTION. See Oxidation and Reduction.

REDWOOD. See Sequoia.

REED, WALTER (1851-1902), a U.S. physician who discovered that yellow fever germs are transmitted by mosquitoes. He was born at Belroi, Va., and studied medicine at the University of Virginia, from which he received an M.D. in 1869 at the age of 17. He then studied medicine at Bellevue Hospital Medical College, in New York City, and received his second M.D. from that institution in 1870. He became an assistant surgeon in the U.S. Army Medical Corps in 1875 and directed an investigation into the causes and means of transmission of typhoid fever in army camps in the United States during the Spanish American War.

In 1900 Reed was sent to Cuba to direct an investigation into the causes and means of transmission of yellow fever among U.S. soldiers stationed in Havana. After conducting many experiments he concluded that yellow fever germs were transmitted from one human being to another by mosquitoes of a certain species. After measures were taken to eliminate these mosquitoes, the incidence of yellow fever in Havana and other infested regions was greatly reduced.

REEL, a lively dance common in Scotland and Ireland. It is danced usually by two couples but sometimes by more. The rhythm, with four beats to the measure, is smooth and flowing. The Highland fling is a vigorously athletic form of the reel. In the late 18th century an adaptation of the Scottish reel became popular in the English ballrooms. Another form, the Virginia reel, was transplanted to the American colonies and remained popular well into the 20th century.

REFERENCE BOOK, usually a collection of information made easily available to the reader by a systematic arrangement of subject entries. Most libraries have a collection of such works in a reference room. See Atlas; Bibliography; Dictionary; Encyclopedia.

The kind of reference works one should use depends on the type and quantity of information desired. Some of these works are so basic that few people can afford not to own them. Many families own a dictionary, an atlas, a cookbook, a child-rearing guide, and some kind of encyclopedia. Depending upon the special interests in the family, such other guides as a thesaurus, a dictionary of quotations, or a Bible concordance may be owned.

Dictionaries should be used whenever there is uncertainty about the meaning, spelling, or origin of a word. A thesaurus should be used with a dictionary if one is at a loss for a word. Atlases are to be used whenever one reads about unfamiliar locations. A general reference encyclopedia gives some basic information in every field.

For a special interest there are available such specific guides as foreign-language dictionaries, cookbooks, dictionaries of mythology or of musical terms, encyclopedias of literature, agricultural handbooks, sportsmen's guides, motion picture handbooks, and field guides for various interests and hobbies.

If a question is of abiding interest, one will want to read books dealing with it in detail. To find out what books are available on a particular subject bibliographies should be used. Some bibliographies list magazine articles; some list books. Some cover the whole range of knowledge, and some cover only special areas. There are even bibliographies of bibliographies. The subject indexes of library catalogues are sometimes complete enough to be good bibliographies.

Finally, a warning: Even the best reference books contain mistakes. For accurate information a person should always double check in another source.

REFINERY, an industrial complex with equipment for removing impurities from, and separating the various components of, petroleum. In petroleum refining physicochemical processes are employed to segregate hydrocarbons according to either boiling-range or hydrocarbon types. Fractional distillation separates hydrocarbons into groups that have similar boiling ranges. Cracking carries out a similar operation but under high temperatures and pressures that crack, or smash, the oil molecules and produce an increased yield of gasoline.

The major equipment required for distillation consists of stills, in which the charge is heated; towers, in which the various boiling fractions are separated; and condensers, in which the gases are cooled to liquids. In straight refining the oil is heated so that the lighter fractions, such as gasoline, kerosene, and naphtha, boil off into the distillation tower, where in their gaseous state they are collected, condensed, and piped to other parts of the refinery for further processing. The remaining hydrocarbons are utilized as fuel in the refinery or are converted into byproducts. These gaseous byproducts of the refining process often serve as the building blocks in the manufacture of petrochemicals, among which are many kinds of plastics and fertilizers.

REFLEX, a nervous response that results in the functioning of a gland, muscle, or organ of the body. The mechanism of the reflex is known as the reflex arc, which may be divided into three parts: the afferent pathway; the nerve center; and the efferent pathway. The afferent pathway includes a receptor organ and the nerve cell or cells that transmit impulses to the nerve center. The nerve center includes one or more cells in the central nervous system. The efferent pathway includes nerve cells that carry the impulse to the organ that effects a response. A good example of a reflex is observed when the tendon just below the knee is tapped while the subject is sitting with his legs crossed. Impulses pass through the reflex arc and return to muscles in the leg, which contract and cause the leg to extend.

Reflexes are of two kinds: conditioned and unconditioned. Conditioned reflexes are acquired in the course of living, and their arcs pass through the cerebral cortex of the brain. Unconditioned reflexes are fixed, and their arcs pass through the lower parts of the brain and the spinal column. All of the activities of the glands, muscles, and organs of the body are produced and integrated by combinations of conditioned and unconditioned reflexes under control of the central nervous system and especially of the cerebral cortex. See CONDITIONED REFLEX; NERVE AND NERVOUS SYSTEM.

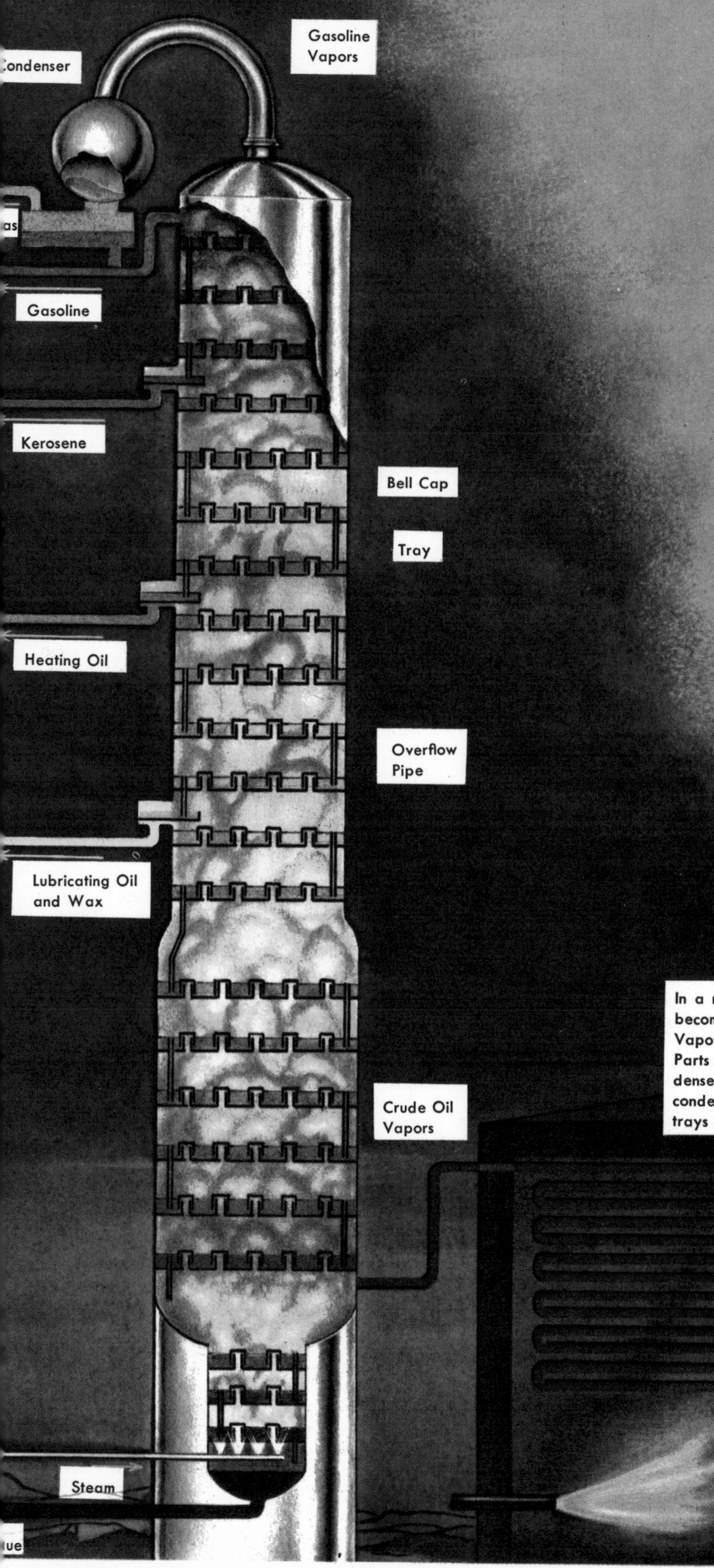

In a refinery crude oil is heated in a pipe still until it becomes vapor, which goes to a fractionating tower. Vapor rises through bell caps in trays to the tower top. Parts of the oil vapor that have high boiling points condense in lower trays; parts with low boiling points condense in higher trays. The liquids that collect in some trays are piped from the tower.

REFORM, LAWS OF, in politics, laws intended to introduce changes for the better. Reform laws of some kind have been introduced continuously in all countries, although some countries have found change more acceptable than have others. Many reform laws have been necessary and successful, but others have made conditions worse and have represented the opinions of a small but vocal minority of reformers. In democracies there is a tendency to regard reform as proceeding toward more freedom and well-being for the individual. This is erroneous. The series of laws passed by the Nazis to produce a totalitarian state in Germany were also reform laws, but democrats would suggest that they altered society for the worse.

A list of reformers would include most of the great leaders of history. Plato's *Republic* and *Laws* had among their intentions the reforming of Greek political society. The motives of many reformers have been to produce the better society. Sometimes, however, as was the case with Czar Nicholas II's acceptance of laws introducing a constitutional monarchy in Russia, reform is an expedient to retain or to gain political power. The following reformers are only a few among those of modern history. Nikon was a religious reformer who introduced ceremonial and textual reforms in the Russian Orthodox Church in the 17th century. Peter the Great introduced into 18th-century Russia many reforms designed to westernize and strengthen the nation. John Howard's exposé of English prison conditions in the 18th century caused corrective reform laws to be passed in England. Florence Nightingale is famed for her 19th-century reforms of hospital nursing. Alexander II, although strongly conservative, was responsible for the 19th-century laws emancipating the Russian serfs. The American Wendell Phillips spoke for many reforms in the 19th century, including labor legislation and the abolition of slavery. Benito Juárez of Mexico led the 19th-century movement called *La Reforma,* which introduced necessary political and social reforms that benefited the Mexican peasants. Emmeline Pankhurst, the English suffragette, worked vigorously for equal voting rights for women, which were granted by a reform law in 1928. Nikolai Lenin was responsible for the portentous socialistic reforms that established the Soviet Union. A great number of reform laws were passed in the New Deal years of President Franklin D. Roosevelt's administration. In England such reform laws as the National Health Service were passed while Clement R. Attlee was prime minister.

The need for reforms is continuous, as most liberals and conservatives agree. Radicals and revolutionaries are not reformers, because they want the transformation of society to be radical (that is, to the root of things), while reformers seek to build on the present society. Differences of opinion exist on the extent and nature of the changes introduced by reform laws. The reason why reform laws are needed is that technical and social changes occur that render the old laws no longer adequate to deal with new situations. The Industrial Revolution, for example, made necessary innumerable reform laws dealing with safety devices on machines, workmen's compensation, and unemployment insurance. Otto von Bismarck, although a strict conservative, was responsible for Germany's pioneering social-insurance laws to protect workers. The development of political awareness on the part of the Moslem population of Algeria made necessary the reform laws advocated by Charles de Gaulle in 1960.

The machinery for instituting reform laws differs in each society. In a democracy reformers work to influence public opinion. Once a large part of the public is aroused in favor of reform legislation, it chooses from two or more political parties those representatives that support reform. These representatives operate, in accordance with the governmental machinery, to legislate and to execute reform laws. If a large part of the public decides the legislation was unsuccessful, it has an opportunity to retract its decision in future elections. In a dictatorship reform laws emanate from the top of the hierarchy down. The dictator may decide on a course of action, set in motion the government's propaganda machine to stir up favorable public opinion, and then act upon his decision. An aroused public opinion that has not been prepared by the channels of communication controlled by the government has no other recourse to initiate political reform than mutiny, revolt, or revolution. Such was the case in the Hungarian revolt of 1956.

Reform laws have been both successful and unsuccessful. All reforms are in a sense experiments. The secret ballot, developed in Australia, was so successful in preventing certain types of vote fraud that it was adopted by the United States and many other nations. The drive for more democracy in the 19th-century United States resulted in the adoption of the long ballot, which presented the voter with numerous candidates for many offices and with many issues to be voted on. The long ballot, in practice, was a burden on the voter, for he could not possibly be informed on the many candidates and issues. Democracy suffered as a consequence, and the reform laws instituting the long ballot were repealed in many states. The drive to repeal the long ballot and replace it by a short one can be considered a reform in its own right.

The success or failure of reform legislation is sometimes a matter of opinion. The laws collectivizing Soviet peasants in 1930 resulted by 1936 in the collectivization of some 90 percent of the peasant population. The cost of the effort, however, was half of the Soviet Union's livestock and millions of human lives. Yet the collectivization of the peasants enabled the government to control and limit their use of consumer goods and to divert the saving to the production of more capital.

The general direction of most reform legislation in democratic countries seems to have been toward more democracy and toward increasing the welfare of the people. The British reform laws of 1832, 1867, 1884, and 1885 and the woman-suffrage law of 1928 are good illustrations of this trend. All these laws extended the vote to more and more British citizens. The United States, France, Canada, Australia, and Scandinavia have shown a similar development. See COUNTER REFORMATION; NEW DEAL; REFORM ACTS OF 1832, 1867, 1884; REFORMATION; WOMAN'S RIGHTS.

REFORM ACTS OF 1832, 1867, 1884, laws passed by the British Parliament that transferred political power from the landowning aristocracy to the industrialists and the working class. This was accomplished through the extension of voting rights.

The act of 1832 was introduced by the Whig government of Earl Grey. It took away parliamentary representation from boroughs with fewer than 2,000 people and removed one of the two representatives of the boroughs with 2,000 to 4,000 people. The 143 seats thus released were distributed to new industrial cities and towns such as Manchester, Bir-

Chicago Public Library

Martin Luther, above, appearing before the Diet of the Holy Roman Empire assembled at Worms in 1521, refused to retract his writings and was afterward banned from the Empire.

On the Reformation monument at Geneva, Switzerland, from left to right, are the figures of Guillaume Farel, John Calvin, and Théodore de Bèze, successive leaders of the Reformation at Geneva, and John Knox, who adhered to the Geneva model.

Swiss Natl. Trav. Off.

mingham, and Sheffield, which had no representation at that time. The franchise was extended by lowering the property requirements.

The act of 1867 was sponsored by the Conservative leader Benjamin Disraeli, but it was also supported by the Liberal Whigs. It gave the vote to thousands of working-class men of the cities and practically doubled the number of voters.

In 1884 the franchise was further extended to include all farm laborers and tenants. As a result of the three reform acts almost every male citizen in Britain had the right to vote. The vote was not given to women until 1928.

REFORMATION, that period in Western history when Protestantism arose. Traditionally, the Reformation began Oct. 31, 1517, the day Martin Luther nailed to the door of the court church at Wittenberg his 95 theses against the Roman Catholic Church's selling of indulgences. Previously, however, Luther—as well as a number of other men, notably John Huss and John Wycliffe—had questioned the church's authority on several matters. In fact, the church had never been without rebellion against its authority, but it had always been able to deal effectively with its opponents. By 1500 that was no longer true.

The Babylonian Captivity (1305-1378), during which the papacy sat at Avignon under the domination of the French monarchy, and the Great Schism (1378-1417), the period when two—and sometimes three—rival claimants vied for the pontifical throne, resulted in the church's diminished prestige. Furthermore, during its residence at Avignon the papal court became large and luxurious, and this tendency toward luxury eventually spread through much of the higher clergy. The papacy recognized the dangers arising from such a display of wealth, but attempts at reform were feeble. Thus those humanists of the Renaissance who desired simplicity of worship and a return to primitive Christianity used the new critical scholarship to expose many of the abuses.

Yet the Reformation might not have succeeded had the new spirit of patriotism not changed the relationship between church and state. Everywhere secular princes were denying the international claims of the papacy. Although patriotism was probably the most powerful factor working on the side of the reformers, it was not the sole one. A budding capitalism, which found in the theology of the Protestant Reformation a code of ethics favorable to the *bourgeoisie* and a pretext whereby secular rulers might seize much of the church's great landed wealth, also appeared in this period of transition from medieval to early modern times.

The Protestant Reformation, however, was not particularly a sign of progress nor of modernity. Nor was it a reaction of old-fashioned minds against the Italian Renaissance. Instead, it was essentially a modification and a simplification of the medieval religious system, of which Luther's ideas may be considered the last great flowering.

New York Public Library

Martin Luther posts his 95 theses.

Luther based his theology upon the quotation from St. Paul's Epistle to the Romans that "the just shall live by faith" and upon many of the teachings of St. Augustine. From these precepts he concluded that the church of his day was wrong in assuming that man could merit salvation by a virtuous life (good works). On the contrary, Luther contended, man could be saved only by divine grace, for man was too depraved and too corrupt to achieve salvation otherwise. Out of this thinking emerged the idea that every man was his own priest, having direct access to God through Jesus Christ and not needing the intermediary powers of a priest. For Luther, the priest became the minister, whose significance lay in his function and not in his office.

Despite these attacks upon fundamental doctrines of the church, Luther still regarded himself as a good Catholic. However, in a debate with the Catholic theologian Johann Eck at Leipzig in 1519 Luther admitted that his views concerning man's direct relationship with God were the same as those held by John Huss. He then acknowledged that a general council as well as a pope might err. Luther now had no choice but separation from the church, and this was accomplished in 1520 by Pope Leo X's bull of excommunication. In 1521 the Diet of the Holy Roman Empire pronounced Luther an outlaw.

Like the other religious reformers of the period, Luther insisted that he was no innovator but was returning to the teachings of Jesus and the early church, the true Christian church. With that in mind he set about organizing a system of belief for his followers, who came to be called Protestants because of their protestations over the Diet's attempts in 1529 to prevent the introduction of "religious novelties." In 1530 the Lutheran creed was defined in the Augsburg Confession, the work of Luther's colleague Philipp Melanchthon. In 1555 the Peace of Augsburg, ending a nine-year civil war between the Catholics and the Protestants, granted the latter religious toleration. But the settlement gave each prince the right to dictate the religion of his subjects and prohibited toleration for Protestants other than Lutherans.

Elsewhere in northern Europe Lutheranism was also on the march. In Denmark Frederick I and his son Christian III desired to increase the royal power. The ecclesiastical organization preached by Luther, which was to be subservient to the state, fitted their purpose better than did the church of Rome. Despite vigorous public protest Lutheranism was placed on an equal footing with Catholicism in 1527, and ten years later it became the state religion. It was then promptly extended to Iceland and Norway, which were governed by Denmark.

Politics also played a large role in the establishment of Lutheranism in Sweden, for the breach with Rome was initiated by the papacy's refusal to remove the antinationalist archbishop of Uppsala from his post. In 1527 all ecclesiastical property was transferred to the crown, and two Catholic bishops were put to death. But not until the reign of Charles IX (1604-1611) did Lutheranism triumph. In 1593 the Confession of Augsburg was adopted as the creed of the Church of Sweden, and in 1604 Catholics were deprived of their offices and estates and were banished from the kingdom.

Meanwhile, a second type of Protestantism arose. It was generally known as Calvinism and was to exert a far greater influence on the whole development of Western civilization than was Lutheranism. The way for the success of Calvinism was prepared by the Catholic priest Huldreich Zwingli, who, after being installed as preacher in the Cathedral of Zurich in 1518, repudiated the papacy and proclaimed the Bible the sole guide of faith and morals. In 1523 when the papacy asked Zurich to abandon Zwingli, it refused and broke with the Roman church. The revolt spread through most of Switzerland, and unsuccessful efforts were made to unite with the Lutherans. In 1531 Zwingli was killed in the civil war that he brought on by his desire to force his views upon those areas of Switzerland that had remained Catholic. A truce followed, which granted each canton the privilege of determining its own religion, thus establishing a religious division that has lasted into the 20th century.

The movement initiated by Zwingli did not die because of lack of direction. In 1536 the French reforming priest John Calvin went to Geneva and, except for a brief period when he was exiled, guided this division of Protestantism until his death in 1564.

Unlike Luther, who was satisfied to leave in the church many of the practices not prohibited by Scripture, Calvin refused to tolerate anything not expressly scriptural.

He returned to St. Augustine's doctrine of predestination, insisting that an all-powerful and all-knowing God had, from before the creation of the world, determined who would be saved and who would be damned. Although the work failed to provide a common religious rule for all Christians in rebellion against Rome, it exerted a tremendous influence on Protestants everywhere, stating in an orderly and concise manner the principal Protestant dogmas.

In addition to—and bound up with—its emphasis on simplicity of worship and austerity in morals, Calvinism held special attraction for the *bourgeoisie*, for it condemned idleness and sanctified the new acquisitiveness by insisting that prosperity was one of the marks of a person's election to heaven. However, the aim of Calvinism, like Lutheranism, was religious reformation, and its contributions to the rise of capitalism were unintentional, just as were the whole Reformation's contributions to the secularization of the world.

This appeal, plus the founding of such important schools as the University of Geneva, which attracted numerous foreign students, and Calvin's correspondence with would-be reformers in all parts of Europe, helped carry Calvinism, known as the Reformed religion, over much of the Continent and eventually to North America. In The Netherlands it replaced Lutheranism and became known as the Dutch Reformed faith; however, it had little appeal for the people living in the great trading area known as the Spanish Netherlands (now Belgium). It crept into southern Germany, but not until after the Thirty Years' War did it gain formal recognition. In France it attracted numerous adherents, known as Huguenots, who engaged in a series of religious wars with the Roman Catholics from approximately 1559 to 1598, when Henry IV granted them political and religious liberty in the Edict of Nantes. In Poland and Hungary Calvinism also made great strides, most of which were eventually lost again to the Catholics. Eastern Hungary, however, remained the stronghold of a very severe Calvinism. In Scotland the feudal reaction against the crown, which was championed by the Roman Catholic clergy, was taken advantage of by John Knox and his reformers, who prevailed upon the nobles to accept Calvinism and to deal a decisive blow against the monarchy. That blow was struck in 1560, when the Presbyterian Church was set up after the model of the church at Geneva and when the "Lords of the Congregation" and the troops of Elizabeth I of England ousted the queen, Mary Stuart. Calvinism also exerted a great influence in England, even before the revolutionary and Cromwellian periods (1642-1660). Toward the end of Henry VIII's reign (1509-1547) Calvinism inspired the theology, if not the organization, of a number of small sects, and under Edward VI (1547-1553) it influenced the theology of the Anglican Church. However, the moderating policies of Elizabeth I (1558-1603) tended to fix a gulf between the Anglicans and the Calvinists.

Anglicanism, which was more conservative in its adherence to Roman Catholic theology than Calvinism or Lutheranism but which probably did more to further intellectual freedom, had its main roots in political rather than doctrinal discontent. Upon the ascension of Henry VIII to the throne the only serious obstacle to royal absolutism was the independence of the Roman Catholic Church in England. But the English church would probably not have immediately broken away without the added impetus of Henry's marital difficulties with his queen, Catherine of Aragon, for the pope had given Henry the title "Defender of the Faith" in reward for his championship of Catholicism against Luther. But Henry greatly desired a male heir, which he knew Catherine could not give him, and he was in love with Anne Boleyn. Henry turned to the papacy, requesting a dispensation permitting him to divorce Catherine and to marry Anne. The papacy refused. Although Henry then declared his independence of the bishop of Rome and set himself up as head of the Church of England (a title to which the popes had referred in addressing the English clergy for more than 1,000 years), he did not become a Protestant. While the Catholic who denied royal supremacy was beheaded, the Protestant who denied transubstantiation was burned.

Later more basic changes were effected. Monasticism, against which there was much popular sentiment, was uprooted (1539). The monks had generally opposed Henry's pretensions to royal supremacy, but the deciding factor in the suppression of the monasteries was economic. Henry claimed much of the confiscated property for himself, for his foreign and domestic policies were a constant drain upon his resources. With the remainder he astutely bribed the nobles, thereby committing them to the new order. Under Edward VI the terms "Holy Communion" and "Lord's Supper" were substituted for the term *Mass*, and during the long reign of Elizabeth I (1558-1603) the Church of England assumed the character that is now generally associated with Anglicanism. The Thirty-nine Articles and the Scriptures were made the sole rule of faith, faith was made the only road to justification, and the sacrifice of the Mass was repudiated.

Although Anglicanism, Calvinism, and Lutheranism were the major Reformation movements, they were not the only ones. Opposed to these conservative creeds, as well as to Roman Catholicism, were a number of radical Protestant sects. Most of them considered Christianity less a creed vouched for by theologians than a way of life revealed by an "inner light." Known as evangelicals, they emphasized the emotional elements in Christianity, rejected any extensive organization, and preached voluntary membership by adults. One of the most influential of these groups was the Anabaptists, who received their name from the belief that baptism should not be administered to infants but only to converted adults. Eventually, the principles of the evangelicals divided the Calvinists; they also gave rise to pietism among Lutherans and to Puritanism and Methodism among the Anglicans; and they provided the basis for modern fundamentalism.

Distinct from the evangelicals, though a radical sect, were the Unitarians, who denied the Trinity and appealed to a strict rationalism. In time Unitarianism contributed to the development of deism and to a critical attitude toward religious authority, including the Bible. In this respect it paved the way for that sort of Christianity known in the 20th century as liberal.

By 1700 the Reformation was over. Protestantism had achieved enough success to be no longer rebellious and to be tolerated generally. While the Reformation had attempted to deepen the spiritual meaning of the individual life and to make the world more consciously religious by correcting what it felt were the abuses of the Roman church, it actually had the opposite results. Its attacks on the supremacy of the papacy, as well as its criticisms of other fundamental doctrines of the church, dealt a shattering blow to the ideal of a universal Christian civilization, which had been most fully realized during the Middle Ages. While this action was not a step into the modern world, it was a step toward that world, the realization of which was primarily a result of the efforts of the 18th century. Educated men of the 16th century, such as Luther, continued to believe in witches; and great Protestant poets, such as John Milton, still accepted the medieval geocentric theory of the earth's relationship to the universe.

REFRIGERATION can best be defined as the removal of heat from an object or system to produce and maintain subambient temperatures. Any material that is used to absorb heat is called the refrigerant. There are three methods of refrigeration: the natural, the mechanical, and the thermoelectric. Natural refrigeration includes the use of ordinary ice, cold ground waters, or Dry Ice (carbon dioxide). All of these are used to some extent in food preservation, but they have a distinct disadvantage—the spent refrigerant cannot be used again. Mechanical-refrigeration methods use the refrigerant over and over again. Such methods include vapor-compression systems, absorption systems, and steam-jet systems. Common refrigerants used in mechanical-refrigeration systems include ammonia, halogenated hydrocarbons, and sulfur dioxide.

Vapor-compression systems are the most widely used. In such systems the refrigerant is changed from a liquid to a vapor by heat absorption. The vapor is passed through a compressor and is then changed back into a liquid by heat removal.

Absorption systems resemble vapor-compression systems, but they lack a refrigerant-compressor stage. In one, the ammonia-absorption system, heat is removed as ammonia is passed through water at different temperatures. The system is effective because ammonia is highly soluble in water at low temperatures and is less so in water at elevated temperatures.

Steam-jet systems utilize the material being cooled (in such systems this is usually water) as the refrigerant. High-pressure steam is passed through a device (an ejector) to remove water vapor and to create a very low pressure. The low pressure lowers the boiling point of the water, which begins to boil. The heat the water uses to boil is supplied by the water itself. The temperature of the water is reduced. Steam-jet systems are not extensively used. See REFRIGERATOR.

In the vapor-compression refrigeration system the refrigerant is compressed and cooled until it condenses under pressure. The liquid refrigerant absorbs heat from the material to be refrigerated; it then vaporizes and returns to the compressor and condenser to be cycled in the same manner again.

Amer. Motors Corp.

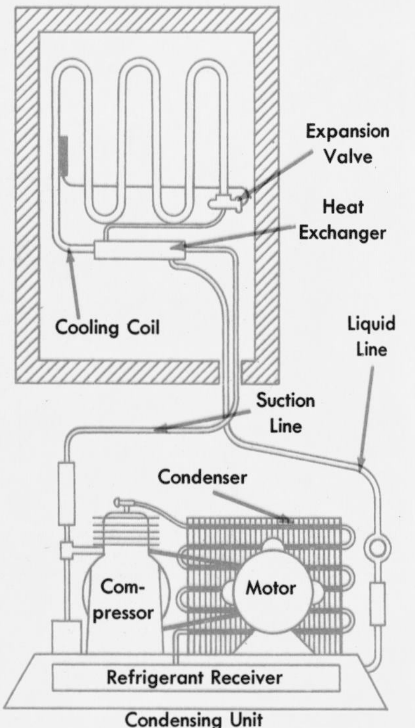

REFRIGERATOR, an insulated cabinet or room in which a temperature of about 40° F. is maintained for the removal of heat from objects placed therein and for keeping those objects from spoiling. Freezers are specialized types of refrigerators, in which the temperature is held at about −20° F. Ships, railroad cars, and trucks are also frequently built as refrigerators. The primary purpose of all of these kinds of refrigerators is to prevent, or at least to delay, decay and other biological changes in the goods stored. For example, most foods with a high water content, such as milk, lettuce, and strawberries, keep fresh for days and even weeks in a tight refrigerator; but there are a few foods, such as sweet potatoes and ripe bananas, that decay even more rapidly when they are placed inside a refrigerator.

Until 1920 most U.S. refrigerators were cooled by ice. The temperature of this type of refrigerator rarely got below 50° F., the maximum for safe storage. However, the ice refrigerators had the advantage that they did not dry out meats and vegetables to such an extent as the mechanical refrigerators do.

About 1920 the mechanical refrigerator started to supplant the icebox. The first mechanical refrigerators were merely converted iceboxes in which the evaporating unit was placed; the compressor and the motor were left outside on the floor. Within ten years this makeshift type was in turn supplanted by the self-contained mechanical refrigerator with the motor and compressor placed either on top of the cabinet or in the bottom with the heat-diffusion unit running up the back of the cabinet.

All refrigerators are "natural" in that they work in essentially the same way and according to the known laws of physics. Heat flows from the food or other warm objects to the cake of ice or Dry Ice (solid carbon dioxide) or to the very cold coils of the evaporator of the electrical powered machine. In absorbing heat the ice or Dry Ice melts into either water or harmless gaseous carbon dioxide and flows away. In electric refrigerators the cold liquid refrigerant (generally ammonia or a type of Freon) in the evaporator coils absorbs the heat, and the refrigerant returns to a gaseous state and flows back through tubes to the compressor, where its heat is expelled again into the air, and the cycle of refrigeration is resumed. SEE REFRIGERATION.

REFUGEE, a person forced to flee his nation because of war or for other reasons. To distinguish between the refugee and the immigrant is difficult. However, the refugee is often dependent upon the host country for support. If the refugee has a special skill, it is not unusual for a country to accept the individual refugee willingly. The refugee may make important contributions to the culture of the host country. Albert Einstein, who left Germany when the Nazi party came to power and entered the United States, is one famous example.

A greater problem than the individual refugee, however, is that of the great masses of refugees who are forced from their homes for one reason or another. Great movements of people have been common in all ages. German tribes sometimes fled to the Roman Empire, where they were given land along the frontiers. In the Middle Ages several hundred thousand Comans fled to Hungary after a terrible battle against the Mongols on the Volga River. The newcomers strengthened Hungary's armies, but they also plundered the peasants. Refugees often bring gifts of knowledge to the host country.

Religious refugees were common after the Reformation. Many colonists in America, such as the Pilgrims, may be called religious refugees. Protestant refugees were fortunate, for Protestant nations gladly accepted such people as the Huguenots. The Moors and Moriscos expelled from Spain with their meager belongings suffered far more, and most of them died in the Barbary States. Since the destruction of Jerusalem A.D. 70 by Rome, the Jews have been forced to flee as refugees from one nation after another.

Few periods have seen a greater refugee problem than that of World War II and after. Families carrying with them only what they could cram into carts, autos, or packs fled before the German armies. After the war Germany was filled with ten million German refugees from eastern Europe. At least eight million nationals of other countries had been released from the labor camps and concentration camps and had no place to go.

The immense job of resettling refugees was taken over in 1946 by the UN's International Refugee Organization (IRO). The most recent tasks of this organization have been the care of Arab refugees from former Palestine and the care of some 140,000 refugees from Hungary in 1956.

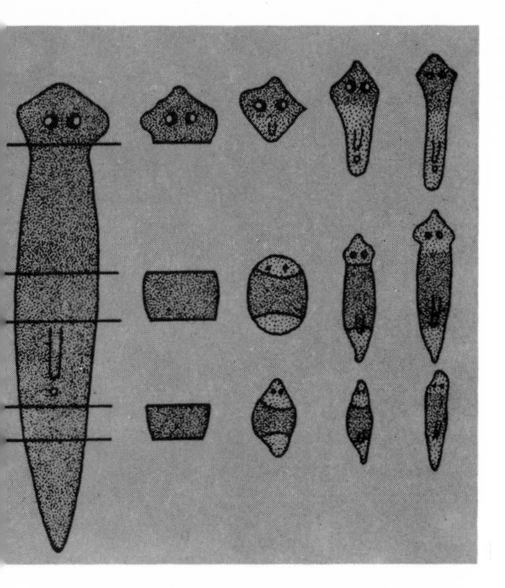

The head of a planarian, or flatworm, was severed from the body. Two short segments were also cut from the body. The head and each body segment were gradually regenerated into complete but smaller planarians.

REGENERATION, the capacity of animals to regrow body parts that have been amputated or to replace body tissues that have been injured. Although all animals are capable of regeneration, the simpler ones that are lower in the evolutionary order can accomplish it to a much greater extent than can the higher, more complex ones.

Regeneration occurs most extensively in certain invertebrates. If the body of a starfish is cut in half, each half will completely regenerate the amputated portion. If a single ray is cut from a certain species of starfish so that some of the central disc is included with it, this single ray will regenerate an entire body that cannot be distinguished from a normal starfish. Crabs and crayfish can regenerate an amputated leg or antenna. If an eye of a crab or a crayfish is removed, a leg is usually regenerated in its place. If a planarian (a member of a class of flatworms) is cut into many small fragments, each one will be regenerated into a complete but slightly smaller planarian. If a few segments are cut from the anterior and posterior ends of a common earthworm, the amputated portion of each end will be regenerated. In one experiment a sponge was cut into tiny pieces and then strained through a fine cloth. Soon afterward, these microscopic fragments combined into larger ones and developed into a complete, normal sponge of adult size.

Certain salamanders and lizards, which are vertebrates, can completely regenerate their long tails after they have been amputated. However, these animals cannot regenerate a new head or eye after its removal.

The regenerative capacity of mammals, the highest and most complex of vertebrates, is comparatively limited. Regeneration in mammals is restricted to the complete healing of small wounds, the partial healing of large ones, the regrowth of small areas of injured tissue in internal organs, and the regrowth of nails and hair.

The causes of regeneration are as yet unknown to biologists. They cannot explain, for instance, how the cells of the planarian, which have assumed specialized functions as members of a certain tissue or organ, can possess the power to regenerate the animal's entire body, which includes many tissues and organs with different specialized functions. Biologists assume that the causes of such regeneration are related to the physiological or chemical factors that cause the original growth of the animals during their embryological development.

REGINA, the capital of Saskatchewan, is situated in the heart of the Canadian wheat belt. Located in the southern part of the province, it is an important distributing point. Important petroleum deposits are in the region. The city has a population of about 100,000.

Leading industries include food processing, oil refining, and the manufacture of metal and lumber products. The legislative buildings and the Provincial Museum are of special interest.

Regina was founded in 1882 and became the capital of the Northwest Territories the following year. The headquarters of the old North West Mounted Police, now the Royal Canadian Mounted Police, are here. Regina was proclaimed the provincial capital in 1905.

REGULUS is one of the 20 brightest stars of our sky. It appears as a first-magnitude star in the constellation Leo, the Lion, and is also known by the formal name Alpha Leonis. See LEO.

Regulus is actually a system of three stars too close together to be distinguished separately without a telescope. They are located about 84 light-years from the sun. Two of the stars revolve around each other as a double star. These two revolve together around the third star. Their combined light is over 100 times greater than the light of our sun.

REIGN OF TERROR. See FRENCH REVOLUTION.

REINDEER, a domesticated caribou that in northern European countries is used to pull sleighs. Caribou are large deer, whose legs are relatively short. Both male and female caribou have large, branching antlers. Wild caribou, which live together in large, migratory herds, are native to arctic and subarctic regions of Scandinavia, Siberia, and North America.

Many centuries ago caribou were domesticated by the Laplanders of northern Scandinavia and Siberia. The domesticated descendants of these caribou are called reindeer. Reindeer, either singly or in teams ranging from two to ten, draw sleighs. In one day a single reindeer can pull a sleigh weighing 450 pounds a distance of 40 miles. In one day a team of several reindeer can pull a heavy sleigh a distance of 100 miles over the frozen snow. Laplanders eat reindeer meat, drink reindeer milk and also make cheese of it, and make parkas, trousers, and shoes from the hides.

Female reindeer are the only female deer to have antlers. Reindeer pull heavy sledges swiftly and sure-footedly over the snow and ice of the arctic tundra. The Laplanders could not survive without the reindeer. They depend upon it for most of their food and clothing and for their transportation.

Reindeer are usually manageable and easily trained. However, during mating season the stags fight each other fiercely with their antlers for supremacy over a harem of does. Sometimes human beings are killed by enraged stags during the mating season.

RELATIVE HUMIDITY. See HUMIDITY.

The theory of relativity predicts the bending of light in a gravitational field. During a solar eclipse, above, stars may be observed whose light has passed through the strong gravitational field near the sun. Compared with their usual positions, these stars appear to be displaced outward from the sun, indicating that their light has followed a curved path. The displacement is very nearly that predicted by Einstein.

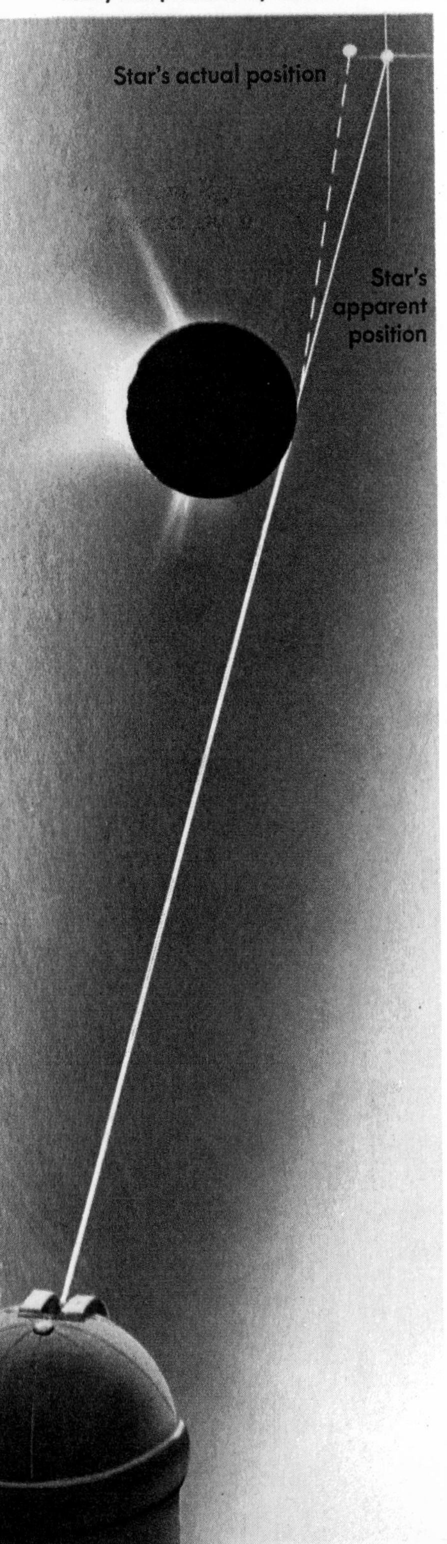

RELATIVITY, THEORY OF, a theory of physical reality, published in two parts by Albert Einstein—the special theory of relativity in 1905 and the general theory of relativity in 1916. (See EINSTEIN, ALBERT.) The theory set forth new and far-reaching conclusions about the general nature of space, time, motion, gravitation, inertia, mass, and energy and relations between them. It is accepted today as superseding the general laws of physics introduced by Isaac Newton, although for most practical purposes Newton's laws give sufficiently accurate results.

In the latter half of the 19th century scientists were puzzled as to how electromagnetic waves (including light waves) could be transmitted across apparently empty space, while water waves or sound waves required a substance of some kind for their transmission. One proposed explanation was that all space might be filled with a strange substance, called the ether of space, that had an infinitely low density and was absolutely at rest. Electromagnetic waves might then be transmitted by the ether.

The Michelson-Morley experiment attempted to measure the earth's absolute motion through this ether. It was expected that, if the earth were in motion in the ether, a light ray traveling forward into the ether and then back to its source would take a slightly different length of time to accomplish this distance than would a light ray traveling at right angles to the ether current across the same distance. Existing instruments were capable of detecting differences far smaller than would be produced even by the known velocity of the earth relative to the sun. The surprising result of the experiment was that the two light rays took exactly the same time. The velocity of light was apparently independent of the motion of its source. This being true, then it was impossible to detect absolute motion through space. Einstein accepted both of these conclusions as fundamental postulates of his theory of relativity.

The detailed steps in Einstein's reasoning are far too many and complex to present here. However, it is possible to describe some of his major conclusions about physical reality. As a general introduction, it can be said that the special theory of relativity considers physical systems moving at uniform velocity relative to each other and the effect of this motion upon the measurement of space and time. It also states a definition of mass that includes a component of velocity. The general theory of relativity considers physical systems moving at a changing velocity. It introduces an effect of matter on space and time, which constitutes a new theory of gravitation.

The special, or restricted, theory of relativity states that, if two physical systems are moving at constant velocity toward or away from each other, certain measurements made for events on one system are not equal to measurements of these events as observed from the other system. The particular measurements that differ are distances measured in the direction of motion, and time. Compared with measurements by the observer on the system where the events take place, the measurements by the distant, moving observer will show distance in the direction of motion as shorter and elapsed time as greater.

For example, imagine two space ships identical in size and shape, one painted black, the other white, both floating beside each other in space. Men on each ship find that their measurements of time and space are identical. Now the ships fire their rocket engines and move apart in exactly opposite directions, their lengths aligned in their direction of motion. After a certain time they establish a constant velocity of separation at, say, half the speed of light. A man on the black ship now moves from one end of his ship to the other, measuring the distance he moves and the time it takes him. According to the special theory of relativity, a man on the white ship will measure the distance and time of this movement differently. He will say that it was shorter in length and took a longer time. In effect, he will be saying that the black ship appears to have shrunk in length and that its clocks are keeping time more slowly. However, according to the theory, observers on the black ship will notice no change whatsoever on their own ship, and they will observe that the white ship appears to have shrunk in length and that its clocks are keeping slower time. Einstein stressed that no preference can be given to one observer's measurements over another's. The important point is that motion relative to an event affects observations of the event.

The restricted theory of relativity also introduces a definition of mass that relates it to velocity. It states that the mass of an object increases with an increase in velocity. One important assumption of the theory in this connection is that nothing can move at a velocity greater than that of light.

The special theory gives exact equations that connect the observations of one physical system with those of another moving relative to it. They are called the Lorentz transformations. The existence of so many different, possible observations of the same event raises the question of whether any physical measurement can be found that is the same for all observers, regardless of their relative motion. Einstein found that such a measure does exist—the square of the time measurement minus the square of the length measurement (in the direction of relative motion). This constant of nature he called separation. He found also that all objects moving through space and time at uniform velocity move in such a way that the separation measurement between events is at all times a maximum. Away from large masses such paths of maximum separation are what we call straight lines.

Perhaps the major burden of the general theory of relativity, which is really Einstein's theory of gravitation, is the statement that the nature of space and time near large masses differs in such a way that lines of maximum separation are not straight lines. According to the theory, paths of the planets around the sun, for instance, represent lines of maximum separation at their velocity in the distorted space-time near the sun.

The equations of Einstein's general theory have been found to describe and predict the behavior of physical bodies more accurately than those of Newton's theory of gravitation. Three experimental tests for the theory have borne it out. First, Einstein's equations account for a part of the planet Mercury's motion that was not explainable in terms of Newton's theory of gravitation.

A second test concerns the path of light in a gravitational field. Einstein predicted a bending of a light ray near the sun in excess of the amount predicted by Newton's theory. Observations that were made at times of total eclipse of the sun, when light rays passing very near the sun can be observed, agree with Einstein's prediction.

Another effect predicted by the general theory is the slowing of an atom's vibration near a large mass. The slower vibration would be evident in a slightly shifted spectral line of the light emitted by the atom. Such shifts have been observed in the case of stars of unusually great mass. The effect has also been verified on the earth by a highly refined method of measuring the difference in wavelength of gamma rays emitted and absorbed by atoms located merely yards apart, one higher than the other and consequently subject to slightly less gravitational effect.

RELIGION, those human beliefs that deal with the supernatural, or divine. Religion is the belief that beyond what men can see and observe is a power or powers that influence life on the earth. These beliefs are held by faith.

The dawning of the religious experience is similar to an esthetic experience, such as a person has when he gazes at a fine work of art. Perhaps religion began in prehistoric times, when primitive men were struck with awe at the spectacular workings of nature in thunderstorms or floods. They may have attributed the workings of the elements to some power or spirit that was greater than themselves and to which they addressed themselves with reverence and the invention of sacred rituals.

The religious experience is not confined to primitive men, however, for to modern men the recognition of a higher reality wells up from what is not disclosed to the ordinary senses. Men feel that their actions are not meaningless but that they are a significant part of an eternal order. The religious sense of ethics and of respect for others as morally awakened beings is joined with religious awe. This religious feeling of oneness with other people and of a relationship to an external power releases men from their feeling of utter isolation. The complete realization of religion is reached when people feel that all of life is the result of the spiritual power. Religions have intellectual as well

Representative local leaders in Western religions are the Jewish rabbi (left), Protestant minister (center), and Roman Catholic priest (right).
Harold J. Flecknoe—Monkmeyer Aigner—Monkmeyer T. Sheenan—Monkmeyer

as emotional content. Many people base their religious beliefs on reason. The scholasticism of the Middle Ages is one example of a balance between intellectual and emotional aspects of religion.

There are many points of view from which to study religion. In one respect religion cannot be studied objectively, for it is bound up with the inner life of men, which is difficult to communicate. Theology, through logic, seeks in some of its branches to study the religious experience of a particular group. Religion may be studied historically because it has expressed itself by customs, ideals, and institutions. We may even arrive at some idea of primitive religions by means of archaeology, ethnology, and comparative studies. The science of religions seeks to explain what is discovered by historical studies. It can deal only with religion from the human side. Psychology attempts to trace the origins of religious emotion. The philosophy of religion studies the basis for those beliefs revealed by the science of religion.

Historically, there have been many ways in which religions have coped with explaining the supreme power and its relation to man. Pantheism has considered the supreme power and the world as one. Monotheism and polytheism have considered one God or several gods to be above and outside the everyday world. Nature religions hold that the sacred resides in natural objects, such as trees, mountains, or rivers. Religions of revelation hold that knowledge of the supreme power has been given man through prophets, teachers, or sacred writings. Some religions are confined to particular peoples or tribes. The great universal religions, however, stress the oneness of all people with relation to the supreme being. The theory of an evolution of religion from animism through fetishism to primitive monotheism has not been proved.

It would be impossible to enumerate the contributions of religion to the culture of all nations or groups of people. Religion has had a profound effect in determining the most fundamental content of cultures. From religion, cultures have derived their ideas of individual worth and purpose, of the good life, and of the objectives of the whole society.

Religion has also made contributions to many specific areas of culture. Early astronomy owes much to religion, for the skies were first studied in order to set dates for religious festivals. The science of law developed from the priesthood, which constituted the first legal body. Religious zeal played a part in the expansion of the Arab peoples and in the Crusades. Man's ethical sense developed from the religious feeling. In literature the mythologies of peoples, the Greek tragedies, and the work of innumerable writers (Dante, John Donne, Goethe, Nathaniel Hawthorne, Leo Tolstoi, Rainer Maria Rilke, Gerard Manley Hopkins) have been inspired by religious belief. Religious art has enriched the culture of all societies. By way of example, Lorenzo Ghiberti, who helped to inspire the artistic Renaissance, considered the purpose of his art the illustration of religious truths. See GOD; RELIGIONS OF THE WORLD.

OCCUPATION: Clergyman

NATURE OF WORK: Serving the spiritual needs of others

PERSONAL FACTORS—ABILITIES, SKILLS, APTITUDES: The ability to speak and write clearly, emotional stability, high moral character, and the desire to serve others are essential. Good health is a valuable asset.

EDUCATION AND SPECIAL TRAINING: From three to eight years of theological training, depending upon the denomination, are required after high-school graduation. Advanced studies are helpful in all denominations.

WORKING CONDITIONS:

1. **INCOME:**
   COMPARED WITH OTHER CAREERS WITH EQUAL TRAINING: Low
   COMPARED WITH MOST OTHER CAREERS: Low
2. **ENVIRONMENT:** Varying, from place of worship to private homes, outdoors, congregation meetings, and so forth
3. **OTHER:** Possible irregular hours; excellent opportunities (women ministers in some denominations, nuns in some denominations)

RELATED CAREERS: Social worker, family and vocational counselor, psychologist

WHERE TO FIND MORE INFORMATION: Jewish Institute of Religion, 40 West 68th Street, New York, N.Y.; American Association of Theological Schools, 744 Jackson Place NW, Washington 6, D.C.; The National Catholic Welfare Conference, 1312 Massachusetts Avenue NW, Washington 6, D.C.

RELIGIONS OF THE WORLD. Religion is a belief in man's relationship to a supernatural power or powers. Even the most primitive groups in the world seem to have had a religion of one kind or another. For all people there seems to be an area of knowledge and experience that remains inaccessible to the scientific method of observation and statistics. Men attempt by religion to develop a relationship with the divine, perhaps by revelation or by philosophic deduction. Religion is certainly as old as man. The most ancient monuments, the Egyptian pyramids, and the megaliths, such

Christians form the largest single religious group but are outnumbered by non-Christians.

MAJOR WORLD RELIGIONS	ESTIMATED MEMBERSHIP (millions)	AREAS OF CONCENTRATION
Christian Religions	850	Western Europe, North and South America, Australia
Roman Catholic	525	Western Europe, South America
Eastern Orthodox	125	Eastern Europe, Near East
Protestant	200	Northern Europe, North America, Australia
Jewish	12	United States, Israel
Islamic	425	Africa, Indonesia, Pakistan, Near East
Hindu	325	India
Confucian	300	China, Korea
Buddhist	150	Southeastern Asia, Korea, Tibet, China, Japan
Taoist	50	China
Shinto	50	Japan

as Stonehenge in England, had a religious purpose.

There are some 12 major religions that are considered dead, for there is no longer a widespread belief in them. The once-living religions of ancient Egypt, Greece, Rome, Babylonia, and Scandinavia are now called mythologies. The religions of the Aztec and Inca are no longer adhered to. In the days of St. Augustine, Manichaeism vied with Christianity, but it is no longer a vital religion.

Eleven religions play a vital role in the present world and are considered living religions. All of them were born in Asia. The following list gives the names of these living religions, together with a date (very approximate in some cases) of their founding: Hinduism, about 1500 B.C.; Judaism, about 1500 to 1200 B.C.; Shinto, about 660 B.C.; Zoroastrianism, about 660 B.C.; Taoism, about 604 B.C.; Jainism, about 599 B.C.; Buddhism, about 560 B.C.; Confucianism, about 551 B.C.; Christianity, about 4 B.C.; Islam, A.D. 570; and Sikhism, 1469. Of these living religions six were originally theistic (stressed a belief in a deity or deities): Sikhism, Taoism, Judaism, Zoroastrianism, Christianity, and Islam. Jainism and Buddhism placed no stress on a deity, although the founders came to be worshiped. Hinduism, Confucianism, and Shinto began as nature worship. Christianity, Buddhism, and Islam are universal religions in the sense that they actively seek converts by extensive missionary efforts. The other living religions tend to be traditional. Shinto is found, for example, only in Japan; Hinduism is concentrated in India. The living religions have several points of contact: They all claim to possess a divine revelation of truths; all have sacred books, such as the Bible or the Taoist Canon of Reason and Virtue; and the golden rule is taught in all of them.

The major difference among the religions lies in what they teach about the relationship between man and a supreme being. Only Christianity, Judaism, Islam, and Sikhism have always been genuinely monotheistic. Although all the living religions teach some sort of existence after death, they are widely different in their interpretation of what sort of existence this might be. See ANCESTOR WORSHIP; BUDDHISM; CHRISTIANITY; CONFUCIANISM; HINDUISM; ISLAM; JAINISM; JUDAISM; RELIGION; SACRED BOOKS; SHINTO; TAOISM.

RELIGIOUS WARS, FRENCH, a series of eight civil wars between the Roman Catholics and the French Protestants, or Huguenots, lasting from 1560 to 1598. The Protestant leaders were the three Coligny brothers, Admiral Gaspard de Coligny, François de Coligny, and Odet de Coligny, allied with the Bourbon king of Navarre and his kinsman Henry I de Bourbon, prince of Condé. The chief Catholic leaders were François de Lorraine, duke of Guise (murdered 1563), and his sons, Henri I de Lorraine, duke of Guise; Charles de Lorraine, duke of Mayenne; and Louis II de Lorraine, cardinal of Guise.

The wars consisted of surprise attacks, sieges, and cruel massacres. Neither of the parties was strong enough to crush the other, and each one called in allies from outside France. At different times the royal power was exerted on one side or the other. Protestant power was strongest in the west, south, and southeast. Paris and the northeast were at all times firmly Catholic.

The first three wars were really one struggle interrupted by periods of truce. Treaties, which temporarily halted the fighting, were signed at Amboise (1563), Longjumeau (1568), and Saint-Germain-en-Laye (1570). Despite defeats at Dreux (1562), Jarnac (1569), and Moncontour (1569), the Huguenots gained an advantage. They were given freedom of worship and possession for two years of the strongholds of La Rochelle, Cognac, Montauban, and La Charité. Catholic resentment at this favor shown to the enemy resulted in the slaughter of thousands of Protestants on St. Bartholomew's Day (Aug. 24, 1572) in Paris and the provinces. Henry I de Bourbon, prince of Condé, and the king of Navarre both escaped death by temporarily renouncing Protestantism. The massacre led to the fourth war, which was highlighted by the successful defense of La Rochelle against the siege of Henry, brother of the king, Charles IX. The Edict of Boulogne (July 8, 1573) ended the war favorably for the Huguenots.

The fifth war (1573-1576) ended with conditions more favorable for the Protestants than any they had yet won. This Peace of Chastenoy (May 6, 1576) caused great dissatisfaction among the Catholics, who formed the Holy League for the complete destruction of Protestantism and the elevation of the Guises to the throne. The league worked in full harmony with the pope and with Philip II of Spain. The new king, Henry III, fearing the league, proclaimed himself its head and abolished the privileges previously granted to the Huguenots.

In the sixth war (1577) and the seventh war (1580) the king's forces and those of the league were again victorious, but easy terms were made with the Huguenots because the king was anxious to prevent the league from becoming too powerful. The death of François, duc d'Anjou, the younger brother of Henry III, in 1584, made Henry of Navarre the logical heir to the throne and drove the league into open opposition to the royal authority.

The eighth war, called the War of the Three Henrys (1585-1589), was a three-way conflict among Henry of Guise and the league, King Henry III, and Henry of Navarre. Against the orders of the king, the duke of Guise entered Paris, and the people rose and besieged the king in the Louvre palace and forced his flight to Blois. On Dec. 23, 1588, he invited the duke and his brother to visit him and had them both murdered. With this news a revolt of the Catholic party broke out, and the king fled to the camp of Navarre, where he was murdered at Saint-Cloud by a monk, Jacques Clément, on July 31, 1589. Henry of Navarre made good his claim to the throne, partly by arms and partly by renouncing his Protestant faith; and the religious wars came to an end with the issuance in 1598 of the Edict of Nantes, which gave the Huguenots equal political rights and granted freedom of religious practice to Huguenot nobles and to the citizens of certain towns.

REMBRANDT (1607-1669), in full Rembrandt Harmensz van Rijn, Dutch painter and engraver, born in Leiden. The son of a prosperous miller, Rembrandt began studying painting at the age of 12 with Van Swanenburch and later studied in Amsterdam, Holland, with Pieter Lastman. He settled permanently in Amsterdam in 1630 and soon became extremely popular as a portrait painter and as a teacher. In 1634 he married the wealthy Saskia van Uijlenburgh. After her death in 1642 he was made trustee of her fortune, which was to go to their son, Titus, if Rembrandt should remarry. He suffered financial reverses as a result of general economic conditions, made great expenditures in amassing a large collection of paintings, and underwent a general decline in the popularity of his paintings. In 1656 he was declared

European Art Color Slides

"The Night Watch," painted in 1642, is one of Rembrandt's most famous group portraits.

bankrupt. To satisfy his debtors his collection was seized and sold. After 1660 Rembrandt found employment in an art shop set up by his son Titus and by his housekeeper, Hendrickje Stoffels. Nevertheless, the artist's last years were spent in poverty and semiseclusion.

Today he is recognized as the greatest of the Dutch painters and also as one of the greatest of all etchers. Although perhaps best known for his many single portraits and group paintings, Rembrandt was a master of the still-life study and the landscape. He was especially noted for the humanity and characterization in the portraits, the use of light and shadow, and his great skill in modeling. In addition to the numerous portraits of himself (between 40 and 50) and of his immediate family, his paintings of contemporary subjects included "The Lesson in Anatomy," "Sortie of the Banning Cocq Company," "Syndics of the Cloth Hall," and "Girl at the Open Half-Door." Paintings of religious and mythological subjects include "The Repose of the Holy Family," "Presentation in the Temple," and "Danae." Etchings include "Tobias and the Angel," "Ecce Homo," "Descent from the Cross," and "Three Trees."

REMOTE-CONTROL SYSTEM, a system that includes the control from a distance of any mechanical operation. Remote control is used with various kinds of machinery and in industrial processes as a whole. The principal elements of a control system are a control mechanism and a final-control element. The control mechanism may be operated by a worker, such as in the remote control of a hydroelectric station from a central location. In this instance valves and circuits are opened or closed electrically. The control mechanism may also be automatic, in which case it receives signals for the measurement of some element in the process to be controlled, such as the temperature or pressure. The control mechanism then operates to correct any change from a predetermined value. Examples of such automatic controls are found in the chemical industry. The integration of automatic controls with computer systems is a part of the process of automation. See AUTOMATION.

RENAISSANCE, a French word meaning "rebirth," or "reawakening." When capitalized, the term generally refers to the period of great cultural activity that began in Italy in the 14th century and spread northward during the two following centuries. In a more restricted sense the term *Renaissance* applies only to the general European movement, while the purely Italian movement of the 14th and 15th centuries is classified as the *Rinascita* (Rebirth).

All periods in history are transitional, but in some—such as the Renaissance—the rate and quality of transition has a more profound effect than in others. The thousand years of the Middle Ages was an era of great but slow and painful accomplishment, beside which the activity of the 15th century was like a sudden explosion. Yet the distinction between the Middle Ages and the Renaissance was neither sudden nor absolute. Men were still religious, at times naively so, and alongside every modern element in their characters existed a medieval one. But the quality of worldliness was gaining strength. Man had a new consciousness of himself as an individual. He considered immortal fame on earth worthier of pursuit than immortal life in eternity, and he regarded with contempt the sort of hypothetical theological questions advanced by the narrow and arid thought of the late Middle Ages. Such secularism was indicative of the entire Renaissance outlook.

The great wealth that poured into northern Italy as a result of the revival of commerce created a *bourgeoisie* independent of the feudal nobility and made possible a rich and varied communal life. Numerous cities came into existence, and those of Florence, Milan, and Venice became hubs not only of commerce and culture but also of political power, for the temporary collapse of the Holy Roman Empire and the absence of the papacy from Italy during the Babylonian Captivity (1305-1378) of the church enabled them to free themselves from external control, even though such freedom only meant quarreling among themselves. The medieval ideal of unity, peace, and status did not die, but the reality of endemic war, divided authority, and a scramble for wealth and position, which had existed for so long, now became generally recognized. Status by birth, which had been of such importance during the preceding era, was still important, but wealth and political power often meant more, and where these were missing great artistic or literary ability would suffice to gain a man more fame and social position than piety and force of arms ever did.

Not even the church escaped the secular spirit. Many high ecclesiatics, including such popes as Clement VII (1378-1394), Alexander VI (1492-1503), Julius II (1503-1513), and Paul III (1534-1549), in their desire for wealth and power, often forgot Christian ideals and not infrequently succumbed to pagan vices. Human failures of this sort heightened the skepticism produced among the intellectuals of the period by the revived interest in classical Latin and Greek. Medieval texts, including the Vulgate, were subjected to scrutiny, and humanists like Boccaccio and Rabelais frequently satirized the lack of faithfulness of certain clerics to their vows of chastity, while the great Dutch scholar and cleric Erasmus, although never opposed to the authority of the church or of the pope, used his *Praise of Folly* to ridicule many ecclesiastical practices and the great credulity and ignorance of many of the clergy.

All of these criticisms indicate the degree to which the prestige of the church suffered, but one of the strongest criticisms directed against Rome was the attack upon its temporal authority. For centuries the papacy had exercised direct political control over the city of Rome and the area around it, basing its right to such power upon the *Donation of Constantine*, a document supposedly presented by the Roman emperor Constantine I to Pope Sylvester I, granting the latter the government of the territory. Lorenzo Valla, an Italian humanist, contended that the document was a forgery, pointing out the anachronisms in it and thus undermining the church's principal legal claim to secular power.

The humanist, despite his attacks on the inequalities arising from the prerogatives of birth, always argued in favor of the prerogatives of *virtù*, an Italian word meaning "a combination of talent and intellect," and advocated—as Thomas Jefferson and James Fenimore Cooper later did—the rule of a nation by a natural aristocracy.

Nor were the people of the Renaissance overly interested in natural science or respectful of authority. Only a few of them, such as Leonardo da Vinci, concerned themselves with experimental science, for the great emphasis on classical antiquity generally served to convince the humanist that most of what was valuable to know could be learned from books, from ancient Greek and Latin manuscripts, or from commentaries on them. Only in removing some of the stigma of original sin, without embracing the 18th-century theory of the natural goodness of man, and in reviving the works of such ancient scientific writers as Hippocrates and Galen did the humanist spirit make any real contribution to the scientific revolution initiated by Copernicus, Sir Francis Bacon, and Galileo.

Yet Renaissance education was by no means devoid of originality or of contributions to the main stream of Western thought. As a result of the new emphasis on the active life—as opposed to the purely contemplative one—and a new optimism about human nature, men came to view the ideal education in terms of the classical rule of proportion in harmonizing the claims of the heart, the head, and the body. This was the ideal stated by Baldassare Castiglione in *The Courtier*, and this was the aim of such academies as that maintained at Florence by the Neoplatonist philosopher Marsilio Ficino, where music, gymnastics, oratory, the ethical concept of *virtù*, Latin, Greek, and dancing were taught. Perhaps the most perfect example of the ideal Renaissance man was Da Vinci, philosopher, painter, musician, sculptor, architect, engineer, and inventor, but Henry VIII—with all his excesses—was a more typical one, being an excellent horseman, an able wrestler, a patron of the arts, an astute politician, a capable administrator, and a champion of the Catholic faith, although not of papal supremacy.

Just as Henry VIII often lacked the degree of moderation so important to men like Castiglione and Erasmus, so did the whole Renaissance. Not only was the period confronted with the frustrations accruing from the conflict between the new spirit of secularism and the old spirit of otherworldliness but also from a conflict between the ideal of simplicity and a tendency to exuberance. But this was understandable in an age where tradition and custom were rapidly crumbling and where men's horizons were being constantly broadened by astounding geographical explorations—such as Columbus' discovery of America and Magellan's expedition resulting in the circumnavigation of the globe—and the formulation of startlingly new scientific theories—such as Copernicus' contention that the sun and not the earth was the center of the universe.

Perhaps the most obvious example of this conflict between moderation and excess is found in the architecture of the period. But architecture was not the sole example of this struggle. Critical scholarship, which was one of the humanists' greatest contributions to Western thought, began as a reaction against the excessive barrenness of scholasticism and the extreme conservatism of the universities, only to become as doctorally pedantic as scholarship ever got to be. Also Renaissance literature, which was closely related to humanist scholarship, partook of the conflict. Some writers, such as William Shakespeare, although exuberant humanists, were sufficient masters of their craft to employ great opulence of language without succumbing to affected elegance. But many other

This decorative gold and enamel cup is the work of the 16th-century Florentine goldsmith Benvenuto Cellini, who made many such items for wealthy Renaissance princes.

Metropolitan Museum of Art, Bequest of Benjamin Altman, 1913

writers were less fortunate, and during the late 17th century various literary movements, taking some of their inspiration from such Latin satirists as the 1st-century Martial, wrote in a style that was excessively ornamented and precious.

Nor was moderation the guiding principle of Renaissance politics. Despite the admonitions of such tender-minded Neoplatonists as Ficino and Castiglione, the Renaissance was the time of despots, exemplified by Ferdinand II of Aragon, who was the husband of Isabella I, and Cesare Borgia. But the political writers were reluctant to face the realities of the situation. Not before Machiavelli did anyone take a historical and sociological approach to politics, amplifying and interpreting conclusions by observing the realities of the day. Machiavelli did so, and the result was *The Prince*, which was a realistic—if somewhat cynical—guide to the game of politics. The immediate hope of the book was to inspire some prince who, like Borgia, possessed sufficient intelligence and ruthlessness to unify Italy, to end the petty bickerings of the city-states, and to present a united front against the rising powers of Spain and France. But Italy was not ready for unity; mutual suspicion ran too high among the petty states. The situation was further aggravated by the fact that, since citizenship was denied many of the people living in the countryside, the defense of the city-states was in the hands of hired troops, who, in order to keep their jobs, sought to perpetuate the political chaos. Poorly trained and equipped and given to plundering both friend and foe, they were decidedly more of a menace to the Italian states than to any invading power. Yet the five major states of Italy—Venice, Florence, Milan, the Papal States, and the Kingdom of Naples, all of which were decidedly imperialistic toward each other—continued to intrigue. In 1492 Florence and Naples forced a secret alliance for the spoliation of Milan, which led Lodovico Sforza, the duke of Milan, to appeal to Charles VIII of France for help. In 1494 the French invaded Italy, and within a few months they were in control of the peninsula. But their success led Milan, Venice, the Holy Roman Empire, Pope Alexander VI, and Ferdinand of Aragon to join against them. Thus was opened the international struggle for Italy, which at first occupied Spain and France and afterward France and Austria. Only at the end of the 19th century did Italy become independent and united.

For over a century Italy had been the focal point of Western culture, the envy of all other Europeans. But the French invasion of the peninsula and the discovery of America marked the beginning of the decline of the Renaissance in Italy. The great centers of banking and trade were transferred to northern Europe and to the Atlantic seacoast, and the rise of the national states of France, Spain, Portugal, and England dominated the political scene. However, the period between Columbus' first discovery and the beginning of the Reformation in 1517 may be considered a period of great accomplishment in the history of the whole European Renaissance. The general increase in wealth and a greater firsthand knowledge of the culture of Italy contributed to the rapid propagation of humanistic ideals throughout Western Europe.

RENAISSANCE ART, properly speaking, is the art of Italy from about the 15th to the 17th century, a period that witnessed vigorous and productive bursts of activity in sculpture, architecture, and painting. In the Western world only the art of classical Greece rivals that of the Italian Renaissance, and nothing of equal beauty and excellence has appeared since. As Italy was the birthplace of the Renaissance, so it was here that the arts first reached their maturity, then lapsed into mannerism, and finally gave way to the grand, sweeping movements of baroque art. From Florence, to Rome, to the north of Europe, the vital impulses spread, and in the meantime other Italian city-states continued to develop their own individual styles. See RENAISSANCE.

On the Continent, particularly in Germany, the spirit of the Renaissance was closely bound up with the Reformation. (See REFORMATION.) But in the visual arts the important European painters and sculptors could not help feeling drawn to the compelling and expressive works of the Italians. Dürer traveled extensively in Italy, and through him Holbein and Cranach felt the new liberalizing influence from the south. The Flemish painters Brueghel and Rubens, somewhat later, also spent time in Italy. Italian artists worked in the court of Francis I. A number of the French medieval chateaux along the Loire River were decorated with Renaissance motifs. England's shining art in the Renaissance was literature, but in its Jacobean and Palladian architecture borrowing from Italian originals is evident.

The rebirth men think of as the Renaissance began with a rebirth of reason and of the pagan ideal *humanitas*. Briefly, this includes the graces and refinements of an educated, well-bred man. Since the Italian peninsula had been the homeland of the Roman Empire, it is no wonder it was in Italy that the classical pagan ideals were first revived. But the Renaissance man also had a legacy from the Middle Ages—his church and Christian faith. For the most part the awakening critical intelligence did not threaten religious beliefs, although it may well have made the prevailing attitude more secular. More important than this was the weakening of the medieval sense of mystery and irrational depths in the universe, for the Renaissance mind was as robust and affirmative as it was restless and inquiring. The world, life, the arts, man himself were subjected to rational scrutiny. See MEDIEVAL ART AND ARCHITECTURE.

Early in the 14th century the painter Giotto had foreshadowed the new conception of painting. He broke away from the decorative surfaces and symbolic figures of Byzantine art and began to paint bodies with mass and to arrange figures with definite spatial relations to each other. This was an important concession to visual appearance. Yet before the Renaissance painters of Florence took up their brushes where Giotto had left off, the sculptor Donatello had already carved a very fine marble statue of St. George. It showed his familiarity with classical forms and his grasp of the current scientific writings on the anatomy of the body. He studied the proportions of its parts, their volumes, and the surface textures of bone, joint, and muscle. He and Ghiberti revived the technique of bronze casting. They and their contemporaries Verrocchio and Pollaiuolo brought back the life-size nude in sculpture. They made the posture of a figure, its facial features, even its drapery show character. Although the ideal physical type tended to be slender, with graceful contours, the range of expression embraced such extremes as Verrocchio's plump, smiling cherubs and Pollaiuolo's violently twisted figures of Hercules and Antaeus. Beside the elongated and rigidly stylized figures of medieval sculpture, those of the Renaissance show much more variety in character types, emotion is more visible, and the body more realistically rendered. From a technical point of view, the Renaissance sculptor was interested in the structure of the figure; hence he was confronted with the problems of organizing volumes in space to make form three-dimensional. Michelangelo handles these problems with special reference to movement. Sometimes he combines movements of striking contrast. The Virgin in his *Pietà*, for example, sits upright; her expression is serene, but her grasp on Christ's shoulder is realistically firm. His body, stretched over her lap, is limp and twisting; his head hangs back over her arm. The later sculpture of Michelangelo shows intense energy and movement. Again and again he puts the human body in positions showing physical activity or unrest.

The Florentine architect Brunelleschi, like Donatello, had explored the ruins of Rome, but being an architect, he focused his attention upon ground plans, columns, cornices, and ornamental motifs. In his design for the *duomo*, or cathedral, of Florence he combined the basilica floor plan with a domed roof. Although the combination was daring, the structures themselves were certainly familiar to the ancient Romans. Other churches in northern Italy kept the more typical classical balance of vertical and horizontal masses. Arch and lintel systems were used together; classical columns decorated the interiors; round arches stretched over doorways and windows. Classical features were even more evident in the total design and ornamentation of secular Renaissance buildings.

The principal architects of the High Renaissance, Bramante and Michelangelo, worked at the papal court as well as for the nobles of Rome. Their designs for St. Peter's (which were never carried out in

This is Leonardo da Vinci's "Adoration of the Magi," the artist's first important commission and one that he never completed.

Uffizi, Florence (Scala)

Isabella Stewart Gardner Museum, Boston

The Florentine profile portrait above, "A Young Lady of Fashion," is believed to be the work of the 15th-century painter Paolo Uccello.

full) provided for a central dome over a Greek-cross ground plan, rather than the basilica plan of Brunelleschi's *duomo*. This was a deliberate attempt to create interior space and at the same time to display a powerful and impressive external symbol. As one might expect from these grandiose conceptions of architecture, the churches and palaces of the High Renaissance are massive, spacious, and rich in decoration. In parts of northern Italy, however, the academic style of Palladio prevailed.

To return again to the early Renaissance, while Donatello and Brunelleschi were unearthing antique ruins, the painter Masaccio was studying perspective and the anatomy of the body. He was the first of the Renaissance painters to develop the visual, tactile aspect of forms and objects that Giotto had begun a century earlier. Masaccio's figures have solid flesh; their proportions correspond to those of the actual human body. He subtly contrasts light and shadow to make outlines definite and to emphasize volume and mass. Through the use of perspective, Masaccio gives his figures definite position in space. Their feet touch the ground. One man really appears to stand behind another instead of merely being glued to the flat canvas surface. The backgrounds recede into deep space, so that trees, rocks, and hills seem to be far away. (See PERSPECTIVE.) When comparing Masaccio and some of his contemporaries—Castagno, Uccello, Piero della Francesca, Pollaiuolo—with the Gothic painters of the Middle Ages, one is immediately struck by the essential unity of early Renaissance canvases. All the parts are grasped at the same time, whereas in medieval paintings the parts seem to unfold one at a time: first Madonna, then Child, then surrounding objects. Sometimes details attract too much attention. But Renaissance painters carefully subordinated less important elements to the dominating ones, and their compositions are meant to please the eye, figures are placed in harmonious groups, and even scenes showing energetic activity have been balanced by strong countermovements.

What is more, the people in Renaissance canvases have flesh and blood. The Virgin Mary is a real woman. Her face reflects her temperament, and her arms hold Christ as a mother would hold a real child. The Christ child is no longer the wizened, undersized old man of Gothic painting but is an infant with round limbs and soft flesh. As in sculpture, the features typical of Florentine figures, especially women, are delicate and narrow.

Florentine painters of the High Renaissance—Da Vinci, Michelangelo, Raphael, Andrea del Sarto—worked on a larger scale. Their canvases are filled with groups of figures, and the figures themselves are imposing. In the hands of Michelangelo bodily anatomy becomes more detailed: Muscles ripple under the flesh; bent arms and legs have noticeable joints; hair is tousled, flowing, or windswept in accordance with bodily movement. As he matures, movement in Michelangelo's canvases becomes more sweeping and dynamic, ultimately to the point of asymmetry and harshness.

The work of the Venetian painters Il Giorgione and Titian shows a love of rich textures and colors. Their portraits, classical scenes, and landscapes are bathed in golden light, so that colors seem to melt into the very canvas. By the end of the Renaissance, Tintoretto and Correggio have become absorbed in dramatic contrasts and heightened emotional effects. From them, as from Michelangelo, Da Vinci, and others, the baroque painters of the next generation took their cue.

RENOIR, PIERRE AUGUSTE (1840-1919), was born in the French city of Limoges, the son of a tailor. He began his artistic life as an apprentice, but in 1862 he enrolled at the Atelier Gleyre as a student. Although his work of this period shows the influence of Courbet, Renoir's meeting the painters Claude Monet and Alfred Sisley was highly significant, for it was these painters who formed the nucleus of the group later called the impressionists.

Renoir fought in the Franco-Prussian War of 1870, and after the war he exhibited in the famous exhibition of 1874. With other painters, he was bitterly attacked for his work in this exhibit. In the years following, Renoir produced some of his most striking work, such as "The Swing" and his portrait "The Henriot Family."

On a visit to Italy when he was 40 years old, Renoir made a study of the classical masters, especially the frescoes of Raphael. Under this influence Renoir entered a new and fruitful period, called by some "Ingresque" but by Renoir himself the "harsh manner." In his paintings of this period a new discipline is evident, seen in such works as "Les Grandes Baigneuses" and "The Braid."

In his last period Renoir displayed a boldness in color, line, and choice of themes that astonishes. In these works, mostly nudes, and in the sculpture of this period he demonstrated an intense interest in creating works that were spontaneous and natural. He was disabled physically in the first decade of the 20th century and completed his masterpieces of sculpture with the aid of the sculptor Richard Guino. His "Venus" and "Washerwoman" date from this period.

Renoir painted many of his intimate friends—below, "Mme. Charpentier and Her Children."
Courtesy of The Metropolitan Museum of Art, Wolfe Fund, 1907

RENT, the price paid for the services of any factor whose supply is fixed for the period under consideration. When the factor is land as such, its price is rent. For other resources whose supply is fixed in the short run, the price is called quasi-rent. Many economists treat rent in a much more restricted sense, considering it to be the income from land after all the costs have been paid. Rent is a handy indication of the uses to which land should be put. For example, a farmer would be foolish to grow wheat on a small plot of land near a city, for he would not be able to pay the entire cost of the land he uses. If he grows vegetables, however, he may be able to make a profit.

The owner of such a rentable possession as a house must decide how much rent he will charge for its use. He figures out about how long the house will last; how much he must expect to pay on repairs, taxes, and insurance; and how much he originally invested. From these figures the owner will arrive at a periodical rent that will allow him to recover his original investment and earn an adequate return on that investment. This rent will include the rent return from the ownership of the land as well as the return from the use of his capital invested in the house.

The person renting goods must decide whether his use of the goods warrants purchasing them or whether it would be best to rent them from the owner. Since he will have to make periodic payments for goods such as an apartment, he must reach his decision on the basis of his future needs and earnings and the alternative uses of his money.

Like prices, rents change according to time and place. A location may become more desirable because a school has been built nearby, and the rents of new houses in the area may rise. The construction of a railroad may make markets more readily available to a farm community, with the result that the rents of farmland may increase. If many people desire to move out of cities and into suburbs, the rents in the center of the city may decrease. See LOAN AND INTEREST; PRICE.

REPRODUCTION, a vital process by which an animal or a plant of a particular species produces offspring like itself. All animals and plants are capable of reproduction. Reproduction in both the animal and the plant kingdom is accomplished either sexually or asexually. Sexual reproduction, which occurs principally in higher animals and plants, differs fundamentally from asexual reproduction, which occurs principally in more primitive animals and plants.

In sexual reproduction a male germ cell, called a sperm, unites with, or fertilizes, a female germ cell, called an egg. The fertilized egg, or zygote, then develops into an adult animal or plant by means of cell division and cell differentiation. The sperms and eggs of most animals and plants cannot by themselves develop into new organisms.

Asexual reproduction is not accomplished by the union of male and female germ cells. Unicellular animals and plants reproduce asexually by the division of their single cell into two halves, each of which then develops to adult size. In the asexual reproduction of multicellular animals and plants a small portion of the organism separates from it and then develops into a complete adult organism.

The details of the various types of sexual and asexual reproduction in various types of animals and plants are discussed in other entries. See ANIMAL; EGG CELL; FERTILIZATION; FISSION; PLANT; POLLEN AND POLLINATION; SPORE.

REPTILE, one of several types of air-breathing, principally terrestrial, usually scaly vertebrates that occupy a position on the evolutionary scale above that of amphibians and below that of birds and mammals. Present-day reptiles comprise five groups: the turtles and tortoises; the New Zealand tuatara; the lizards; the snakes; and the crocodiles and alligators.

The first reptiles to appear on earth evolved from the amphibians about 225 million years ago. The fossilized skeletons of these reptiles have many characteristics that are distinctly amphibian as well as many others that are distinctly reptilian. Zoologists think that reptiles of this group, as for example *Seymouria*, were the first animals to become adapted anatomically and physiologically for living all their life on dry land. Reptiles like *Seymouria* were ancestors of modern reptiles.

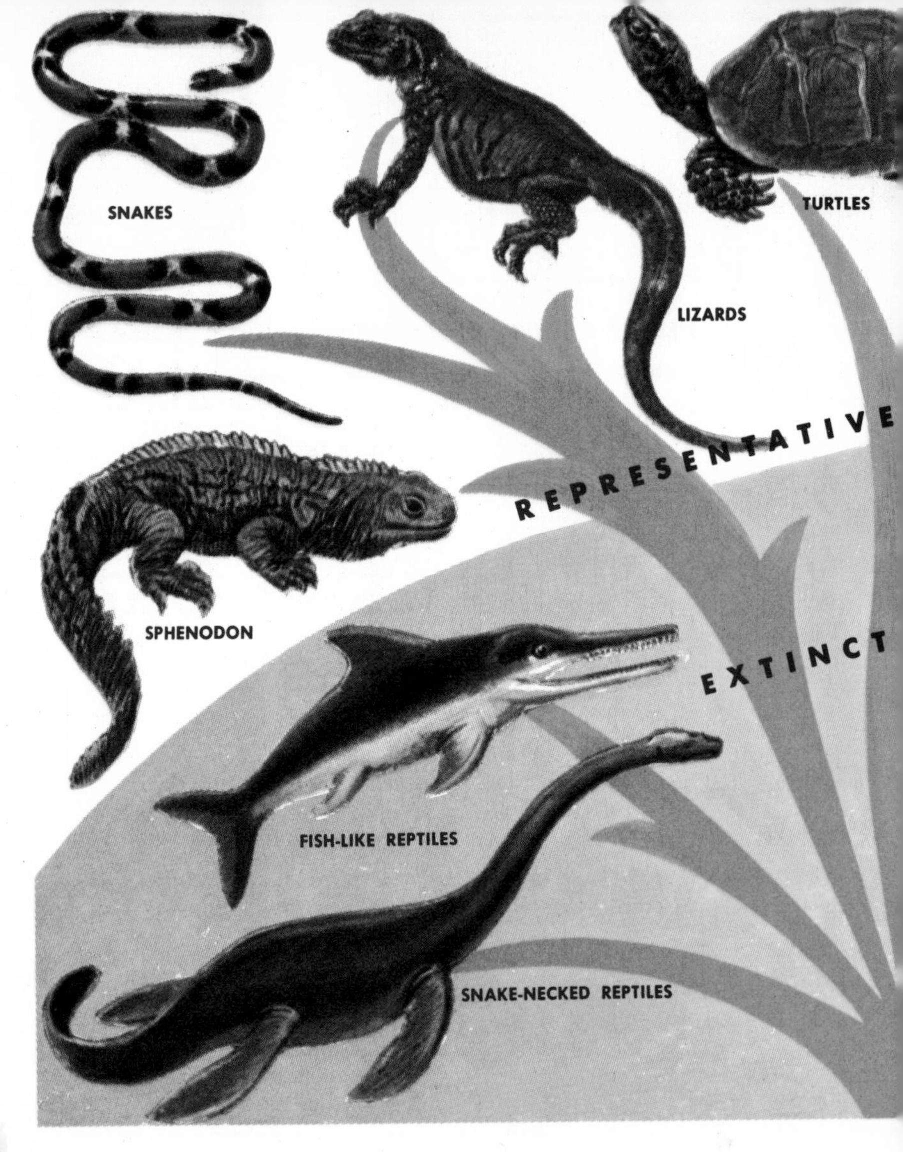

Representatives of several different reptilian types, both living and extinct, are shown in this diagram. Certain extinct aquatic reptiles had fishlike fins and inhabited the oceans.

Alligator eggs are laid in a large nest built of weeds and sticks. Baby alligators hatch from the eggs (below) by cutting the shell with the temporary egg tooth.

Crocodile

Crocodiles and alligators have a long, broad body, a long, laterally compressed tail, and a large head with long, strong jaws that open widely. The short limbs extend sideways and terminate in clawed, webbed toes.

The turtle's shell consists of sutured platelike bones covered by large cornified scales.

Another extinct reptile, the ancestor of the birds, had wings and could fly. The extinct dinosaurs dominated some regions of the earth many millions of years ago.

Lizards inhabit fields, forests, swamps, caves, and deserts; some lizards live in trees.

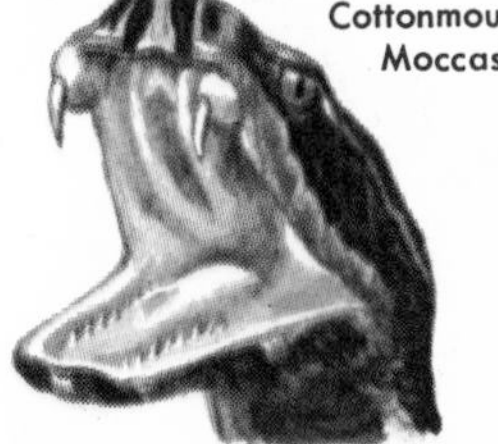

Lizard Eggs

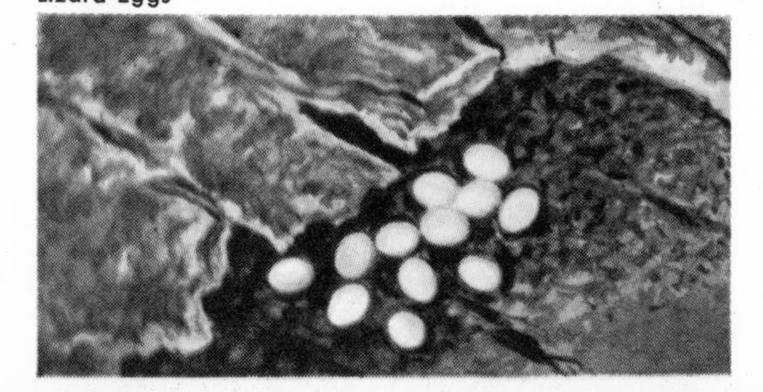

Snakes lost their limbs during the course of their evolution from lizard-like ancestors. The ears of snakes have no external opening. The eyelids are immovable. The tongue is long and forked and serves as an organ of touch. The poison fangs of venomous snakes are modified teeth. While growing, snakes molt their skin at least once a year.

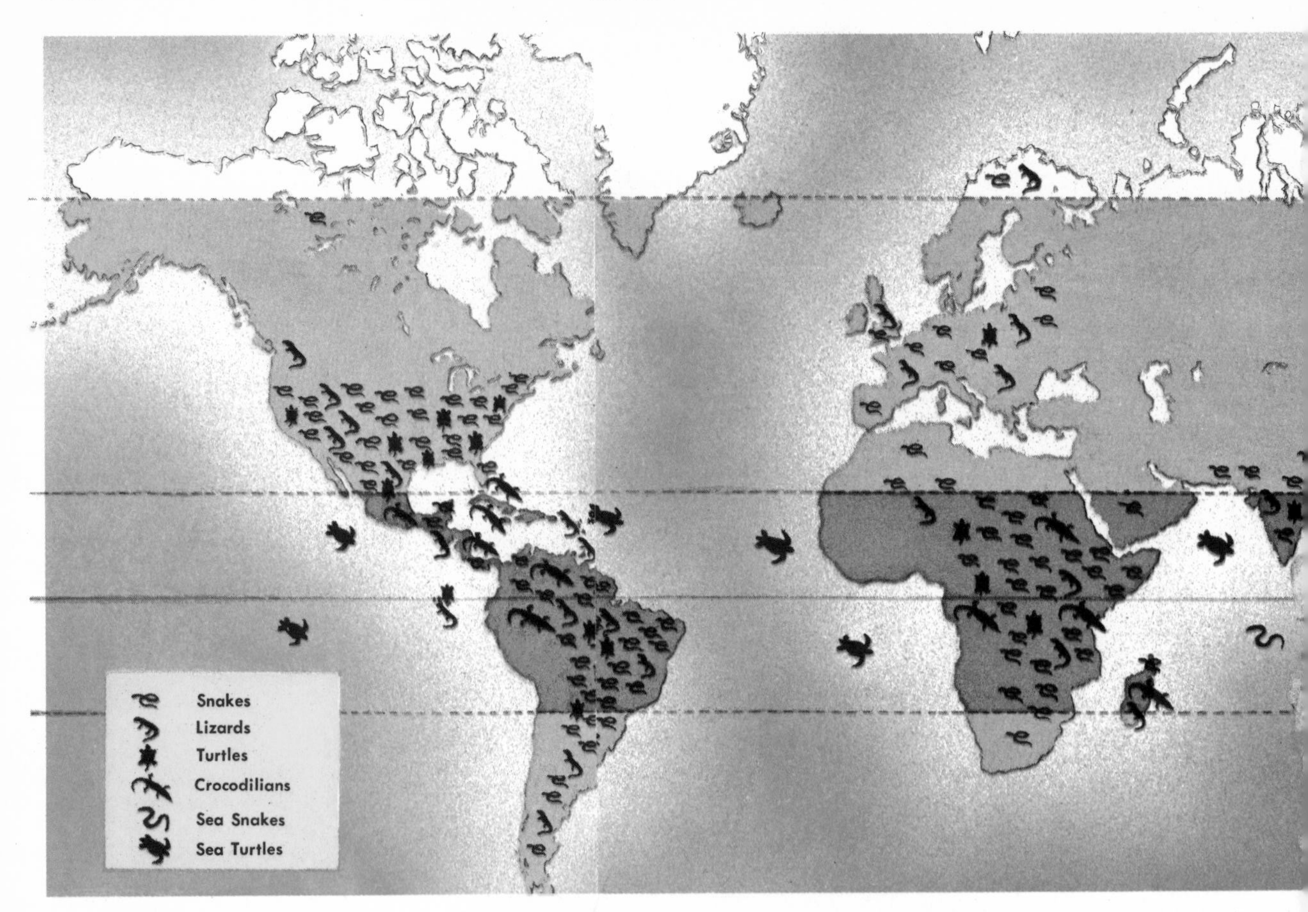

This map shows the worldwide distribution of present-day reptiles. They are more abundant in tropical and subtropical regions than in temperate ones. Relatively few reptiles are found in the northern parts of the North Temperate Zone or in the Arctic Regions.

Reptiles are above amphibians on the evolutionary scale. Reptiles during their development do not pass through a larval stage as amphibians do. Newly hatched larval amphibians usually have fish-shaped bodies with gills and live and breathe under water. Newly hatched reptiles are shaped like adult ones, and they breathe air through lungs and can live on dry land. Although some reptiles do live in water, they always breathe air through lungs.

However, reptiles are beneath birds and mammals on the evolutionary scale. Reptiles are not always warmblooded, as birds and mammals are. The heart, skeleton, and appendages of reptiles are more primitive and less efficient than those of birds and mammals. The overall anatomy, physiology, and behavior of reptiles are much more primitive and limited than those of birds or mammals.

The three principal groups of modern reptiles differ considerably from each other. The lizards and snakes have long, narrow, rounded bodies, whose thick, dry skin is covered with continuous scales. In general, they either creep on four short limbs or are limbless and move by wriggling their bodies along, in, or under the earth. The turtles and tortoises, which are both aquatic and terrestrial, have an extremely hard, thick, protective shell on the back and belly. They can withdraw the head, neck, and tail under the shell for protection. The crocodiles and alligators, which look like big lizards, are the largest of living reptiles. They are related to the dinosaurs of old. Although they spend most of their lives in the water of tropical rivers and swamps, they have short, clumsy legs for crawling on land. They have huge mouths and stout, conelike teeth that help to overpower their prey.

Each of these reptilian types is highly specialized for a limited way of life. Although modern reptiles constitute a small, unimportant minority in the animal kingdom, their ancestors of about 200 million years ago were the gigantic dinosaurs that dominated all other living creatures in their prehistoric world.

REPUBLIC, a state in which the head of the government is elected. Theoretically, all things of interest to the people are decided upon by the people in a republic. But in the ancient republics of Greece and Rome these decisions were made by the citizens; slaves did not vote.

The word *republic* is frequently misused. In the Middle Ages governments were often referred to as republics, when in reality they were hereditary monarchies. Even Jean Bodin, a French political economist of the 16th century, used the word to refer to a government under an absolute king. Napoleon also misused the word, although probably to some purpose. The coins of France during Napoleon's time bore the inscription, "French Republic, Emperor Napoleon."

However, republics have existed since the fall of Rome. Venice was a republic until the closing of the great council restricted voting privileges to the aristocracy. The republicans of Florence carried on a long but futile battle against the Medici family. At the time of Philip II the

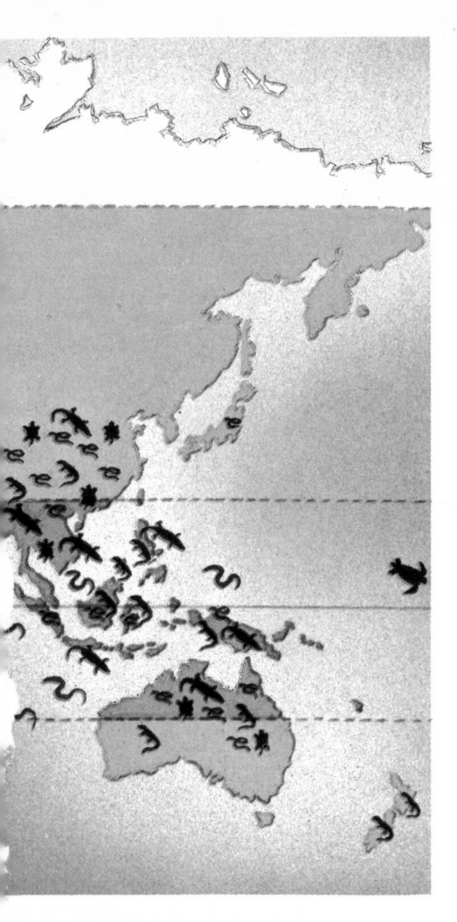

seven states of the confederation of the United Netherlands were republics. However, belief in the political rights of men was not strong until the Declaration of Independence in 1776 and the French Revolution of 1789. Thereafter, republican ideas of democracy replaced the old monarchical traditions. The 19th century was the era of battle between republicanism and monarchy. Republicanism won. After World War I, however, the problem was not whether democracy should be instituted in a nation, but in what form it should be instituted. Mussolini's Fascist government in Italy came into power in the beginning in the guise of a republic. See DEMOCRACY.

REPUBLICAN PARTY, one of the two major political parties of the United States. Prior to the formation of the Republican party, the two major parties in the United States were the Democrats and the Whigs. The immediate cause for the new party was the Kansas-Nebraska bill, which came under debate in Congress in 1854. The bill would have opened to slavery territories that had for over three decades been free because of the Missouri Compromise. The first meeting of a group to discuss a new party took place in a small frame building on the Ripon College campus in Wisconsin. The meeting was organized by Alvan E. Bovay, a young friend of Horace Greeley. It was attended by Conscience Whigs, Abolitionists, Anti-Nebraska Democrats, and Free-Soilers. The day after the Kansas-Nebraska bill passed the House of Representatives (May 8, 1854), a group of congressmen, mainly Conscience Whigs, agreed upon a new party to be called the Republican party. On July 6, 1854, the Republican party was launched at Jackson, Mich., and was an immediate success. It displaced the Whig party and almost split the Democrats in the North.

The first national convention of the Republican party took place in Philadelphia on June 17, 1856. John C. Frémont was nominated for the presidency on the first ballot. Abraham Lincoln lost the nomination for the vice presidency to William L. Dayton. Frémont was defeated in the election of 1856 by the Democrat James Buchanan. However, he ran well ahead of the Know-Nothing candidate, Millard Fillmore.

The Republican national convention at Chicago in 1860 nominated Abraham Lincoln for president, and Hannibal Hamlin for vice president. The campaign was bitter. However, Lincoln won a majority of the electoral vote against the candidates of three major parties, the strongest of whom was the Democrat Stephen Douglas. The policy of commercial advancement, Hamiltonian principles of government, "sound money," a protective tariff, and a homestead land policy for the West composed the Republican party's platform. The party was strongest among Northern industrialists and Western agriculturalists. The Republicans enjoyed one election victory after another. Ulysses S. Grant, Rutherford B. Hayes, James A. Garfield, Benjamin Harrison, and William McKinley were Republican presidential victors. Only the campaigns against Democrat Grover Cleveland in 1884 and 1892 were lost, the first largely because an important group of Republicans—the Mugwumps, who opposed corruption in government—refused to support the Republican candidate, James G. Blaine. When Theodore Roosevelt became president in 1901, he stressed social and economic reforms. Roosevelt formed the Bull Moose party in 1912, and the more conservative ranks of the Republican party backed William H. Taft (running for reelection) in the election of 1912. The split resulted in the Democratic victory of Woodrow Wilson. After World War I the orthodox Republicans Warren G. Harding and Calvin Coolidge were elected. Herbert Hoover held the presidency from 1929, when the depression of 1929-1933 began. This misfortune resulted in the overwhelming Democratic victory of 1932. The Republicans entered a slump period, from which they began to emerge by 1938. They constructed a middle-of-the-road policy that opposed only some aspects of the New Deal. In 1948 the Republican candidate for the presidency was Thomas E. Dewey. He stressed domestic issues, such as economy in government. The Republicans met defeat at the hands of Harry S. Truman. In 1952 and 1956 the Republicans successfully elected Dwight D. Eisenhower to the presidency, but the president faced a Democratic Congress after 1954. So-called modern Republicanism seemed to have replaced for a while the more conservative elements in the party, which had aligned themselves with Senator Robert A. Taft. See DEMOCRATIC PARTY; POLITICAL PARTY.

RESEARCH is the careful examination of things, concepts, or symbols in order to extend knowledge. Research may be divided into two areas—scientific research and literary research—but the areas overlap, and their methods are often used in conjunction. Research may sometimes be classed as either pure or applied.

Scientific research is the particular activity of physical and social scientists, but it is undertaken to some extent by anyone who tries to solve a problem systematically by direct examination. The chief method of scientific research is experimentation, or the manipulation of things under controlled conditions. For example, a scientist may observe the behavior of various gases under extreme pressures or the occurrence of red eyes in several generations of fruit flies. In each case the scientist observes the experiment as carefully as possible and records data for his own use or for the possible use of other scientists in future research.

Particularly in the social sciences, the experimenter may not be able to control the conditions. For example,

Wilson & MacPherson Hole

A literary researcher (above) searches through bound volumes of old newspapers.

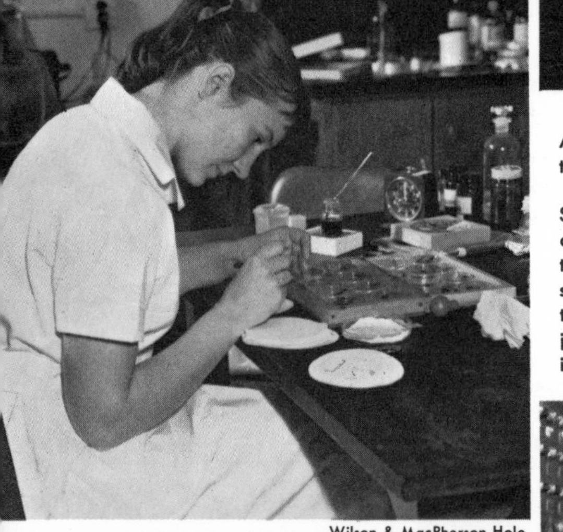

Wilson & MacPherson Hole

Scientific research involves many kinds of activities. A biologist (left) stains a culture of cells so that chromosomes may be seen under a microscope. The superintendent of a plant laboratory (below) adjusts a switchboard that controls climates in growing rooms for plant research.

Wilson & MacPherson Hole

in studying the buying habits of a particular community the social scientist will not be able to control such factors as the ages, economic status, and political affiliations of his subjects. However, he can thoroughly study such factors and, by comparing his results with the results of similar experiments, try to evaluate the effect of each factor on the results of his own observations. Statistical methods are vital to research under conditions that cannot be controlled.

Another aspect of scientific research is gathering data from a number of experiments and accounting for the data in a general hypothesis. Such research may involve delving into already written materials, such as reports on experiments by other scientists. This phase of scientific research involves the methods of literary research.

Literary research is the special domain of creative writers and journalists, but its methods are used by the student every time he looks up a word in a dictionary or checks a date in a history book. Literary research is the gathering and ordering of concepts and information from published and unpublished writings, interviews, and the like. Some kind of report, such as a book or a newspaper article, is usually the end product of literary research.

The methods of good literary research are as painstaking as those of good scientific research. The literary researcher must be able to account for sources of all his materials. He must check each bit of information against all the other information he has collected, and he must consider the reliability of every source of information.

Traditionally, research is divided into pure research, or research undertaken solely to extend knowledge, and applied research, or research undertaken with the further purpose of developing practical applications of the results. Actually the distinction is rarely a clear one. Research undertaken for purely scholarly reasons may turn out to have unforeseen practical applications. On the other hand, research undertaken with a practical goal but yielding no practical results may yield results of purely theoretical value.

Research is often thought of as a solitary activity, but today researchers often work together in great centers of research. Such centers are usually financed by governments, industrial organizations, universities, or foundations.

RESERVE OFFICERS TRAINING CORPS, or ROTC, an organization for the training of Army, Navy, and Air Force reserve officers, with units in military and civilian colleges and secondary schools. The educational institutions that participate in the program provide military studies as a part of the curriculum leading to academic degrees. Those students who register for the ROTC program on entering college are required to devote three hours per week during the first two years and five hours weekly during the last two years to the study of military science. During the summer following his junior year the ROTC student attends a six-week camp for field training in military tactics or joins a naval training cruise. After being graduated he may receive a commission as second lieutenant in the Army or the Air Force reserve or as an ensign in the Navy. Uniforms are provided by the national armed services. The military and naval studies are taught by qualified professional instructors, and the entire program is under the supervision of the chief of the U.S. Army Reserve and ROTC Affairs of the Defense Department.

The ROTC was established under authority of the National Defense Act of 1916.

RESERVOIR, a natural or artificial basin for storing water. The term is applied to a wide range of objects, from a 100-gallon storage tank to an artificial lake. Early in his history man found that a constant supply of water could be maintained, even in arid areas and places where the distribution of water resources was uneven, by collecting water when it was readily available and storing it until needed. Reservoirs were built by the Egyptians of ancient times along the Nile River to store water for crop irrigation during the dry season. Somewhat later in history similar storage places were built in India for the same purpose. The Romans during the time of the Empire built artificial lakes in the mountains surrounding Rome to assure the city of an adequate water supply.

Today's reservoirs, created in most cases by the damming of valleys, serve not only as sources of water for irrigation and for human consumption, the reservoir's traditional functions, but also figure in flood control and hydroelectric-power production. Many reservoirs have been developed as recreational sites. In the terms of volume capacity the world's largest reservoir is the Salto de Aldeadavilla Reservoir in Spain (150 million acre-feet). Other reservoirs of note are the Kariba Reservoir on the border between Southern Rhodesia and Northern Rhodesia; Wainganga Reservoir in India; and the Glen Canyon and Lake Mead reservoirs in the western United States.

An adequate water supply is of great importance to modern cities. Reservoirs are built to store water so that it can be used as needed. Below, a sewage-disposal system is made possible by an additional water supply drawn from a lake reservoir.

Hartley Alley

RESINS, in general, the sap of many kinds of trees and shrubs used for making paints, varnishes, drugs, aromatics, dyes, and naval stores. Synthetic resins, made from wood alcohol and coal tar, are important in the plastics industries and are combined with natural resins in the manufacture of adhesives.

Man's use of natural resins dates from the very beginnings of religion, when primitive men burned fragrant woods while worshiping their gods. The ancient Egyptians used resins in the process of mummifying bodies and also in finishing the exteriors of the mummy cases. Resins and resinous woods were used in ancient Palestine and India for the preparation and ceremonial burning of the dead. Gatherers of the resinous woods were held to be sacred persons, especially by the Romans. Myrrh and frankincense are resinous products. Resins have long been used as caulking and waterproofing on wooden sea vessels.

Natural resins are classified by some chemists as hard resins, oleoresins, and gums. Hard resins quickly lose their volatile oils and are odorless and tasteless. As they ooze out of a break in the bark of a tree, they dry into hard lumps (sometimes as heavy as 100 pounds), fall to the ground, and remain there for thousands of years. In the coalbeds of Utah great lumps of hard resins are dug out. Copal gum, which is not a gum at all, is frequently found as a fossil in tropical swamps. Copal dissolves in alcohol and makes a most durable varnish. Amber is another important resin. It is picked up on the eastern shores of the Baltic Sea. Amber is used for cigar holders and jewelry.

The oleoresins dissolve in volatile oils. In Asia the oleoresins are the foundation of the lacquer industries. Oleoresins include the class of balsams, which generally have medicinal properties. Balsam of Peru, balsam of Tolú, and balm of Gilead are medicinal balsams. Dragon's blood is a brownish black resin used to make crimson lacquer. It was formerly used as medicine in the Middle East. Canada balsam, obtained from the balsam fir tree of the United States and Canada, is used medicinally and also in microscopy as an optical cement.

Gum resins are extracted from many plants and are widely used in perfumes and flavorings.

Rosin is the resinous residue of the sap of pine trees after the volatile oil of turpentine has been distilled off. See TURPENTINE.

RESPIRATION, the process by which living organisms absorb oxygen and give off the products of oxidation. Most cells of higher plants and animals obtain energy by oxidizing foods. In this form of combustion tissue cells use molecules of oxygen to convert foods into carbon dioxide, water, and energy. Governed by respiratory enzymes in the cells, however, respiration proceeds more rapidly and at lower temperatures than in laboratory oxidation. Sunlight, chemically incorporated into molecules of carbohydrates in the process of photosynthesis, is the original source of all energy released in respiration.

In many simple aquatic plants and animals all cells are in contact with the water that supplies their oxygen and receives their carbon dioxide. In higher forms these gases must be exchanged through the surface and transported to the tissue cells. Processes that accomplish these steps are called external respiration, while tissue oxidations are called internal respiration. Higher plants have pores (stomata in leaves and lenticels in stems) through which oxygen enters to be distributed by diffusion and osmosis to all tissue cells. Carbon dioxide produced in internal respiration leaves by the same route. Insects and some other arthropods have a system of branching tubes through which air passes from the exterior to the tissue cells. Other animals have some thin, moist membrane (respiratory epithelium), through which oxygen and carbon dioxide are exchanged, and a circulatory system, in which these gases are transported between this membrane and the tissue cells.

In man, air passes from the mouth or nose (where it is filtered, moistened, and warmed) into the pharynx. From there it passes into the trachea (windpipe), a tube that extends downward in front of the esophagus (gullet) and branches into two bronchi, one for each lung. Each bronchus branches into smaller and smaller tubes (bronchioles), the final branches of which form clusters of alveolar sacs. The larger air tubes, made rigid by open rings of cartilage embedded in their walls, are lined with cells that secrete mucus and other cells whose rhythmically beating cilia force particles upward. Exchange of carbon dioxide and oxygen takes place across the alveolar walls, composed of thin, flat cells in contact with similar cells forming the capillary walls of the pulmonary circulatory system. Passage of oxygen and carbon dioxide between alveoli and capillaries is a process of diffusion regulated by differences between the concentration of these gases in the air and in the blood, each passing from a region of high concentration to one of lower concentration. Most of the oxygen and some of the carbon dioxide is carried by the hemoglobin of the red blood cells. The blood plasma carries most of the carbon dioxide. When blood reaches the capillaries in the tissues, where the lymph has a high concentration of carbon dioxide and a low concentration of oxygen, these gases diffuse through the capillary walls in the direction of low concentration. The total epithelial surface of the lungs of a man is about 630 square feet; of this about 500 square feet is respiratory; this is over 25 times the surface area of the skin. See CIRCULATION; LUNG.

Various protective reflexes may temporarily stop breathing movements. Stimulation of sensory nerves in the larynx (as by the presence of irritating particles) will inhibit the nervous center for respiration, tending to prevent the inhaling of harmful dust, gases, and other substances. Swallowing stimulates sensory nerves in the pharynx that inhibit the respiratory center and make it impossible to breathe while swallowing. However, the breath cannot be held for long. Carbon dioxide in the blood produces upon the respiratory center a stimulating effect that overcomes any neural inhibiting effects.

During exercise, when the body needs more oxygen, more carbon dioxide is produced, which in turn automatically increases the rate of breathing so that more oxygen is taken in. However, as muscles increase their energy output, a point is reached where increase of respiration is insufficient to supply the body's need for oxygen. Other resources must be drawn upon. Muscle cells obtain additional energy from the breakdown of glycogen into lactic acid. (See MUSCLE.) This lactic acid accumulates in the muscle and in the circulating blood and must eventually either be oxidized into carbon dioxide and water or be reconverted into glycogen. Since neither of these reactions releases energy for muscle contraction, and both require oxygen, the reactions are not completed during intensive exercise. The resultant accumulation of lactic acid is called the body's oxygen debt. To pay off this debt increased respiration is continued after exertion until enough additional oxygen has been supplied to complete the delayed reactions of lactic acid.

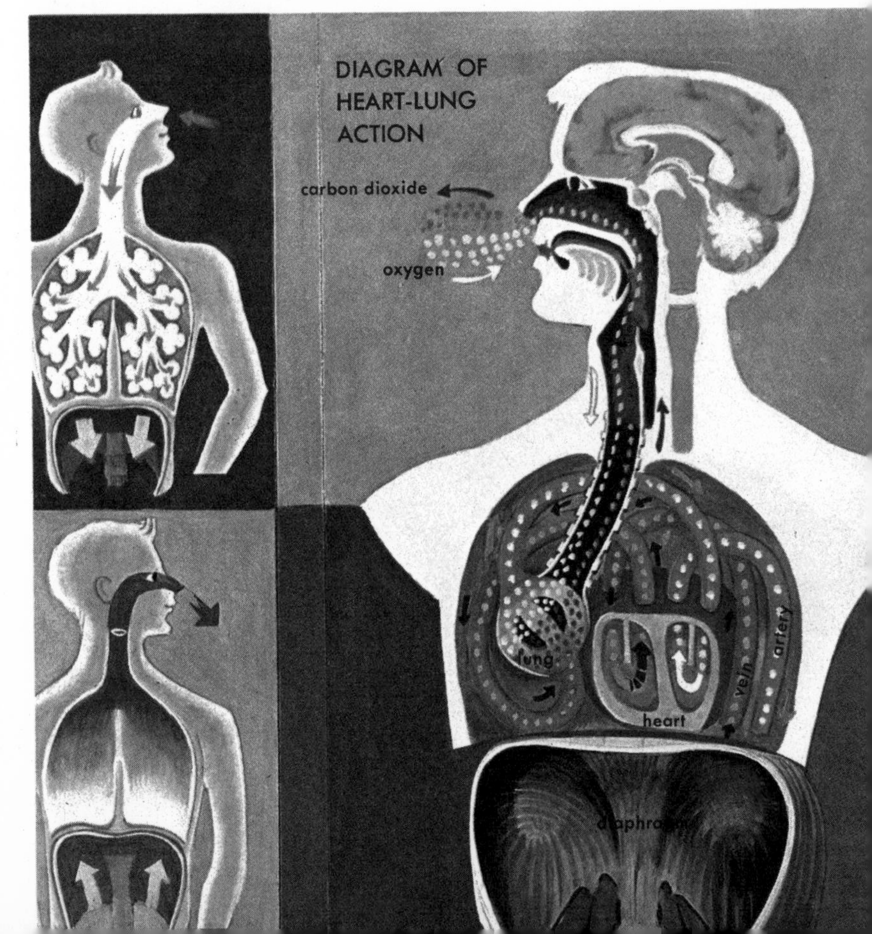

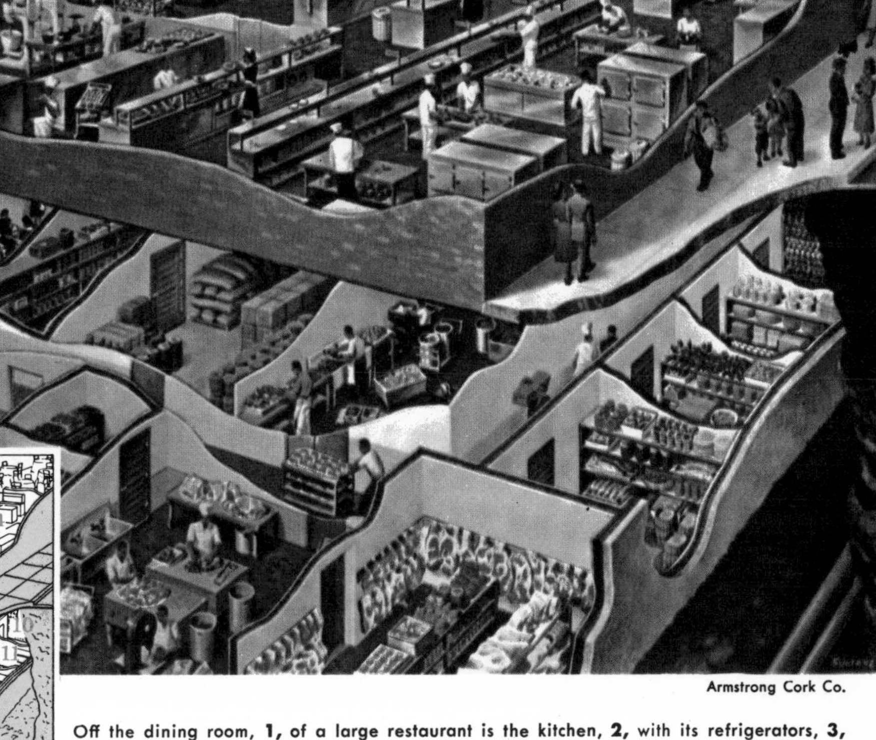

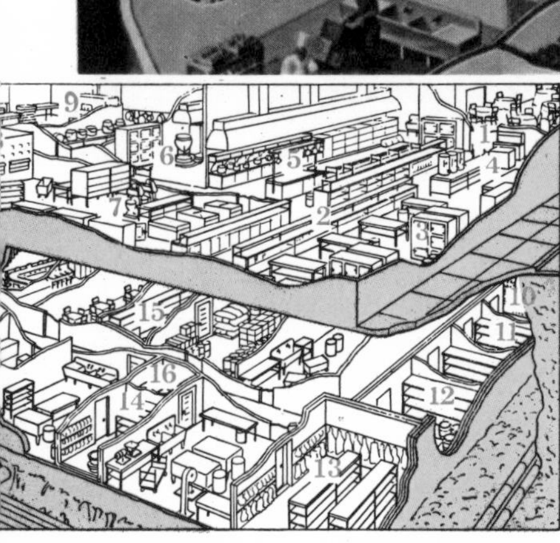

Armstrong Cork Co.

Off the dining room, **1,** of a large restaurant is the kitchen, **2,** with its refrigerators, **3,** ice cream cabinet, **4,** and cooking area, **5.** Soups are cooked in a special kitchen, **6.** In the bakery, **7,** bread and pastries are baked in a large oven, **8.** Dishwashing is done by machine, **9.** In the basement are storerooms for beverages, **10,** dairy products, **11,** seafood, **12,** meat, **13,** poultry, **14,** fresh vegetables, **15,** and frozen foods, **16.**

RESTAURANT, an eating establishment. The term *restaurant* was first used in Great Britain and the United States in the 19th century to refer to those fashionable establishments that had originated in France. However, the term is generally applied to lunchrooms, diners, tearooms, coffeehouses, cafeterias, family restaurants, restaurants for the epicure, hotel restaurants, specialty restaurants (foreign-food restaurants, fried-chicken houses, seafood restaurants), and roadside stands.

There was a time when few people thought of "eating out"; meals were traditionally prepared and eaten in the home. Railroad and automobile travel made people more mobile; often it was necessary for them to eat away from home. In cities many people have no cooking facilities, or, at least for the noon meal, they find themselves far from home. Women in industry sometimes do not have time to cook. Finally, for variety, many people like to dine out on Sundays and holidays.

Although the growth of cities has caused a great demand for restaurants, the restaurant business has a high mortality rate among new establishments. The restaurant owner must know more than how to prepare food properly. Knowledge of purchasing, dietetic science, cost accounting and pricing; judgment of patrons and their needs; and the ability to adjust to seasonal fluctuations are requisites for good restaurant management. Compared with other retail trades, restaurants have a high expense ratio.

There is a great variety of labor in the restaurant business. Hours are usually long for everyone, with heavy workloads around mealtimes. In the fashionable American restaurants there is a chef, who traditionally is of French, Austrian, Swiss, or German origin. Skilled cooks work under the chef, preparing their specialties. Busboys and dishwashers are generally unskilled and transient. Waiters in the exclusive establishments are usually men, and their job requires a great deal of skill and experience. Many women work as cooks or as waitresses in more modest establishments.

Until the 17th century, travelers ate at inns, hotels, or monasteries. The tavern, the part of the hotel where food and drink were served, gradually became a separate establishment, serving local residents as well as travelers. French cafés and English coffeehouses appeared in the 17th century. America had its inns based on the English pattern. The first restaurant, or cookshop as it was called, in the colonies was established in Boston in 1643. The restaurant as a place for dining in style was a French invention, and Paris is still a city of many famous restaurants.

In Europe many restaurants serve beer or wine and an incomplete menu, for they are primarily places where people may gather to converse, talk politics, read the newspapers, or write. America's contribution has been the type of eating place that serves food cheaply and quickly, such as the cafeteria (the first was the New York Exchange Buffet in 1885), the fountain lunch, and the sandwich shop. The automat was first used in Germany, but it had its greatest popularity in the United States. In the cities of the Soviet Union much of the population is served in large communal restaurants.

Courtesy of Watkins Products, Inc.

A restaurant manager and waiter

OCCUPATION: Restaurant Management

NATURE OF WORK: Directing the operation of an establishment that serves food to the public

PERSONAL FACTORS—ABILITIES, SKILLS, APTITUDES: Poise, self-confidence, and the ability to get along with people are desirable.

EDUCATION AND SPECIAL TRAINING: Although no specific educational requirements exist, participation in management-training programs offered in vocational schools may be helpful. Experience in lesser positions is desirable.

WORKING CONDITIONS:

1. **INCOME:**
   COMPARED WITH OTHER CAREERS WITH EQUAL TRAINING: Average to high
   COMPARED WITH MOST OTHER CAREERS: Average
2. **ENVIRONMENT:** Restaurant of varying size, capacity, and quality
3. **OTHER:** Irregular hours; 40 to 48 hours per week; free meals; usual benefits; good opportunities

RELATED CAREERS: Hotel manager, caterer, maître d'hôtel

WHERE TO FIND MORE INFORMATION: Educational Director, National Restaurant Association, 8 South Michigan Avenue, Chicago 3, Ill.; The National Council on Hotel and Restaurant Education, 777 14th Street NW, Washingon 5, D.C.

First-class service by a restaurant waiter
Courtesy of Watkins Products, Inc.

OCCUPATION: Waiter and Waitress

NATURE OF WORK: Taking food orders, serving food and beverages, making out checks

PERSONAL FACTORS—ABILITIES, SKILLS, APTITUDES: An aptitude for simple arithmetic, a friendly manner, neatness and cleanliness, and reasonably good English speech are needed. Manual dexterity is helpful.

EDUCATION AND SPECIAL TRAINING: A high school graduate with some vocational courses usually receives on-the-job training. Promotion from busboy or busgirl is usual. A health certificate is frequently required.

WORKING CONDITIONS:

1. **INCOME:**
   COMPARED WITH OTHER CAREERS WITH EQUAL TRAINING: Low
   COMPARED WITH MOST OTHER CAREERS: Low
2. **ENVIRONMENT:** Modern dining room, luncheonette, railroad dining car, other restaurants
3. **OTHER:** Long, irregular hours; split shifts; much walking and carrying of trays; some benefits; unionized; good opportunities

RELATED CAREERS: Busboy, maître d'hôtel, wine steward, dining car attendant, bartender

WHERE TO FIND MORE INFORMATION: National Restaurant Association, 8 South Michigan Avenue, Chicago 3, Ill.; Hotel and Restaurant Employees and Bartenders International Union, 525 Walnut Street, Cincinnati 2, Ohio

The efficient, smiling restaurant waitress
Courtesy of Hilton Hotels Corp.

Courtesy of Hilton Hotels Corp.

A chef of one of the better restaurants

OCCUPATION: Cook and Chef

NATURE OF WORK: Preparation of food in large quantities

PERSONAL FACTORS—ABILITIES, SKILLS, APTITUDES: Cleanliness, the ability to work under pressure during peak periods, physical stamina, and a keen sense of taste and smell are needed.

EDUCATION AND SPECIAL TRAINING: A high school graduate who may have taken courses in restaurant cooking needs either informal on-the-job training or an apprenticeship of an indefinite period. Experience is essential. A health certificate is required by state law.

WORKING CONDITIONS:

1. **INCOME:**
   COMPARED WITH OTHER CAREERS WITH EQUAL TRAINING: Average to high
   COMPARED WITH MOST OTHER CAREERS: Average
2. **ENVIRONMENT:** Varying from modern kitchen with latest equipment to smaller and older kitchens
3. **OTHER:** Irregular shifts; 40 to 48 hours per week; meals free; some danger from burns, knives, and so forth; unionized; good opportunities

RELATED CAREERS: Restaurant manager, waiter and waitress, railroad chef

WHERE TO FIND MORE INFORMATION: Educational Director, National Restaurant Association, 8 South Michigan Avenue, Chicago 3, Ill.; Hotel and Restaurant Employees and Bartenders International Union, 525 Walnut Street, Cincinnati 2, Ohio

RETAILER, one who sells goods directly to consumers. The retailer generally sells in small quantities to individuals. The field of retailing is a large one in all nations, and it employs numerous people. In Great Britain, for example, there were in 1950 well over 500,000 retail establishments employing a total of about 2,225,000 people (out of a total working population of about 23,000,000). These retail establishments include stores selling groceries and meats, confections, tobacco, clothing, hardware, books and stationery, magazines and newspapers, drugs, photographic supplies, furniture, jewelry, leather goods, sports equipment, general merchandise (department and variety stores), fuel, feed, and builders' materials. Retailing includes specialty shops, peddlers or hawkers, chainstores, large department stores, automatic vending machines, mail-order houses, and cooperative stores.

Retailing is one of the oldest of man's occupations. As early as 2000 B.C. there were numerous retail shops and peddlers. In ancient Greece and Rome the retailer displayed his wares in booths along the street or in the outer room or on the porch of his home (as retailers still do in many countries of the Middle East and the Far East). Some of the early retailers were not always honest. The butcher's thumb was often dishonestly weighed with the meat. For that reason the patron god of the retail trade was Hermes, who also took care of thieves and pirates.

In capitalistic and in many socialistic nations retailing is an area of private enterprise. It would seem easy for the small shopkeeper to set up his grocery store, his shoestore, or his tobacco shop, and then to wait for customers. It is not easy, however, and demands planning and long hours of work. The location of a shop is very important. A shop in the wrong area, or even on the wrong side of the street, may do little business. The retailer must also try to have a large turnover so he can buy his goods more cheaply from the wholesaler. The retailer must be able to build up a large group of loyal customers, to buy goods wisely and at the right time (many a shopkeeper has been stuck with a surplus of cranberry sauce after the holiday seasons), and to display goods in a pleasing manner. Some retailers through hard work are successful, but lack of success results in many bankruptcies among retail establishments each year.

Persons interested in the retail trade may want to own their own small shop. In that case they will be owner, manager, salesman, buyer, and displayer. Others may want to specialize in one aspect of retailing. These persons may want to work as salesmen, buyers, managers, or advertising personnel for large department stores. The good retailer must be able to get along with people. "The customer is always right," but he is often very exasperating. Some retailers learn the problems of the retail trade by means of part-time work in such jobs as that of grocery boy. Buyers, of course, must have special knowledge of the goods they buy, which comes with study and experience.

In Communist countries retailing is a state-owned enterprise. The New Economic Policy (NEP) of the Soviet Union in the early 1920's allowed private retail merchants. By 1931, however, the temporary NEP concessions were terminated, and Soviet retailing became a state enterprise. In 1932, in fact, private retailing was made a criminal offense. The distribution of goods is the task of the ministry of trade. Within this ministry the main retail sales unit is the *torg*, which is located in each Soviet republic. Its officials are appointed by the ministry of trade. Staff departments manage the stores and the wholesale buying, the planning, and finance. The large stores within each *torg* have a large degree of autonomy, but the policies of the small stores are decided by the *torg*. Each large city has a large department store, comparable with those in Chicago, New York, London, Copenhagen, or Paris. Some retail stores are subordinate to other ministries—the drugstores, for example, are operated by the ministry of health. A mail-order house began operations in 1949. By 1960 the Soviet Union's state-owned retail stores were devoting more attention to selling techniques and to attractive displays, an aspect of retailing highly developed in countries where retailing is a private sector. See CHAINSTORE; DEPARTMENT STORE; WHOLESALER.

REUTHER, WALTER (1907-), president of the United Automobile Workers and president of the Congress of Industrial Organizations division of the AFL-CIO. He began his career as a labor organizer at the age of 17 after being fired from his first job in the steel industry. He moved from Wheeling, W. Va., to Detroit, rose to foreman of tool-

Brown Brothers

Walter Reuther, U.S. labor leader

and-die makers in the Ford Motor Company, completed his education in night classes through the third year in college, and was fired again for union activity. He worked in the Soviet Union as a machinist and returned to the United States in 1935 to take an active part in the sitdown strikes out of which grew the United Automobile Workers and the unionization of the automobile industry.

Soon after the attack on Pearl Harbor in World War II Reuther advocated full and immediate mobilization of both capital and workers to produce 500 planes a day and a no-strike program to be administered by both labor and industry. This program held down hours lost by strikes in General Motors during the war to $\frac{1}{160,000}$ total production time.

After the war Reuther led a successful 113-day strike in the automobile industry. His basic program for the U.S. labor movement is acceptance by business of unions as partners, the gearing of wages to productivity and to living costs, and intense hostility to Communists, both at home and abroad.

REVERE, PAUL (1735-1818), American silversmith and patriot, was born in Boston, where he attended grammar school and learned his trade from his father. About 1765 he added copper engraving to his skills and was soon busy producing highly effective political cartoons as well as such items as seals, certificates, coats of arms, bookplates, and picture frames.

Because he was the acknowledged leader of a large segment of Boston workers, he became an important associate of such Revolutionary leaders as John Hancock and Samuel Adams. He was one of the committee of three that determined upon the Boston Tea Party and was one of its participants. After making several long trips on horseback for various causes connected with the colonial resistance, he was appointed official courier between the Massachusetts Provincial Assembly and the Continental Congress in 1774. Messages carried by Revere were responsible for the successful raid on British supplies and munitions at Fort William and Mary. This raid supplied the powder and shot used six months later at Bunker Hill.

On Apr. 16, 1775, Revere rode to Concord to warn the patriots there to move their military stores because of the pending British raid. Two days later he made his famous midnight ride that warned the countryside and the people of Lexington that the British were in fact on the march. While the Battle of Lexington was in progress, Revere was occupied with the important task of removing to a safe place a trunk of important documents that had been left behind by Hancock.

During the Revolutionary War Revere designed and printed the first Continental money, learned to manufacture gunpowder and for a time supervised a powder mill, served on several Boston committees of patriots, and participated in one ill-fated military expedition. After the war he devoted greater attention to his trade and produced much fine silverwork, for which he is famous. He also opened a foundry in which he cast bells, cannon, and much of the metal equipment used in building *Old Ironsides*. He discovered a new copper-rolling process and made the copper plates for one of Robert Fulton's earliest steamboats. He also participated actively in Boston civic affairs, most notably working for the ratification of the Constitution.

REVOLUTION, in political science, a violent overthrow of a ruling group by a new group of leaders with the purpose of creating a new government. The revolution follows the pattern of criticism of existing conditions, amassing of military power, defeat of the opposition, seizure of power, reduction of the power of the old ruling groups, rebuilding of a new power, and possibly the promulgation of a new constitution. Revolutions begin as a new, enthusiastic, and determined group begins to attract previous resistance groups or aggrieved classes by the use of compelling slogans. Ideologies elaborating social utopias often play a decisive role, especially in the most important revolutions. These social utopias are frequently forgotten by the new rulers, who strive only to retain power after the revolution. The revolution may continue with internal strife within the new ruling groups, perhaps between a conservative group and a radical group that wants more change, or between individuals seeking personal power. Because of modern technology and bureaucracy the revolutionary forces will try to seize the means of public authority, communication, transportation, and supply. The precariousness of the power of the new regime may make necessary a reign of terror.

There are several kinds of revolution. In one type the aristocratic classes rise against an absolute monarch. The Magna Charta was gained in this way. In the middle-class revolution, the third estate rises against a feudal-clerical monarchy. The French Revolution is an example. In a proletarian revolution the farmers and workers rise against a constitutional, middle-class government. The revolution in Russia in 1917 established first a middle-class regime under Kerensky and then a dictatorship of the proletariat under Lenin. A counterrevolution may displace a revolution that has succeeded in establishing a new government if the latter is weak and divided. In the 20th century, revolutions of "the right" were led by the Fascists under Mussolini and the National Socialists under Hitler. The world revolution, in which all the workers and peasants of the world would rise against middle-class constitutional governments, was long a goal of Communists.

Most revolutionary groups attempt to base their overthrow of the old government on some legal or moral grounds. Natural law and natural rights played a part in establishing the moral necessity for the American Revolution, according to Thomas Jefferson's stirring Declaration of Independence. See CHINESE REVOLUTION; DECEMBRIST UPRISING; DECLARATION OF INDEPENDENCE; FRENCH REVOLUTION; GLORIOUS REVOLUTION; HUNGARIAN REVOLT; LATIN AMERICAN INDEPENDENCE; MEXICAN REVOLUTION; REVOLUTIONARY WAR; RUSSIAN REVOLT OF 1905; RUSSIAN REVOLUTION.

REVOLUTIONARY WAR, the conflict in which 13 North American colonies, which later became the first states of the United States, gained independence from Great Britain. Although the war itself lasted from 1775 to 1783, the revolutionary period began much earlier.

Upon the conclusion of the French and Indian War in 1763 Great Britain was the undisputed master of eastern North America, but the problems of organization, administration, and defense of the area were pressing. Furthermore, the hostility of the Indians, made fully apparent by Pontiac's Rebellion (May 7–Nov. 28, 1763), complicated all three issues. The result was the government's issuance of the Proclamation of 1763, which was originally conceived as a provisional measure prior to opening the western territories to colonization but which, in its final form, was designed to prohibit all settlement west of the Allegheny Mountains. This meant that not only were all colonial western land claims abolished but also that those settlers already in the area, principally around the forks of the Ohio River, were "to remove themselves." The British government hoped that this measure would quiet the Indians and that land-hungry settlers would be driven northward into Canada, where they would submerge the French in an English-speaking population. But Quebec failed to appeal to the settlers, who continued to push westward and who were angered by the failure of the colonial governments to provide more adequate protection.

This unpopular proclamation was succeeded in 1764 by the American Revenue Act, generally known as the Sugar Act, which was the first law passed by Parliament for the specific purpose of raising revenue in the colonies. More important than this act, however, was Chancellor of the Exchequer George Grenville's determination to end the policy of salutary neglect by enforcing the trade laws and reforming the American customs service, which then collected only about one-fourth the cost of the service. The chief motive behind the new policy was the government's need for revenue to help defray the cost of the war with France and to assist in maintaining in America an army to protect the colonists.

James Otis immediately raised the question of taxation without representation, which he insisted was out of keeping with the British constitution, but the ministry in

London was unwilling to back down and proceeded to impose additional unpopular laws. The colonies were prohibited from printing legal tender, and a vice-admiralty court, with jurisdiction over all the American provinces, was established at Halifax, Nova Scotia. Instead of taking suits to a local court, prosecutors and informers could take them to Halifax, where there was no jury and where the accused had not only the burden of proof but also the necessity of posting a bond to cover the cost of the trial. In 1765 colonial civil authorities were required to furnish barracks and supplies for British troops, and in 1766 provision was made for quartering British troops in inns, taverns, and unoccupied dwellings.

But the most odious measure yet taken was the Stamp Act, the first direct tax levied by Parliament upon the colonies. Designed to raise £60,000 annually, the Stamp Act placed fees on newspapers, almanacs, pamphlets, broadsides, legal documents, insurance policies, ship's papers, licenses, dice, and playing cards. The reaction against the law was immediate. The Sons of Liberty were organized to direct opposition; the records of the vice-admiralty court in Boston were burned; the home and library of Chief Justice Thomas Hutchinson were looted; and all the stamp agents were forced to resign before the act went into effect. Also, a meeting, known as the Stamp Act Congress, was held at New York on Oct. 7, 1765, to protest this attempt at taxation. Attended by 28 delegates from all of the colonies except New Hampshire, Virginia, North Carolina, and Georgia, the congress drew up memorials to both the king and Parliament and also a Declaration of Rights and Liberties. But perhaps the most effective protest was made by many of the leading colonial merchants, who refused to trade with Europe until the act was repealed. The resulting decline in British exports to America persuaded many British merchants of the need for repeal, which was accomplished by Parliament on Mar. 18, 1766. On the same day, however, it also passed a law declaring its power to make laws binding the colonials in any way.

The Bettmann Archive

Paul Revere is shown here as he spreads the alarm of the coming of the British. His famous ride on the night of Apr. 18, 1775, roused the countryside from Boston to Concord.

Colonists paraded to protest the Stamp Act, a direct tax passed by the British Parliament without colonial representation.

Brown Brothers

In 1767 the Townshend Acts were passed, imposing duties on imports of lead, tea, paper, glass, and painter's colors. A meeting was held in Boston, and an agreement of nonimportation was adopted. The following year the Massachusetts General Court registered its disapproval in a petition to the king, in a message to the ministry, and in a circular letter to the other colonies.

Shortly after the assembly's action a detachment of British troops arrived in Boston. The town refused to quarter them, and on Mar. 5, 1770, the town's hatred of them led to a brawl, the Boston Massacre, in which several citizens were killed or wounded.

In that same year, the tension between the colonies and the home government was somewhat lessened by Lord Frederick North's repeal of the Townshend Acts, with the exception of the tax on tea, and Parliament's failure to renew the Quartering Act. But the temporary truce was disrupted by the government's decision in 1772 to pay the governor and judges of Massachusetts from the royal Exchequer, thus depriving the General Court of the power of the purse.

Another disquieting move on the part of the British government was the passage of the Tea Act (May 10, 1773), which was designed to save from bankruptcy the East India Company, important to England because of its hold upon India. Parliament removed all duties on tea exported by the company to the

Yale University Art Gallery; Courtesy TIME

John Trumbull's painting depicts Washington offering his hand to mortally wounded Colonel Johann Rall, commander of the Hessians who surrendered at Trenton.

This naval flag was flown on the American frigate *Alliance* in 1779.
Chicago Historical Society

A portrait of Benedict Arnold shortly after his unsuccessful Quebec campaign
Collection of Mrs. John Nicholas Brown

Guilford Court House National Military Park

At the outbreak of the Revolutionary War the commander of the British troops in North America was General Thomas Gage (right).

Drums, such as that at left, were used to transmit orders governing camp routine and battle maneuvers; they took the place of bugles.

Alexander Hamilton is depicted below as he directed a brilliant attack against one of the two major British redoubts at Yorktown.

Museum of the City of New York

This cartoon, created in 1774 by Benjamin Franklin, shows his opinion of the outcome of disunity among the colonies.

Library of Congress

Collection of R. V. C. Bodley—Chailey, Newburyport, Mass.

The seizure of Newport, R.I., in December, 1776, was excellently directed by Sir Henry Clinton. The five frigates shown below laid down a barrage, while landing craft waited in the harbor. The landing met with no opposition. Newport thereafter was used as a British base for attacks on American ships and on other seaports.

National Maritime Museum, London, England

colonies but retained the 3-pence import tax in America. The most disturbing aspect of the act was the provision for the company to sell tea directly to agents in the colonies rather than at public auction in England. This granted the company a virtual monopoly, for it could now undersell all other dealers. Because of this threatened monopoly, the colonials protested, forcing all of the tea consignees, except those of Boston, to resign. But the citizens of Boston, determined that the tea be returned to England without payment of a duty, refused to allow the ships in their harbor to unload. Since Governor Hutchinson refused to submit to their demands, a group of citizens, disguised as Indians, held the Boston Tea Party (Dec. 16, 1773); they boarded the ships and dumped 342 chests of tea into the harbor.

This resistance provoked the ministry, at the insistence of George III, to get through Parliament the Intolerable Acts. These laws were followed by a new quartering act (1774), which legalized the quartering of troops not only in deserted houses and taverns but also in occupied dwellings. And before all of these five laws were passed, on May 13, 1774, General Thomas Gage supplanted Thomas Hutchinson as governor of Massachusetts, virtually placing that province under military rule.

Deeply aroused, the colonies, with the exception of Georgia, called the First Continental Congress, which assembled at Philadelphia, Sept. 5, 1774. On September 17 the assembly adopted the Suffolk Resolves, which declared the Intolerable Acts unconstitutional, urged Massachusetts to form a government to collect taxes and to withold them from the ministry until the repeal of the acts, advised the people to arm them-

At Saratoga John Burgoyne (left) surrenders his sword and some 5,000 of Britain's best troops to Horatio Gates. Daniel Morgan (in white, center) led a force of riflemen. After Burgoyne's surrender France entered the war on the side of the Americans.

Yale University Art Gallery

The Henry Francis du Pont Winterthur Museum

The American delegates signing the peace treaty were (left to right) John Jay, John Adams, Benjamin Franklin, Henry Laurens, and William T. Franklin. Benjamin West was unable to finish this painting because the British commissioners refused to pose.

selves and to form a militia, and recommended stringent economic sanctions against Great Britain. To implement the latter resolve, the Continental Association was organized in October with the purpose of adopting a policy of nonimportation of British goods after December 1, and if the acts were not repealed by Sept. 1, 1775, the colonies were to refuse to export their products to Britain.

The threat of war was now actual. Lord North made an attempt at reconciliation but the plan, a scheme that the colonists would not have obeyed, reached America after the shooting had begun. As the spring of 1775 advanced, the New Englanders organized military companies. The colonial leaders favored a defensive policy: The militiamen were to attack only if the British struck first. As if to test this policy Major John Pitcairn led a contingent of British soldiers from Boston to Salem. The group went unmolested. General Gage, convinced that a show of British force was all that was necessary to discourage and scatter the rebels, decided to send a force to Lexington and Concord, both in Massachusetts, where the militia was collecting military supplies. At the same time Gage would carry out his orders to arrest John Hancock and Samuel Adams, who were in the area of Lexington. On Apr. 19, 1775, Pitcairn and his trained soldiers were defeated by an undisciplined group of minutemen in the first battle of the war. Talk of reconciliation with Britain died out as all colonies made war preparations and the Second Continental Congress met in Philadelphia in May.

The first important action of the congress was to provide for a Continental army and a commander. The militia units constituted the army; in George Washington, a former officer, the patriots found their man. The congress assumed the powers of a revolutionary government. Little more was done before news reached Philadelphia of the Battle of Bunker Hill (June 17, 1775). The raw militiamen technically lost the battle, but they lost it only because they ran out of ammunition. The British losses, which were heavy, included Major Pitcairn among the dead.

Washington's cannon, mounted on Dorchester Heights, caused General William Howe to evacuate Boston. Howe went to New York, where he received reinforcements. Washington followed and was defeated on Long Island. The American army, pursued by the British, retreated across New Jersey and into Pennsylvania. In a surprise move Washington took his army back across the icy Delaware River and captured almost 1,000 Hessians at Trenton on Dec. 26, 1776. After defeating a British detachment at Princeton on Jan. 3, 1777, the Americans settled into winter quarters.

The year 1776 was important for the colonists aside from battles. The rulers of France and Spain had ordered that munitions be supplied to the colonies, and from them the Americans received much of their war matériel, including most of their gunpowder. Congress took a step toward independence in April by opening American ports to the trade of all countries but Britain. Most important, the congress voted on July 2 for complete independence. The Declaration of Independence, largely the work of Thomas Jefferson, was approved on July 4 and was proclaimed in Philadelphia on July 8.

The British plans for 1777 included capturing Philadelphia and severing the colonies by joining the British forces in Canada with those in New York. General Howe moved on the American capital, defeated Washington at Brandywine Creek on Sept. 11, 1777, and occupied Philadelphia as Congress fled to York, Pa. Washington was again unsuccessful against Howe in October and retired to Valley Forge.

The action in the north was more favorable to the American cause. British General Burgoyne, coming south from Canada, captured Ticonderoga in July, 1777. But Burgoyne moved his army so slowly that the Americans had time to rally. Under General Horatio Gates the colonial forces won a spectacular victory against Burgoyne at Saratoga on Oct. 17, 1777. The Battle of Saratoga, in which Burgoyne surrendered 5,700 men, had far-reaching consequences. Lord North made another attempt to reconcile the colonies with Britain. His offer came too late—the Americans would be satisfied with nothing short of complete independence. North's proposal, however, frightened the French, who feared a reconciliation would result in the loss of the French colonies in the West Indies. Benjamin Franklin skillfully negotiated with France and won recognition of American independence. The treaties between France and the new United States put England's old rival into the war on the American side. The Spanish and Dutch later followed France into war against Britain. The little rebellion in the colonies came to assume international importance.

The victory at Saratoga did little to help Washington during the winter at Valley Forge. Many farmers around Philadelphia, eager for hard cash, supplied General Howe's army, while Washington's soldiers starved and froze only 20 miles away. Despite the privations the veterans of Valley Forge became the nucleus of a new army. A Prussian volunteer, Baron von Steuben, taught the men the arts of drill, tactics, and maneuver. In the dreadful winter the Americans learned to be real soldiers.

The announcement of the alliance with France brought a new turn of events. The British in Philadelphia, now commanded by Sir Henry Clinton, were ordered to evacuate the city and return to New York. In June, 1778, Clinton began the march. Washington followed, hoping to cooperate with the French navy in an attack on the British. Plans for coordination failed, however, and Washington ended the year 1778 at White Plains, N.Y., not far from where he had been two years before. The Americans seemed to be back where they had started.

In the West the American outlook was brighter. With a group of Virginia frontier militiamen George Rogers Clark captured Fort Kaskaskia on the Mississippi (July, 1778). Clark quickly won the support of the French in the area and was able to extend his authority to Fort Vincennes on the Wabash. When the British retook Vincennes, Clark and his tiny army marched 180 miles across flooded land and defeated the king's garrison. About this time the British made special efforts to gain the friendship of the Indians. Loyalists participated in raiding parties that terrorized the frontier settlements. The Wyoming Massacre in Pennsylvania and the Cherry Valley Massacre in New York were accomplished by Tories and Indians in 1778.

The British also raided in the South, where they captured the port of Savannah in 1778. Washington, still unable to launch a full-scale attack on Clinton in New York, had to be content with waiting.

Hopes for an American victory dimmed in 1780, when Clinton left New York by sea and, in May, captured Charleston, S.C., and all the American forces in that city. It was the greatest defeat of the war. Clinton then returned north, leaving Lord Cornwallis in charge at Charleston. Cornwallis, a ruthless commander, defeated the Americans at Camden, S.C., in August and moved northward, fighting all the way, until he reached Yorktown, Va. Here, at the small port city, he would be safe as long as England ruled the sea.

Washington had been hoping for months to utilize the French navy against the British in New York. The fleet had brought a French army under Comte de Rochambeau to aid the Americans. But the British had blocked Newport harbor, and the French were unable to sail out. When Washington learned that the fleet had finally managed to escape and was headed for Chesapeake Bay, he quickly adjusted his long-held plans. The combined Franco-American army started southward toward Cornwallis. When the British admiral in the Chesapeake sighted the numerous French ships, he saw the odds against him and headed north. Now in full command of the area the French fleet was able to transport the allied troops down the bay. On Sept. 30, 1781, the siege of Yorktown began. Cornwallis, outnumbered two to one, surrendered the British garrison on Oct. 19, 1781, as bands played "The World Turned Upside Down" and "Yankee Doodle."

Yorktown was the last battle of the war in North America. The British people were tired of the interminable struggle and were shocked by the defeat at Yorktown. In March, 1782, Lord North resigned, and a new government was formed. On Sept. 27, 1782, formal negotiations for peace began. The final treaty was signed in Paris on Sept. 3, 1783. The other countries involved in the war all signed treaties with Britain the same day. England acknowledged the independence of her former colonies and established generous, but vague, boundaries for the new republic. The United States was also granted rights in the Newfoundland fisheries. The struggle for independence was over.

This picture depicts American feelings as the British evacuated New York in 1783.
The Bettmann Archive

REVOLUTIONS OF 1848, a chain reaction of revolutions in Europe, starting in France, that brought to a climax the liberal and nationalist movements that had been growing in Europe at least since the days of Napoleon.

Napoleon's conquests both spread the political ideas behind the French Revolution and aroused feelings of national unity among many of the conquered peoples. In addition, national consciousness had been stimulated among many European peoples by revivals of their languages and cultures. (See PATRIOTISM AND NATIONALISM.) Persecution and repression by Prince Metternich and his allies, while temporarily successful, eventually strengthened the liberal and nationalist movements. (See CONGRESS SYSTEM; METTERNICH, PRINCE VON.) Additional factors peculiar to the revolts in Paris and Vienna were the problems caused by industrialization—long working hours, low wages, and mass unemployment in time of depression.

The French revolution, begun in February, 1848, by liberals, Socialists, and workers of Paris, was ignited by the government's prohibition of a political protest meeting (disguised as a banquet). Though the rebels declared a republic, their aims differed—the liberals desiring only representative government and civil liberties, the workers, led by the socialist Louis Blanc, wanting the government to remove the evils accompanying industrialization. In response to the demands of the workers the new government set up work projects called national workshops. Supposedly modeled on Louis Blanc's plans for government-run industries, they were sabotaged by their moderate administrators. Unemployment increased, but free nationwide elections in April returned a socially moderate government that decided to close the workshops. Therefore, the Paris workers revolted in June. The suppression of this revolt marked the failure of the French revolution; for though the Second French Republic lasted another three and a half years before being replaced by the Second Empire under Napoleon III, it became increasingly conservative and repressive.

The February revolt, besides encouraging a rebellion already in progress in the Kingdom of Sicily, inspired a series of revolts among the peoples of the Hapsburg Empire. The Hungarian patriot Louis Kossuth denounced the Hapsburg regime, and Viennese workers and students demonstrated against it. Prince Metternich fled to England, and Emperor Ferdinand I promised the Austrians constitutional government, accepted the March Laws and other Hungarian demands that made Hungary an independent constitutional monarchy with the emperor as king, and granted similar status to Bohemia (inhabited mainly by Czechs and Germans). The Croats, a Slavic minority living in Magyar-dominated Hungary, then demanded autonomy, and the revolution spread to other Slavic groups within the empire. By the end of March the revolution had spread to the Hapsburgs' Italian possessions of Venetia and Lombardy and to the local monarchies dominated by Austria; Sardinia, the most independent Italian state, had declared war on Austria.

In March, too, rioting occurred in Berlin, capital of Prussia. The Prussian king promised constitutional government, as did the other German monarchs. Delegates from all the German states then met in Frankfort on the Main to write a constitution for a unified Germany. However, the Frankfort Assembly was divided by disagreement over the form of government and over the territories to be included. It was also distracted by a war with Denmark over that country's possession Schleswig, which had a large German population. By the time the assembly completed a constitution in March, 1849, the prerevolutionary governments had been restored; first Austria and then Prussia opposed the new state, and the assembly disbanded. The failure of the Frankfort Assembly marked the failure of liberal nationalism in Germany.

The revolutions in Germany, Italy, and the Hapsburg dominions began to collapse in June, 1848. One reason was the divisive nature of nationalism. The recognition the Magyars desired for themselves they would not grant the Croats and other minority groups, which composed at least half the population of Hungary. There was friction between the Germans and the Czechs in Bohemia.

Furthermore, both liberalism and nationalism lacked the backing of a large or strong segment of the population. The middle class, from which most of the revolutionaries came, was smaller and less well developed than in western Europe. The same was true of the working class, which, in addition, most of the middle-class liberals distrusted. Finally, the great landowners and the peasants whom they controlled were, except among the Magyars, antiliberal and antinationalist. Because the antiliberals and the antinationalists made up the armies, the troops also remained loyal to the monarchs.

The first victory of the counterrevolution occurred in June in Bohemia. A Czech demonstration in Prague, during which his wife was accidentally killed, provided the Austrian commander Prince Windischgrätz with an excuse to conquer the city, thus ending Bohemian autonomy. The next month Austrian forces defeated the Sardinians (who had been deserted for various reasons by most of the other Italians) at Custoza. Finally, in September the Austrian emperor accepted the Croatian leader Baron Jellachich's offer to put down the Hungarian revolution. The Viennese revolutionaries, rioting against the government, called on the aid of the Hungarian revolutionaries. However, in October the Austrian forces of Windischgrätz and the Croatian forces of Jellachich joined to subjugate Vienna.

The Prussian king, Frederick William IV, encouraged by the Hapsburg successes, dissolved the Prussian constituent assembly in December and declared his own constitution. This document, which left control of the government in the hands of the conservative landowners and wealthy businessmen, remained in effect until 1918.

Though the prerevolutionary governments were firmly in power by the end of 1848, the revolutions continued until August, 1849. A new revolt created the Roman Republic, and Sardinia resumed the fighting against Austria, but Austrian troops defeated the Sardinians in March, French troops suppressed the Roman Republic in June, and Austrian troops forced the surrender of Venice in August. After the restored Austrian government revoked the Hungarian constitution in March, 1849, the Hungarian Diet declared Hungary independent. However, in August the Austrians, with the aid of the Russians, forced the Magyars to surrender.

The failure of the revolutions of 1848 was only a temporary setback to the tide of nationalism. The subsequent decades witnessed the unifications of Germany and Italy; and, in addition, the problem of the national minorities in the Hapsburg Empire set off World War I.

REVOLVER, a type of pistol that, by a revolving cylinder, fires a number of shots, usually six, without reloading. In 1836 Samuel Colt, an American, patented the first revolver to have wide general use. The Colt revolver was first used in Texas. The Texas Rangers carried it in the Mexican War. The Colt became essential to the mounted frontiersmen of the western plains. Here the long, muzzle-loading rifle, so useful to the unmounted pioneer of the woodlands, did not equal the Indian bow and arrow. The revolver restored the superiority of the plainsman and played a significant part in the conquest of the West. The automatic pistol competes with, but has not superseded, the revolver, as the latter responds to direct control and is easily kept in working order. Modern revolvers vary in bore from .22 to .45 caliber.

REYNOLDS, SIR JOSHUA (1723-1792), English portrait painter, was born in Devonshire. In 1746, following an apprenticeship under the portraitist Thomas Hudson, Reynolds established a London studio and soon afterward began acquiring patrons. Between 1749 and 1752 he traveled and studied on the Continent. Reynolds enjoyed great success as a painter of fashionable portraits from the time of his return to London until his retirement in 1790.

Reynolds was a prominent participant in the intellectual activity of his times. The famed Literary Club, which numbered among its members Samuel Johnson, Oliver Goldsmith, James Boswell, David Garrick, and Richard Sheridan, was founded in 1764 upon Reynolds' suggestion. He was also the first president of the Royal Academy. He was knighted in 1769 and became painter to the king in 1784. In addition to portraits of leading personalities of the day, including members of the Literary Club, his paintings include "The Strawberry Girl," "The Age of Innocence," and "The Infant Hercules."

National Gallery of Art, Washington, D.C., Mellon Collection

Sir Joshua Reynolds' "Lady Caroline Howard"

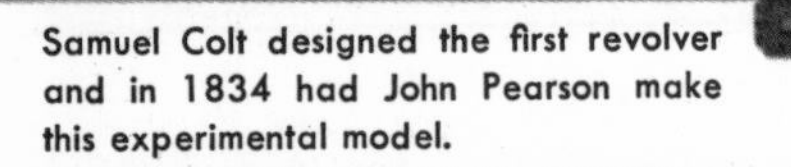

Samuel Colt designed the first revolver and in 1834 had John Pearson make this experimental model.

The Paterson Colt, which was an improved version of John Pearson's model, was manufactured by Colt in Paterson, N.J. This revolver, which was the first Colt pistol offered to the public, sold poorly.

This U.S. Army Colt, model 1860, was given to Lieutenant Charles Morton by the Territory of Arizona for bravery against Apaches. It is now in the West Point Museum.

Frontier Scout .22 cal.

Python .357 Magnum.

RHEA, the largest bird in the New World, found only in South America. It is known as the American ostrich and is an anomaly in the bird world. It has wings, but it cannot fly. It fights courageously, but it is also a household pet in South America and takes well to life in a zoo. It can run at racehorse speed, but one of its defenses when harassed by hunters is to double back and fall flat on the ground. The male has a deep, booming voice, and at courtship time he fights with other males until he has assembled a harem of six or so females; but then, after the females have laid several dozen eggs in the communal nest, he incubates the eggs and cares for the young while the females wander about the plains.

Rheas are about 4 feet tall, but they are smaller than the true ostrich of Africa. They also differ from the ostrich in having three toes instead of two and in having feathers on the head and neck. Rheas have a slender neck, a large, flat bill, long legs, and no tail. They are brownish or blue gray. Their sight is keen, and they swim well, with the body almost submerged. Their food consists of mollusks, worms, lizards, seeds, grass, and roots. They have a habit of swallowing all sorts of small, shiny objects.

Two species exist—the common rhea of the pampas and highland savannas of Brazil and Argentina and the long-billed rhea of the mountains in western South America.

RHEE, SYNGMAN (1875-), Korean politician, descended from the Ri Dynasty, which ruled Korea from 1486 to its overthrow by the Japanese in 1910. Rhee grew up to be an intense nationalist, conservative, and autocrat. He tolerated political corruption and suppression of political dissent. It was these policies that led to his downfall.

To promote his political advancement Rhee acquired a classical Chinese education and a knowledge of English. He began his active political career in 1894 by founding Korea's first daily newspaper, in which he advocated opposition to expanding Japanese influence. Three years later he was caught, tortured, and imprisoned by the Japanese. He won a release in 1904 and escaped to the United States, where he acquired a Ph.D. in theology at Princeton University.

For the next 25 years Rhee fought the Japanese, mainly from bases in China, against which Japan was waging wars of conquest. With the defeat of Japan in 1945 the United States allowed him to return to South Korea. Three years later the National Assembly elected him president of the Republic of Korea, which extended only as far north as the 38th parallel. This division of Korea resulted in 1950 in the Korean War. (See KOREAN WAR.) At the end of this conflict Korea was divided much as it had been before the war. Rhee ignored warnings by the United States against autocracy. He drove his political opponents from the National Assembly, allowed them to be beaten and murdered, stuffed ballot boxes, and forced upon the country the election of his friend Lee Ki Poong to the vice-presidency.

A revolt, led by students, broke out in March, 1960. After 140 were slain, the police and soldiers surrendered their tanks and rifles to the students. The vice-president's son, who was also Rhee's adopted son, shot himself, his father, and the rest of his family. Thereupon the United States Department of State suggested that Rhee retire at once. He resigned the presidency and fled to Hawaii.

Brown Brothers

Syngman Rhee, Korean statesman and patriot

RHETORIC, the basic art of the communication of ideas, usually in order to persuade. It may be divided into two subordinate arts: composition and oratory. Composition is the shaping of a speech or a written work, including the application of the rules of grammar and syntax. Oratory is the art of delivery of speeches. It includes elocution and gesture. Elocution is the art of speaking well. Gesture is the art of appropriate carriage and movement in public speaking.

Composition is basic to oratory. Even a speech that is to be delivered has to be composed. Since the invention of printing the majority of compositions have been read silently rather than delivered before audiences. Composition may be extemporary or carefully prepared and revised. All prepared composition requires, first of all something to say and, second, a consideration of the character of the audience. The author also must decide what kind of impression he wants to make on his audience. Then an outline should be made of the general organization of the composition. This should combine clarity with devices to engage the interest of the audience.

The essay is the main form of organized communication of ideas in persuasive reading material. Usually the term *essay* is applied only to works that can be read at one session, but the term can include longer writings. Part of the effectiveness of the famous essays of Joseph Addison and Charles Lamb stems from their intensely personal character.

The speech is the traditional rhetorical composition and can be one of many special forms, such as the sermon, the political speech, the eulogy, and the plea. The sermon is a religious address. Among the great masters of the sermon were J.B. Bossuet in France, Jeremy Taylor in England, and Jonathan Edwards in America. The political speech may be a report or a campaign speech. The campaign speech sometimes takes the form of a debate. A eulogy is a speech in commendation of a person, institution, work of art, or the like. A plea is a legal speech.

Radio and television have stimulated a new interest in oratory. Because *oratory*, like the word *rhetoric*, often carries with it the unfortunate connotation of "pompous and inflated language," we often use the term *public speaking* instead. The composition of a speech is intimately connected with its delivery. Therefore, public speaking classes also teach speech composition.

Speakers sometimes read their compositions, though this is seldom very impressive. Usually, a speaker works from notes and is aided by memory and previous practice. The notes give the outline of the speech and other hints. Even if a speech is completely extemporaneous, it should be delivered with care.

Both aspects of oratory, elocution and gesture, depend greatly on the mental attitude of the speaker. Instead of centering his attention on himself, he should direct his attention to the audience. In this way the speaker will act naturally and effectively. See SPEECH.

The common rhea (left and center) and the long-billed, or Darwin's, rhea (right) are the only species of this large bird. They are related to the ostrich.

RHEUMATIC FEVER is a serious complication of an infectious disease that attacks the joints and the heart. It may result from an infection with a specific germ called group A beta-hemolytic streptococcus. In acute rheumatic fever characteristic nodules develop, particularly in the valves and muscle of the heart. Also joints become red and swollen and tender. When the leg tendons are affected, there are "growing pains." The first attack of rheumatic fever usually occurs in childhood. Later attacks occur when there is reinfection with the specific streptococcus organism. Accordingly, it is important to prevent reinfection. Sulfonamides may be prescribed for this purpose.

The usual symptoms of rheumatic fever are fever, perspiration, fatigue, and inflammation and pain in the joints. When the heart becomes inflamed, there are symptoms of heart failure. The symptoms of rheumatic fever are relieved by salicylic acid (aspirin). A most important feature of treatment is bed rest, along with proper diet.

RH FACTOR, a substance in human blood cells that is similar to a substance in the blood cells of the Rhesus monkey—hence the use of the symbol Rh. Those people having this substance are Rh-positive; those not having it are Rh-negative. There is considerable variation among ethnic groups throughout the world in the relative proportion of Rh-positive and Rh-negative people. In the United States it is estimated that 85 percent of the Caucasoid population is Rh-positive.

A blood transfusion from an Rh positive to an Rh negative may have serious consequences. After such a transfusion the blood of the recipient develops an anti-Rh factor in about 12 days. Another transfusion after this time may result in a serious reaction, sometimes fatal, brought about by the destruction (hemolysis) of the transfused cells by the anti-Rh factor.

Complications related to the Rh factor may occur in pregnancy and childbirth. For example, a dangerour reaction may be produced when an Rh-negative mother is sensitized by the blood of an Rh-positive fetus and then receives Rh-positive blood in transfusions. Also, the blood of an Rh-negative mother may produce an anti-Rh factor that readily passes across the placenta and reacts with the blood of an Rh-positive child, causing hemolytic disease of the newborn, which may end in death. The disease does not always occur with the first child, and a large number of Rh-negative mothers do not produce a high quantity of anti-Rh factor. Treatment of the disease is exchange transfusion, or the complete replacement of the infant's blood, preferably with Rh-negative blood. There is a variety of Rh factors. There are also similar substances known as Hr factors, which are weaker but produce similar reactions.

RHIND PAPYRUS, one of the two oldest known mathematical works. The Rhind papyrus is named after A. Henry Rhind, a Scottish antiquary who bought it in Luxor, Egypt, in 1858. The papyrus is nearly 18 feet long and 13 inches high.

The papyrus was said to have been found in ruins at Thebes. It was broken in two parts, and a few missing fragments prevented it from being completely understood. Fifty years after it was bought, many of the missing fragments turned up at the New York Historical Society, and the work was then easily read.

The papyrus was written about 1700 B.C. It is a handbook of ancient Egyptian mathematics. It contains mathematical exercises. It also contains computations of the areas of such geometrical forms as triangles, rectangles, circles, and cylinders.

The Egyptians achieved great skill in solving practical mathematical problems. Their methods remained cumbersome in comparison with those of the Greeks, the latter having a more extensive facility for abstraction. For example, almost all fractions had to be expressed as the sum of several fractions having 1 as the numerator. To express $\frac{3}{8}$ they wrote $\frac{1\,1\,1}{8\,8\,8}$. They did have a special symbol and understanding for $\frac{2}{3}$.

The Egyptians applied their mathematical knowledge to everyday life and work with great success. Evidence of this ability is seen in the building and transportation of such great monuments as the pyramids and obelisks. The Rhind papyrus is now at the British Museum.

RHINE RIVER, a major river of central and western Europe. It enters or borders on Switzerland, Liechtenstein, Austria, Germany, France, and The Netherlands. It is connected to Belgium and Eastern Europe through canals. It is commercially and culturally one of the most important rivers in the world. The river is formed in the Alps of eastern Switzerland, near Chur, by the union of two headstreams. It flows north to Lake Constance, turns west to Basel, Switzerland, then flows north between France and Germany, until at Karlsruhe it fully enters Germany. There it is

Barges move up the Rhine below castles that were once the strongholds of robber barons.
Courtesy of TWA—Trans World Airlines

Rhinoceros skin resembles plates of armor.

joined at Mainz by the Main River and at Coblenz by the Moselle River. At The Netherlands border the river divides into three distributaries, the Waal, Lower Rhine, and Ijssel rivers. The Rhine has a total length of approximately 820 miles.

The Rhine handles a great amount of trade. It carries large quantities of coal, iron ore, and grain. Basel is the head of navigation. The principal inland port is Duisburg, Germany, and the chief cities include Mannheim, Cologne, Strasbourg, and Bonn, all in Germany, and Rotterdam in The Netherlands.

In ancient times the Rhine formed the boundary between the Roman Empire and the Teutonic hordes. During the Middle Ages it lay within the borders of the Holy Roman Empire. In 1648 France obtained territory along its left bank, lost it with the cession of Alsace-Lorraine after the Franco-Prussian War, and finally regained it after World War II. In March, 1945, during World War II, the Rhine was first crossed at Remagen, near Bonn, by U.S. troops.

RHINOCEROS, a large, thick-skinned mammal that lives in the tropical swamps and forests of Asia and Africa. It is 8 to 10 feet long, not counting its tail, and 5 to 6 feet high at the shoulder. It weighs as much as 6,000 pounds. Among land animals the rhinoceros is said to be surpassed in size and weight by only the elephant and the hippopotamus.

Its body is thick and bulky and is covered with a hard, rough, nearly hairless, almost boardlike skin, which usually is blackish gray. Sometimes the skin is so loose that it lies in great folds on parts of the body. The legs are short and stout, almost like pillars. The head is large and long, with erect ears placed far back. The Indian rhinoceros has one horn on the top of its nose, while the African rhinoceros has two. The horns are usually sharp and sometimes 2 or 3 feet long. They make powerful weapons of defense for the rhinoceros, which is stupid and timid, but which, when attacked or brought to bay, will fight fiercely. Its great weight makes it a match for even the elephant. Even though it is extremely ungainly, it is able to run as fast as 28 miles an hour. It is exclusively herbivorous. It usually lies hidden during the day but comes out at night to feed and roam about.

Usually only one rhinoceros is born at a time; twins are rare. The newborn calf, which weighs about 75 pounds, can walk after a few hours. It is suckled for about two years and then remains with its mother until it is more than half grown. The calf of the central-African white rhinoceros walks in front of its mother wherever she goes. She steers the calf by prodding her horns against its rump.

RHODE ISLAND, nicknamed Little Rhody because it is the nation's smallest state in area, is located in the northeastern United States. It is also one of the original 13 states. The capital, Providence, is Rhode Island's commercial and industrial center, as well as an important port. Chief cities include Pawtucket, Woonsocket, and Cranston. Newport, located on an island near Providence, gained national prominence as a society resort. Industrial magnates built lavish mansions here in the mid-19th century. The city is the site of the Naval War College and a naval training station. The state population in 1960 was 859,488.

Rhode Island is the most densely populated state, with about 708 persons per square mile. This New England state measures 40 miles east-west and 47 miles north-south. It covers an area of just over 1,200 square miles.

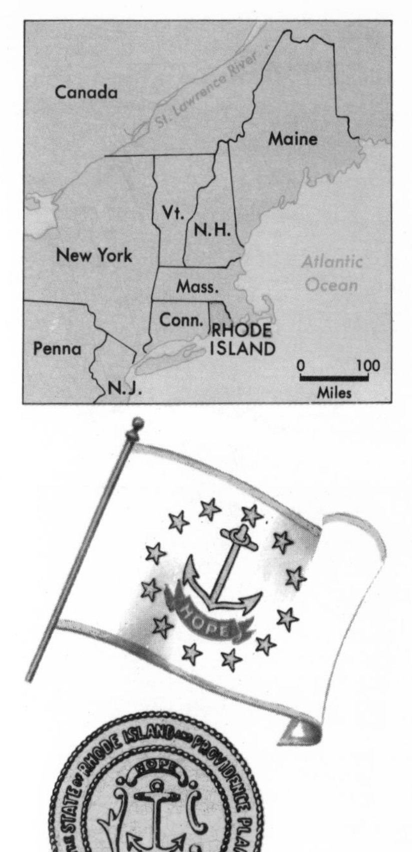

Rhode Island's motto, "Hope," appears on the state's flag and seal.

Narragansett Bay dominates the eastern third of Rhode Island. The west and central sections of the state are hilly and rocky. Barrier beaches and sandspits mark the coastline.

The state has a humid continental climate, influenced by its proximity to a large body of water. Providence has an average temperature of 30° F. in January and 74° F. in July.

Rhode Island is mainly an industrial state, producing many high-grade specialty products. There is also a sizable fishing industry carried on at several centers along the bay.

In 1636 Roger Williams, a religious exile from Massachusetts, purchased some land from the Indians and established Providence, the first permanent settlement in Rhode Island. Other colonies sprang

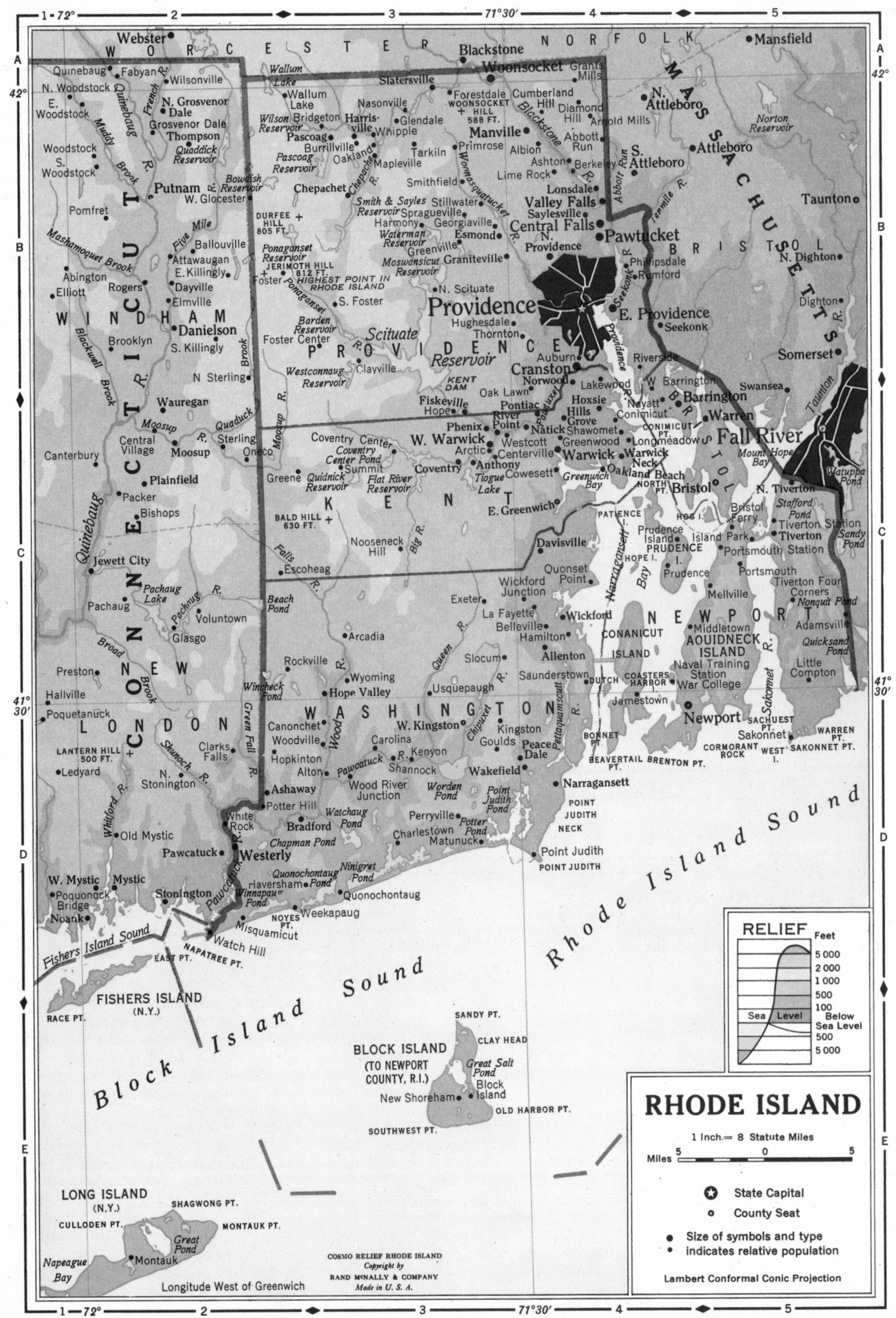

For map index, see Volume 20.

New Haven R.R.

The Rhode Island State House in Providence, built of white marble, was completed in 1900.

Frank Donato—Photo Researchers

The Slater textile mill, Pawtucket, R.I., was the country's first factory, 1793.

Rhode Island Development Council

The manufacture of jewelry is one of the most important industries of Rhode Island.

The state flower and bird of Rhode Island

up, many composed of Quakers and Jews who found here a haven from persecution. In 1663 Rhode Island was given its second royal charter, but as in the other colonies, there was friction between Rhode Island and England. Rhode Island was the first to declare its independence. It became the 13th state in 1790.

Since its early days the state has turned more and more from shipbuilding and commerce to manufacturing, particularly textile milling. It is also a famous resort area.

RHODE ISLAND

Nickname: Little Rhody
Seal: Anchor with motto above
Flag: 13 gold stars surrounding anchor and motto
Motto: Hope
Flower: Violet
Bird: Rhode Island Red hen
Capital: Providence
Largest city: Providence
Area: 1,214 sq. mi. (including 156 sq. mi. inland waters)
Rank in area: 50th
Population: 859,488
Chief universities: Brown University, University of Rhode Island
Chief rivers: Pawtuxet, Blackstone, Pawcatuck
Chief lake: Scituate Reservoir
Average temperature: Providence, 30° F. (Jan.), 74° F. (July)
Average annual rainfall: 45 inches
Chief economic activities: Manufacturing, agriculture (principally dairying and poultry raising)
Chief crops: Truck crops, hay, potatoes
Chief manufactures: Textiles, machinery, metal products
Notable attractions: Newport, Easton's Beach, Providence's colonial churches
Important historical dates:
1524 Narragansett Bay explored Giovanni da Verrazano
1636 First settlement founded at Providence by Roger Williams
1663 Colony granted royal charter
1776 Rhode Island first colony to declare independence from England
1790 First successful U.S. cotton mill established at Pawtucket by Samuel Slater
1790 13th state to enter Union

RHODES, CECIL JOHN (1853-1902), English financier and colonial statesman. Rhodes, the son of a clergyman, was born at Bishop's Stortford in Hertfordshire. In 1870 he was sent to South Africa to recover his health. There he resided for a time on a farm owned by his brother. In 1871 he and his brother moved to Kimberley, where diamonds had been found. Successful prospecting and speculation in mines and land founded Rhodes's fortune.

Rhodes returned to England and was admitted to Oriel College, Oxford. Although not an avid scholar, Rhodes read extensively in his favorite classics: Aristotle, Plato, Plutarch, and Marcus Aurelius. He was also impressed by Charles Darwin's *On the Origin of Species*. Several absences from England for reasons of health delayed his degree until 1881, just after he had been elected to the Assembly of Cape Colony.

In 1884 he became resident deputy commissioner of Bechuanaland, and in the next year southern Bechuanaland was declared a British protectorate. In negotiations with the Boers toward this end Rhodes met his great antagonist Paul Kruger, who stood stubbornly against Rhodes's plan for a British federation in South Africa. When gold was discovered on the Witwatersrand in 1886, Rhodes founded a company to mine it, which was known as the Gold Fields of South Africa. He also controlled the De Beers Consolidated Mines, which was an amalgamation of the South African diamond interests.

In 1890 Rhodes became prime minister of Cape Colony. In December, 1895, Leander S. Jameson, with the support of Rhodes led a filibustering expedition into the Boer Transvaal. Jameson's raid was crushed by Boer guerrilla tactics, and Rhodes, as a result of public indignation, resigned all his posts. In 1896, at great personal risk, Rhodes prevented by negotiation a revolt of the Matabele in Southern Rhodesia. He turned his attention to the development of the Rhodesias and to his scheme for a Cape-to-Cairo railroad.

Rhodes died a month before the end of the Boer War. His last words were "So little done, so much to do." Rhodes had added some 800,000 square miles to British territory. His last will established the Rhodes scholarships, which provide scholarships to Oxford for students from the British Commonwealth and the United States. See KRUGER, PAUL.

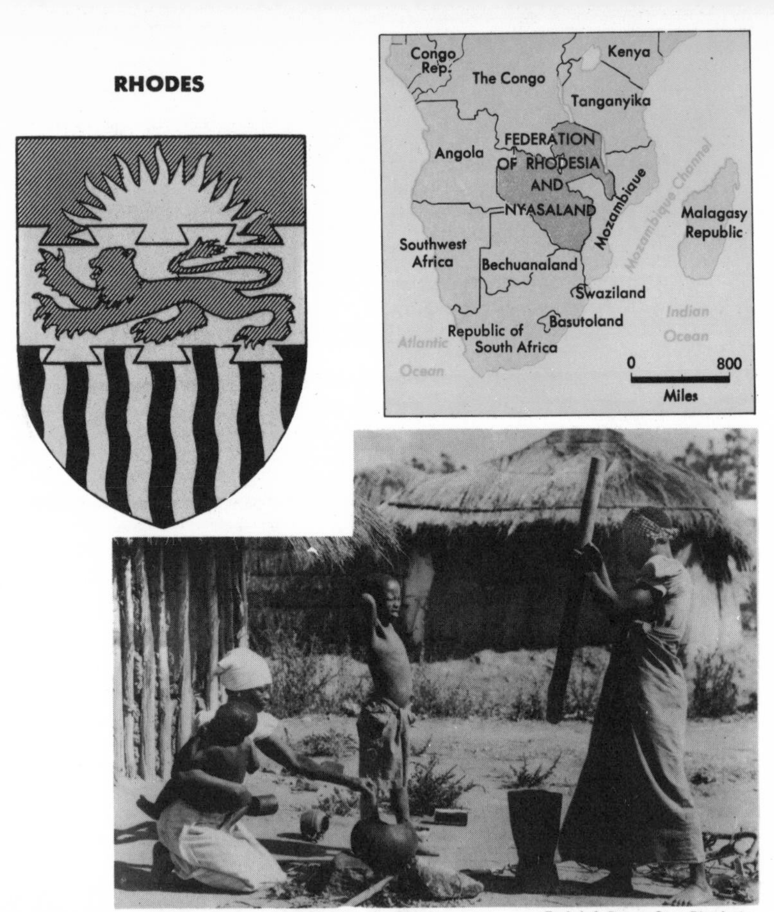

Fed. Inf. Dept., Sou. Rhodesia

The large majority of Rhodesians live in tribal areas and practice communal agriculture. A meal is being prepared (above). Europeans run the plantations, the mines, and most of the large industry.

RHODESIA AND NYASALAND, FEDERATION OF. The self-governing colony of Southern Rhodesia and the protectorates of Northern Rhodesia and Nyasaland comprise this British Commonwealth area. The federation, located in southern Africa, was established in 1953.

The executive power rests with the appointed governor-general, who exercises it through the prime minister. The Parliament consists of 47 Europeans and 12 Africans. It is the declared government policy to give Africans a greater voice in government as the ability and standard of the African population warrants it.

Salisbury in Southern Rhodesia is the federal capital. The total area, over 485,000 square miles, has a population of about 8,000,000.

Southern Rhodesia, covering an area of approximately 150,000 square miles, is mostly high plateau country. A broad ridge, the high veld, crosses the territory in a southwest-northeast direction. This section, where most Europeans settle, varies from 4,000 to 6,000 feet in height. Two-thirds of the colony lies in the middle veld at an elevation from 2,000 to 4,000 feet. A small section in the north and southeast is low veld—below 2,000 feet.

The colony has a population of about 200,000 Europeans, 2,500,000 Africans, and 14,500 Asians and mixed. The largest European population is at Salisbury, the capital.

Southern Rhodesia has been a self-governing colony since 1923. An appointed governor, a Parliament of 29, and a council of ministers rule. The government is almost entirely in the hands of the Europeans.

The original inhabitants of south-central Africa were primitive peoples, Bushmen and Hottentots. The more highly developed Bantu tribes settled in the Rhodesias and Nyasaland. In the early 19th century gold prospectors came, and the explorations of David Livingstone in the region encouraged missionaries. In 1889 Southern Rhodesia came under the influence of the British South Africa Company, headed by Cecil Rhodes.

Northern Rhodesia has an area of about 288,000 square miles, which is entirely within the tropics. Its elevation is generally over 3,000 feet, giving it a subtropical climate. Lowland areas along rivers are usually infested with the tsetse fly.

European settlement is along the

railroad line and in the industrialized copper belt of the north. About 74,000 Europeans, 2,200,000 Africans, and 7,700 Asians and mixed live here. Northern Rhodesia, as a protectorate, is governed by an appointed governor, a 19-member legislative council, and an executive council.

Missionaries came to the territory in the middle of the 19th century. Arab slave traders were driven out by the British in the 1890's. In 1889 the territory applied for a British protectorate and came under the British South Africa Company until it was annexed to Southern Rhodesia.

Nyasaland has an area of about 46,000 square miles and consists mainly of high plateau country ranging from 3,000 to 10,000 feet. The climate of the highlands is equable and healthy, but the low area near Lake Nyasa is humid and tropical.

About 8,000 Europeans, 2,700,000 Africans, and 11,000 Asians and mixed inhabit the territory. A governor and an 11-member legislative council make the laws.

The history of the territory is similar to Northern Rhodesia's. In 1858 David Livingstone visited Nyasaland. The territory became a British protectorate in 1891. For detailed map see SOUTH AFRICA, REPUBLIC OF.

RHODESIA AND NYASALAND

Area: Southern Rhodesia, 150,000 sq. mi.—Northern Rhodesia, 288,000 sq. mi.—Nyasaland, 46,000 sq. mi.
Population: Southern Rhodesia, 2,800,000—Northern Rhodesia, 2,300,000—Nyasaland, 2,700,000
Capital: Salisbury
Largest cities: Salisbury, Bulawayo
Highest mountains: Mlanje (about 9,800 feet)
Chief rivers: Zambezi and tributaries
Chief lakes: Nyasa, Tanganyika, Bangweulu
Climate: Generally subtropical—tropical in lowlands—rainy season with moderate rainfall
National flag: Blue, with Union Jack in upper left quarter—shield of coat of arms in lower right
Form of government: Federation within British Commonwealth—Southern Rhodesia, self-governing—Northern Rhodesia and Nyasaland, British protectorates
Unit of currency: Pound
Languages: English, native tribal languages
Chief economic activities: Mining, agriculture
Chief minerals: Copper, lead, zinc, cobalt, asbestos, gold, chrome
Chief crops: Tobacco, cotton, tea, corn
Chief exports: Copper, tobacco, asbestos, tea, chrome ore, other minerals
Chief imports: Vehicles, machinery, textiles

RHODODENDRON, one of a large group of mostly evergreen shrubs of great garden value for their spectacular masses of large flowers and attractive foliage. They are often called rose trees because *rhododendron* is derived from the Greek words for "rose" and "tree." The azaleas are correctly included with the rhododendrons, but in common garden practice they are usually separated.

Rhododendrons and azaleas are found throughout the north temperate regions of the world. Several important species are native to the mountains of the eastern United States and those of the Pacific northwest. The most colorful and showy species are native to Asia, particularly the Himalayas. Most types grown today are hybrids.

The five-lobed flowers are generally bell-shaped or funnel-shaped and vary in size from ½-inch to over 4 inches. They are borne in clusters, usually at the ends of the stems, and are surrounded by whorls of the generally large, smooth-edged, glossy leaves. Most varieties flower in late spring or early summer. Colors include white, many shades of pink and rose, lavender, purple, and red. Rhododendrons require some shade, particularly in the winter until well established. The soil should be loose, well drained, and covered with a continuous mulch of leaves. Many azaleas are grown in pots and are forced for flowering in the winter and early spring.

Rhododendron flowers grow in clusters, which in most species are large. The flowers are blue, yellow, red, pink, or purple.

RHUBARB, a perennial flowering herb that is cultivated for its edible leaf stalks. Native to Siberia, rhubarb belongs to the same family as beets and buckwheat. Rhubarb leaves, which are about 18 inches wide, are coarse and oval shaped and often have wavy margins. The leaves are never eaten by man. The thick green or red leaf stalks are from 12 to 30 inches long.

The young, tender stalks are cooked and sweetened and then either chilled and eaten as a sauce or else baked in pies, cobblers, or other fruit desserts. The flavor of cooked and sweetened rhubarb is tart as well as sweet and is quite palatable. Rhubarb is cultivated both commercially and in home gardens in most regions of North America and Europe and also on other continents.

RHYME, similarity of vowel sounds in words and of any consonant sounds that follow. In the *you* and *hue* the vowel sounds rhyme; in the words *bright* and *light* the rhyme includes both the vowel and consonant sounds of the syllable, *ight.* Two rhyming syllables, as in the words *bitter* and *glitter,* are called double rhymes. Three rhyming syllables, as in *hideous* and *fastidious,* are called triple rhymes. The bulk of English poetry uses single or double rhymes. Triple rhymes are more appropriate for limericks and other kinds of light verse.

Rhyme, although not as essential to the movement of verse as are accent and meter, has been a marked characteristic of English poetry since the 11th century. In Anglo-Saxon poetry, alliteration was the basis of rhythm in verse. (See ALLITERATION.) The stanza forms traditionally used by English poets are based on patterns of rhyme, sometimes called rhyme schemes. The couplet, being the shortest and simplest stanza form, has a rhyme scheme of *a a.* The ballad rhyme scheme is *a b c b* or *a b a b;* that of the Shakespearean sonnet is *a b a b c d c d e f e f g g.* In each of these forms the rhyming words come at the ends of lines, for which reason they are called end rhymes. This couplet from A. E. Housman uses end rhymes: "And early though the laurel *grows* / It withers quicker than the *rose.*" Internal rhymes, on the other hand, appear within a line or lines. The following line by W. S. Gilbert illustrates the use of internal rhyme: "Go *away,* madam, I must *say,* madam, you *display,* madam, shocking taste."

Rhyming words having single, stressed syllables, as *stark* and *mark*, are known as masculine rhymes. In feminine rhymes, the stressed syllables are followed by one or more unstressed syllables, as in *winging* and *singing*. Two short words may also rhyme with a single word if the accent falls in the right place. T. S. Eliot writes: "Oh, do not ask, 'What *is it?*' / Let us go and make our *visit*." From a popular song come the lines, "A tinkling piano in the next *apartment*, / Those stumbling words to tell you what my *heart meant*."

Poets use certain kinds of irregularities in rhyme. Identical rhymes, such as *flour* and *flower* or *knight* and *night*, differ only in spelling. Conversely, visual rhymes are similar in spelling, but different in pronunciation: *dour* and *sour*, *rough* and *though*, and *glove* and *move* are all visual rhymes. Words are sometimes wrenched out of shape to make comic rhymes. Ogden Nash writes: "One kind of sin is called a sin of commission, and that is very *important*, / And it is what you are doing when you are doing something you *ortant*." Such licenses as these can be effective if they are sparingly used. See POEM.

Ripened rice is being harvested by machine in a field in Colombia, South America.

Annan Photo Features

RICE, a cultivated grain that belongs to the grass family. The rice plant grows from 2 to 4 feet tall. Its edible grains are its ripened seeds and their adherent pericarps, which are borne in clusters, like those of oats, at the top of the stalk.

There are both wetland and dryland forms of rice. Dryland rice requires no irrigation.

Wetland rice grows best in subtropical or tropical regions that have a heavy annual rainfall. It is planted in low, level fields or on terraced hillsides. Since these plants can grow only if they are standing in water, the fields are flooded with 3 to 6 inches of water when the plants reach a height of 8 inches. The fields are drained when the grains begin to ripen. The hard rice grain, which is pure white, is enclosed in a yellowish-brown hull. After being cut and threshed, the grains may or may not have their hulls removed.

Although hulled white rice is preferred in the markets of the West, its food value is comparatively slight, as it consists chiefly of carbohydrates. Because the hulls contain proteins and vitamins, their food value is higher.

Rice has been cultivated in China for more than 4,000 years. Cultivated rice was probably derived from a wild ancestor that is native to southern China. Rice is the principal food of the majority of the people of China, India, Japan, and Indonesia, which are among the world's leading ricegrowing countries. Pakistan, Burma, and the Philippine Islands are other leading rice producers. About one-third of the world's inhabitants subsist chiefly upon rice.

Rice was first cultivated in North America near Charleston, in South Carolina, in 1694. Now the chief ricegrowing states are Louisiana, Texas, Arkansas, California, and Mississippi. In the United States rice is steamed and eaten as a vegetable and is made into breakfast cereals and puddings.

RICHARD II (1367-1400), king of England 1377-1399, was the son of Edward the Black Prince, England's ideal fighting man, and grandson of Edward III, an immensely popular king who had kept his nobles fighting in France and his people at home amused with showy pageants. But these diversions had cost so much that the royal authority had fallen under the financial control of Parliament, which was packed with unscrupulous nobles who did not hesitate to murder and exile each other. Richard's reign was filled with the fighting among these nobles, some on his side, some against him.

When Richard was only 14 years old and had been king four years, he displayed great bravery and tact in breaking up a rebellion of 100,000 peasants led by Wat Tyler. See WAT TYLER'S REBELLION.

From about 1382 to 1389 Richard tried to rule England with the aid of some of his nobles but ran afoul of others who forced him to accept a ruling committee called the lords appellant. These men exiled the king's friends, murdered them, and confiscated their estates.

In 1389 Richard regained the upper hand and ruled despotically for seven years. By setting his will completely above the law he defied the medieval ideal of the supremacy of law—under which both king and Parliament ruled.

Richard was so sure of his absolute power that he left England for a campaign in Ireland. Meanwhile, Henry of Bolingbroke, the king's cousin and former councilor, collected an army of nobles whose lives and estates had been threatened by Richard. Richard's friends deserted him. He was captured, forced to abdicate, and died in prison.

The net result of Richard's reign was the establishment of the idea that the king could be controlled by Parliament, could be deposed, and could be killed, and meanwhile the government would continue.

Rice grows in these flooded Chinese fields. In the Orient a rice field is called a paddy.

Ruth V. Bair

RICHARD III (1452-1485), the last Yorkist king of England, was born at the outbreak of the Wars of the Roses. These dynastic civil wars among the descendants of Edward III were waged so mercilessly that they all but exterminated the legitimate royal lines of descent. Richard grew up in the midst of unlimited and cruel family violence. Some scholars now doubt whether Richard was the monster that Shakespeare portrayed. They feel that his murderous career was merely typical of a dying feudalism and that his memory was blackened by propagandists in the pay of Henry VII, the first Tudor king.

In 1461, on the coronation of his brother, Edward IV, Richard was made duke of Gloucester and was sent to the Scottish border, where invasion and revolt were endemic. He proved to be a popular administrator and an able individual fighter, which hardly fits the historical picture of him as a bitter hunchback with a withered arm. But before Edward IV died, Richard was implicated in the murders of the Lancastrian king, Henry VI, and of the Prince of Wales and of the Duke of Clarence, Richard's own brother.

When Edward IV died in 1483, he left, by will, the 12-year-old Edward V and his younger brother under the protection of Richard. Richard took the two children from their mother, a leader of a rival faction in the struggle for power, and locked them up in the Tower of London. He accused the queen mother of sorcery, packed Parliament with his supporters, and had them declare Edward IV's marriage invalid, thereby making the two little princes in the Tower illegitimate. The boys were never seen alive again, and it has been assumed, but not proved, that they were murdered on the orders of Richard. At the request of his Parliament Richard then accepted the throne as Richard III.

Richard's reign lasted only two years. The Wars of the Roses continued when Henry Tudor, a distant cousin, returned from exile in France and raised an army to which most of Richard's forces deserted. On Bosworth Field Richard was slain, battleax in hand. According to his enemies, he was a terrific fighter to the last.

Henry Tudor, soon to be Henry VII, married Richard's niece Elizabeth. He thereby brought together in marriage the House of Lancaster and the House of York and so ended the Wars of the Roses.

In his justification for killing the alleged tyrant king of England, Henry VII never mentioned the fate of the two little princes in the Tower. Whoever killed them, the death of these two legitimate claimants to the throne was as advantageous to Henry as it had been to Richard.

The Bettman Archive

King Richard III at Bosworth Field

The story of the killing of the princes was probably written originally in Latin by John Morton, who had been a deadly enemy of Richard III. Henry VII gave Morton the archbishopric of Canterbury as a reward for his years of conspiring and fighting to make Henry king of England. In Morton's palace Thomas More served as a page and won Morton's admiration and friendship. Thirteen years after Morton's death in 1500, More translated into English Morton's account of Richard's killing of the two little princes. At the time More was working for Henry VIII. More, himself a very kindly man, was fully aware of the murderous proclivities of his master, whose life was haunted by the need to establish the legitimacy of his claims to the throne. It was very much to More's advantage to paint Richard III in the blackest colors. Strangely, More's translation of Morton's account was not fully published until 1557, long after Henry VIII had had More killed.

RICHARD THE LION-HEARTED (1157-1199), king of England and a famous warrior, was the third son of Henry II and his wife Eleanor of Aquitaine. With his brothers Henry and Geoffrey, he was in constant conflict with his father. In 1173 Richard joined them in open rebellion against the king. With the help of Philip II, king of France, Richard forced Henry II in 1188 to recognize him as the successor to the throne following the death of his older brother Henry. The old king's death in the following year made Richard king of England. He stayed in England only long enough to be crowned and to raise money for the crusade he had already planned. Early in 1191 he set out, with a large army, for the East.

The exploits of Richard the Lion-Hearted—his march to Jaffa (now in Israel) along the seashore, his approach to Jerusalem at Christmas, his capture of Acre, his second advance on Jerusalem in the summer of 1192, and his relief of Jaffa—made his name known throughout the East but accomplished nothing of value to the crusading cause. On the other hand his conceit and high-handed manner so offended the other princes that they became his permanent enemies. One of them, Philip II, returned home to intrigue against him with Prince John, Richard's younger brother.

Hearing of this, Richard left his army in October, 1192, and hastened toward England. While crossing in disguise the territory of the duke of Austria he was captured and turned over to Holy Roman Emperor Henry VI. He was held prisoner for more than a year in the castle of Dürenstein. He regained his freedom only after the payment of a large ransom by the English people. Arriving home in March, 1194, Richard remained only a few weeks before sailing for Aquitaine to war against Philip. He was killed by an arrow while besieging the castle of Châlus.

The city of Acre surrendered to Richard the Lion-Hearted and the Crusaders in 1191.

Cardinal Richelieu, French statesman

RICHELIEU, CARDINAL (1585-1642), the title of Armand Jean du Plessis, French prelate and statesman. He was born in Paris. Renouncing a career in the army, he was educated for the church. He became bishop of Luçon in 1607 and was created cardinal in 1622. After serving in the Estates-General as a deputy of the clergy and on the king's council he attained the position of principal minister of Louis XIII in 1624. From that time until his death he exercised complete control over Louis and the French government. From time to time Richelieu's position was threatened, but not seriously. He was officially appointed first minister of the state in 1629 and acquired the title of Duc de Richelieu in 1631.

During his administration Richelieu pursued three major objectives: the separation of the crown from the influence of the French nobility, the suppression of the French Huguenots, and the defeat of the House of Hapsburg. All three of these objectives he accomplished with remarkable success. The Thirty Years' War, which coincided roughly with the period of Richelieu's administration, saw France allied with Sweden and Protestant Germany against the Hapsburg-dominated countries of Italy, Spain, and Austria. The war resulted in the emergence of France as the foremost power in Europe. Although the Peace of Westphalia, which ended the war, was not signed until six years after Cardinal Richelieu's death, the treaty was consistent with principles that had been laid down by him.

RICHMOND is the capital of, and largest city in, the state of Virginia. It is situated on the James River in east-central Virginia. The city is a great tobacco market and seaport and is a financial, cultural, and commercial center of the South. In 1960 the population was 219,958. The principal industries are tobacco processing and the manufacture of chemicals, textiles, fabricated metals, paper and food products, and agricultural equipment.

Points of interest in this historic city include many old homes, such as those of John Marshall and Robert E. Lee; the White House of the Confederacy, once occupied by Jefferson Davis; and St. John's Church, dating from 1741, where Patrick Henry spoke the famous phrase, "Give me liberty or give me death!" A cemetery contains the graves of John Randolph, Jefferson Davis, and two presidents, James Monroe and John Tyler.

Richmond was first settled as a trading post in 1637. It was not formally laid out until 100 years later, when it was done so according to plans by William C. Byrd. It became the capital of Virginia in 1779. During the Civil War Richmond was the capital of the Confederacy and was under heavy threat of Union attack throughout the war. Its eventual fall came in April, 1865, when the city's inhabitants evacuated and burned Richmond. The Richmond National Battlefield, established in 1944, includes the battlegrounds of several engagements fought near the city. Belle Isle, in the James River, was the site of a Confederate prison. There is a national cemetery in the vicinity.

RICKETS, a nutritional disease with defects in the structure and the shape of bones. In rickets the body does not properly use calcium and phosphorus, and the bones do not contain the mineral that gives hardness to the bones. The cause is lack of vitamin D in foods and lack of exposure to ultraviolet light (sunlight). Widespread bone deformities affect the ribs, chest, head, legs, and pelvis. Prevention of the disease depends on providing 400 to 800 International Units of vitamin D a day. Common food sources of vitamin D are fish-liver oil, eggs, and milk. Milk containing 400 IU of vitamin D—the standard for all milk fortified with vitamin D—will prevent rickets in children. Overdosage with vitamin D can cause injury that may be fatal.

RIEL, LOUIS (1844-1885), was a leader of the midwestern French-Canadian-Indian trappers, or métis, during the period when English-speaking farmers were pushing the frontier westward along the lines of railroad construction. His life and execution by hanging epitomized two of the deepest divisions of Canadian life.

In 1869 the Canadian government bought most of the lands of the old Hudson's Bay Company, over which Riel's fellow trappers and squatters were scattered. Riel came forward as chief to oppose the British regulars and the Canadian militia. (See RED RIVER REBELLION.) Though driven out of Canada, he was elected and reelected to the Parliament in Ottawa, but because of an alleged murder he never took his seat and was finally outlawed in 1875 and fled to the United States.

In 1885 Riel led the Northwest Rebellion of his métis against 7,000 soldiers. At the Battle of Batoche in Saskatchewan he was captured and later was hung as a traitor. He went to his death so fearlessly that around his memory grew up a folklore of unselfish patriotism.

RIFLE, a firearm in whose bore are cut spiral, parallel grooves, which impart a twisting motion to the elongated, closely fitting bullet. This rotary motion causes the bullet to travel steadily on its longer axis, point foremost, thereby greatly increasing the accuracy of its flight and its penetrative power. A hand firearm with a spirally grooved bore, the first rifle, was invented in Vienna about 1500.

Rifles probably were first brought to America by Swiss and German immigrants. Settlers in what is now Lancaster Co., Pennsylvania, began manufacturing rifles as hunting arms as early as 1754, and a few such weapons were used by American frontiersmen who served during the Revolutionary War. This rifle was fairly accurate up to 150 yards, while brown Bess, the military musket of those days, could not be relied upon beyond about 70 yards. Muzzle-loading rifles, which were very accurate up to about 500 yards, were made in the United States during the first half of the 19th century. The repeating, or magazine, rifle was introduced in America just before the Civil War. The cartridge magazine ran the length of the barrel and was capable of holding 15 bullets end to end and pressed toward the breech of the gun by a spring. The cartridge was projected into firing position by a lever. The Winchester rifle, first made between 1860 and 1866, was a great improvement over the early repeating gun. Later improvements eliminated the feeding lever, and a bolt was designed to eject the used cartridge, insert another in the breech, and cock the hammer, all in one operation. In 1873 the United States War Department adopted the Springfield breech-loading, single-shot rifle of .45 caliber, which was superseded in the Spanish-American War by the Krag-Jorgensen smokeless-powder repeating rifle (six shots). The Krag in turn was displaced by the 1903 model of the Springfield, adopted in 1904, also a six-shot, smokeless-powder rifle, which remained the standard arm for infantry for many years. Similar weapons were used during and after World War I by the infantry of other nations. Automatic and semiautomatic rifles have been produced since 1903 by private companies for use in hunting and for law-enforcement agencies. No such weapon rugged enough for army usage had been perfected, however, until 1939, when the United States Army, after extensive tests, adopted the Garand rifle as a regular combat weapon. This rifle holds a clip of 8 cartridges; as many as 12 clips can be fired per minute. Because of the automatic loading and ejection, an entire clip can be fired without removing the gun from the shoulder.

RIGA, the capital, largest city, and chief seaport of Latvia, on the Western Dvina River, 10 miles from its mouth on the Gulf of Riga. It has a population of about 600,000.

The old town has narrow streets and medieval buildings, but the new sections and the suburbs are laid out in broad streets with modern buildings. The main industries of Riga are the manufacture of furniture, paper and other wood products, bicycles, hydroturbines, measuring instruments, glass, textiles, rubber and leather goods, and electrical machinery.

Among the historical buildings of the old city are the cathedral, founded in 1215 and rebuilt after a fire in the 16th century; St. Peter's Church (1406); and a castle dating partly from 1515. Cultural centers include the Latvian State University, agricultural and art academies, a teachers college, and a conservatory. Riga Jurmala is a suburb.

Riga was founded in 1158 as a storehouse by merchants of Bremen. During the first half of the 13th century the city was under the control of the bishop of Livonia. It joined the Hanseatic League, and from 1253 to 1420 Riga was an independent city under its own magistrates. The bishop reestablished his authority in 1420 and maintained it until 1566, when it was abolished as a result of the Reformation. Riga belonged to Poland from 1561 and to Sweden from 1621 to 1710, when it was taken by Russia. Under Russian rule Riga became an important seaport and commercial center. The city was occupied by the Germans during World War I, and many of her industries were destroyed. In 1919 Riga became the capital of the independent republic of Latvia. Troops of the Soviet Union occupied the city and the country in June, 1940, and in July Riga became the capital of the new de facto Soviet republic. The city was again taken by the Germans in 1941 and was recaptured by the U.S.S.R. in 1944.

RIGEL, or Beta Orionis, a prominent star in the constellation Orion. (See ORION.) Rigel is a double star with one component of first magnitude and the other of seventh magnitude. The fainter component is itself a multiple system of three stars, making Rigel actually a quadruple star. The system is about 900 light-years distant from our sun. Its combined light is some 18,000 times brighter than the light of the sun.

Below is a Marlin Model-336 carbine, .30/30, with a scope sight. It weighs less than 7 pounds and has a 20-inch barrel.

Wide World Photo

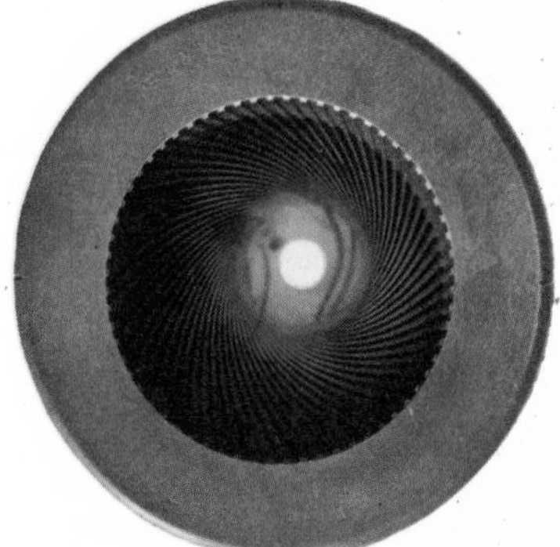

Courtesy of the U.S. Army—Ace Williams

Above is a view through the bore of a U.S. Army howitzer. The spiral grooves cause the shell to spin and increase its accuracy. Ridges between grooves are called lands. The grooves and lands together make up rifling. Rifling is also a feature of the 280-millimeter atomic cannon at left.

RIGHT ASCENSION, one of the two measurements used to locate the direction of objects in space. The other measurement is called declination. (See DECLINATION.) Measurement of right ascension involves certain elements of the celestial sphere. (See CELESTIAL SPHERE.) These are the celestial equator and hour circles, which are circles passing through the celestial poles perpendicular to the celestial equator.

Right ascension measures the angular distance between two hour circles, one passing through the vernal equinox and the other passing through the position of the star or other body to be located. (See EQUINOX.) This angular distance is measured eastward along the celestial equator from the vernal equinox. The distance is usually expressed not in units of degrees, as in degrees of longitude on earth, but in units of time—hours, minutes, and seconds. This is accomplished by dividing the 360 degrees of the celestial equator into 24-hour units, each equal to 15 degrees. One degree is then equal to $\frac{1}{15}$ hour, or four minutes. The choice of hour units derives from the fact that, as the earth rotates, the stars appear to rotate through a full circle in 24 hours.

The right ascension of the star Castor is given as 6 hours 32 minutes. This means that the hour circle passing through Castor crosses the celestial equator at a point 6 hours and 32 minutes east of the vernal equinox. The same distance would equal 98 degrees.

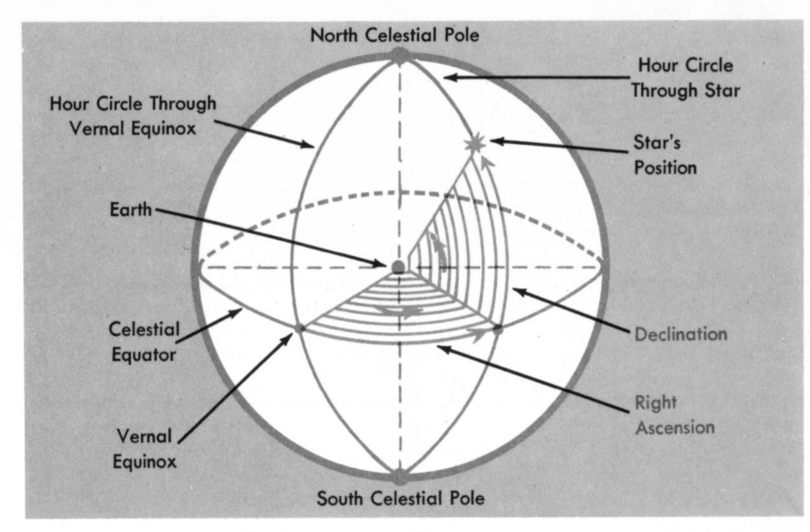

Right ascension is measured eastward along the celestial equator from the vernal equinox to a star's hour circle. Declination is measured northward or southward along this hour circle.

RIGHT-TO-WORK LAW, a law such as those passed in 18 states since 1944, which provide that no one shall be required to be a member of a labor union in order to keep a job. Such laws have been presented to the voters in some other states but have been rejected. Union contracts with employers usually state that anyone taking a job with the employer under contract must join the union within a specified time after being hired. The right-to-work laws outlaw such contract clauses. Employer groups usually favor these laws, and organized labor opposes them. In 1960, right-to-work laws were in effect in Alabama, Arizona, Arkansas, Florida, Georgia, Indiana, Iowa, Mississippi, Nebraska, Nevada, North Carolina, North Dakota, South Carolina, South Dakota, Tennessee, Texas, Utah, and Virginia.

RIJEKA. See FIUME.

RILKE, RAINER MARIA (1875-1926), German poet, born in Prague, Bohemia (now in Czechoslovakia). After an unhappy childhood, during which he attended a number of schools (in Linz, Austria, and in Prague), including two military academies, Rilke took up residence in Munich, Germany. His early poems were written in the romantic tradition of Heinrich Heine. Best known of his early works was the sentimental and melodramatic prose poem *Tale of Love and Death of Cornet Christopher Rilke*. After 1899 Rilke commenced his wanderings, which were to take him throughout Europe. Although Rilke's work achieved general popularity during his lifetime, he chose to remain aloof from society. Nevertheless, Rilke was often forced by financial need to seek patronage. *Poems from the Book of Hours* and *Stories of God*, inspired by trips to Russia, reveal a sophisticated sense of imagery and the influence of Russian mysticism. After residing at an artists' colony in Worpswede, Germany, Rilke moved to Paris, where he made the acquaintance of Auguste Rodin. Rilke was the sculptor's secretary in 1905 and 1906. *New Poems* and the prose narrative *The Notebook of Malte Laurids Brigge*, both written in the poet's mature style, reflect his association with the French impressionists and symbolists. During World War I he worked in the Austro-Hungarian War Department. His last seven years were spent in Switzerland. His major postwar works include *Duinese Elegies* and *Sonnets to Orpheus*. Rilke is often considered the foremost German poet of the early 20th century.

RIMSKI-KORSAKOV, NIKOLAI (1844-1908), Russian composer, was born in Tikhvin. Although his musical talent was evident at an early age, he was prepared for a career in the Russian navy. Nevertheless, while attending the naval college at St. Petersburg (now Leningrad), he managed to receive instruction in music. While on a postgraduate naval cruise Rimski-Korsakov composed his first major work, a symphony. Returning to St. Petersburg in 1865, he renewed his friendship with the Russian composers who, with himself, were to comprise The Five of Russian nationalistic music. On the merit of a symphonic poem, he won a professorship at the St. Petersburg Conservatory of Music in 1871. He retired from the navy in 1873 but served as inspector of naval bands from that year until 1884. During his years at the conservatory he gained a reputation as a conductor as well as a teacher and composer.

Like other nationalistic composers Rimski-Korsakov drew his inspiration from the cultural tradition of his own people. Not only did he utilize Russian folk music itself, but in the case of his operas he drew upon episodes in Russian history. His symphonic music is marked by brilliant orchestration, which heightens its descriptive nature. His work includes three symphonies; several operas, including *The Snow Maiden*, and *The Maid of Pskov;* chamber music; songs; and program music, including *Scheherazade* and *Antar*. *Le Coq d'Or*, one of his best known works, was finished in 1907, but it was not performed until after his death.

RING, a circular adornment, usually metallic, worn on the fingers, wrists, arms, neck, nose, ears, ankles, or toes. The earliest Egyptian tombs show that finger rings, sometimes made of glass, but more often of metal, were worn as ornaments as well as symbols of authority. The early Roman citizens, like the early Greeks, wore iron finger rings as a sign that they were free men; while, later on, an iron ring around the neck was the sign of a slave. As time went on, rings became badges of authority, each ring bearing some special device belonging only to the owner. We find the giving or lending of a ring often mentioned in history and in the Bible as a sign of conferring personal authority on the bearer, as when Pharaoh made Joseph ruler over Egypt by giving him his own ring (Gen. 41:42).

The gold ring soon became a badge of rank; and at Rome only men of, or above, the equestrian (knightly) order were allowed to wear rings. When Hannibal, the Carthaginian general, annihilated a Roman army at the Battle of Cannae (216 B.C.), he sent back to Carthage three bushel-baskets full of knights' rings taken from their bodies on the field. Under the Empire, Roman senators and high officials all wore massive and elaborate rings of gold as a sign of rank or office. Christian bishops, after the official adoption of Christianity as the state religion by the Emperor Constantine, wore large gold rings as a sign of their rank. The episcopal ring, worn on the first finger of the right hand, became so important that in the Middle Ages a bishop was not considered to be properly entitled to exercise his duties if he had not been officially presented with his ring by the pope or the king. The pope wears a ring called the Fisherman's Ring, which on the bezel bears a figure of St. Peter in a boat. This ring is given to a new pope by the city of Rome and is broken when he dies. The pope presents a new cardinal with a massive gold ring, and nuns wear a wedding ring as a symbol of their spiritual marriage to Christ.

The use of the ring in marriage is very ancient, dating from Roman times, when rings were exchanged between man and woman as a sign of betrothal. In many countries men as well as women wear wedding rings. Seal rings, with the bezel incised with a monogram, are also very ancient. During the Middle Ages the seal ring usually carried the knight's coat-of-arms so that he could use it for signing (by seal) documents or letters written for him by others.

The ring still bears a ceremonial significance today in the wedding ceremony of many lands, in the coronation of kings, and in the investiture of bishops.

RINGLING BROTHERS, five circus men who, as musicians, actors, and dancers, organized and managed with brilliant success the Ringling Brothers Circus. Albert C. (1852-1916), Otto (1858-1911), Alfred T. (1861-1919), Charles (1863-1926), and John (1866-1936) grew up in the home of a Baraboo, Wis., harnessmaker. Their love of playing and singing together developed by 1880 into the Ringling Brothers Classic and Comic Concert Company. Charles was the fiddler; Albert, the juggler; John, known as Mr. John, the clown. Otto and Alfred took in the money and danced, sang, and played 12 different musical instruments. Every move was decided by majority vote, and all earnings went into one family account. During the period 1880 to 1890 they acquired a wagon, a mangy horse, a dancing bear, a "hideous hyena," a knock-kneed elephant, and "Yankee" Robinson, a great clown. The show grew rapidly, and by 1890 it was put onto 18 railroad cars. Prosperity allowed the Ringlings to have a private family railroad car equipped with a five-octave piano, around which they continued to live in the world of popular and classical music. They bought out the Forepaugh-Sells Circus in 1906 and the Barnum and Bailey Circus a year later and in 1919 merged them all into the world's greatest circus.

Because of the depression and because of unwise financing the show that had been a great moneymaker went into technical bankruptcy in 1933. Three years later Mr. John, the last of the brothers, died. However, their nephew John Ringling North and Robert E. Ringling, son of Charles, reorganized and carried on the circus.

RINGMASTER, a leader of acts or stunts performed in the circus ring. (See CIRCUS.) Since the late 18th century, particularly in France and England, when equestrian acts were directed by a leader dressed in a riding habit, the ringmaster has always been associated with this circus performance. The association of ringmaster and equestrian director continued through the 19th century, both on the Continent and in the United States. Even as more animal acts were included in the circus repertoire, it was always the director of the equestrian acts who was thought of as ringmaster. Dressed in a riding habit, top hat, and white gloves, he announced his acts from the center ring or sometimes by loudspeaker. Bareback performances were, or course, a favorite of circus audiences, although the ringmaster worked more often with an act known as high-school horses. The most colorful of American ringmasters was Fred Bradna, who worked for Ringling Brothers and Barnum and Bailey Circus.

This is a collection of rings from various times and countries: **1,** Egyptian signet, 2d century B.C.; **2,** Ionian-Persian signet, 5th century B.C.; **3,** Etruscan signet, 4th-3d centuries B.C.; **4,** Roman legionary's ring, 3d century; **5,** Nordic, 9th and 10th centuries; **6,** Italian, 14th century; **7,** German engagement ring, 17th century; **8,** Greco-Roman signet, 1st century B.C.—2d century A.D.; **9,** Ostrogoth or Lombard, 5th-7th centuries; **10,** English, 12th and 13th centuries; **11,** origin unknown, 17th century; **12,** Austrian, 18th century; **13,** English, 19th century; **14,** Russian, 20th century; **15,** German Freemason's ring, 19th century; **16,** Russian, 16th-17th centuries; **17,** Indian or Persian, 17th and 18th centuries; **18,** Chinese mandarin, 18th century; **19,** Lapland reindeer-bone ring, 19th century.

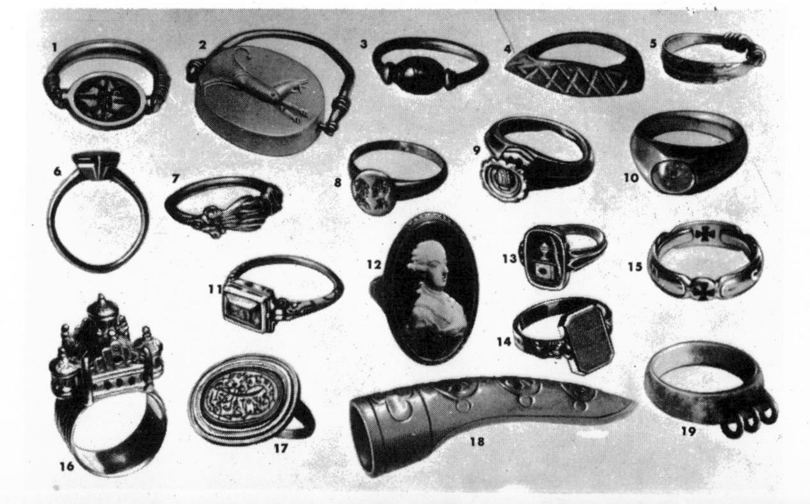

RING NEBULA, one of the best known planetary nebulae. Located in the constellation Lyra, the Ring Nebula is a shell of expanding gas surrounding a central star of 14th magnitude. The gas is made luminous by the central star's ultraviolet radiation. The Ring Nebula is not visible to the naked eye. In a telescope it is revealed as a glowing ring of green and orange light.

The Ring Nebula is shown below as photographed through the 200-inch telescope.
Mount Wilson-Palomar Observatories

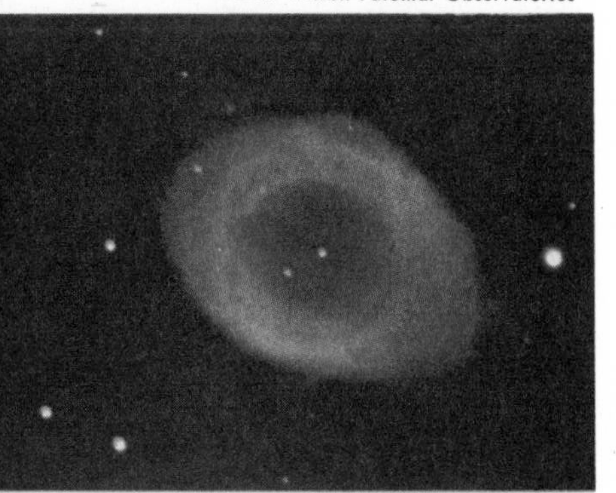

RINGWORM is a contagious skin disease caused by infection with fungi. It may affect any part of the body. The commonest type is ringworm of the foot, or athlete's foot. The appearance of the disease and the treatment differ with the part of the body affected. The eruption may consist of scales, blisters, pustules, or discolored patches. Itching is often present. There are specific fungicidal ointments for treatment of the disease.

RIO DE JANEIRO is a seaport city located in a beautiful setting on the western shore of a landlocked harbor in southeastern Brazil. Until 1960, when the new capital, Brasília, was completed, Rio de Janeiro was the seat of the federal government. The city is a commercial, financial, cultural, and tourist center of Brazil. Its long harbor, with approximately 2 miles of wharves, is near the center of the city and handles a large share of the country's imports. Rio de Janeiro has a population of about 3,000,000.

Although not the country's industrial center, the city produces a wide variety of manufactures, such as textiles, clothing, tobacco products, and leather products. The items are produced largely for domestic use.

Rio de Janeiro has a hot, humid climate. It has a mean temperature of 75° F., with a slight annual variance. The annual rainfall is about 44 inches; yet Rio de Janeiro is one of the most healthful tropical cities. This condition was achieved through urban sanitation and drainage of the surrounding insect-breeding areas. Nearby mountain resorts, such as Petrópolis, are popular for their cool climate. Rio de Janeiro's fashionable Copacabana Beach, in the form of a crescent, has a fine beach, with tall, modern apartment buildings in the background. The annual festive pre-Lenten carnival is a highlight for the *Cariocas* (Rio de Janeiro's citizens) and also for visitors and tourists.

In 1502 Portuguese navigators discovered the land-locked bay, which they named River of January. In 1567 Portuguese settlers occupied the harbor. By the early 18th century Rio de Janeiro was Brazil's leading city. In 1763 it became the seat of the Portuguese viceroyalty. The city's growth was further enhanced from 1808 to 1821 when the exiled Portuguese government was established here. Rio de Janeiro became capital of the Brazilian Empire in 1822.

RÍO DE LA PLATA is a wide estuary of South America, between Uruguay on the north and Argentina on the south, through which the waters of the Paraná and Uruguay rivers flow to the ocean. It is the major indentation on South America's eastern coast.

The river extends approximately 170 miles from the junction of the Paraná Bravo and Uruguay rivers in Uruguay to its mouth. It has a maximum width of about 140 miles at its mouth, between Punta del Este and Cape San Antonio. The tributaries of the Río de la Plata drain an area estimated at 1,500,000 square miles.

The Río de la Plata is an important navigation route, giving access to the interior. Navigation is hampered by shallow water and sandbanks, and the river must be continually dredged. Principal ports include Montevideo, Uruguay, and Buenos Aires. The Río de la Plata was discovered in 1516 by Juan Diaz de Solís. Its name sometimes refers to the entire river system (Paraná-Paraguay-Uruguay) of southeast-central South America.

A panoramic view of Rio de Janeiro, a great tourist center, may be enjoyed from an observation point far above the city.
Alfred O. Holz

RIO GRANDE, known as the Río Bravo in Mexico, flows through the southwestern United States and along the northern Mexican border. It rises in the San Juan Mountains of southwestern Colorado and follows a southeasterly direction for approximately 1,800 miles. It flows south through New Mexico and then southeast to form the international boundary between Texas and Mexico. The river empties into the Gulf of Mexico 22 miles east of Brownsville, Tex.

An international agreement forbids all navigation. Irrigation and flood-control projects are located along the Rio Grande's course.

RIVERA, DIEGO (1886-1957), a Mexican artist, was born in Guanajuato. He studied at the School of Fine Arts in Mexico City and in France, Spain, Italy, and the U.S.S.R. His work was influenced by El Greco, Goya, Cézanne, and Picasso.

Although he was not a consistent member of the Communist party, it impressed him to the extent that his philosophy of art changed. He came to believe that art should alter with the times, should belong to the people, and should be put in public buildings. For that reason he turned to murals, which are found in Mexico in the Building of Public Education, the Building of Public Health, the Agricultural School of Chapingo, the Cortes Palace at Cuernavaca, and the National Palace of Mexico at Mexico City. He did frescoes in the San Francisco Stock Exchange and in the San Francisco School of Fine Art, in the Detroit Art Institute, in the New Workers School in New York, and in Rockefeller Center in New York. A fresco at Rockefeller Center, which was unacceptable because it included a portrait of Lenin and was the source of controversy, was repainted in the Palace of Fine Arts in Mexico City. Rivera wrote *Portrait of America.*

RIVER AND STREAM, terms applied to a body of running water flowing across a land surface from a higher elevation toward a base, generally the sea. A stream can be small or the size of the Mississippi River or larger. All streams begin originally as rainfall. Rainwater that runs off the land collects into streamlets, and these join to form larger streams or rivers. Smaller streams flowing into larger ones are called tributaries. A river with all of its tributaries is a river system. The beginning of a stream is called its source; this may be a spring from underground, a lake or marsh, or simply falling rain. The path of a stream is its course. For water to collect and form streams it is necessary that the land have a slope. As the stream flows down the slope, it gradually cuts into the surface and forms a valley. Precipitous-walled valleys are called canyons or gorges. Where the bedrock consists of layers that differ in their resistance to stream erosion, waterfalls and rapids may occur. River valleys are separated from one another by ridges of higher land; the ridges separating river systems are known as watersheds.

All rivers have a constant tendency to cut their valleys deeper and wider as they approach sea level. The widening is caused by changes in the flow from a straight line. These changes, called meanders, result in cutting into the banks on either side of the riverbed. In addition to eroding or wearing away the land surface, streams also deposit material. Stream deposits occur where the transporting power of a stream decreases. Such deposits include bars, flood plains, alluvial fans and cones, and deltas. River water is fresh except for the short stretch of tidal water above the mouths of rivers that empty into the sea or where rivers are polluted by man.

RIVER PO, THE (constellation). See ERIDANUS.

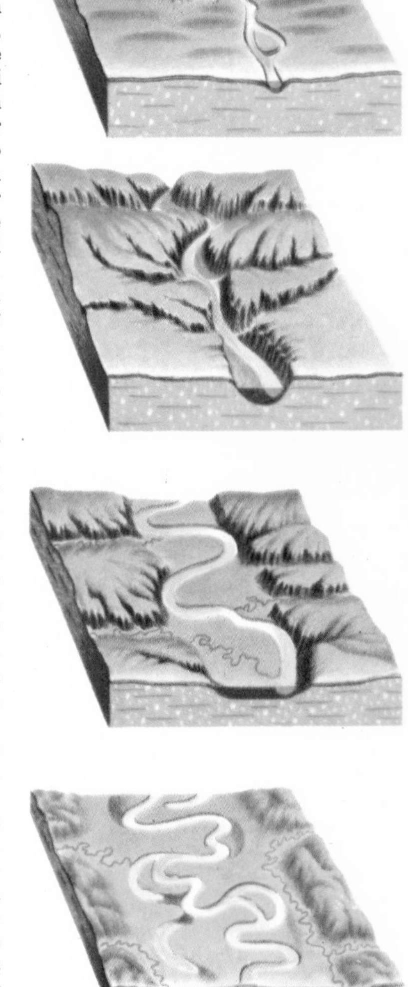

Above are four stages, starting at the top, in land sculpture by a stream. Rivers that flow swiftly through hard material, as in the diagram below, expend more energy deepening their channels than widening them. At left is a picture of the different ways rivers can transport rock particles. Larger pieces are rolled or bounced along the river bottom; smaller pieces are carried by water.

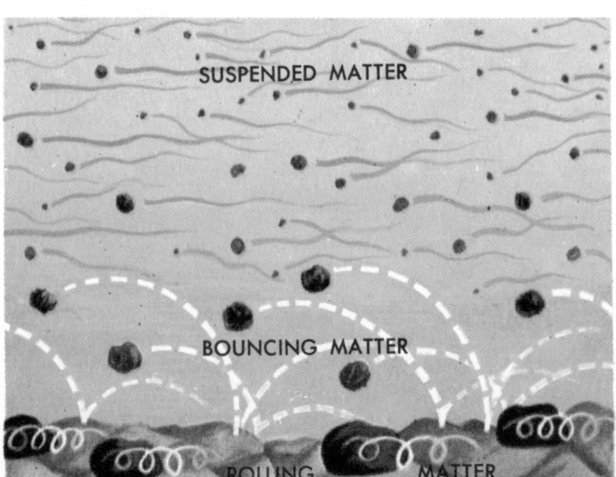

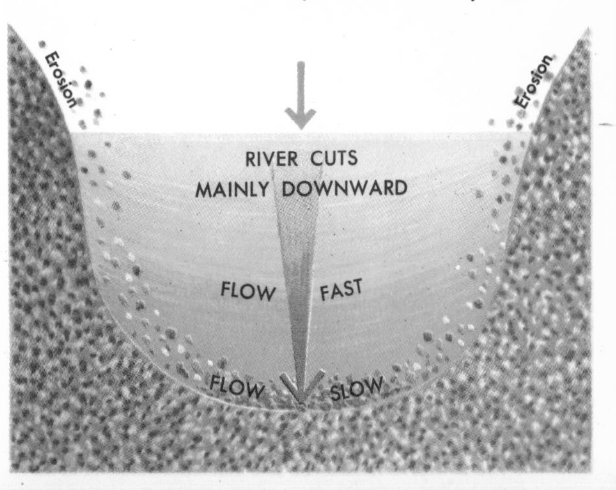

New Jersey Turnpike Authority

The New Jersey Turnpike extends from near Wilmington, Del., to New York City.

Title Insurance and Trust Co., Los Angeles

The relative slowness of activity on Spring Street, Los Angeles, in 1885 (above) contrasts with the high speed of traffic today on the city's interwoven system of freeways.

Union Pacific Railroad

ROAD. Highways for traveling and for the transportation of merchandise were constructed at a very early period. The Egyptians had to transport over land for short distances the immense blocks of stone needed for the pyramids; according to the Greek historian Herodotus, 100,000 men worked for ten years on a causeway for the great pyramid of Khufu. Although there were short stretches of paved road in many parts of the ancient world, the construction of a nationwide system of roads, according to some writers, belongs to the Carthaginians or the Romans.

It was the Romans, however, who were the great roadbuilders of antiquity. Their roads, built chiefly for military and administrative purposes, connected Rome with the provinces. Immense sums were expended in their construction. They were laid out, as far as possible, in a straight line, the nature of the ground being disregarded. Mountains were cut, valleys filled or spanned with masonry, and streams bridged. The first great Roman road, the Appian Way (Via Appia), built 312 B.C. by the censor Appius Claudius, is worthy of admiration even now in its ruined state, for portions of this wonderful work still exist. The Romans built thousands of miles of similar solidly constructed roads, not only throughout Italy but also in Gaul, Spain, and Britain and in parts of Africa and Asia, wherever they carried their victorious arms.

Almost equal to the Roman highways were the great military footroads built by the Incas of Peru, the remains of which still attest their magnificence. There were many of these roads, but the most remarkable was that which extended from Quito to Cuzco and thence southward toward Chile, more than 1,500

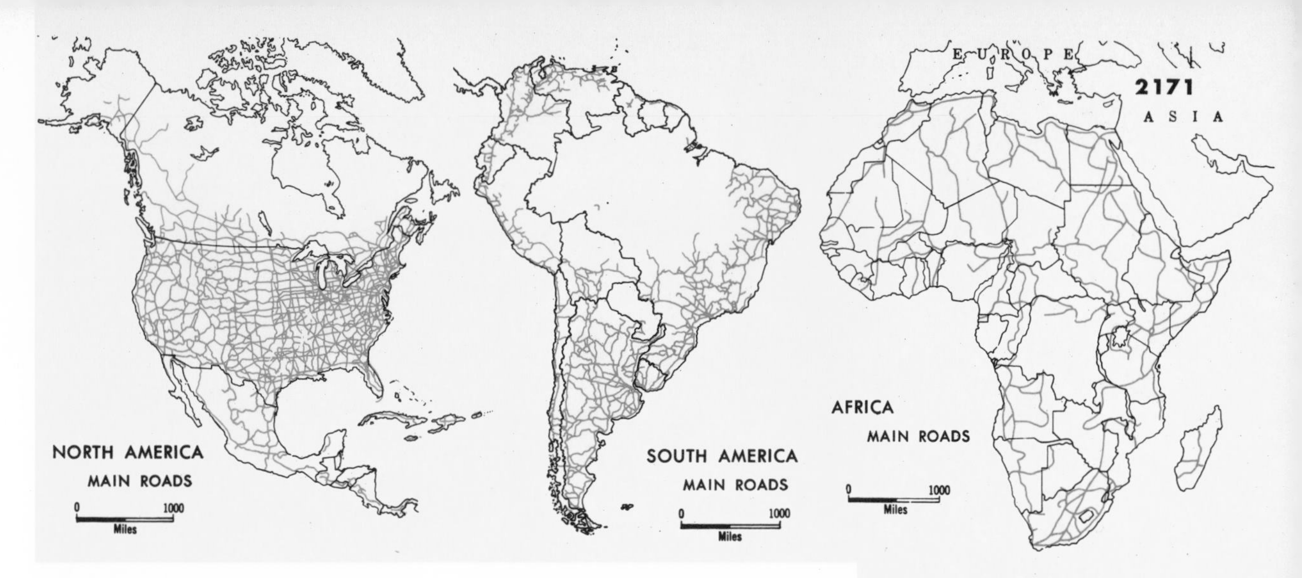

miles. It ran through a mountainous region, where the natural difficulties to be overcome might appall even a modern engineer. Galleries were cut for miles through the solid rock, ravines were filled with solid masonry, and rivers were crossed by suspension bridges hung on great ropes made of fiber or wool. The roadbed, about 20 feet wide, was formed of heavy flags of freestone, and in some parts was covered with asphalt.

In the Middle Ages in Europe roads were sometimes made or were kept in repair by noblemen, who charged tolls on all traffic to repay the cost; sometimes the great religious houses built or maintained roads as a pious service; but scientific roadbuilding did not really revive until the middle of the 18th century. At the end of that century, the Scottish engineer John L. McAdam introduced the broken-stone construction that still bears his name (macadam), and France under Napoleon laid out a splendid series of national highways.

It was about the end of this century, too, that the first general interest in good roads was awakened in the United States, when it was felt necessary to knit the scattered communities into a nation. From the first years of the 19th century, turnpikes began to be constructed in all directions, until there were nearly 5,000 miles of them. These were privately owned roads, made with private capital, and like the European toll roads they had tollgates every few miles. They had gravel or crushed stone, and in some cases plank, surfaces. The rapid expansion of the country to the west made roads—any sort of roads—necessary. Famous westward routes, such as the Oregon Trail, were merely tracks across the plains and mountains. Not until the coming of the automobile and truck did the United States devote itself seriously to its roads and the need for developing an improved road network. See MACADAM ROAD.

Roads within towns and cities are called streets, which, in modern cities, are paved. In Rome streets were not paved until about four or five centuries after the city's founding. The streets of Paris were first paved in the 12th century, but paved streets did not become common in London until the 16th century. Córdova, Spain, however, may have had paved streets as early as 850. In the early 19th century English travelers in Italy were impressed by the fine pavements of Florence, Siena, Milan, and Rome. Streets in these cities sometimes had specially laid wheel tracks of durable stone. The early street pavements in England were mainly cobblestone. In the 19th century London experimented with granite, wood, and rock asphalt. New York streets were mainly cobblestone until about 1850, when Belgian block (and on one street cast-iron block) came into use.

There are six important elements in designing streets: width of pavement, which depends on the necessary traffic capacity; longitudinal grades, or slopes of the center line of the pavement, the gutters, and the curbs, which are determined by vehicular travel and drainage requirements; the crown, or the elevation in the center of the pavement, which slopes toward the gutter and allows drainage and facilitates street cleaning; intersections; surface drainage; and curvature. The design of the sidewalks that flank the street is relatively easy. Most sidewalks are made of portland-cement concrete. Pavement serves to facilitate vehicular traffic and to drain water from the street and surrounding area into an under-

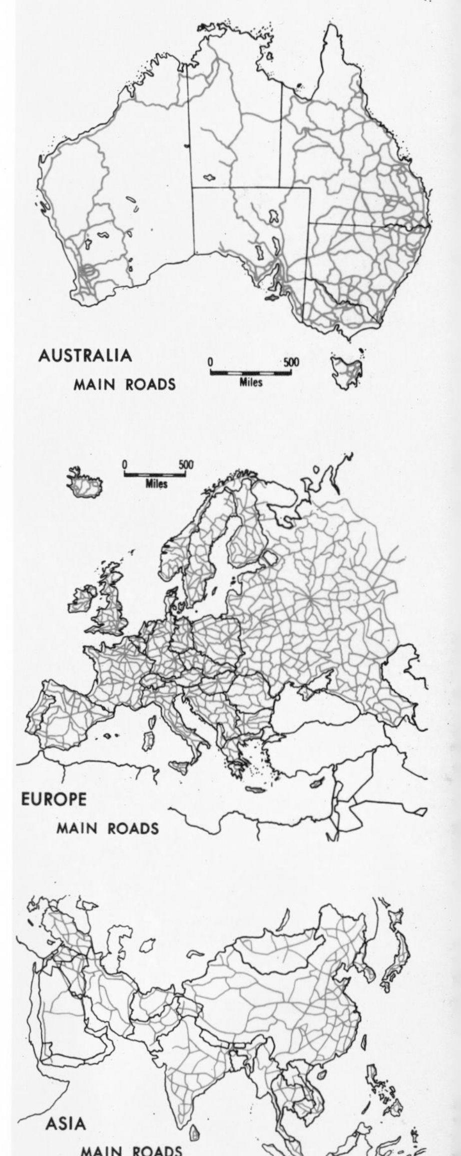

ground drainage system. An ideal pavement is cheap, durable, easily cleaned, nonslippery, cheaply repaired, and favorable to travel. One common type consists of asphaltic concrete laid on a portland-cement concrete base. This base is cast in slabs on a well-graded bed. Coarse material, sand, and filler are mixed at a plant. Hot asphalt is added to the mixture, and this asphaltic concrete is carried in trucks to the paving site, where it is dumped into the hopper of a mechanical spreader. The spreader distributes (and sometimes tamps) the asphaltic concrete to the correct uncompacted thickness. Heavy rollers compact the surface.

The major part of a modern city's paving program consists of building arterial expressways and freeways, as well as resurfacing old pavements. Roadways must also be widened to accommodate increasing arterial traffic. In many large cities the conversion to bus transportation in the 1950's meant that the cobblestone or pavement between streetcar tracks had to be resurfaced. The annual inspection and repair of pavements would be an ideal paving program, but city budgets sometimes do not allow such wear-preventing maintenance of streets.

ROADRUNNER. See CUCKOOS, ANIS, ROADRUNNERS.

ROAD SIGNAL. Before roads were well traveled, there were few signals or signs to regulate traffic or to direct the traveler to his destination. The situation was gradually improved as roads became more crowded. Today, traffic lights are used to control the flow of vehicle and pedestrian traffic at busy intersections, and signal devices, employing flashing red or amber lights, warn drivers of hazards, such as railroad crossings and pedestrian crosswalks. Red and amber lights are recognized universally as danger warnings.

United States stop signs are octagonal in shape and red in color; warning signs are diamond shaped, and their color is yellow; and directional signs have a rectangular shape, and their color is black and white. Most European countries have adopted a common code concerning the shape of road signs. For example, a triangular-shaped sign warns the motorist of a specific hazard, such as a sharp curve, while a circular sign bears a specific instruction, such as a speed limit.

ROANOKE ISLAND is on the east coast of North Carolina, where Sir Walter Raleigh tried twice to found an English colony. The first group, consisting of 108 persons under the command of Sir Richard Grenville, landed in 1585. They built Fort Raleigh and explored the countryside. Food became scarce, wars with Indians ensued, and many of the settlers became discouraged. In 1586 they sailed back to England with Sir Francis Drake, who had anchored his ships off the coast.

Raleigh dispatched another group in 1587, consisting of 150 men, women, and children, governed by John White. When White returned with the supply ship in 1591, after a delay in England, he found no trace of the colony.

It is thought that the colonists went to the friendly Croatoan Indians who lived inland, or that they left camp, suffered from sickness and war, and the survivors were absorbed by the Indians. However, the tragic mystery of what became of the "Lost Colony" has never been solved.

ROBBIA, DELLA, a family of Italian artists.

Luca della Robbia (1400?-1482) was a Florentine sculptor. Between 1431 and 1440 he did ten panels for the cathedral in Florence. These panels, of angels and dancing boys, have been called one of the finest works of sculpture of the 15th century. Another great work of his was a bronze door, with ten panels of figures in relief, for the sacristy of the cathedral, done between the years 1448 and 1467. This sculptor's name was closely associated with the production of figures in glazed or enameled terra cotta, made by a process he did not discover but did perfect. Using this process, he executed numerous medallions and reliefs.

Andrea della Robbia (1435-1525), a nephew and pupil of Luca della Robbia, was born in Florence. He used a glazed terra cotta with blue and white the dominant colors. His best works were the medallions and figures for the Foundling Hospital at Florence and bas-reliefs for churches in Florence, Arezzo, and Prato.

Giovanni della Robbia (1469-1529?), a son of Andrea della Robbia, continued his father's work. His most noteworthy work is a fountain in Santa Maria Novella in Florence.

Girolamo della Robbia (1488-1566), the second son of Andrea della Robbia, became an architect and was especially known for his use of Della Robbia ware in architecture. He built the Château de Madrid in France, a structure since destroyed but surviving in drawings.

Brown Brothers

This is a Della Robbia relief sculpture.

ROBESPIERRE, MAXIMILIEN FRANCOIS MARIE ISIDORE DE (1758-1794), French statesman who took a leading part in the so-called Reign of Terror during the French Revolution. Robespierre was born in the city of Arras. His mother died while he was still small, and his father deserted him. Through the help of a few friends, among them the bishop of Arras, he was given scholarships to study in Paris. In 1781 he returned to Arras to practice law and became a well-known provincial lawyer. In 1789 he was elected a deputy to the Estates General. After the dissolution of this body he became a member of the Constituent Assembly (1789-1791). Realizing that his ideas would not be acceptable in the Assembly, he turned for a following to the Jacobin Clubs, a society of extreme revolutionaries with branches all over France. He spoke often in the Assembly and advocated universal suffrage and the abolition of the death penalty.

In August, 1792, the king and the royal family were imprisoned, a revolutionary commune or municipal government was set up in Paris, and the mob massacred over a thousand persons. Robespierre opposed this unnecessary violence. A new government, called the National Convention, was set up in September, 1792.

The Convention was at first dominated by the moderate Girondists, such as Danton. But the more radical party, which was called the

Mountain, and of which Robespierre was the leader, carried the votes in the Convention in condemning the king, Louis XVI, who was guillotined in January, 1793. Robespierre became the idol of the masses. By June, 1793, the Mountain purged the extreme terrorists, or Hébertists, as well as the party of Danton, which was more moderate than the Mountain. In April, 1793, the Committee of Public Safety had been set up, and Robespierre had become one of the spokesmen. This committee of 12 members had a democratic program and tried to initiate economic controls. Robespierre introduced the "worship of the supreme being," acknowledging the existence of God and the immortality of soul. This satisfied neither the Roman Catholics nor the atheists. The Committee's highhanded actions and the continuing terror antagonized everybody. The Convention outlawed Robespierre, and he was guillotined, with 21 of his supporters, on July 27, 1794.

Robespierre was called the Incorruptible.

ROBIN. See THRUSHES, ROBINS, BLUEBIRDS.

ROBIN HOOD (about 1160- ?), a legendary English outlaw and hero of a cycle of ballads. The period to which most of the ballads refer is the latter part of the 12th century. Robin Hood lived in the forest with his band of gay and adventurous men and, according to tradition, robbed the rich to help the poor. Sherwood Forest in Nottinghamshire is usually given as his place of abode, and the sheriff of Nottingham is his great enemy. The band of "merry men" included Little John, Friar Tuck, Will Scarlet, and Allan-a-Dale. Later ballads add the figure of Maid Marian, Robin Hood's lady.

The ballads and later prose tales tell of the band's compassion for the poor and oppressed and their exciting escapes from the sheriff's men after robbing some rich merchant or abbot. Robin Hood was always chivalrous toward women, was an irrepressible prankster, and was an archer of great skill and renown. According to one tradition he met his death as an old man at the hands of a treacherous prioress of Kirklees Abbey in Yorkshire.

The facts behind the legends are uncertain, and Robin Hood may have been a purely imaginary person. He is first mentioned in the records of Yorkshire in 1230, where there is a reference to a "Robertus Hood fugitivus". The first detailed history is *Lytell Geste of Robyn Hoode*, printed about 1495. Some accounts identify him with the outlawed Earl of Huntingdon, who is supposed to have lived in the reign of Richard I.

ROBINSON, EDWIN ARLINGTON (1869-1935), American poet, born in Head Tide, Maine. Most of his boyhood and youth were spent in Gardiner, Maine, which became the Tilbury Town of his poems. Robinson entered Harvard in 1891 but withdrew two years later because of financial difficulties. After 1899 he was a resident of New York, where for several years he found employment with the city subway system. His first volume of poems, *The Torrent and the Night Before*, as well as his second, *The Children of the Night*, were published privately. His next volume, *Captain Craig*, which appeared in 1902, attracted the attention of President Theodore Roosevelt, who appointed him a clerk in the New York Customs Office. With the appearance of *The Town Down the River* in 1910 Robinson was assured a modest income that permitted him to devote his entire energies to writing poetry. Most of his writing was done at the MacDowell Colony, an artists' and writers' summer colony near Peterboro, N.H. The collection of poems *The Man Against the Sky* brought to the poet a popular audience. During the next decades he was recognized as one of America's major living poets. Robinson won the Pulitzer prize for poetry three times—for *Collected Poems* (1921), *The Man Who Died Twice* (1924), and *Tristram* (1927). Subsequent volumes included *The Glory of the Nightingales*, *Amaranth*, and *King Jasper*. Many of his most famous short poems, such as "Miniver Cheevy" and "Richard Corey," are psychological studies of New England eccentrics who are unable to adjust to a society that has turned from its transcendentalist tradition.

ROBINSON CRUSOE, the tale of a headstrong boy who went to sea against his parents' wishes. When his first ship sank in a storm, the ship's captain told him that this was a warning to return home. But instead the stubborn lad boarded another ship, and this time made a successful journey to Africa. On his third voyage, however, Crusoe was captured by pirates and made a slave to their captain. After several years, he managed to escape and to reach "the Brazils." There he cultivated a plantation. After this enterprise was well founded, Crusoe undertook a journey to the African coast to secure slaves for himself and for his neighbors. After a series of misfortunes, he was shipwrecked on a lonely island near America. All his companions were lost. Crusoe was left to live as best he could—one man against all the forces of nature.

Daniel Defoe, the author of *Robinson Crusoe*, based the story on a true episode. In 1704 Alexander Selkirk, a boy who had ran away to sea, quarreled with his captain. At his own request, Selkirk was put ashore on an uninhabited island. He lived there, all alone, until he was rescued by another ship five years later. Daniel Defoe, a man with a vivid imagination, elaborated on the facts of this case to write the story of Robinson Crusoe. This exciting adventure has been translated into many different languages and has been read by generation after generation.

Robinson Crusoe discovers Friday's footprint.

ROCHESTER, a city in western New York on Lake Ontario at the mouth of the Genesee River, 65 miles northeast of Buffalo. It is an important lake port, an educational and industrial center, and one of the largest cities in the state. According to the 1960 census Rochester had a population of 318,611.

Manufactures include machinery, photographic and optical supplies, clothing, thermometers and other instruments, chemicals, and business machines. Bausch and Lomb, Eastman Kodak, and Taylor Instrument companies are here. The city handles freight from the lake and the Barge Canal, which passes through Buffalo.

Places of interest include the flower gardens in Highland Park and the numerous nurseries and fine parks, the Rochester Museum of Arts and Sciences, the Memorial Art Gallery, and Rundel Memorial Building, housing the public library and an art gallery. The city is a noted musical center. It is the seat of the University of Rochester, with its famed Eastman School of Music, the Rochester Institute of Technology, Colgate-Rochester Divinity School, and Nazareth College of Rochester.

The city was settled in 1812. The construction of the Erie Canal through Rochester and the Civil War and World Wars I and II brought industrial expansion.

ROCKEFELLER, JOHN DAVISON (1839-1937), an American capitalist, was born in Richford, N.Y. He engaged in business when he was 19 years old. After making a small fortune in Civil War grain speculation, he entered the oil business, then in its infancy, in 1863. In 1870 he became president of the Standard Oil Company of Ohio. By enlarging this enterprise, driving out and absorbing rival companies, and establishing the Standard Oil trust, he secured by 1879 a virtual monopoly in the petroleum-refining industry. By 1902 he had relinquished active control of his widespread financial interests. In 1911 the U.S. Supreme Court dissolved the trust.

The fortune he had accumulated at the time of his retirement was valued at over a billion dollars. In the years that followed he made numerous gifts, only the largest of which are mentioned here. The Rockefeller Institute for Medical Research, incorporated in 1901, has specialized in the prevention and cure of disease. The General Education Board, founded in 1902, promotes education in the United States and has concentrated on the South with special Negro studies. The University of Chicago was founded in 1890 with a large endowment from Rockefeller, and through the Baptist Church he made many other gifts and donations for various institutions. He also established the Rockefeller Foundation in 1913, and in 1918, in memory of his wife, he established the Laura Spelman Rockefeller Memorial, devoted to child welfare and social science.

UPI

John Davison Rockefeller, U.S. capitalist

ROCKEFELLER, JOHN DAVISON, JR. (1874-1960), American industrialist and philanthropist. He was born in Cleveland, Ohio, and attended Brown University. After graduation, he entered his father's business. He had been associated with some of his father's philanthropic endeavors, and in 1910 he resigned the directorship of Standard Oil and other companies to devote himself to this vocation.

It has been estimated that Rockefeller donated some 500 million dollars to various causes. Among his philanthropies were the restoration of Colonial Williamsburg in Virginia, Acadia National Park in Maine, the Jackson Hole section of Wyoming, and the donation of land in Manhattan to the UN. He built Rockefeller Center in New York.

ROCKET, commonly a projectile-shaped vehicle driven through air or space by a reaction motor that operates without air. Rockets, originally propelled by gases formed from the combustion of gunpowder, now burn various solid and liquid fuels for propulsion. All long-range and most short-range rockets employ complex guidance systems to reach their destination. Since their propulsion units operate most efficiently at high speeds and high altitudes, rockets are most practicable as transport vehicles in space or over long distances on earth.

Rockets were first used in 1232, when the Chinese fired black-powder skyrockets against invading Mongols. In the War of 1812 British iron rockets inspired the "rockets' red glare" in the "Star Spangled Banner." During the later 1800's artillery shells superseded the rocket because of their greater accuracy. Modern rocketry started with Russia's K. E. Tsiolkovskii, who wrote on astronautics (science of space travel) in the late 19th century. In the early decades of the 20th century Robert Goddard in the United States made the first scientific rocket experiments and developed a liquid-fueled motor in 1926. H. Oberth was Germany's rocket pioneer. His work was the basis of the large, liquid-fueled V-2 rockets with which Germany bombed London during the closing weeks of World War II.

A rocket motor consists essentially of a combustion chamber, where the fuel is burned, and an escape port. The escape port is a nozzle at the rear of the rocket, through which the propulsion gases are ejected. The nozzle is shaped to accelerate the gases coming from the combustion chamber. A De Laval nozzle is the common type. The diameter of this nozzle is first narrowed, which causes the gases, then moving at subsonic speeds, to accelerate to the sonic level. The rate at which the propellants are burned and the size of the nozzle throat, or minimum area, determine the combustion-chamber pressure. The nozzle then flares outward, further accelerating the gases to supersonic speeds. Escape velocity of the gases approximates 5,000 to 7,000 feet per second for solid fuels and 8,000 to 10,000 feet per second for liquid fuels.

Special materials are required in the motor's construction, since combustion temperatures of 5,000° F. and pressures of several hundred pounds per square inch are common. Kinds of materials used include ceramics, recrystallized carbon, fiberglass, and alloys of molybdenum, iron, or nickel. The best materials degenerate under combustion conditions, especially during the longer firing period of a liquid fuel. As a result, the motor's walls are often cooled by circulating the fuel through a jacket surrounding the chamber.

Official U.S. Air Force Photo

George C. Marshall Space Flight Center

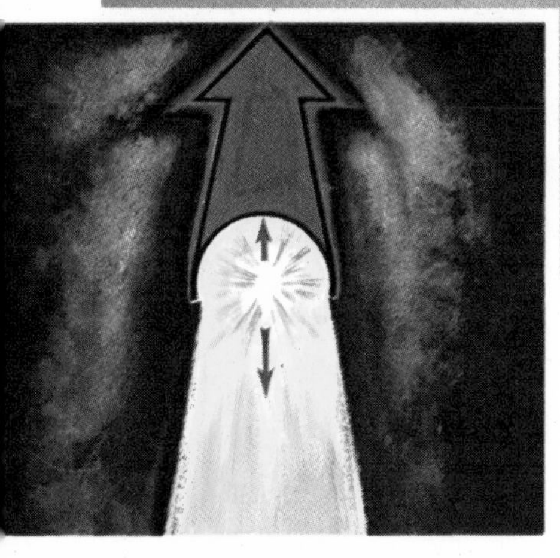

The reaction principle is illustrated above. Expanding gases exert force in all directions. If the gas is allowed to escape in but one direction, the net force exerted on the container is in the opposite direction. Small, disposable rocket engines, right, above, called jato units (*j*et-*a*ssisted *t*ake*o*ff) are attached to large airplanes to increase power temporarily. A rocket engine, right, is tested at a rocket-launching site. Instruments will measure the power, or thrust, developed by the engine before it is used to power a rocket in flight.

A rocket is propelled by either a solid propellant that is cast as a hard core (the grain) in the combustion chamber or by a liquid fuel and oxidizer stored in tanks outside the chamber. Solid propellants are usually burned at higher pressures than the liquid propellants. They are generally composed of a hydrocarbon plus an oxidizer that supplies oxygen for burning the basic fuel. Most solid propellants consist of an oxidizer dispersed through a polymerized fuel, which together form the grain. Fuel components include synthetic rubber, plastics, and asphaltic-type compounds. They are used with such oxidizers as potassium perchlorate, ammonium perchlorate, or any of several nitrates.

Most liquid fuels are petroleum compounds, bipropellants (fuel plus oxidizer). Common fuels are alcohol, hydrazine, and liquid hydrogen. These are used with such oxidants as liquid oxygen, fluorine, or hydrogen peroxide. Liquid fuels and oxidizers are stored separately in tanks and are injected into the combustion chamber by pumps or by pressure from inert gases. In the chamber, ignition may be caused by an electrical apparatus, such as a spark plug, or no ignition may be needed if the fuel and oxidizer are hypergolic (bursting into flame spontaneously upon contact.) In nuclear rockets, heat derived from thermonuclear reactions will be used to convert liquid hydrogen to a high temperature gas.

For conditions outside strong gravitational fields, such as during interplanetary trips, rockets with low-thrust systems operating over long periods will be practicable. Such systems use thermal plasma or ions as a propellant and may produce added acceleration by electromagnetic processes. See SPACE TRAVEL.

The propulsion power of fuels is called thrust and is measured in pounds. The maximum present thrust is in the several-hundred-thousand-pounds range. The relative thrust of different fuels is measured in terms of specific thrust or specific impulse. Specific impulse is the amount of thrust developed by 1 pound of solid propellant and is measured in pound-seconds per pound. The term "specific thrust" is used to compare liquid propellants and is defined as the thrust, measured in pounds, produced when the propellant is consumed at the rate of 1 pound per second.

A rocket engine is a reaction-type engine. Newton's third law of motion states that for every acting force there is an equal and opposite reacting force. In a rocket engine a huge mass of gases that results from

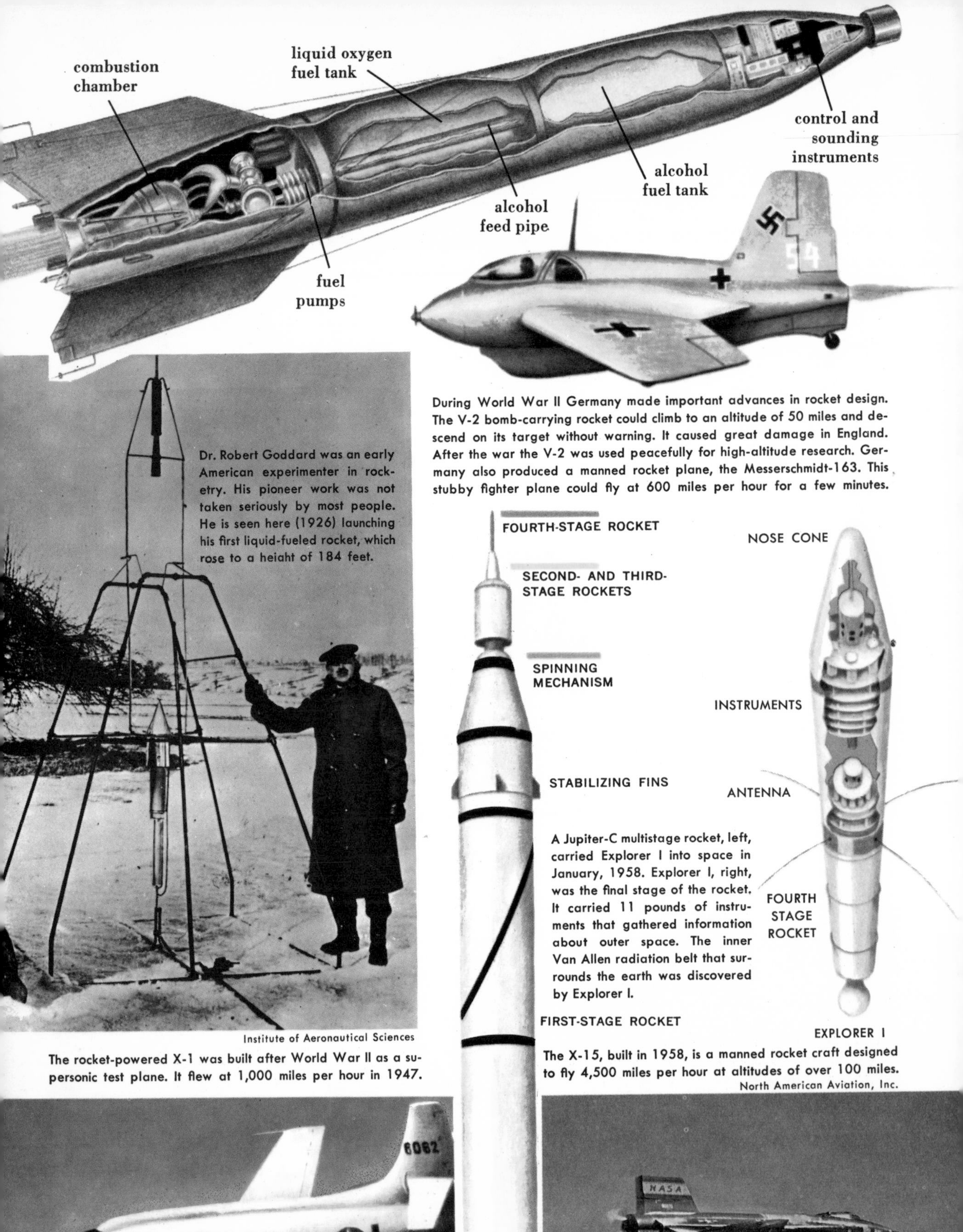

During World War II Germany made important advances in rocket design. The V-2 bomb-carrying rocket could climb to an altitude of 50 miles and descend on its target without warning. It caused great damage in England. After the war the V-2 was used peacefully for high-altitude research. Germany also produced a manned rocket plane, the Messerschmidt-163. This stubby fighter plane could fly at 600 miles per hour for a few minutes.

Dr. Robert Goddard was an early American experimenter in rocketry. His pioneer work was not taken seriously by most people. He is seen here (1926) launching his first liquid-fueled rocket, which rose to a height of 184 feet.

Institute of Aeronautical Sciences

A Jupiter-C multistage rocket, left, carried Explorer I into space in January, 1958. Explorer I, right, was the final stage of the rocket. It carried 11 pounds of instruments that gathered information about outer space. The inner Van Allen radiation belt that surrounds the earth was discovered by Explorer I.

The rocket-powered X-1 was built after World War II as a supersonic test plane. It flew at 1,000 miles per hour in 1947.

The X-15, built in 1958, is a manned rocket craft designed to fly 4,500 miles per hour at altitudes of over 100 miles.

North American Aviation, Inc.

Official U.S. Navy Photo

The Polaris guided missile is a two-stage rocket that is launched underwater from a submarine. The Polaris is ejected from the submarine by compressed air and ignites after popping out of the water. It is guided by inertia.

The Nike-Zeus rocket, right, is a defense rocket designed to detect, intercept, and destroy an attacking ballistic missile as it reenters the atmosphere. The Nike-Zeus uses a solid-fueled engine and has a range of 200 miles when carrying a nuclear warhead.

Official U.S. Army Photo

Official U.S. Air Force Photo

An Atlas liquid-fueled rocket has just been fired, right, and is rising from its launching pad. The Atlas, designed as an intercontinental ballistic missile, is also used in space research; it is a component of larger multistage rockets, such as the Vega.

The Jupiter-C liquid-fueled rocket, below, is a purely experimental rocket design developed from the Redstone solid-fueled guided missile. The Redstone was in turn developed from the German V-2 rocket of World War II. The Jupiter-C has been used extensively in space research; it is seen here launching an Explorer instrument package into orbit.

Official U.S. Army Photo

the combustion of fuel is accelerated rearward from the engine. The forces that accelerate the gases are the result of the heat of combustion and the pressure exerted on the expanding gases by the internal surfaces of the combustion chamber and nozzle. The reaction forces exerted by the gases on the inside of the combustion chamber and the nozzle are equal to the original forces but act in the opposite direction. The reaction forces push the rocket forward by acting on the internal surfaces of the combustion chamber of the rocket. The presence of air retards the movement of any object propelled by the action-reaction principle. This impeding effect is caused by air friction. The local atmospheric pressure acts as a drag force on an area equal to the rocket exhaust area. This makes the thrust of a rocket in a vacuum greater than the thrust in the atmosphere.

ROCKNE, KNUTE (1888-1931), a famed football coach, was born in Voss, Norway, but was brought to the United States when he was very young. He grew up and was educated in Chicago. After high school Rockne worked four years in the Chicago Post Office and saved enough money to enter the University of Notre Dame in 1910. At Notre Dame he was an all-round athlete and was especially noted as a football player.

After being graduated, Rockne received an appointment as chemistry instructor at Notre Dame and was also assistant football coach. In 1918 he became head coach upon the retirement of Jesse Harper. Rockne coached the Notre Dame team for 13 years, during which time 105 games were won, 12 lost, and 5 tied. Little in football strategy was originated by Rockne, but his use of the forward pass and spinner plays won him a great reputation as a coach. Rockne died in an airplane crash.

ROCKY MOUNTAIN NATIONAL PARK is located in one of the most majestic and diversified sections of the Rocky Mountains, in northern Colorado. It covers just over 400 square miles of the Front Range of the Rockies. The Continental Divide, separating slopes draining to the Pacific Ocean from those draining to the Gulf of Mexico, runs through the park.

The park, which was established in 1915, is famous for its rugged gorges, broad valleys, spectacular peaks, flowered meadows, abundant

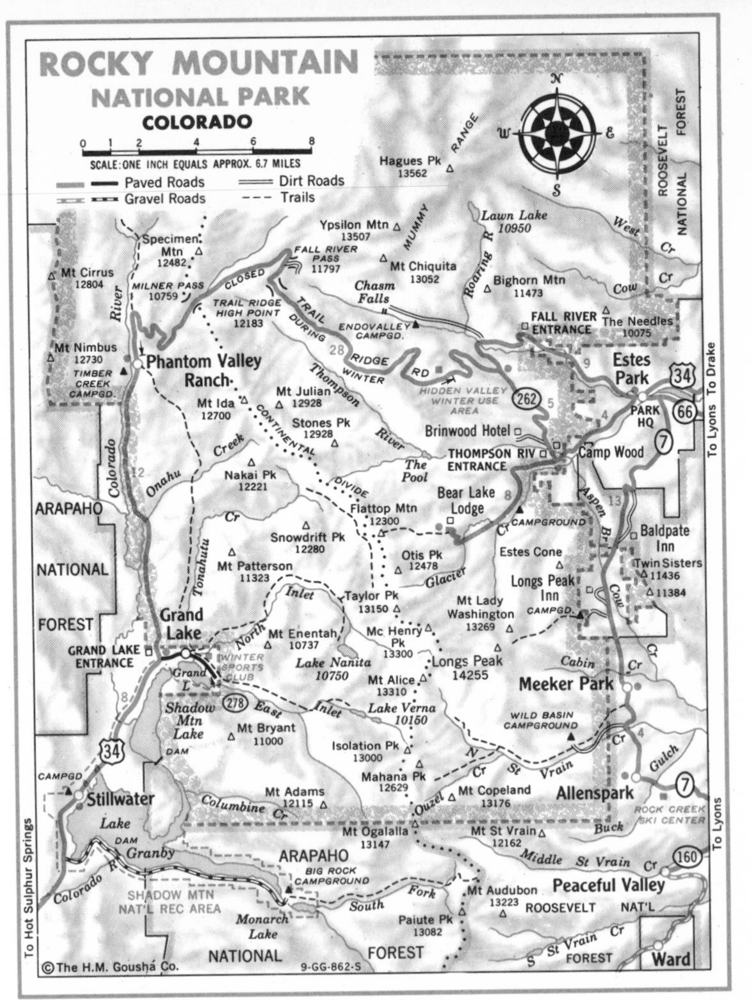

Vacationers fish at Bear Lake (below) in Rocky Mountain National Park. The park's chief attractions are its numerous peaks, one of which (Longs Peak) towers to a height of 14,255 feet.

Union Pacific Railroad Colorphoto

wildlife, and many small lakes and streams. The region is a wildlife sanctuary. Elk and Rocky Mountain mule deer are numerous. With a wide range of elevations represented, a variety of plantlife occurs within the park. More than 700 species of flowering plants have been identified. The scenic Trail Ridge Road, which reaches an altitude of 12,183 feet, winds high above the deep, forested canyons and the picturesque gorges.

ROCKY MOUNTAINS. This mountain system of western North America is known also as the Rockies. The system extends more than 3,000 miles in a generally northwest direction from eastern Mexico, across the western United States and Canada, and into the state of Alaska. The Rocky Mountains consist of rugged topography carved by stream and ice erosion. The highest peaks are in the Colorado section.

The Rocky Mountains are composed of several generally parallel ranges and may be divided into the

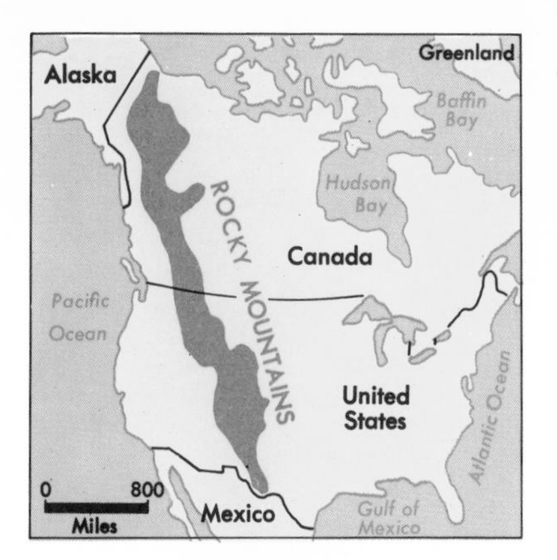

Southern Rockies, the Middle Rockies, the Northern Rockies, and the Arctic Rockies. The Southern Rockies extend from eastern Mexico to northern New Mexico through Colorado to southern Wyoming. The Middle Rockies run throughout Utah, northwestern Wyoming, and southern Idaho. They are separated from the Southern Rockies by the Wyoming Basin. The Northern Rockies, which are heavily glaciated, stretch into Idaho, Montana, northeastern Washington, and deep into Canada. The Arctic Rockies are the least known group, and many parts of this region are unexplored. They are found across the width of Alaska and in the Northwest Territories and the Yukon Territory of Canada.

The Rocky Mountains form the Continental Divide, which separates the Atlantic (Gulf of Mexico) and arctic drainage system from the Pacific drainage system. Among the many major continental rivers rising in the mountains are the eastward-flowing Rio Grande, Missouri, Arkansas, and Saskatchewan and the westward-flowing Colorado, Fraser, Columbia, and Yukon.

The mountains are very rich in mineral resources. Some of the important minerals mined are gold, copper, lead, zinc, uranium, tungsten, and molybdenum. Coal, petroleum, and natural gas are also found in vast reserves. Lumber is plentiful.

In both the United States and Canada extensive areas of the Rocky Mountains have been set aside as reserves where the natural resources and the wildlife are protected. Among the national parks in the region are Rocky Mountain, Glacier, Yellowstone, and Grand Teton in the United States and Jasper and Banff parks in Canada.

ROCKY MOUNTAIN SHEEP. See BIGHORN.

RODENT, an order of mammal whose teeth are specialized for gnawing. Rodents, most of which are small in size, include the rat, mouse, squirrel, chipmunk or ground squirrel, woodchuck or groundhog, gopher, beaver, porcupine, muskrat, prairie dog, chinchilla, and flying squirrel. These rodents occupy diverse habitats. The woodchuck, gopher, chipmunk, and prairie dog spend much of their lives in extensive burrows, which they dig themselves. Although rats and mice live naturally in open fields and underground burrows, a few of their species have adopted human habitations as their own. These species live in houses, cellars, barns, sewers, ships, and wharves. The squirrel lives in trees. The beaver and muskrat, which are modified anatomically for an aquatic existence, inhabit fresh-water ponds and streams. The flying squirrel cannot really fly but is able to glide a long distance through the air by means of two horizontal flaps of skin that extend between its fore and hind limbs. In the number both of species and of individuals the rodents are the most abundant of present-day mammals.

The most distinctive anatomical characteristic of a rodent is its peculiar teeth. It entirely lacks the dagger-like canine teeth with which the dog and cat seize and tear apart their prey. In place of canines the rodent has a wide gap between its front incisors and its first premolars or molars. Its long incisors are continually worn off by gnawing. However, they never waste away because they are continually growing from their roots. A rodent's molars are specialized for grinding. The upper and lower ones can be moved forward, backward, and sideways while being pressed together. A rodent's peculiar teeth equip it excellently for gnawing grain, nuts, grass, leaves, or roots.

Most rodents multiply very rapidly. Many of them have two or more broods of several young each year. Many rodents are intelligent and can readily learn new behavior. They are capable of adapting to unfamiliar habitats and of assuming new and unprecedented ways of life within these habitats. The rat, mouse, gopher, and other rodents are notorious pests to man, who continually tries to exterminate them.

RODEO, originally, among cattle herders, a celebration after the annual roundup, at which feats of bulldogging, riding, roping, and shooting were exhibited by cowboys from various ranches. Rivalries developed among the ranch groups, and the first intercamp rodeo was held about 1870, with the cowboys betting on their comrades against the best of another camp. These rodeos drew large crowds, and in 1888 the competing cowboys decided that an admission fee should be charged, the resulting fund to be

This diagram shows many of the different types of present-day rodents. These diverse types are thought to have evolved from a primitive ancestral rodent called Paramys.

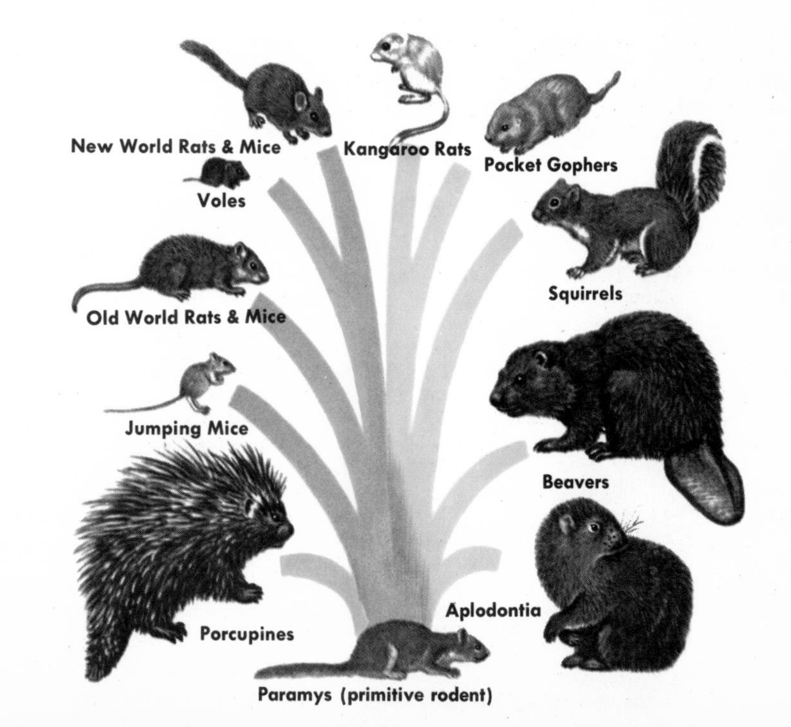

Bob & Ira Spring

Bronco riding is one of the most spectacular of all the contest events in today's rodeo.

split as prize money among winners of the events. In 1928 the Rodeo Association of America was founded by a group of men interested in the welfare of the increasingly popular sport. The association standardized the events making up a rodeo program and arranged for the promotion of rodeos in key cities, with the meets scheduled so that they did not conflict. A contestant could thus participate in most of the major rodeos in the United States and Canada. A regulation program includes bareback broncho riding, saddle broncho riding, calf roping, steer wrestling, bull (or steer) riding, and steer roping, as well as special features. The cowboy scoring the most points in these events during the year becomes the all-round champion. The amount of the prize money is based on his point total. Outstanding rodeos are the Round-Up at Pendleton, Ore., and Frontier Days at Cheyenne, Wyo. The indoor rodeo was pioneered with great success at Madison Square Garden in New York.

Richard Rodgers, American composer

Lynn Farnol Agcy.

RODGERS, RICHARD (1902-), American composer and theatrical producer, was born in New York. After attending public schools Rodgers entered Columbia University. His talent was recognized when, as a freshman, he wrote the score for *Fly With Me*, Columbia's annual varsity show. As a result he was introduced to Lorenz Hart, a lyrics writer who had previously attended Columbia. Rodgers left Columbia at the end of his sophomore year to work with Hart and others on several Broadway shows, but with limited success. From 1921 to 1923 Rodgers studied under Walter Damrosch at the New York Institute of Musical Art. *Garrick Gaieties*, produced in 1925, was the first successful Broadway show by Rodgers and Hart, although the team had contributed songs to other shows. During the following 17 years Rodgers and Hart wrote 21 musical shows, including *Dearest Enemy*, *The Girl Friend*, *Connecticut Yankee*, *Simple Simon*, *Jumbo*, *On Your Toes*, *Babes in Arms*, *The Boys from Syracuse*, *I'd Rather Be Right*, *Pal Joey*, and *By Jupiter*.

Shortly before Hart's death in 1943, Rodgers began collaboration with lyrics writer Oscar Hammerstein 2d to adapt the Lynn Riggs play *Green Grow the Lilacs* to the musical theater. The resulting production, *Oklahoma!*, which opened on Broadway in 1943, not only was a phenomenal success commercially but soon was recognized as a milestone in the evolution of the musical drama. The show was awarded a special Pulitzer prize in 1944. Subsequent Rodgers and Hammerstein productions included *Carousel*, *Allegro*, *South Pacific*, *The King and I*, *Flower Drum Song*, and *The Sound of Music*. *South Pacific*, perhaps the most popular musical in the history of the modern theater, received the Pulitzer prize for drama in 1950. The partnership of Rodgers and Hammerstein was terminated by the latter's death in 1960. See HAMMERSTEIN, OSCAR, 2D.

Rodgers is also noted for his contributions to other areas of show business. In addition to several of his own shows Rodgers coproduced the dramas *I Remember Mama* and *Happy Birthday* and Irving Berlin's musical *Annie, Get Your Gun*. He has also written scores for a number of motion pictures and television programs.

RODIN, AUGUSTE (1840-1917), French sculptor, was born in Paris. At the age of 14 Rodin entered the drawing class of Lecoq de Boisbaudran. After three unsuccessful attempts to enter the Ecole des Beaux Arts, Rodin resumed study under Antoine Louis Barye and others. Rodin's first major work of sculpture, "The Broken Nose," completed in 1863, was rejected when it was sent to Le Salon in Paris for exhibition. During the next seven years he worked as an artisan in Marseilles and Strasbourg and studied in the studio of sculptor Carrier-

This bronze head is a study Rodin made for one of the six figures of "The Burghers of Calais," a work that required some ten years. It was commissioned by Calais to commemorate the heroism of its citizens against the English in the 14th century.

Courtesy of The Art Institute of Chicago

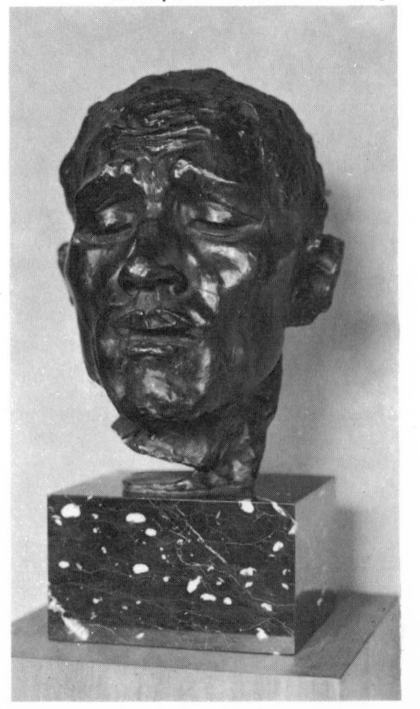

Belleuse. After service in the Franco-Prussian War Rodin rejoined Carrier-Belleuse in Brussels, Belgium. Rodin then journeyed to Italy, where he studied the works of Michelangelo, Donatello, and other Italian masters. Two years after Rodin's return to Paris in 1877 he won recognition with his "Saint John the Baptist." In 1882 he was commissioned to create bronze doors for the Musée des Arts Décoratifs. Several of his most famous pieces, including "The Thinker," "Adam," and "Eve," were originally conceived as elements of this project. Later works include "The Kiss," "The Hand of God," "The Burghers of Calais," and the busts of Antonin Proust, Jean Paul Laurens, and Victor Hugo. Today the Musée Rodin, the Louvre, and the Luxembourg Museum (all in Paris), as well as New York's Metropolitan Museum of Art and the Victoria and Albert Museum in London, contain important Rodin originals. Although once the subject of controversy Rodin's work is now considered of great significance, representing a culmination of the various artistic trends—pictorialism, naturalism, impressionism—that had been developing in sculpture during the 19th century.

ROEBLING, JOHN AUGUSTUS (1806-1869), an American civil engineer who designed the first suspension bridge to be erected in the United States. Born in Mühlhausen, Germany, he studied civil engineering at the Royal Polytechnic Institute of Berlin. After immigrating to Pennsylvania in 1831, he began in 1841 to manufacture wire rope in his own factory.

In 1846 Roebling designed and supervised the construction of a suspension bridge for a highway over the Monongahela River at Pittsburgh, Pa. The two cables from which the bridge was suspended were made of his own wire rope. This suspension bridge was the first one to be constructed in the United States. He subsequently designed and constructed a railroad suspension bridge over Niagara Falls and another suspension bridge over the Ohio River at Cincinnati, Ohio. He also designed a bridge to span the East River between Brooklyn and Manhattan in New York City. However, before the construction of this bridge—later named the Brooklyn Bridge—was begun, Roebling died of tetanus resulting from a severe foot injury received while he was inspecting the bridge site.

ROEMER, OLAUS (1644-1710), a Danish astronomer who discovered that the velocity of light is finite. He was born in Aarhus. He was in Paris between 1672 and 1676 and tutored the dauphin, the eldest son of the king of France. In 1681 Roemer became a professor of mathematics at a Danish university and was appointed director of the astronomical observatory at Copenhagen.

Roemer derived his hypothesis of the finite velocity of light from observations of eclipses of the satellites of the planet Jupiter. He calculated the times when future eclipses should occur, but sometimes they occurred slightly later than at their predicted times. He conjectured that this apparent tardiness was due to the fact that light required some time to travel from Jupiter's satellites to the earth. He then calculated the velocity of light but not accurately. Prior to Roemer's observations scientists thought that light traversed great distances instantaneously.

Roemer also improved the telescope and invented other astronomical instruments.

ROENTGEN, WILHELM CONRAD (1845-1923), born at Lennep, a German physicist who discovered X-rays. In 1869 he obtained a Ph.D. in physics from the Polytechnic School of Zurich, Switzerland. He served as professor of physics at the University of Würzburg, Germany, from 1885 to 1899 and at the University of Munich from 1899 to 1923.

Roentgen inadvertently discovered X-rays in 1895 while experimenting with the passage of electricity through a vacuum. These rays penetrated thick layers of opaque solid substances, such as paper, wood, and human flesh, and even penetrated thin layers of metal. They affected photographic plates as ordinary light does. If these rays could be directed through the human body and onto a photographic plate placed behind it, shadowy pictures of the bones would be impressed upon the plate. Roentgen named these rays X-rays because he knew little of their nature or cause. They are also called Roentgen rays in his honor.

In 1901 Roentgen was awarded the Nobel prize in physics for his discovery of X-rays. He also conducted research on the absorption of infrared rays by moist air, on the compressibility of solutions, on the optical and electrical properties of quartz, and on the effect of the pressure of fluids on their viscosity.

Brown Brothers

Will Rogers, American humorist

ROGERS, WILL (1879-1935), American humorist, entertainer, and author, was born near Oologah, Indian Territory (near what is now Claremore, Okla.), and attended Kemper Military School, in Booneville, Mo. After traveling with a circus and a wild-West show, Rogers made his debut as a vaudeville entertainer in 1905, when he performed a lasso act in a show at Hammerstein's Roof Garden in New York. To this act he added a humorous monologue. In 1914 Rogers joined the *Ziegfeld Follies* and at once became one of its most popular performers. Subsequently, he appeared in a number of motion pictures, including *They Had to See Paris*, *Judge Priest*, and *Steamboat Round the Bend*. Through a daily newspaper column, his books, and his ventures as an entertainer he became known as one of America's foremost humorists. His humor was basically a combination of homely philosophy, satire, and shrewd commentary on the contemporary scene. Rogers was killed in a plane crash with pilot Wiley Post near Point Barrow, Alaska. Rogers' books included *The Cowboy Philosopher on Prohibition*, *The Illiterate Digest*, and *Letters of a Self-Made Diplomat to His President*.

ROLAND, hero of the 11th-century French *chanson de geste* entitled *La Chanson de Roland*, or *Song of Roland*, part of a cycle of poems recounting the real and legendary history of Charlemagne. According to medieval romance Roland was the nephew of Charlemagne and the most stalwart of the French emperor's 12 paladins, or honor guards. The most famous passages of the poem are those that deal with Roland's death, which occurred in the battle at Roncesvalles Pass in northern Spain in 778. Because of the treachery of Ganelon, also a paladin, Roland and the French rear guard were cut off from the rest of Charlemagne's army by a band of Saracens. Roland failed to blow his magic horn to summon help until it was too late. As a result, Roland and all his comrades perished. Roland appears as the hero Orlando in the works of several later authors.

The Roland legends have historical basis in the career and person of a Breton count named Hrodland, who accompanied Charlemagne on his disastrous Spanish campaign and who was slain in battle at Roncesvalles Pass.

ROLFE, JOHN (1585-1622), English colonizer of Virginia, was born at Heacham, Norfolk. In June, 1609, he sailed for Virginia in the *Sea Adventure*, which was wrecked at Bermuda. After several months there, the company escaped to Virginia. Rolfe's first wife died shortly after their arrival.

Rolfe made two contributions of great importance to the young colony. By developing a method of cultivating native tobacco, he established the product that made the colony prosper; and by marrying the Indian princess Pocahontas, he established a peace with the neighboring Indians that lasted for eight crucial years. See POCAHONTAS; POWHATAN.

In 1616 Rolfe returned to England, where Pocahontas died. In May, 1617, he returned to Virginia. For five years he was the colony's secretary and recorder, and shortly before his death he became a member of the Council of State. Rolfe remarried and settled at Bermuda Hundred, where he is presumed to have been murdered during an Indian uprising.

This historic print depicts the marriage of John Rolfe and Indian princess Pocahontas.
Chicago Hist. Soc.

ROLLER BEARING. See BALL AND ROLLER BEARINGS.

ROLLER COASTER, a popular riding device at amusement parks all over the world. It consists of a track raised on a wooden framework, over which passenger-carrying cars travel, largely by the force of gravity, around curves and up and down hills. A powered chain drive between the tracks of the roller coaster catches the cars and draws them up at least the first grade. There may be additional grades where power is needed.

The earliest form of the roller coaster was an artificial ice slide, first built in Russia and very popular as early as the 17th century. A Frenchman traveling in Russia early in the 19th century enjoyed the amusement and took the idea back with him to France. The difference in climate made the ice slide impractical, and a wooden track and cars with wheels were substituted. This structure, the first roller coaster, called the Russian Mountain, was set up in 1804 in a public garden in Paris.

The French inventors made several improvements on the device, and roller coasters in various forms were constructed at amusement parks all over the country. Americans first showed an interest in the new sport in the 1870's. The first gravity pleasure ride in the United States was the famous switchback railway at Mauch Chunk, Pa. For many years railroad cars had been carrying coal from an open mine on Sharp Mountain down a 9-mile stretch of mountain and valley slope to the canal in the Lehigh Valley. In 1844 a power cable was installed to pull the empty cars back up the slope to the mine. When the railroad was abandoned as a coal carrier in 1870, a group of enterprising citizens took it over and turned it into a scenic railway for passengers. The Mauch Chunk Switchback Railway then became one of the most popular tourist attractions in the nation, and it continued to provide pleasurable thrills for sightseers and honeymooners until it was discontinued in 1939.

Wide World Photo

The roller coaster is a thrilling amusement.

The first roller coaster at Coney Island Amusement Park in New York was built in 1884 by LaMarcus Adna Thompson, who became famous as a designer of coasters. The first roller coasters consisted of either one or two, long, straight slopes. The first one built on the plan of an oval was constructed at Coney Island in 1885 by Charles Alcoke.

Modern coasters usually have a track from 2,000 to 4,500 feet long, including hills and curves. The general public has an exaggerated notion of the speed of the cars. The speed is actually only about 25 miles per hour on the curves and from 35 to a maximum of 40 miles per hour in the valleys.

Coasters are the longest rides at major amusement parks; often they also are the most popular and profitable and the most costly to install. For decades most coasters were custom built for each installation. After the end of World War II amusement parks enjoyed new prosperity, and several parks installed new coasters or improved cars. In addition, manufacturers perfected standardized models of smaller coasters that could be added to kiddielands and other smaller parks. Portable roller coasters were also designed and constructed in various sizes. They were intended principally for use by the traveling carnivals. In the 1950's German makers exported a variation called the Wild Mouse, and soon American copies of it appeared. It uses a coaster track with sharp curves and steep dips and two-seated cars that have the appearance of mice. The cars dart along the track, giving the ride its name.

ROLLER SKATING, moving about by means of roller skates—skates that have small wheels or rollers instead of runners and are designed for use on a hard, smooth surface. As is true of ice skating, the majority of roller skaters skate simply for the fun of it. There are many public rinks throughout the United States, in most of which skates can be rented.

Figure skating on roller skates by experts compares favorably with figure skating on ice. Holland is credited with having produced the first roller skates in the 18th century. These consisted of large wooden spools attached to the shoes with strips of leather. In 1863 an American designed a skate with four little wheels made of boxwood. Later came a skate with pin bearings, and still later the ball-bearing skate with metal casters, which was the most important improvement. The newest skates for indoor use have plastic wheels. The United States Amateur Roller Skating Association, with headquarters in New York, conducts annual contests.

ROLLING MILL, those sections of a steel mill in which the hot malleable steel ingots are compressed, lengthened, and shaped by great pressure between sets of steel rollers, the clearances between which can be varied. Rolling steel is now the cheapest method for reducing the spongy steel ingot as it comes from the soaking pit (a huge furnace for equalizing the temperature of the ingot from surface to center); but irregular steel shapes, such as crankshafts, and steel products with small cross sections, such as wire, are still hammered, pressed, or drawn.

A rolling mill, costing many millions of dollars, is one vast machine consisting of at least three sets of machinery. The first set of machinery is a conveyer system on which the massive chunk of hot steel is carried to the second part of the rolling mill, the great grooved steel rollers, through which the steel is pressed. Just before and behind the bank of rollers are elevating and lowering tables that bring the piece of steel into perfect alignment with the rollers. These tables might be regarded as part either of the conveyer system or of the rolling system. Sometimes the rollers are arranged in banks of three so that steel can be rolled in both directions at once.

In this rolling mill aluminum ingots are being rolled into smaller cross sections of aluminum.
Kaiser Aluminum & Chem. Corp.

The third part of the rolling mill is the immense amount of electrical machinery, cranes, and controls that shift the steel back and forth, up and down, and around as fast as possible before it cools. If the steel cools before it can be fully rolled, it must be returned to a furnace to be thoroughly heated (but not melted) for further rolling. Railroad rails, armorplate for tanks and warships, and structural steel for buildings are rolled into shape and strength in rolling mills.

ROMAN ARCHITECTURE, the architecture of ancient Rome and, to a certain extent, Roman provinces. It was influenced by Greek and Italic architecture but achieved a character and a greatness of its own, partly because of the Romans' engineering skill.

Greek architecture excelled in the simplicity and perfection of its proportions. Roman architecture was influenced by the Greeks, but its greatness lay in its variety of forms and its technical execution rather than in classic simplicity.

Throughout Italy from early times Greek architectural traditions were evident. The Etrurians adapted the Doric column, with some modifications, to form the Tuscan order. Their temples resembled the Greek but were originally built of wood. The columns did not have to support a heavy stone roof and could be spaced farther apart, but the different spacing of the columns resulted in inferior proportions. The temple was placed on a high platform, called a podium. The Roman temple of Mars Ultor on the Forum of Augustus was built in the Etrurian style. The Romans developed the Composite order from the Corinthian and Ionic orders and invented the figured capital.

Roman architecture did not fully develop until after the Republic. Sulla, Pompey, and Caesar attempted to give Rome a more monumental character. But not until the reign of Augustus Caesar did Roman architecture acquire its own style.

This style was characterized by great technical skill, the use of circular structures and curved walls, and the prominence of vaults and domes. The ancient Italic hut had been circular, with a fireplace and a smoke hole in the middle. The cir-

E.N.I.T.

Above are the Colosseum of Rome and the Arch of Constantine. The Colosseum is the largest surviving ancient Roman edifice.

The Roman ruins in the city of Baalbek, Lebanon, are very impressive, especially the ruins of the temples of Jupiter and Bacchus.

Pan Amer. World Airways

The Metropolitan Museum of Art, Purchase, 1891, Levi Hale Willard Bequest

Left is the Arch of Constantine. Triumphal arches of ancient Rome commemorated the deeds and personalities of the emperors.

Below is the ruined interior of the Colosseum of Rome, once the scene of bloody struggles between gladiators and wild beasts.

E.N.I.T.

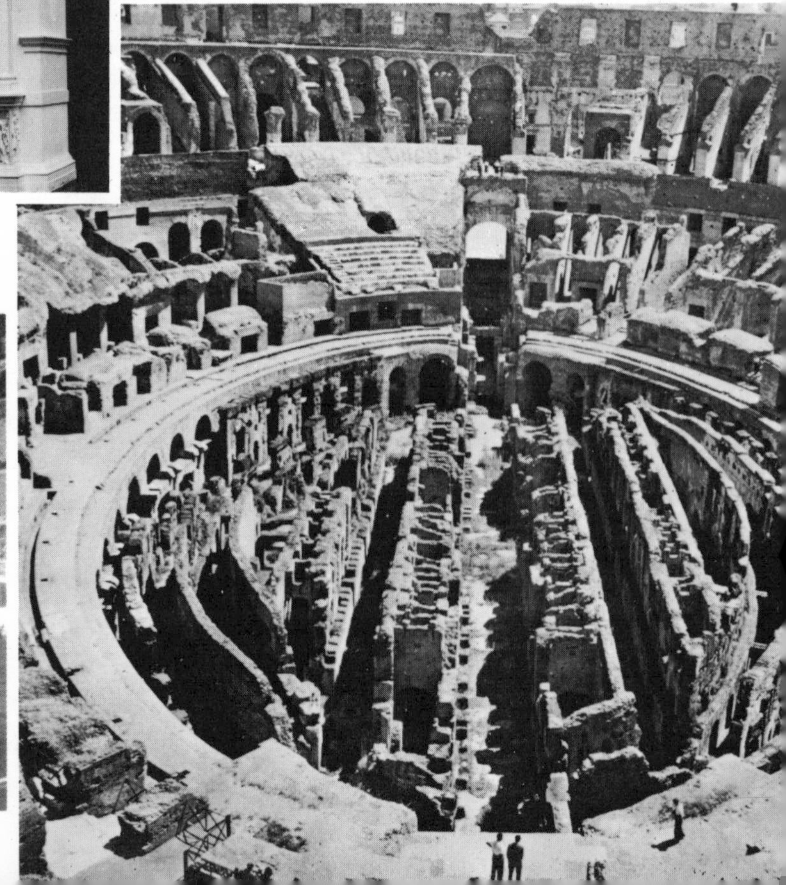

Hadrian's villa, located near the modern city of Rome, was the largest and most sumptuous of the ancient Roman imperial villas.

Artha Hornbostel

Courtesy of The Art Institute of Chicago

The Pantheon in Rome is an imposing example of the ancient Roman circular temple.

cular temple of Vesta, with its altar fire in the middle, resembled the ancient huts.

The Romans had a perfect command of the problems of lateral thrust in the construction of vaults and domes. They also knew the use of building materials that were unknown to the Greeks: concrete, bricks, and irregular pieces of stone fitted together with mortar. Marble was used to line wall surfaces made of these materials, but in the 2d century A.D., the art of masonry had developed to such perfection that walls composed of bricks of various colors could rival the beauty of marble. The Romans also became masters of the art of mosaic.

The Colosseum, built under the emperors Vespasian and Titus, shows the engineering genius of the Romans. Roman palaces and public buildings had central heating and plumbing. Very complicated ground plans were skillfully arranged. Only in recent times has modern architecture equaled the technical sophistication of the Roman builders.

During the reigns of Nero and the Flavian emperors great imperial palaces were constructed, with delicate interior light effects and ground plans combining straight lines with the curved lines of vaults. Under Emperor Trajan, Apollodorus of Damascus, probably the greatest Roman architect, must have been the foremost designer of the Forum of Trajan.

The Forum of Trajan was a large square with a market hall and great shopping arcades on one side against the slope of a hill. On the other side were magnificent thermae (public baths and a recreational palace, somewhat comparable to the palaces of culture in many Soviet cities) in which a stunning variety of halls, rooms, and corridors for a multitude of different purposes and activities were combined into one great architectural whole.

This was the great Roman style that lasted through the time of Emperor Constantine until the decline of the Western Empire. The remains can be found today, not only in the ruins of Rome itself but in the traces of thermae, theaters, aqueducts, and bridges in all those vast areas of Europe, northern Africa, and western Asia where once the Romans ruled.

ROMAN LAW, one of the two great systems of law upon which all the leading law systems of the present day are based. The other is the English. Roman law was based originally on custom, and there was not much legislation until the time of the later Empire. The first code of laws, called the Twelve Tables, was written down between 451 and 448 B.C. It was the code of an agricultural community and was of a specific nature dealing with current problems.

In the period of the Roman Republic the law was gradually shaped by the praetors, two officials who were elected annually, one in charge of cases concerning Roman citizens and the other handling the cases of aliens. At the beginning of the year the praetor would publish his edict stating the legal principles that he would follow during his term of office. Each praetor took over many of the rules and regulations of his predecessor but also added new ones and dropped some of the old ones that had been found unsatisfactory. Thus the system allowed for annual revision of the laws.

The body of laws that developed in this way was consolidated A.D. 131 by the emperor Hadrian. Under the Empire there were two sources of law: new laws made by the emperors, and the opinions of jurists and other legal experts. Between about A.D. 150 and A.D. 250 a famous group of jurists, through their published works, greatly influenced the development of Roman law. Among them were Gaius, who wrote the *Institutes* for his students in 161; Papinian, who was put to death by Emperor Caracalla; Ulpian; Julius Paulus; and Herennius Modestinus. Although the Western Empire broke up in the 5th century, the Eastern Empire, centered at Constantinople (now Istanbul, Turkey), continued for a thousand years. By 528 the number of laws was so huge that Emperor Justinian I ordered a single, clear, and comprehensive code to be compiled. This very important *Corpus Juris Civilis* (body of civil law) was known also as the Justinian Code. It included 50 books of the condensed opinions of jurists, a textbook, and a collection of Justinian's own ordinances.

After the 5th century, Roman law appeared lost in Western Europe, but it reappeared in the 11th century, when there was a great revival of learning, and jurists in Italy began working on the old texts. At the end of the Middle Ages a movement began in many European countries to apply Roman law in the courts in place of their own customary laws. The Roman law that was used was not the exact code of Justinian, but the law as explained and brought up to date by the scholars who had been working on the texts. In this form it was combined with customary laws of France, Holland, Germany and other countries. From Europe the influence of Roman law spread to the European colonies in the New World. It has also had some effect even on English law.

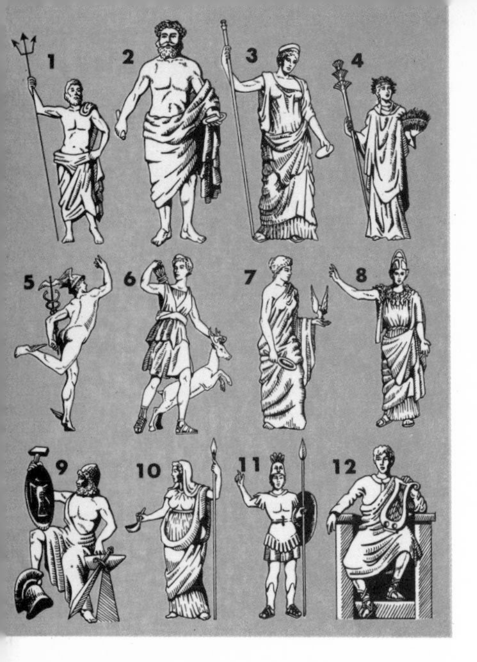

The Roman gods above are **1**, Neptune; **2**, Jupiter; **3**, Juno; **4**, Ceres; **5**, Mercury; **6**, Diana; **7**, Venus; **8**, Minerva; **9**, Vulcan; **10**, Vesta; **11**, Mars; and **12**, Apollo. Their Greek counterparts are Poseidon Zeus, Hera, Demeter, Hermes, Artemis, Aphrodite, Athena, Hephaestus, Hestia, Ares, and Apollo.

ROMAN MYTHOLOGY. Properly speaking the Romans had no mythology of their own. In the early days of the republic the lares and the penates, spirits of the household and of the cupboard, were worshiped. The household was thought of as under the care of these spirits. The spirits of the dead, the manes, were also worshiped collectively and later, individually. No stories were told about these or about the other old Roman gods—Mars, Jupiter, Quirinus, and so forth—until they were identified with the gods of Greece. See GREEK MYTHOLOGY.

ROMAN NUMERAL, the term applied to letters used in a system of representing integers that was first used by the Romans. In this system the letter I means 1; V, 5; X, 10; L, 50; C, 100; D, 500; and M, 1,000. When two or more letters are used, and the lesser value follows the greater, the values are added (XVI =16). If the lesser value precedes the greater, they are subtracted (IL =49).

ROMANTICISM, a 19th-century European and American cultural movement that opposed the classicist ideals of the previous age. It developed new philosophies and ideas that deeply affected our own times. Romanticism stressed the importance of nature, imagination and emotion over the reason, proportion, and polite cultivation that, according to classicism, were the ideals of ancient Greece and Rome.

Many 18th-century developments contributed to romanticism: a revival of interest in nature and in the Middle Ages; the ascendancy of the middle classes and their chief literary form, the novel; the fashion of sentimentalism; and the religious revival that in England produced Methodism and in Germany produced pietism.

During the Renaissance both romantic and classic tendencies existed in European culture, but in the 17th century classicism generally triumphed, accompanying the rise of absolute monarchy in national government. In France classicism was strongest during the reign of Louis XIV. In England, where absolutism failed to take hold, the classic era started with the restoration of Charles II.

The reaction against absolutism came soon. Advocates of the Enlightenment denied the divine right of kings and favored deistic religion and a materialistic philosophy. At the same time there was a reaction against the overcultivation of manners. In France Rousseau objected to the practice of forcing young children to act and dress like polite little grownups. In 18th-century England society ceased to pattern its manners after the royal court. Gentlemen often dispensed with their periwigs. The middle classes became socially prominent.

In art and literature deviations from classicism became increasingly frequent. Classic rural poetry had imitated the ancient pastorals. But 18th-century poets like James Thomson and Oliver Goldsmith substituted the oak for the cypress and the English peasant for shepherds and shepherdesses. The interest in humble people led to the collection of folk ballads. The English garden lost its formal symmetry and imitated free nature.

Historians became interested in the Middle Ages, which had been considered barbarous by the classicists. Enjoying great popularity were the epics attributed to the ancient Irish bard Ossian but actually composed by James Macpherson. In England Thomas Chatterton, whom poverty drove to suicide at the age of 18, achieved a similar hoax by attributing a number of masterful poems that he himself had secretly composed to the imaginary 15th-century poet Thomas Rowley. The Gothic horror story and the medieval romance came into fashion. (In the United States Edgar Allan Poe wrote stories in the Gothic style.)

The Gothic romances appealed to morbid sensitivity. Possibly in reaction to the rationalism of the age the 18th century was afflicted with, oversensitivity. Sentimental plays and novels sought out the pathetic and the pitiful. In Germany Goethe's sentimental novel *The Sorrows of Young Werther* caused a wave of suicides. In England "graveyard poets" like Robert Blair and Edward Young wrote their melancholy verses.

The rationalism of the 18th century tended to make religion empty and formalistic. In reaction John Wesley led the revival in England and Jonathan Edwards, in America. In Lutheran countries the pietists stressed individual faith. Some poets, like Christopher Smart and William Blake in England, expressed their deep religious mysticism.

By the end of the 18th century European culture had strayed far from classicism. In 1789 the French Revolution began, and in 1791 the new order abolished absolutism in France. But in literature and art no new aesthetic theories had yet replaced classicism. One of the first contributions of the romantics was the formulation of the romantic creed.

In England this was first done in 1789 in Wordsworth's preface to *Lyrical Ballads*. Wordsworth denounced the extravagance of the sentimental writings and condemned poetic diction—the use of stilted, ornamental language in poetry. For him, the poet was the man who felt deepest and digested his emotions well, recapturing them in ordinary language, "dignified and variegated, and alive with metaphors and figures."

The sentimentalists had indulged in emotion for its own sake, but most romantics saw in emotions the intimations of a deeper reality. From the beauty of nature and the torments of the soul arose feelings that seemed to be perceptions of the divine. Romantics like the philosopher Friedrich Schlegel and the poet Novalis made mysticism, especially in Germany, important. The idea that God could be found in nature led to pantheism, the belief that God is in all his creations. In the United States the transcendentalist movement was pantheistic. In 1836 Emerson formed the Transcendental Club and started the publication of *Nature*. In Germany Schopenhauer developed a pantheistic philosophy.

During the 18th century poetry was written according to strict rules. In England the heroic couplet was the favored form. (See POEM.) Most plays followed the dramatic unities strictly. (See PLAY.) Painters idealized reality in standard ways. Generally, content was often sacrificed to a beautiful and ornamented surface. Typical classic poetry was witty and instructive but usually failed to stir the emotions.

Most romantics could not accept the old rules. Blank verse was used widely, and some poets, like Walt Whitman, dispensed with regular meter and wrote free verse. But other romantic poets, including Byron, still wrote heroic couplets. Great composers like Beethoven, Schubert, Brahms, Chopin, and Berlioz developed new forms in music. The elaborate and ornamental counterpoint of 18th-century music disappeared. Often a single melody was played against a background of bass chords. Painters like Delacroix did not hesitate to picture the ugly.

The greater intellectual freedom was accompanied by greater individualism. The heroes of novels were often outsiders to society. In Victor Hugo's *Les Misérables* they were the downtrodden. The hero of Emily Brontë's *Wuthering Heights* was solitary and obsessed. Poetry became more personal and introspective. Some romantics, like Byron and Heine, were estranged from society and preferred homelessness to their native countries.

The dirt and poverty of the Industrial Revolution made many romantics antagonistic to the civilization of their own time. Increasingly, men were drawn to nature as a contrast to the sordidness of city life. Henry David Thoreau wrote in *Walden* about his solitary life in his handmade hut in the wilderness near Concord, Mass. Shelley wrote "To a Skylark" and many other nature poems; Keats, his "Ode to a Nightingale." William Wordsworth wrote some of the finest English nature poetry in poems like "Ode on Intimations of Immortality" and "The Prelude." Painters like Camille Corot and Courbet excelled in landscape painting.

Folklore and primitive cultures offered an escape from the harshness of 19th-century society. Henry Wadsworth Longfellow wrote his *Song of Hiawatha*. Composers started imitating folk melodies and exotic music. The ballad became a major art form. Novelists like Herman Melville introduced primitive characters from exotic countries.

Many people turned away from their own time. Hawthorne was fascinated with early colonial New England. Sir Walter Scott wrote the first real historical novels. The influence of medieval philosophy reasserted itself. Many Roman Catholics abandoned the rationalism of Descartes in favor of the realism of the medieval philosopher Thomas Aquinas. Idealists desired a return to medieval craftsmanship and to the guild system. Reformers like Saint-Simon designed utopian societies for the future and laid the basis for modern socialism. Others, like the Frenchman Gobineau, thought modern man racially perverted. The German philosopher Nietzsche went back to the ancient warlike Aryan tribes to find racial and moral purity. Richard Wagner dramatized the mythical past of the Germans in operas.

ROMANTIC MUSIC begins about the time of Von Weber and continues until the arrival of Debussy and Stravinsky. For the sake of convenience one might say that the period of romanticism in music extends from 1800 to 1900. Yet romantic expression can certainly be heard in the compositions of Beethoven and Schubert, and a surprising number of 20th-century composers can accurately be called romantic. Richard Strauss, Elgar, Bruckner, the early Schönberg, and the Italian operatic composers Puccini and Mascagni are some of them.

Of course, romantic music has overlappings with classical and modern music, historically and otherwise, and like all music it is written to move the emotions. What distinguishes Mendelssohn or Berlioz from Bach and Haydn is that the former make a powerful appeal to the feelings in a direct and detailed manner. Moreover, they make this appeal at the expense of regularity and form in music. This is why romantic music is so often described as less formal than classical music, less intellectual than modern music, and more expressive than medieval church music. Its emotion is more intense, more changeable, and more likely to run to extremes. Even the classically minded composer Brahms indulges himself in some of the typical romantic feelings—a sense of grandeur and triumph, melancholy, tenderness, and compassion.

In a way, it was the settling of musical forms during the classical period—the fugue, sonata, symphony, and string quartet—that gave the romantics their freedom; at any rate they began to turn their

This is a scene from Act II of Giacomo Puccini's romantic opera *La Bohème*.

Cincinnati Summer Opera Assoc., Inc.

attention elsewhere. They read the romantic novels of Scott and the poetry of Byron, just then appearing on the Continent, and studied contemporary painters. The symphonic poem began to undermine the traditional symphony in four movements. In a type of musical composition that Liszt referred to as program music, romantic composers tried to incorporate literary ideas and pictorial images in their work. Although this mode of expression was not a new one, earlier composers had made more limited use of it.

While still in his teens, Mendelssohn set parts of Shakespeare's *Midsummer Night's Dream* to music. Berlioz wrote a dramatic symphony with chorus based on Shakespeare's *Romeo and Juliet.* Chopin, in exile, wrote musical pieces inspired by the poems of his countryman Mickiewicz. The French poet Lamartine was the literary source of Liszt's inspiration. And Wagner, perhaps the most culture conscious of them all, himself wrote both the music and dramatic settings for his operas. Norse drama provides themes for *Lohengrin, The Ring of the Nibelungs,* and *Tristan and Isolde.* In his search for national identity Wagner exemplifies another aspect of romanticism as expressed in music—a fervent patriotism.

At the close of the Napoleonic domination Europe is broken up into political rivalries and alliances centering around France and Austria. Farther east, Russia chafes at her Austrian borders and strikes out at kingdoms in central Europe. Chopin mourns for a captive Poland in his polonaises. Liszt pours out a love of country in his Hungarian rhapsodies. The later romantics, Mussorgsky and Tchaikovsky in Russia, Granados and De Falla in Spain, Grieg in Norway, and Dvořák in Bohemia, bring native songs and folk melodies into their tone poems, suites, symphonies, ballets, and miscellaneous pieces. Even the string quartet is affected by national consciousness.

Debussy's experiments with the whole-tone scale at the turn of the century place him in the modern musical setting, but his dreamy, suggestive moods reflect a kind of refined romanticism. Igor Stravinsky's break with the romantics, on the other hand, has amounted to an open and determined quarrel ever since the completion of his *Rite of Spring* in 1913. See Classical Music; Modern Music; Romanticism.

ROMBERG, SIGMUND (1887-1951), American composer, born in Szegedin (now Szeged), Hungary. After attending schools in his native country Romberg moved to Vienna to complete his education in civil engineering. While there he began to study music. In 1909 Romberg came to the United States, where he found employment as a musician and orchestra leader in several New York cafés and restaurants. His career as a composer of popular music began when he was commissioned to write the score for *The Whirl of the World* (1914), the first of a series of revues produced at the Winter Garden by J. J. Shubert. *Maytime,* produced in 1917, was the first of the operettas that established his name in the American musical theater. Later successes included *Blossom Time, The Student Prince, The Desert Song, Rosalie,* and *Up in Central Park.* Romberg also wrote scores for motion pictures, radio, and television. Among the noted composers and librettists who collaborated with Romberg during his career were George Gershwin, Oscar Hammerstein 2d, and Otto Harbach.

ROME, often called the Eternal City, is the capital of Italy and the site of Vatican City. It is one of the most interesting cities of the world, offering a wealth of history and art, and is also a great intellectual, cultural, and religious center. It stands on both sides of the Tiber River, about 15 miles from the Tyrrhenian Sea, in central Italy. The city has a population of about 2,000,000.

Ancient Rome in the reign of Augustus is believed to have had a population of somewhat over one million. The city was adorned with a vast number of splendid buildings, including temples, palaces, public halls, theaters, amphitheaters, baths, porticoes, and monuments. The oldest and most sacred temple was that of Jupiter Capitolinus, on the Capitoline hill. The Pantheon, now a church, is still excellently preserved. Other temples included the temples of Apollo, Minerva, Peace, and Venus. The principal palace of ancient Rome was the Palatium, adopted as the imperial residence by Augustus.

Among the theaters, those of Pompey and Lucius Cornelius Balbus were the most celebrated. The most magnificent of the amphitheaters, completed by Titus A.D. 80, is now known as the Colosseum. The principal circus was the Circus Maximus, which was capable of holding 200,000 spectators.

Robert J. Bezucha

On the left is the beautiful cloister of St. Paul's Outside the Walls, the second largest church in Rome. This church was built by Constantine I over St. Paul's tomb.

Below is the circular Piazza San Pietro as seen from St. Peter's. In the center of the square is an Egyptian obelisk; the two wings of Bernini's colonnade are also visible.

Robert J. Bezucha

The four great Roman leaders represented above are, from left to right, Pompey the Great, Augustus, Mark Antony, and Julius Caesar.

The public baths were very numerous. The largest were the Thermae of Titus, the Baths of Caracalla, and the Thermae of Diocletian. Imposing ruins of the Baths of Caracalla may still be seen.

Among the educational institutions the first place is claimed by Rome's university, founded in 1303. The Collegio de Propaganda Fide is well known as the training school for Roman Catholic missionaries. Several institutions in Rome are maintained by foreign nations.

Before modern times the city was protected by walls. They were built of brick and stone and reached a height of about 55 feet. They are partially preserved. After Rome became the capital of united Italy, great changes took place in the city's appearance. It lost much of its ancient, picturesque appearance and became a great modern city. Extensive excavations laid bare the remains of many of the grandest monuments of ancient Rome.

Today Rome is second only to Milan as a center of Italian industry and commerce. Industries include publishing, motion picture production, vehicles, artisan products, and chemicals. Tourism is a great source of income.

The legendary founding of Rome took place in 753 B.C. by Romulus, who with his twin brother Remus, had been abandoned as a child on the banks of the Tiber River. Ancient Rome was built on seven hills. Romulus was the first of seven kings. A republic followed and lasted for half a millennium. It was the first instance of an enduring democratic system of government in the world. Two elected consuls ruled Rome, and the Senate made its laws. The Roman legions proved invincible in their many wars, and the republic rapidly expanded.

In 60 B.C. Pompey, Crassus, and Julius Caesar formed the First Triumvirate. In 48 B.C. Caesar became the first *de facto* emperor, and the republic ended. The Roman Empire continued for another 400 years.

From the downfall of the Empire, Rome's history is mainly identified with that of the papacy. The greatest popes were those of the Renaissance; they made Rome a haven of literature and art. In 1871 Rome became the capital of Italy. In 1929 the Lateran Treaty ended an old feud between church and state and established Vatican City as an independent political entity. After Italy's collapse under Benito Mussolini in 1943, the Nazis seized Rome and held it until 1944.

ROME AND THE ROMAN EMPIRE. During the 8th century B.C. small settlements on the Capitoline, Esquiline, Palatine, and Quirinal hills became one settlement. For a common meeting place they had the valley between; this became the Forum. The early government consisted of an elective king, an advisory senate of 100 elders, and a popular assembly, which conferred upon the king his imperium. The people of the state were divided into two classes: the patricians, who alone could become senators, and the plebeians. The early monarchy was in the hands of the natives. Rome was united only when the Etruscans conquered and ruled the area until the overthrow of the monarchy in 509 B.C.

A republic was established. Its supreme authority was the Senate of 300 members. Two consuls, elected annually, were generals and had little civil power and no criminal jurisdiction. Other officials included two quaestors, who looked after the treasury; two censors, who guarded morals, made assessments, and looked after the census; and two (later ten) tribunes, who protected the interests of the people. For the next 200 years the dominant theme in the domestic affairs of Rome was the plebeians' struggle to gain political and social equality. This struggle culminated in the Hortensian law (287 B.C.), which made the vote of the assembly of the plebeians law without ratification by another body.

For approximately 200 years following the expulsion of the Etruscans the external affairs of Rome centered first upon the necessity of protecting itself against its neighbors and then upon the problem of uniting Italy under Roman domination. By 296 B.C. the Romans controlled the Italian peninsula, with the exception of Magna Graecia in the south. Furthermore, only Magna Graecia and the Carthaginians remained to contest Roman supremacy in the western Mediterranean. But these two rivals were both eliminated by the rising power of Rome. In subduing Magna Graecia Rome received the help of Carthage, but the two allies soon quarreled over the control of Sicily. This resulted in the First Punic War (264-241 B.C.), which ended with the triumph of Rome. Thirty-three years later the two powers went to war again over control of Spain. Although in the Second Punic War Hannibal invaded Italy and won several victories, Carthage was eventually crushed in 202 B.C. at the Battle of Zama (now Jama, Tunisia). The Third Punic War (149-146 B.C.) resulted in the annexation of Carthage as a Roman province.

During the struggle with Carthage Rome had also warred in other areas and had built an empire that included most of Spain, Dalmatia, Greece, Asia Minor, Sicily, Sardinia, and Corsica.

Courtesy of TWA—Trans World Airlines

The most famous of all ancient Roman roads was the Appian Way, built in 312 B.C. under censor Appius Claudius. More than 350 miles long, it connected Rome with Brindisi.

From 133 to 33 B.C. Rome was devastated by a series of civil wars. These wars were the result of a rapid imperial expansion, which created problems with which the Senate was unable to cope. The farmlands of Sicily, of the east, and of Africa flooded Rome with foodstuffs. The small farmer of the Italian peninsula could not compete, and he was forced to sell his land to wealthy patricians, who acquired vast tracts. Furthermore, the conquered areas poured into Rome tribute that was rarely used constructively. Instead it was used by the wealthy for luxury and by the poor as dole. Another problem was that after the Punic Wars the Senate came to rule alone; no longer did the plebs share in the government. Oligarchy replaced democracy, and individual initiative was drowned in luxury, the dole, and circuses. The only apparent solution was a dictatorship.

Tiberius Sempronius Gracchus and his brother Gaius Sempronius Gracchus perceived the difficulty and worked in their capacity as tribunes to remedy the problem of the disappearance of the small landowner and to reassert the authority of the Assembly. Each was assassinated at the instigation of a conservative and frightened Senate.

Another phase of the struggle between the Senate and the Assembly began in 107 B.C. when Gaius Marius, a self-made man and a highly able soldier, appealed to the people over the head of the Senate and secured the consulship; thus did the Assembly claim ultimate authority. But the Senate, which also claimed ultimate authority, countered by making Sulla the supreme general. Sulla marched his army on Rome, from which Marius fled, and forced the Assembly to pass a law making the Senate supreme. Following Sulla's death in 78 B.C. a new champion of the people came to the fore. This was Pompey the Great, who repealed Sulla's laws against the Assembly and temporarily quelled the internal disorders. He was joined in his work by Gaius Julius Caesar, conqueror of Gaul.

But Pompey grew jealous of Caesar's success and popularity. He abandoned his championship of the people, joined with the Senate, and plotted against Caesar. Upon learning of these events, Caesar left his camp at Ravenna, crossed the Rubicon River, and marched on Rome. Terrified, Pompey and most of the senators fled to Greece. Caesar consolidated his position in the west and then turned eastward, where he defeated his rival.

Caesar never abolished the republic, but by 45 B.C. his position was that of absolute monarch, and in order to weaken the Senate he increased its membership to 900. The next year, however, a group of conservative senators, including Marcus Junius Brutus and Gaius Cassius Longinus, killed the dictator. Caesar's friend and master of horse, Mark Antony, took control of Caesar's fortune and aroused the people against the conspirators. He was later joined by Octavian, Caesar's nephew, and the two met the armies of Brutus and Cassius on the plains at Philippi (42 B.C.). Here the would-be protectors of the republic were defeated.

Antony and Octavian now began to quarrel. Antony became involved with Cleopatra of Egypt and threatened the West, supported by Octavian, with Eastern domination. These rivals met in 31 B.C. at the Battle of Actium, where Cleopatra, followed by Antony, fled to Egypt. Octavian followed, Antony and Cleopatra killed themselves, and Egypt became another Roman province.

Returning to Rome (31 B.C.), Octavian was made tribune for life, *princeps* (first citizen among equals), and imperator (leader of the army) and was given the title of "Augustus" (majestic). In theory republican forms were retained, but even though the *princeps* was an elective position, Augustus' government was a virtual one-man rule. This period, coupled with the preceding Ciceronian era, formed the golden age of Roman civilization.

Augustus died A.D. 14 and was succeeded by four descendants of his family. These rulers, Tiberius (reigned A.D. 14-37), Caligula (reigned A.D. 37-41), Claudius I (reigned A.D. 41-54), and Nero (reigned A.D. 54-68), were known as the Julian emperors. For a year after Nero's suicide a struggle raged between contending rulers. Vespasian won and established the Flavian Dynasty, which remained in power until the assassination of Domitian A.D. 96. That year a final, and again unsuccessful, attempt to reestablish the republic was made by appointing Nerva, an elderly senator, to the supreme power. By using the principle of adoption (that is, choosing a favorite instead of a member of the family as successor),

Marcus Cocceius Nerva and his successors gave Rome capable leadership. This group, which also included Trajan (reigned 98-117), Hadrian (reigned 117-138), Antoninus Pius (reigned 138-161), and Marcus Aurelius (reigned 161-180), was called the five good emperors.

Following Marcus Aurelius' death the empire began to decline. The army seized control and made and murdered emperors at will. From 180 until the beginning of Diocletian's reign in 284, Rome had 19 emperors; 14 were slain by their own troops.

Diocletian came to power with the hope of emulating Augustus, but instead he created an oriental despotism. No longer was the title "princeps" used; it was replaced by that of "dominus" (lord). Diocletian's most significant achievement was the thorough reorganization of the empire, which was now divided into two parts—the East and the West. The dividing line ran from the Danube River to a point south of Dalmatia. Each part was ruled by an emperor (Augustus), who had as his assistant and successor a Caesar. The empire was also divided into four prefectures: Gaul, Italy, Illyrium, and the East. Each prefecture, controlled by a prefect, was divided into several dioceses, which were under vicars. These vicars were independent of the prefects and responsible directly to the emperors. The dioceses were divided into provinces, which were under the control of presidents. Furthermore, the civil and military powers were for the first time separated. The supreme military commanders in each region were the counts and the dukes. Diocletian, in his capital at Nicomedia in Bithynia (now Izmit, Turkey), took control of the East, and he appointed Maximian ruler of the West. The latter's capital was Milan in Italy. The city of Rome declined as a center of political power.

In 305 Diocletian and Maximian abdicated, and following a short struggle for power Constantine the Great reunited the empire under his sole rule. In 313 he granted the Christians freedom of worship; in 325 he presided over the first ecumenical council, which met at Nicaea (now Iznik, Turkey), to settle the Arian crisis; and in 330 he dedicated his capital of Constantinople. He died in 337 and was succeeded by his three sons, who struggled among themselves for supremacy.

These civil wars were ended by Julian, who during his reign (361-363) attempted to supplant Christianity with paganism. Jovian, Julian's successor, was succeeded by Valentinian I (reigned 364-375). This emperor ably defended the West against the barbarians' attempted infiltration. In 367 he made his son Gratian coemperor in the West, and when Valentinian died, Gratian succeeded him. In 379 Gratian made Theodosius I co-Augustus for the East. After Theodosius the empire became and remained, for all practical purposes, two empires.

The eastern part of the empire, called the Eastern Roman Empire, or the Byzantine Empire, remained a political entity until 1453, when Constantinople fell to the Ottoman Turks. The western part, however, quickly deteriorated. Britain was evacuated (407), the Goths invaded Italy (409), Rome was sacked (410), Africa became a Vandal kingdom (435), Rome was sacked again (455), and with the deposition of the child emperor Romulus Augustulus in 476 the throne thereafter remained empty, and barbarian chiefs ruled.

This is an artist's reconstruction of the famous Roman Forum, which is now in ruins.

Brown Brothers

Brown Brothers

Erwin Rommel, the Desert Fox, commanded Germany's Afrika Korps in World War II. One of his greatest military victories was the capture of Tobruk, Libya, June 21, 1942.

ROMMEL, ERWIN (1891-1944), a German soldier, born in Heidenheim. After receiving a military education at Stuttgart, he entered World War I as a lieutenant. He served with distinction, winning the highest German military decoration. Later he became attracted to Adolf Hitler's Brown Shirt movement in its early days and was one of the pioneer organizers of the storm troopers. When Hitler came into power, he made Rommel an instructor in the Potsdam War College. While here Rommel wrote his celebrated military textbook, *Infantry Attack*, outlining some of his unorthodox theories of warfare. He later commanded troops in Czechoslovakia and Poland when these countries were subjected and was in charge of the armored divisions that spearheaded the conquest of France and Belgium. After the British had routed the Italians in Libya early in 1941, Rommel was sent to bolster the defense. By late 1942 he had pushed the British far into Egypt. The British Eighth Army, however, began an offensive that, coupled with the U.S. invasion of North Africa, compelled Rommel to evacuate his forces, and he fled to Sicily. He was in charge of the German defense forces in Italy late in 1943, and in 1944 became aid to Karl von Rundstedt, who was commander of all German forces in western Europe. Involved in the July, 1944, bomb plot on Hitler's life, he was shortly afterward forced by the Gestapo to commit suicide by poison.

ROOF AND ROOFING. The covering structure of a building is the roof, designed to protect the building from rain, snow, heat, cold, and falling embers. Some roofs are also objects of beauty, as in the case of those covered with red Spanish tile. Roofing is the outer protective surface of a roof. Roofing, laid on rafters or on any of many kinds of sheathing material, is made from reed, straw or heather thatch, wooden or composition shingles, slate, tile, lead, copper, steel, aluminum, or layers of felt or paper impregnated with asphalt.

A roof is almost a building in itself. The roofs and walls of some buildings, such as storage barns, exhibition halls, and certain modern churches, are built on inverted V-lines merging into the ground with only enclosing end walls to provide the envelope; but generally the roof is built up as almost a separate structure designed to cover the area that is enclosed by the vertical walls.

Since the walls of the building support the roof, the roof must be planned in terms of the outward and downward stresses imposed upon the walls. These stresses include not only the weight of the entire structure but also the pressure and other effects of water, snow, and wind. For example, a roof slanted at 30 degrees must be able to withstand a wind pressure of about 25 pounds per square foot.

The gabled roof is a simple type that illustrates some of the problems of construction. The rafters are laid as A-frames with the lower ends pressing out against the walls of the building. The walls must be relatively heavy to support the outward thrust of the roof, and if the span of the roof is larger (greater than 12 feet) and the slope is slight, the load of a heavy fall of sticky snow can be crushing. To remove from the walls the outward thrust of the roof the rafters are nailed or bolted at their lower ends to the ends of the floor joists of the attic to make the roof act as a self-supporting and self-tying unit. With the addition of many kinds of struts and tie rods a light, strong framework can be built to reduce the need for extra thickness of the supporting walls.

However, this type of construction creates a space at the top of the building that is useful at best only for insulation and ventilation. In order to make this space more useful a 17th-century French architect, Nicolas François Mansart, designed the mansard roof. By clever internal bracing and by slanting inward the top section of the wall of the building to make an almost vertical roof, the mansard roof provides an area in the very top of the building that can be used as living space.

In addition to these types (the gabled roof and the mansard roof), there are many other types of ridgepole roofs with sloping flat and curved surfaces broken by dormer windows, skylights, and, in factories, even great surfaces of glass. Through the use of ingenious bracing and new materials architects are always seeking to decrease the weight and costs of roofs and to increase their strength and span of coverage.

For heavy buildings with internal load-carrying walls, flat or nearly flat roofs can be built up from cement slabs covered with coats of hot tar and layers of felt or paper impregnated with tar. Generally such roofs are finished off with a protective coating of clean gravel or finely chipped stone.

In the United States about 90 percent of all new roofs are now covered with bituminous products in the form of built-up layers of roofing paper or shingles. Some bituminous roofing papers and shingles are colored with chips of slate or similar material on the upper side to increase resistance to weather, sunshine, fire, and corrosive chemicals in the air.

In Europe many roofs are still covered with sheet lead, zinc, copper, or tiles. These materials make beautiful, long-lasting roofs that are highly fire resistant, but they have low insulating value.

Thatch, wooden shingles, and other combustible materials have almost ceased to be used on roofs in technologically advanced countries. A good thatch roof has a life expectancy of about 75 years but needs to be constantly protected against wind, birds, and vermin.

Sheet steel, both corrugated and flat, has been very popular, especially on barns and other farm buildings. They are lightningproof when properly grounded. Aluminum is another popular metal for roofing. It is now being embossed with a diamond pattern to reduce glare.

Insulation batts applied to the inside of a roof should be so stapled to the rafters as to leave an inch or two of free air space between the batts and the roof sheathing. Also, the vapor barrier should face down to the ceiling in order to prevent water vapor from condensing in the insulation.

ROOSEVELT, ELEANOR (1884-), born Anna Eleanor Roosevelt in New York. The niece of Theodore Roosevelt, she was educated privately, and for three years she taught at New York's Rivington Street Settlement House. In 1905 she married Franklin Delano Roosevelt, a distant cousin. Gaining a considerable knowledge of political affairs during Roosevelt's career as a New York state senator and as assistant secretary of the Navy, she protected his political fortunes while he was incapacitated by infantile paralysis. From 1924 to 1928 she was financial chairman for the woman's division of the New York Democratic party, and she was leading speaker in the senatorial campaign for Robert F. Wagner in 1926. In that same year she bought a private school for girls in New York and taught sociology, government, and economics for six years.

In her years as first lady (1933-1945) she was far more active than any preceding president's wife. She was the first president's wife to hold press conferences, and she made extensive travels throughout the United States, from which she brought back her impressions to her husband. She also wrote a daily column, "My Day," which was syndicated in 1936. During World War II she visited Great Britain, the South Pacific, and Army camps in the United States in order to further good will and to improve morale.

From 1945 to 1952 Eleanor Roosevelt was a U.S. delegate to the United Nations General Assembly, to which she was again appointed in 1961. In 1946 she was named chairman of the Human Rights Commission of UNESCO. In both of these capacities she labored ardently to promote understanding and goodwill among all the peoples of the world. During these years after her husband's death she continued to be of great service to the Democratic party, although she herself always refused to seek an elective office.

Former first lady Eleanor Roosevelt

Courtesy of Talmanac, Published by Talman Federal Savings & Loan Association of Chicago

ROOSEVELT, FRANKLIN DELANO (1882-1945), 32d president of the United States, was born at Hyde Park, N.Y., on Jan. 30, 1882. As president he was famous for being elected and reelected for a total of four terms, for leading the American people to utilize their government as a major creative social instrument, and for his successful guidance of U.S. forces in World War II.

Franklin Roosevelt, a distant cousin of Theodore Roosevelt (president of the United States from 1901 until 1909), was born into a family of wealth and social conservatism. As a youth he studied under governesses and attended Groton School, made a creditable record at Harvard as an undergraduate, and attended the law school of Columbia University. His early New York law practice was largely in estate administration. He was an enthusiastic salt-water yachtsman.

Franklin Roosevelt loved "the great game of politics" in which he started as a New York State senator in 1910, elected by the Democrats from a wealthy, overwhelmingly Republican district. Although he was reelected in 1912, he left the state senate to be assistant secretary of the Navy under President Woodrow Wilson, for whose election he had worked in 1912. Roosevelt did an excellent job as leading administrative civilian officer of the Navy during World War I and in 1919 liquidated without scandal the huge accumulations of naval supplies in Europe. He accepted the Democratic nomination for vice president in 1920 and campaigned vigorously, but he was defeated. A year later he was crippled by polio, and it seemed as if his active life was over. However, he accepted his infirmity, not as an excuse to give up and live out the rest of his life as a wealthy country gentleman but as a challenge to master himself and others, especially his domineering mother.

During the next three years, using every bit of his mind and will, he conquered continuous pain and rebuilt his body so that he could swing his legs around on crutches and even drive a specially adapted car. He attended the Democratic National Convention in 1924 and worked for the nomination of New York's governor Alfred Emanuel Smith. Four years later Governor Smith and a group of doctors persuaded Roosevelt to run for the governorship of New York. Smith, the Democratic presidential nominee, failed to carry the state or to win the national election, while Franklin Roosevelt carried the state by 25,564 votes. He won again in 1930.

In political outlook Franklin D. Roosevelt was, by heritage, a Jeffersonian Democrat.

As governor of New York Roosevelt continued Al Smith's policies of using the state's political power to improve the lives of its citizens. Despite a hostile legislature Roosevelt advocated state development of hydroelectric power on the St. Lawrence River, a 48-hour workweek for women and children, and cooperation between the state and the owners of marginal rural lands. Toward political corruption in the New York City government Roosevelt took a cautious attitude in order to let the culprits expose themselves while a reform public opinion developed.

Franklin Roosevelt was elected president of the United States in 1932, committed to almost no program other than that of the positive use of government to help improve the condition of the common man. He started his first term in office in the grip of a paralyzing bank panic and depression and tried many conservative policies. When these policies failed to work, he used other policies, feeling his way all the time in terms of what his electorate would tolerate. His foreign policies were likewise improvised to fit the needs of a rapidly changing world and the desires of voters who were not alalways sure of what they really wanted. See New Deal; World War II.

Franklin Roosevelt died from a cerebral hemorrhage at Warm Springs, Ga., on Apr. 12, 1945. He was buried at his home estate, Hyde Park, which is situated on the banks of the Hudson River.

ROOSEVELT, THEODORE (1858-1919), U.S. statesman and 26th president of the United States, born in New York. He was graduated from Harvard University in 1880 and began the study of law. The next year he was elected to the Assembly from the 21st District of New York and served in the legislatures of 1882, 1883, and 1884. In 1886 he was an unsuccessful candidate for mayor of New York against Abram Stevens Hewitt (elected), Democrat, and Henry George, United Labor candidate. In 1889 Roosevelt was appointed a member of the United States Civil Service Commission.

Roosevelt was called by President William McKinley in 1897 to be assistant secretary of the Navy. At the outbreak of the Spanish-American War he assisted in recruiting the 1st United States Volunteer Cavalry (the Rough Riders), of which he became lieutenant colonel and afterward colonel, being promoted for gallantry in action.

After the war Roosevelt returned to private life. In 1898 he was nominated by the Republicans for governor of New York and was elected. In 1900, against his wish, he was nominated for vice president on the Republican ticket headed by William McKinley and was elected in November. On the death of President McKinley, Sept. 14, 1901, Roosevelt succeeded to the presidency, announcing that his policy would be a continuation of his predecessor's. During this administration McKinley's treatment of the Filipinos was followed out, and they were granted a certain measure of autonomy; reciprocity negotiations with other powers were conducted; naval strength was increased; the Department of Commerce and Labor was established; the Pacific cable was laid; and the construction of the Panama Canal was authorized.

In 1904 President Roosevelt was reelected. His message to Congress in December dealt with many questions, particularly with those pertaining to corporations and to capital and labor. In 1906 Roosevelt received the Nobel peace prize for his action leading to the termination of the Russo-Japanese War. In the same period he influenced Congress to legislate against unfair railway rate discrimination. He succeeded in having the Pure Food Law passed, and he prosecuted various trusts. One of the most colorful presidents in U.S. history, Roosevelt is often quoted as saying, "Speak softly and

Theodore Roosevelt was an ardent sportsman.

carry a big stick; you will go far." After his term ended, he spent nearly nine months hunting in Africa and about six months visiting the principal capitals and large cities of Europe.

In 1912 Roosevelt was nominated again for the presidency, this time by the Progressive party, but he was defeated by Woodrow Wilson. At Milwaukee, Wis., where he had been asked to speak on the campaign issues, he was shot (October 14) in the right breast by a political malcontent, but the wound was not serious. In October, 1913, Roosevelt sailed from New York for a hunting expedition in Brazil, and from February 27 to April 26 he rendered a distinct service to science by his exploration of the unknown Rio da Dúvida, afterward named the Roosevelt River in his honor. He declined the nomination for the presidency by the Progressive party convention at Chicago on June 10, 1916. He advocated an early entrance of U.S. forces in the Allied cause during World War I. His death occurred suddenly, Jan. 6, 1919.

ROOSEVELT COROLLARY. See MONROE DOCTRINE.

ROOT. In mathematics the word *root* is used in two important senses —root of a number and root of an equation.

The *n*th root of a number is a number that, used as a factor n times, produces the given number. The second root (called the square root) of a number is the number that, multiplied by itself, produces the given number. Likewise, the third root (or cube root) of a number r is the number q such that $q \times q \times q$ (or q^3) $=r$. Thus the cube root of 8 is 2 because $2^3 = 8$. Taking the *n*th root is the reciprocal process to raising to the *n*th power. See POWER.

The root of an equation is a number that, when substituted for the unknown in the equation, produces an identity (an equation of the form $1 = 1$). Thus, 3 is a root of the equation $x^2 - 7x + 12 = 0$ since $3^2 - 7.3 + 12 = 0$. The root of an equation is sometimes called the solution, but *solution* more properly refers to the process of finding the root.

ROOT, the organ of a plant that anchors it in the soil and that absorbs water and dissolved minerals from the soil. The root system of many plants consist of a long, thick taproot from which shorter, thinner secondary roots branch in all directions. Such a root system is called a taproot system. The taproot of some plants is longer than their stem; for example, the taproot of alfalfa becomes 15 or more feet long. A fleshy taproot is one that becomes large because of storing food for future consumption by the plant. The carrot, radish, and beet are fleshy taproots that are eaten by man. The root system of some plants, such as corn, oats, and bluegrass, consists of a cluster of thin, equal-sized roots, called fibrous roots, which do not penetrate deeply into the soil. Such a system, in which no taproot is present, is called a diffuse root system. Although the proportion of root size to aboveground size varies considerably for different species, the volume of the roots of most terrestrial plants is equal to or greater than the volume of their aboveground portions.

The lower tip of a young growing root is a hardened rootcap that protects the delicate tip from injury as it grows downward through the soil. A short distance above the rootcap is a 1-inch or 2-inch band of tiny root hairs. Water and dissolved minerals are absorbed through these hairs. As a root grows downward, new root hairs continually form near its tip, while the older ones continually die.

A mature root is composed of several layers of tissue. Just beneath the thin external epidermis is the comparatively thick cortex in which food is stored. Beneath the cortex is the phloem, through which synthesized foods are conducted downward from the stems and leaves. Beneath the phloem is the xylem, which conducts water and dissolved minerals upward to the stem and which, because of its firmness, supports the root. In trees the xylem is hard and woody.

An important function of roots is the absorption of water and dissolved minerals from the soil. Absorption in a large root occurs only near its tip, where it is less than $\frac{1}{8}$-inch thick. Absorption also occurs near the tips of small branch roots and through the root hairs. Water and dissolved minerals are absorbed through the membranes of root tips and hairs and flow through the cortex and phloem to the xylem. They then are conducted upward through the xylem to the stems and leaves. The minerals that roots absorb include nitrates and other nitrogenous compounds, calcium, iron, potassium, and phosphorous. These minerals are assimilated into the cells of plants and are necessary for their life and growth. Botanists have found evidence that roots in their absorption may select some minerals but reject others. For example, if broccoli and peas are grown in the same soil, the broccoli will eventually contain much more calcium than the peas; this indicates that the broccoli selectively absorbed more calcium from the soil than the peas did.

Roots respond positively to the stimulus of gravity. As a result of the influence of gravity on hormone distribution, roots grow downward toward the center of the earth. Such a response is called a tropism. See TROPISM.

The roots of certain hyacinths and other waterplants grow in the water without touching the soil. Epiphytes, or air plants, such as certain tropical orchids, grow on trees and have roots that dangle in the air. The roots absorb moisture from the air. See PLANT.

ROOT-TAKAHIRA AGREEMENT, an exchange of notes between Secretary of State Elihu Root and Japanese ambassador Kogoro Takahira, Nov. 30, 1908, which smoothed over the disturbed relations between the two countries resulting from conflicting interests in the Pacific Ocean area. The two governments agreed to help maintain the *status quo* in the Pacific, to respect each other's territorial possessions in that area, and to uphold the open-door policy in China while supporting Chinese independence. The Japanese interpreted the *status quo* provision as a recognition of Japan's imperialist influence in Korea and southern Manchuria.

ROPE AND TWINE, nonjointed flexible devices of indefinite length for binding objects together or for keeping them at a constant distance, especially for towing. Rope is also used for power transmission. In terms of manufacture, thickness, and strength, this general class of most useful objects includes thread, string, twine, cord, rope, hawser, and cable. Chains serve often in place of rope, but they are jointed.

Rope is made by peoples everywhere from a multitude of materials. Among these materials are vines, vegetable fibers, animal fibers, synthetic fibers, and steel. However, all rope has one basic characteristic: It is built up from twisted strands, and the strands are built up from twisted threads. It is the multitude of strands and the twisting that give strength to rope and twine.

Before the mechanization of the rope and twine industry rope was made in sheds as long as 1,000 feet. These sheds were known as ropewalks because the ropemaker, having gathered a mass of fiber around his waist, walked backward from a fixed revolving hook (known as a whirl) and payed out the fiber as strands of yarn between his fingers. The ropewalk was very long in order to provide as great lengths of rope as possible without splices, which might weaken it. During the 19th century ropewalks disappeared as machinery took over the work of the oldtime ropemaker and produced a better product.

Manila rope is quite coarse but strong. Its strength arises partly from the length of the fibers of the wild banana plant, from which they are stripped, partly from the ability of the fibers to withstand intesne twisting, and partly from the relative imperviousness of the fibers to soaking.

Cotton rope is cheap and easily made, and it stretches. But it does shrink drastically when soaked. Cotton rope, when soaked, can rip a tent apart or pull down clothes posts. Sisal twine is coarse but very strong and durable. Agricultural binding machinery uses great quantities of sisal and henequen twine. Nylon rope is still relatively expensive but of great importance where strength, light weight, flexibility, and stretch are needed. Some types of nylon rope are stronger than certain steel ropes of similar diameter. Parachute shroudlines are made of nylon rope. Other important synthetic ropes are made of Dacron, polyethylene, and polypropylene.

Steel rope, especially when made from plow steel, is the strongest of all rope. Its flexibility is largely a matter of the fineness of the many wires that are twisted to make the strands. Most steel rope is built around an oil-impregnated fiber center, which provides lubrication among the wires and strands so as to reduce internal friction, heat, and wear. Wire rope is widely used for the standing rigging of ships and for power transmission in power shovels and other types of construction machinery.

Robert Leahey—Shostal

Binder twine is made from the strong fibers of henequen, grown chiefly in Yucatan.

In cordage mills raw Manila, sisalana, or henequen fibers are carefully selected, blended, treated with fungicide, oil, and insect and rodent repellents, converted into yarn, and twisted into twine or rope. The machine shown below, called a spinning jenny, combs, straightens, parallels, and staggers the fibers to make yarn.

Amer. Mfg. Co.

Standard Oil Co. (N.J.)

Rope has important uses in many industries, especially, in the maritime industry. Heavy ropes, like the barge line shown above, are used to tie barges and towboats together and to tie large ships to docks.

ROSE, any of a large group of flower ing shrubs and vines. Roses belong to a family that also includes the apple, pear, strawberry, blackberry, and hawthorn.

The rose is probably the world's favorite flower. It has long been associated with man's activities. It was called the Queen of Flowers by the ancient Greeks and was mentioned several times in the Old Testament. It has been associated with romance the world over. Modern rose growing got its start in the early 19th century when the Empress Josephine of France made rose culture fashionable.

Roses have reached their highest development in the Temperate Zones. Many species, mostly from Europe and Asia, have been blended together by many years of breeding to produce the modern rose types and varieties. The most widely grown roses for cut flowers and for garden use are those of the hybrid tea group. These roses are upright shrubs, 2 to 4 feet high; they produce flowers periodically from June until frost. The flowers are double, with pointed buds, and are usually fragrant.

The floribunda types result from the crossbreeding of the hybrid teas with the old polyantha, or cluster, rose types. Floribundas are popular roses for landscape plantings. They are similar in growth to the hybrid teas, but the flowers are borne in clusters instead of singly. Climbing roses of several types are used to cover arbors or trellises. Many types of larger bush, or shrub, roses are especially suitable for planting in masses or groups in parks or other large areas.

The flowers are made up of from 5 to many petals; most hybrid tea types have from 25 to 50 petals. Five green sepals enclose the unopened bud. The fruit, a fleshy structure called a hip, is similar to a small apple. Flower colors include white, yellows, oranges, pinks, and reds. Many varieties have petals of several blended colors. Some are very fragrant; others have little scent. Roses will grow in a great variety of soils, but the soil must be well drained. Roses grow best in cool, but not extremely cold, climates. Southern France, England, Ireland, and the northwestern United States are noteworthy for fine roses. Because of their popularity, roses are important to the florist. The cultivation of various kinds of roses is also a hobby of many home gardeners, who enjoy their beauty and great variety.

Courtesy of Ford Motor Co.

Roses of the New Yorker hybrid tea variety (left) are fragrant and have long stems. Most hybrid tea roses have a minimum of 20 petals. Roses of the Betsy McCall floribunda variety (right) are satiny pink and are smaller than hybrid tea roses.

ROSES, WARS OF THE, a long struggle in England during the 15th century between the House of York and the House of Lancaster—that is, between descendants of two sons of Edward III. The conflicts began with the Battle of St. Albans (1455) and ended with the Battle of Bosworth Field (1485). The name of the wars comes from the identifying badges worn by the leaders of the two groups—the white rose of York and the red rose of Lancaster.

In 1450 there had been an uprising of the common people in Sussex and Kent. They had demanded that Henry VI, the third and the last of the Lancastrian kings, reform the government and restore to power Richard, duke of York, who was heir presumptive to the throne inasmuch as Henry had no children. Richard returned to England from Ireland and forced his admission into the royal council.

In 1453 a son was born to Henry and his queen, Margaret of Anjou, and at the same time Henry lapsed into insanity. Richard was appointed protector of the realm. When Henry recovered, Margaret, who hated Richard and feared that he would take the throne from her son Edward, persuaded Henry to take up arms against Richard. Richard, supported by the earls of Warwick and Salisbury, the heads of the House of Neville, met the royal army at St. Albans and defeated it. Again Henry became insane, and again Richard became protector of the realm, but again Henry recovered, and again he turned against Richard. In 1460 Henry and Richard met on the field at Northampton. Henry's army was defeated, and he himself was taken prisoner to the Tower of London.

Richard advanced his claims to the throne, and the nobles decreed that upon Henry's death Richard would become king, thus barring young Edward from the throne. This turn of events aroused the Lancastrians more than ever, and at the Battle of Wakefield (1460) they defeated the Yorkist army, and Richard himself was slain. The following year Edward, Richard's son, defeated the Lancastrians at Mortimer's Cross but shortly afterward was defeated by the Lancastrians in the Second Battle of St. Albans. However, the House of Lancaster could not take London, which rallied to the support of the young duke of York. Thus encouraged, York crushed his rivals at Towton Field (1461), and Margaret of Anjou fled to Scotland. Parliament now outlawed the House of Lancaster and made Edward king.

In 1469 the earl of Warwick turned against Edward and was joined by Edward's brother George, duke of Clarence. Their forces were defeated by the king at the Battle of Stamford (1470), and Warwick fled to the Continent, where he gained the support of Louis XI of France. Returning to England, Warwick forced King Edward to flee to Burgundy and for a brief period (in 1470-1471) restored Henry VI to the throne. Edward soon returned, defeated the Lancastrians, and slew Warwick at Barnet. In 1472 Margaret returned from Scotland with a large army. Edward attacked and defeated her forces at Tewkesbury. Inasmuch as her son was slain during the battle and her husband was in the Tower, where he was probably murdered, the Lancastrian cause was crushed. The only surviving Lancastrian claimant to the throne was 14-year-old Henry Tudor, earl of Richmond.

Edward IV died in 1483 and was succeeded by his 12-year-old-son Edward V. Before his death, however, he had appointed his brother, Richard, duke of Gloucester, regent during his son's minority. Within two months Richard was given the throne by Parliament, which had declared Edward V illegitimate. England still seethed with turmoil, and Richard's reign was destined to be brief and filled with trouble. In 1485 Henry Tudor landed at Milford Haven on the southwest coast of Wales, gathered an army, and on August 22 defeated Richard on Bosworth Field. By this victory, and later a Parliamentary act, Henry became king as Henry VII. In order to secure his throne he married Elizabeth, the daughter of Edward IV and the sister of Edward V. In this way the House of Lancaster and the House of York were united.

These wars, which were confined almost exclusively to the nobles, resulted in the annihilation of a majority of the English nobility. This group was thus unable to offer much resistance to the virtual absolutism of the Tudor and Stuart monarchs.

ROSETTA STONE, the name given to a tablet found near Rosetta, Egypt, by an officer in Napoleon's army in 1799. When the British forces defeated Napoleon in Egypt, the Rosetta Stone was included in archaeological objects taken as prizes to the British Museum. It is a tablet of black basalt with an inscription made during the reign of Ptolemy V. The inscription is in hieroglyphic, demotic, and Greek scripts and deals with the Egyptian priesthood gathered at Memphis in honor of Ptolemy V. It was finally completely deciphered in 1822 by Jean François Champollion, who used it in establishing the present-day system of deciphering Egyptian hieroglyphics.

The Rosetta stone bears the story of honors that some Egyptian priests paid a Greek king.

ROSH HASHANA, the Jewish festival of the New Year. Rosh Hashana is a solemn holiday celebrated on the first and second days of the first month of the Jewish calendar, Tishri, which falls at the beginning of autumn. New Year's Day is the first of ten days of penitence, which end with Yom Kippur, the Day of Atonement.

Rosh Hashana is traditionally an anniversary of the creation, and it commemorates the annual rebirth of the world. It is a time of remembering the past and of establishing the continuity of generations of mankind. During the morning service in the synagogue the ram's horn (shophar) is blown to symbolize a fanfare before a king (God) and to herald the day when God will drive out the powers of darkness. Although it is a time of festive joy, Rosh Hashana is also the first of ten days of penitence, and Jews refrain from amusements and devote these days to introspection and prayer. At the morning service on Rosh Hashana men customarily wear the kittel, a long white garment that symbolizes purity. See YOM KIPPUR.

ROSS, BETSY (1752-1836), alleged to have been the maker of the first Stars and Stripes, was born Betsy Griscom. In 1773 she eloped with one John Ross, a Philadelphia upholsterer. Early in 1776 Ross was killed by a gunpowder explosion.

Records of the Pennsylvania State Navy Board show that Mrs. Ross was paid to make naval flags. There is no documentary evidence to support the legend that she made the first Stars and Stripes and was at least in part responsible for its design.

Mrs. Ross remarried in 1777 and again in 1783. She was the mother of seven children.

ROSS, SIR RONALD (1857-1932), a British physician and pathologist who discovered that malarial parasites are transmitted by anopheles mosquitoes. He was born in Almora, India. In 1874 he obtained a medical degree from St. Bartholomew's Hospital Medical College of London.

While serving as a medical officer in India he conducted experiments involving various mosquitoes and discovered that anopheles mosquitoes transmit from one human being to another the parasites that cause malaria. He further discovered that malarial parasites spend part of their life cycle in the bodies of anopheles mosquitoes. When anopheles mosquitoes were exterminated in regions infested by malaria, the incidence of this disease among human beings was reduced. Ross planned and directed measures for exterminating these mosquitoes in many malaria-ridden regions of the world.

In 1902 Ross was awarded the Nobel prize in medicine and physiology for his discovery of the means of malarial transmission. From 1902 to 1912 he was professor of tropical medicine at the University of Liverpool in England.

Besides attaining eminence in medicine, Ross also wrote and published poems, plays, and romantic novels.

Medical researcher Sir Ronald Ross

The Bettmann Archive

ROSSINI, GIOACCHINO (1792-1868), Italian composer of operas, was born in Pesaro. His parents belonged to a strolling opera company, and he began his career by playing second horn to his father when he was only ten years old. His father had him study music under an eminent professor. He took the treble parts as a chorister in the Bologna, Italy, churches and soon became an excellent singer and accompanist. The breaking of his voice put an end to his occupation as a chorister, and at the age of 15 he was admitted into the Lyceum at Bologna and received lessons in counterpoint. But his ardent nature turned restive under strict discipline and dry studies, and he set to work assiduously to educate himself—studying intently the best models, Italian and German. He produced some light operatic pieces, of which *Lucky Trick* came out in 1812. *Tancredi*, brought out at Venice in 1813, made his name famous. Rossini produced a number of other works in quick succession. In 1816 he produced at Rome his world-famous *Barber of Seville*. Other works were *Otello*, *Moses in Egypt*, *Cinderella*, *Semiramide*, *The Thieving Magpie*, *The Lady of the Lake*, *Count Ory*, and *William Tell*. This last and most original of his works was written at the age of 37, and with it, except for *Stabat Mater*, ended the career of Rossini as a composer. After holding the post of manager of the Italian Opera at Paris for some time, he returned in 1836 to his native country, where he continued to reside until 1855, when he returned to Paris. After his death, Rossini's body was taken to Florence, and he was buried there with honors.

ROTC. See RESERVE OFFICERS' TRAINING CORPS.

ROTTERDAM is one of the largest ports in the world, often considered second to New York. The city is located in The Netherlands, on the New Maas River, about 14 miles from the North Sea. The port serves as an outlet for the imports and exports of industrial Germany. It is connected with Germany by various Rhine River branches and with the North Sea by a ship canal. Rotterdam has a population of about 700,000.

The port of Rotterdam is a great commercial center, handling the majority of The Netherlands overseas trade. In tonnage it ranks first in Europe. Its port facilities are extensive and up to date. Rotterdam contains shipbuilding yards and petroleum refineries (in suburbs), distilleries, tobacco factories, and large machine shops, but its mainstay is commerce. The city has many places of interest, which include the old East India House, Boijmans Museum, the Town Hall, dockyards, and the churches. The Groote Market has a statue of Erasmus, who was a native of the city. There are fine parks and a large zoological garden.

Frits J. Rotgans, Amsterdam

Grain silos line part of Rotterdam's harbor. The city is intersected by numerous canals, which permit large vessels to moor alongside the warehouses in the center of the city.

The city received its town rights in 1299. Its modern prosperity has been chiefly developed since 1870. During the German invasion of The Netherlands in 1940 all of the old city and the surrounding area was destroyed. The city was completely rebuilt with the emphasis on industrial development.

ROUGE, a reddish cosmetic liquid, cream, paste, or powder used to tint women's cheeks. It consists of small amounts of suitable colors in some sort of base or filler.

Industrial rouge is finely divided iron oxide, Fe_2O_3. It is used for polishing plate glass, plastics, metals, and jewelry. Optical goods are also polished with rouge. Black rouge is powdered magnetite, Fe_3O_4. Green rouge, chromic oxide, Cr_2O_3, is used on stainless steel.

ROUND DANCE, any kind of dance performed in a circle. In folk dances the circle may break up at intervals to give way to solo or couple dances, but at some point the round figure is resumed. Among children the round dance is an early expression of instinctive motions. Many such dances consist of simple walking steps, as in ring-around-a-rosy, which is a favorite of American children.

In primitive societies the circle was the oldest type of formation for ceremonial and ritual dances. Dancers joined hands and grouped themselves around a tree or a sacred object, seeking to incorporate its lifegiving qualities into their own bodies and spirits. The Maypole dances, which became popular throughout Europe in the Middle Ages, were an outgrowth of such magical associations and religious impulses. Sometimes the central object was a fire or a deep pit. Round dances could also symbolize a wish to threaten or banish some evil, the illness of a sick warrior, for example.

Among the most interesting of surviving round dances are the kolos, which are danced in Balkan countries during feast days. Men and women form a circle, moving clockwise or counterclockwise. The dance begins slowly but becomes faster and faster. As it continues, it develops an intricate, rhythmical pattern.

In more complicated round dances men and women separate and form concentric circles. Round dances of this type, containing two or more circles, once had astronomical significance in many parts of the world. They symbolized the contrasting motions of sun, earth, and moon.

Sometimes the term "round dance" is applied to ballroom dances in which couples move around the floor in a circle, as in the waltz or foxtrot. A round dance in this sense is distinguished from the square dance and the line dance.

ROUNDHEADS. See CIVIL WAR, ENGLISH.

ROUNDTABLE DISCUSSION. See DISCUSSION.

ROUSSEAU, JEAN JACQUES (1712-1778), French social and political philosopher. Rousseau was born at Geneva, Switzerland. His father, Isaac, was a watchmaker. Rousseau attended school for a short time and worked briefly for a notary and for an engraver. In 1728, however, he left Geneva and finally was taken under the protection of the charitable Madame de Warens, with whom he resided intermittently for about the next 12 years.

Rousseau developed a love for music, which he studied ardently. In 1738 he began to apply himself to the study of history, philosophy, and science. In 1742 he went to Paris, where he entered literary society. He served for a brief time as secretary to the French ambassador to Venice. In 1750 he was given a prize by the Academy of Dijon for an essay in which he developed the idea that man is naturally free and happy until corrupted by society. His operetta *Le Devin du village* was presented before the French court in 1752.

Rousseau contributed articles on music and political economy to Diderot's *Encyclopédie*. In 1758 he published an attack on an attempt by Voltaire to establish a theater, for Rousseau considered theater immoral. This essay brought out the contrast between the philosophs (like Diderot)—who heralded reason, individualism, and materialism—and Rousseau, who emphasized emotions, social loyalties, and sentimental deism. His novel *Nouvelle Héloïse* was very popular. It is the story of the love of a man of low station for a woman of rank.

In 1762 Rousseau wrote his greatest works. *Emile,* in narrative form, presents Rousseau's views on education. Emile is described as receiving an education that stressed sympathy, spontaneity, and closeness to nature. *Emile* has influenced the development of progressive education. *The Social Contract* is a political work that criticizes the theory of natural right and develops the idea of the general will. Rousseau vacillated between ideas of individual rights and the concept of the general will, a concept that merges the individual will into the will of the group. So abstract is the *Social Contract* that it has been used with equal logic to defend both democracy and totalitarianism, both conservatism and radicalism. The work may have drawn upon Rousseau's memories of Geneva, a strict, theocratic social organization that succeeded in fostering the well-being and happiness of most of its citizens. The most immediate influence of the *Social Contract* was on Robespierre and Saint-Just and on the Jacobin party in the French Revolution. The Declaration of the Rights of Man was probably based on the *Social Contract.*

Rousseau's espousal of deism in *Emile* angered the French clergy and forced him to leave France. In 1766 he went to England, where David Hume offered him a refuge. He began to write his autobiographical *Confessions.* A quarrel with Hume—Rousseau was suffering from a persecution mania—caused him to return to France, where he wrote *Rêveries d'un promeneur solitaire,* one of his finest works.

ROWING, as a sport, enjoys worldwide popularity among men and women; it is the propulsion of a craft by oars. In 1715 races were organized on the Thames River for professional oarsmen. Oxford University traces its sport of rowing from 1815, and the annual Oxford-Cambridge boat race has taken place since 1829. Amateur rowing has flourished at Henley-on-Thames since 1839.

The first recorded race in the United States of America is accepted to be that between a Long Island and a New York crew on the Hudson River in 1811. In 1834 the first organized association of amateur boat clubs was formed by New Yorkers, but it lasted only nine years. Harvard and Yale held the first intercollegiate rowing event in 1852, and in 1872 the National Association of Amateur Oarsmen was formed.

Many inventions have improved rowing through the years. Spoon-shaped oars were designed, but their use was soon discontinued. Aluminum boats became popular in 1923. Many experiments were made with sliding seats, width of blade, length of oar, and actual styles of rowing; and many attribute the successes of the German crews in the 1960 Olympics to a new oar with a shorter, broader blade.

Below is a college rowing team in action. The photograph shows clearly the narrowness of the racing shell, as the boat is called. The crew consists of eight oarsmen and the coxwain.
Courtesy of the University of Wisconsin—Milwaukee Journal Photo

RUBBER, any of a number of natural or synthetic materials that share the following characteristics: elasticity, flexibility, resilience, resistance to electrical current and chemicals, low permeability to gases and liquids, and resistance to abrasion. Latex, the milky fluid from which natural rubber is processed, was at one time extracted almost exclusively from a variety of plants and trees that grew, uncultivated, in the following three general areas of the world: South America and the West Indies, Africa and Madagascar, and southeastern Asia, including the Malay Peninsula. Since about 1910 the Pará rubber tree, native to the valley of the Amazon River in South America but cultivated extensively on plantations throughout the tropical areas of the world, has been the primary source of natural-rubber latex.

Although the existence of rubber was known by the Spaniards at least as early as 1530, commercial processing of the material did not commence until the latter part of the 18th century. At the same time, according to tradition, the English chemist Joseph Priestley gave rubber its name when he discovered its capacity to erase pencil marks. In 1791 another Englishman, Samuel Peel, patented a method for waterproofing fabric by treating it with a solution of rubber dissolved in turpentine. In 1823 Charles Macintosh established a plant in Glasgow, Scotland, for the preparation of waterproof cloth and thus gave his name to a type of garment now widely used. Various other rubber products, including shoes and bottles, were marketed throughout the world. However, it was soon found that all rubber products had basic faults: If subjected to cold, the rubber would become brittle and hard; if heated, the rubber would become soft and give off a foul odor.

In 1839 after many years of fruitless experimentation, Charles Goodyear invented the process called vulcanization, essentially the heating of crude rubber with sulfur. Out

John Strohm

Latex yields are increased by producing new plant varieties. This man inspects new plant grafts in a rubber nursery in Malaya.

Ewing Krainin—Photo Researchers

Latex is harvested on plantations by making thin cuts in the bark of the rubber tree, above, and collecting the oozing latex. The latex is treated with acid to coagulate it, rolled into sheets, below, and hung on frames to dry. The sheets will be pressed into bales for shipment.

Harold Schultz—American Museum of Natural History

The rubber tree was originally native to the New World. These rubber gatherers in the Amazon jungle of Brazil smoke latex to harden it.

Margaret Lang—Shostal

The great demand for rubber products has led to the development of synthetic replacements, largely derived from petroleum. This plant in Sarnia, Ontario, uses locally available materials to make synthetic rubber.

Malak—Anann Photo Features

A major use for rubber is in the manufacture of pneumatic tires.

The Goodyear Tire & Rubber Company, Chemical Division, Akron 16, Ohio

of this development came the whole modern rubber industry. With the increasing consumption of rubber and rising prices for crude rubber came an accumulation of scrap rubber, most of which had been incorporated with textiles in making belting, shoes, boots, and similar products. In 1905 a process was invented whereby rubber could be separated from the fabric and reused. In the following year occurred the discovery of organic accelerators for the vulcanization process. Such accelerators not only cut down time but also brought about substantial savings to the industry, for utilization of organic accelerators made available supplies of lower-priced extracted rubber and also improved the quality of the final rubber product.

Today, a significant part of the rubber-processing operation takes place on the rubber plantation itself. The first step, the extraction of the latex from the Pará rubber tree, is accomplished by means of a groove about $\frac{1}{4}$ inch deep and partially encircling the tree. The latex exuding from the tree is caught in a small cup. Trees are usually tapped every other day after they reach maturity (from five to seven years old). A thin strip of bark is removed from the tree each time the tree is tapped. On a typical plantation from 80 to 125 trees are cultivated on an acre, with from 400 to 500 pounds of dry rubber the average annual yield per acre. However, by employing special methods of grafting, yields have been as high as 2,500 pounds per acre.

After it is collected, the fresh latex, which is about one-third rubber by weight, is diluted with water and coagulated with a solution of either acetic acid or formic acid. The coagulated rubber is then compressed by rollers into ribbed sheets, which are dried over a wood fire in a smokehouse. About 85 percent of the natural-rubber crop is delivered to the processing factory in the form of smoked ribbed sheets. Most of the remaining 15 percent is marketed as pale crepe, which is processed much like the sheet form. In the production of crepe a bleaching agent is added to the latex before coagulation, and the coagulated rubber is rolled and cut into long strips and dried in hot air. A small percentage of the latex is marketed as a pure concentrate.

The crude rubber is shipped to the processing factory, where it is first washed, if necessary, and then run through mills to make the rubber soft and pliable. Various materials, called compounding ingredients, are added to the softened, or masticated, rubber. Compounding ingredients may include pigments, reinforcing agents, sulfur, organic accelerators, fillers, and antioxidants. The rubber is once again kneaded in preparation for the vulcanization process. Rubber may be vulcanized either at high temperatures—the method invented by Goodyear—or at room temperature —the method discovered by English inventor Alexander Parkes in 1841. The vulcanized rubber is then formed in calenders (used to coat fabric with rubber), tubing machines, and other shaping devices. In some cases vulcanization and shaping occur in a single operation.

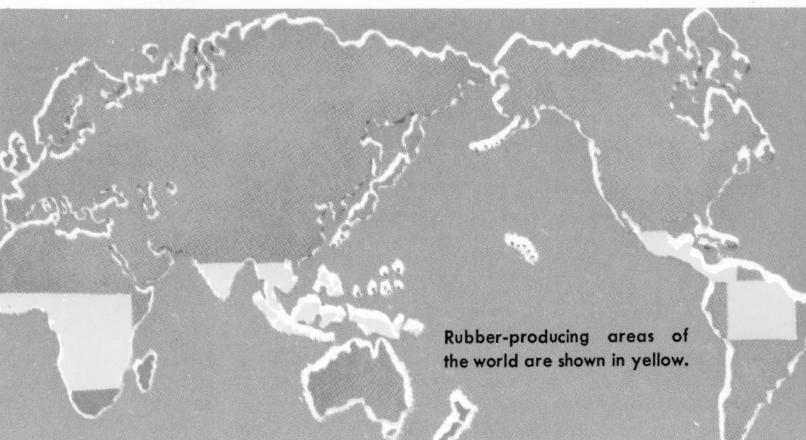
Rubber-producing areas of the world are shown in yellow.

Manipulation of the various ingredients and processes has resulted in the development of a number of rubber derivatives. Among the most significant of these are chlorinated rubber, prepared by passing chlorine into a solution of rubber in carbon tetrachloride, and rubber hydrochloride, prepared by passing hydrogen chloride gas into a solution of rubber in benzene. Hard rubber, also known as ebonite and vulcanite, is produced by using a large percentage of sulfur in the vulcanization process. Most soft natural rubber is vulcanized with 3 or 4 percent sulfur. Hard rubber is vulcanized with as much as 60 percent sulfur.

Scarcely was the natural-rubber industry well established before scientists began to search for methods of producing synthetic rubber. One of the first types of synthetic rubber, developed in England before 1900, was prepared from the hydrocarbon isoprene, which was synthesized from turpentine. By the time of World War I German scientists had perfected a commercial process for producing synthetic rubber from other hydrocarbon compounds. The development of such processes became a matter of grave concern in the United States when the nation's supply of natural rubber from southeastern Asia was cut off by the Japanese shortly before the outbreak of World War II.

Virtually all types of synthetic rubber are obtained from products of the petroleum industry or of allied industries. Important sources are styrene, acetylene, and butadiene. Two of the most important types of synthetic rubber are butyl rubber and the rubber known in the United States as SBR, an abbreviation for "styrene-butadiene rubber." SBR and butyl rubber, together with natural rubber, made up about 90 percent of the world's supply of new rubber used during the 1950's. Also important, however, are the so-called natural synthetic types of rubber. These are synthetics that duplicate the molecular structure of natural rubber and can be used interchangeably with the natural product. Since World War II an increasing number of products, such as foam rubber, have been made directly from natural-rubber latex or from its synthetic equivalent. Today rubber, both natural and synthetic, with its numerous derivatives, is one of the most versatile materials available to industry. About two-thirds of the rubber crop is consumed by the automotive industry for the production of tires and other vehicle parts. The remainder goes into over 30,000 different products, including rubberized-fabric products (tennis shoes, boots, raincoats), building materials (insulation, floor coverings, paint), electrical appliances and insulation, water hose, heels and soles for footwear, medical and surgical supplies, toys, belting, and a variety of foam-rubber products.

RUBENS, PETER PAUL (1577-1640), a distinguished Flemish painter, was born at Siegen, in Westphalia. When he was ten years old his mother, then a widow, returned to her native Antwerp. After studying in his own country under Otto van Veen he went to Italy, where he copied the works of the masters, chiefly Titian, Tintoretto, and Correggio. While in Italy he was employed by Vicenzo Gonzaga of Mantua as an artist. He returned to Antwerp in 1608 and soon after was made court painter to Archduke Albert, governor of the Low Countries. In 1622 he was employed by Marie de Médicis to adorn the gallery of the Luxembourg with a series of paintings illustrative of the principal scenes of her life. He was afterward employed by Philip IV of Spain in some important negotiations, which he executed with such credit as to be appointed secretary of the privy council. He acquired immense wealth. Rubens was one of the most rapid in execution of all the great masters and was one of the greatest perfecters of the mechanical phases of his art. His works were numerous and diversified in subject. His chief works included "The Descent from the Cross" and "Venus and Adonis."

Pinakothek Museum, Munich

This typical Rubens portrait is of his wife, Helena Fourment, and their son Frans.

RUBY, a red variety of corundum (aluminum oxide, Al_2O_3, used as a gemstone. Large rubies without flaws are rare and are more valuable than diamonds of equal size and quality. Small rubies are not so rare or expensive. Star rubies, which display a six-rayed white star when cut in a rounded shape, are very rare. The most valuable rubies are the dark-red pigeon blood rubies.

Rubies are hard and tough. The only mineral that is harder is diamond. Rubies are unusually heavy for their volume for a nonmetallic mineral. Cut rubies are transparent and have a glassy or a brilliant appearance. Rubies are found as rough, rounded or barrel-shaped crystals with a glassy luster. The red color of rubies is caused by small amounts of chromic oxide in the crystals.

Rubies are found chiefly in Burma, Thailand, and Ceylon. The best rubies come from the area near Mogok in Burma. The stones are found in a residual soil resulting from the weathering of metamorphosed limestone. Some rubies are found in the limestone. In Thailand rubies are found near Bangkok on the Gulf of Siam. The rubies are found in a clay formed from weathered and decomposed basalt. In Ceylon rubies are found in stream gravels. In the United States rubies have been found in stream gravels and corundum deposits in North Carolina.

Synthetic rubies have been manufactured for many years. The first successful process fused together small chips of natural ruby into a larger stone, which was called a reconstructed ruby. Since 1902 synthetic rubies have been made by the Verneuil process in France, Germany, and Switzerland. Small amounts of aluminum oxide powder mixed with chromic oxide for coloring are melted in a hot oxyhydrogen flame, and the liquid is allowed to crystallize on a fire-clay support. The procedure is repeated many times, and a boule, or synthetic ruby, is formed. Synthetic rubies are not easy for the amateur to distinguish from natural rubies, but a trained person can distinguish between artificial and natural stones. Since 1947 Linde Air Products Company has made synthetic star rubies.

Rubies that do not possess the required transparency or color to be used as gems are used as jewel bearings in watches and in scientific instruments.

RUDDER, primarily an oar, specifically the instrument by which a ship or an aircraft is steered. It is fitted vertically in the afterpart of the ship or aircraft on a hinge so that it may be turned from side to side. The hinge mechanism consists of the pintle and the gudgeon. A crosspiece is fixed to the rudder so that it may be turned. This piece is the tiller. When the rudder is in line with the keel of a ship or the centerline of an aircraft, the force of the water or air flowing past the rudder is equal on both sides, and there is no tendency to turn. If the rudder is moved to one side, the forces of both pressure and suction are unbalanced, and the stern of the ship or aircraft will move, thus turning the hull or fuselage to a new direction. To steady on a new course the rudder is reversed to stop the turning; it is then brought back to the centerline or amidships. In actual practice the rudder is being constantly moved small amounts to keep the ship or aircraft on course. The rudder is said to be to the right or left depending on the side to which the trailing edge has been moved; thus right rudder will cause a turn of the ship or aircraft to its right. On a ship the entire steering mechanism is called the helm, and the person who controls it is the helmsman.

A plane, **1,** turns left when rudder, **1B,** is turned left by the wire-connected rudder control, **1A.** A right turn, **2,** is made by turning rudder, **2A,** right with control, **2B.**

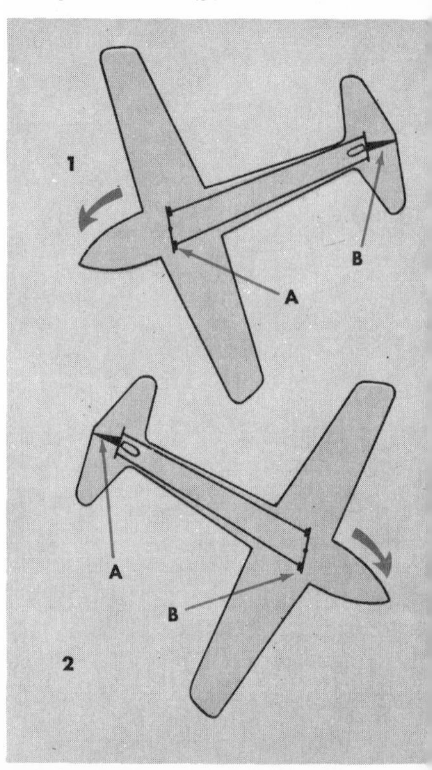

RUG AND CARPET. Both of these terms are applied to a wide variety of floor coverings made from heavy weights of yarns and fibers. Unlike the rug, which is not tacked down and does not cover the entire floor of a room, a carpet is usually tacked to the floor and stretches from wall to wall. Despite these differences, as well as certain differences in construction, the two terms are used almost interchangeably, particularly when referring to oriental floor coverings.

The making of rugs and carpets is an old and honored profession, which has been carried on for many centuries. The weaving of rugs is shown on the walls of Egyptian tombs dating from about 3000 B.C. Rugs were also made at an early period in China, India, Assyria, and Persia. In Persia rug making became a famous art after the 6th century B.C.

In France rug making began in the early 17th century. The Aubusson weavers of France developed tapestries; later they returned to rug making and gave a particular weave the Aubusson name. This and the Savonnerie weave became noted throughout the world. By 1750 Brussels, Belgium, and the towns of Wilton and Axminster in England were producing carpeting that bore their place names. The rugs of the English cities were characterized by patterns adapted from the oriental types.

In America William Sprague set up the first rug-making factory at Philadelphia in 1791. In the 1820's the first New England mills started American carpet manufacturing on a large scale. Two inventions gave the industry its greatest impetus—the power loom and the axminster loom. The former was invented by Erastus Bigelow in 1839, and the second was developed by Halcyon Skinner in 1867. Like the English rugs, American types bore designs that were similar to the oriental.

In rug making, cotton or jute threads, known as the warp, are stretched on a loom, and a second set, called the weft, is laced between the former at right angles. Wool loops are knotted to the warp, with the loose ends forming the pile, or hairlike surface, of the rug. The first power looms could produce only narrow rugs; however, the broadloom was soon developed and produced rugs up to 18 feet wide.

The color and design of a rug is brought about by setting tufts of pile in a predetermined pattern. Almost any design, from the simplest to the most intricate, can be duplicated in a rug. The modern trend, however, is toward single-colored and textured rugs. Texture is obtained by putting tufts of different heights in the weave to give it an embossed appearance.

In these diagrams, showing three methods of producing machine-woven rugs, the dots represent cross sections of the shots, or weft yarns. On the loom the shuttle carries the shots across the fabric. The black lines are warp yarns, running lengthwise. The looped warp, or chain warp, ties the weft together. The straight black lines are stuffer yarns to give the fabric additional strength. The colored threads of the pile are warp yarns. Above is a diagram showing a three-shot velvet with single chain warp and two stuffer yarns; middle, an Axminster with three double shots, a double chain warp, and one stuffer yarn; below, a two-shot tapestry with double chain warp and three stuffer yarns. In tapestry the pile is not cut.

Some rugs are still handmade, such as the oriental and the European hand-tufted rugs. Those that are woven on power looms include the axminster, chenille, Jacquard (brussels and wilton), and velvet. A type of construction called tufting originated in the carpet industry in the early 1950's and already is used in more than 50 percent of the carpets produced. Tufting consists of stretching yarn into a woven jute backing. The tufts are locked into position by the application of a generous layer of latex. Oriental rugs are classed according to the region from which they come and are listed as Persian, Turkish, Turkoman, Caucasian, Indian, and Chinese. The hand-tufted Savonnerie carpets of France are well known, although they are no longer produced.

The axminster has been a popular type of carpet in America. The axminster weave is close to the oriental, and in this respect it can duplicate most of the oriental designs. The axminster loom produces this weave accurately and swiftly. The axminster carpet contains less wool per square inch than most other carpets, which makes it less expensive. A fine-quality axminster carpet has about eight rows of pile to the inch. It can be obtained in widths up to 12 feet. The axminster may be readily distinguished because it cannot be rolled crosswise, only lengthwise.

The chenille carpet is the aristocrat of carpets. In the chenille process two looms are required. The first weaves the chenille fur, or blanket. This is cut into strips, the strips are pressed into a form which resembles caterpillars (French, *chenille*), and these are used as the filling yarn when the rug is woven on a second loom. It is made in sizes up to 30 feet wide and in irregular shapes.

The Jacquard carpet refers to a carpet that is produced on the Jacquard loom and includes the wilton and brussels carpets. The wilton is made of woolen or worsted yarns in a cut-pile or plushlike fabric. These rugs come in widths up to 15 feet. The brussels carpet is a nap fabric of woolen and worsted yarns. The wilton and the brussels rugs are expensive to manufacture, and they make luxurious floor coverings.

The velvet carpet is a cut-pile type, similar to the wilton but less expensive to manufacture. A pattern for the velvet carpet is made in a preliminary process known as drum dyeing. In weaving the velvet carpet resembles wilton.

RUGBY evolved by accident in 1823 when a student at Rugby School, in England, picked up the ball in a game of association football (soccer) and ran with it. This play was contrary to the rules of the game, but soon afterward the carrying of the ball and the tackling of the ball carrier became legal features of the game. A commemorative plaque has been placed on a wall adjoining the field on which the historic game in 1823 was played.

In 1871 the Rugby Football Union was formed by 32 representatives of London and suburban clubs. The game was played with 20 men on each side until 1876, when the rules were radically changed, and only 15 men were allowed on each side. This is so today. South Africa soon adopted Rugby as its national game, as did Wales, Australia, and New Zealand. Every year international matches are played between countries of the British Commonwealth, France, and Argentina.

The game was introduced into the United States soon after its inception in England. However, President Theodore Roosevelt insisted on reform after a particularly rugged match between Pennsylvania and Swarthmore in 1905. It was then that the forward pass was introduced, and so developed the American version of the game. It is true, therefore, that Rugby was the father of the modern American football game. Rugby is still played in the eastern United States and in California.

Rugby is played on a field 110 yards long and 75 yards wide. A goalpost is placed centrally on the line at each end of the field. There are no so-called plays; the game, controlled by one referee, develops as it is played and is stopped only when the ball is unplayable. The ball must always be passed backward; no blocking is allowed as only the person with the ball may be tackled; much kicking is involved; and the game is fast, with many men handling the ball. No substitutions are allowed. Injury means that a team must reorganize on the field and play with fewer men. Players wear no form of protection except boots, socks, shorts, and shirt. The ball is similar to an American football but is larger and less pointed.

A professional form of the game, with 13 players on each side, is played in England, Australia, France, and New Zealand under the rules of the Rugby Football League. This game is even faster than the amateur version of Rugby.

RUMANIA is a country of southeastern Europe. After World War II it fell under Communist control, and since then has been a satellite state of the Soviet Union. Although it is called a people's republic, it is actually a dictatorship, allowing no opposition. The historic regions of Rumania include Moldavia in the northeast, Walachia in the south, and Transylvania in the northwest. With an area of some 91,000 square miles, Rumania has about 18,000,000 inhabitants.

Southern and eastern Rumania lie in the basin of the Danube River, which forms most of the boundary with Bulgaria. Before the Danube flows into the Black Sea through its several mouths, it forms a number of marshy lakes. The Danube is an important national and international shipping route. Of its many Rumanian tributaries, the Prut River on the Soviet border is the chief navigable one.

The climate has great temperature ranges. Summers are hot and dry; winters, cold and snowy. Average temperatures decrease with higher altitudes. The least amount of rain falls on the eastern plain.

Rumania has a great variety of mineral wealth. Petroleum is the principal natural resource. Among the European nations, Rumania ranks second only to the Soviet Union in petroleum production. Coal, natural gas, salt, iron ore, and manganese are among other leading minerals. Extensive forests cover Rumania's mountains. The Danube and the Black Sea provide rich fishing grounds.

The development of industry and hydroelectric power has been actively promoted by the Communist government. Iron and steel, chemicals, machinery, textiles, and foodstuffs are among the country's industrial products. All industry is government owned. Foreign trade is a government monopoly, and nearly all trade is with the Soviet Union and its satellites. Exports consist mainly of petroleum products, lumber, and grain.

Rumanians are descendants of the old Roman colonists, the native Dacians, as well as of the Slavs and the various other peoples who wandered through their land. Besides the Rumanians, there are large groups of other nationalities, including Hungarians, Germans, and Jews. The Rumanian language developed from vulgar Latin, its vocabulary enriched with many Slavic words. The Rumanian Orthodox Church is the largest religious group.

In the 2d and 3d centuries Rumania was the Roman colony of Dacia; during this time it became completely Romanized. When the Romans withdrew, various other peoples wandered through the land. Around 1400 Moldavia and Walachia, the basis of present-day Rumania, became independent feudal states. Although they held off the

Constanta, which is located on the Black Sea, is the principal port and seaside resort of Rumania. The city has several mosques and an open-air archaeological museum.

Eastfoto

Turks for a few centuries, they were finally absorbed into the Turkish Empire. Transylvania was under Hungarian control.

Rumania was formed in 1862, when the union of Moldavia and Walachia was completed, but it did not become fully independent until 1878. Internal strife troubled the kingdom. Taking part in the Second Balkan Wra, it took the southern Dobruja region (in the southeast) from Bulgaria. After World War I, in which Rumania eventually joined the Allies, it received other territories, including Bessarabia (in the northeast) from Russia and Transylvania from Hungary, which nearly doubled its area.

Drawn into World War II on the Axis side, it was occupied by the U.S.S.R. in 1944. After the war some of the lands Rumania had been forced to give its neighbors in 1940 were returned, but Bessarabia was kept by the Soviet Union and southern Dobruja by Bulgaria. Rumania became a Soviet satellite in 1947, when the Communists took control after forcing King Michael to abdicate. For detailed map, see YUGOSLAVIA.

RUMANIA

Area: 91,000 sq. mi.
Population: 18,000,000
Capital: Bucharest
Largest cities: Bucharest, Cluj, Timisoara, Ploesti
Highest mountain peak: Negoi (about 8,300 feet)
Chief rivers: Danube and tributaries
Climate: Hot, dry summers—cold, snowy winters
National flag: Three vertical stripes of blue, yellow, red—coat of arms in center
National anthem: *Te slavim Rominie, pamint parintesc* (We Praise Thee, Fatherland Rumania)
Form of government: Communist people's republic

The national flag of Rumania was adopted in 1948 following communist seizure. The coat of arms depicts the nation's resources.

Unit of currency: Leu (plural, lei)
Language: Rumanian
Chief religion: Rumanian Orthodox
Chief economic activities: Agriculture, mining
Chief crops: Corn, wheat, barley, rye, oats, sugar beets, potatoes
Chief minerals: Petroleum, coal, natural gas, salt, iron ore, manganese
Chief exports: Petroleum products, lumber, grain
Chief imports: Semimanufactured goods, raw materials, machinery, metals

RUMANIAN, the language of the Rumanian people. It belongs to the eastern Romance group of languages, and is spoken principally in Rumania. It is also spoken in a series of localities in Greece, Albania, Yugoslavia, Bulgaria, and Hungary.

The number of people speaking Rumanian on Rumanian territory is 18 million. Rumanian has several foreign dialects, the most important of which is Macedono-Rumanian, distributed in Greece, Albania, Yugoslavia, and Bulgaria and spoken by about 500,000 people. The Rumanian language is based upon the Vulgar Latin spoken by settlers from the Roman Empire, and nearly 90 percent of its modern vocabulary is of Latin origin, though there are numerous words derived from Slavonic, Albanian, Turkish, Hungarian, and Greek as well.

RUMFORD, COUNT. See THOMPSON, BENJAMIN.

RUMINANT, one of many herbivorous mammals that regurgitate swallowed but unchewed vegetation and chew it before swallowing it again. Ruminants belong to the order of mammals that have an even number of functional toes, usually two but occasionally four. Each toe is usually sheathed in a cornified hoof. Ruminants are almost exclusively herbivorous. They either have no canine teeth or else their canine teeth are small. In carnivorous mammals the canine teeth are used for tearing the flesh of prey.

Ruminants take into their mouths large quantities of grass, leaves, or herbs and swallow them without chewing them. This swallowed food passes into a large division of the stomach called the rumen, where it is stored but not digested. Later, the food is forced back, or regurgitated, into the mouth and is thoroughly chewed. While being chewed the food is called the cud, and the animal is said to be chewing its cud. Then the food is swallowed again into a different stomach division, where digestion begins. Soon it passes through the other stomach divisions, and digestion is completed. The stomach of most ruminants consists of four divisions, but some ruminants have only three.

Ruminants include domestic cattle, sheep, and goats and the deer, antelope, buffalo, camel, and giraffe.

RUMMY, the basic card game from which a number of other games, such as gin rummy, 500 rummy, and canasta, developed. Rummy (or rum) is thought to be an American adaptation of a Spanish game, conquian, which was introduced into the United States from Mexico in the middle of the 19th century.

Rummy is played by two to six people with a regular pack of 52 cards, ranking from the king (high) to the ace. In some rummy games the ace ranks either low or high. After cutting for the deal, the cards are dealt around, one at a time, until each player has ten cards if there are two players, seven cards when three or four play, and six cards when five or six play. The remaining cards are placed in a pile face down in the center of the table and become the stock. The top card is then turned face up and placed beside the stock. The object of the game is to get rid of all of the cards in one's hand by melding. A meld is three or more cards, either in sequence in one suit, as jack, ten, nine of hearts, or three or four of the same rank, as four sevens. In basic rummy the ace is in sequence with the two, not with the king.

The player to the left of the dealer plays first. Each player in his turn draws either the top card of the stock or the top card of the discard pile. He adds this card to his hand. He may then meld, if he is able, by laying the meld on the table faceup. The player may meld as many cards as he wishes at each turn. He ends by discarding one card from his hand to the discard pile. The discard pile is kept neatly stacked, and no previous discards may be examined. In melding, a player may either lay down one or more melds of three or more cards each or add cards to melds already laid down—either his own or those of opponents.

The players who first "goes out" by getting rid of all the cards in his hand wins the deal. If he can play all of his remaining cards on melds, he may go out without a final discard. If no one goes out before the last card of the stock has been drawn, the discard pile is turned over (without shuffling) to form a new stock, and the play continues. If a player discards a card that could have been played on a meld, any other player may call "Rummy!" and claim the card. The claimer must then play the card and discard one from his hand, after which the turn is taken in proper order.

When a player goes out, he receives the number of points in his melds plus the points of the cards remaining in the hands of his opponents. Face cards count ten each, aces count one, and the other cards count according to their value. If a player melds his entire hand in one play, without having made a previous meld, he collects double the number of points remaining in his opponents' hands. In scoring, each deal may be counted as a separate game, or the game may be set at 100 points.

RUNE, a letter in the ancient alphabet of the Scandinavians and of the Germanic tribes. The origin of the runic alphabet is uncertain.

The runic alphabet is sharp and angular, and for this reason scientists believe that it was first incised in stone, wood, or other hard material. Runes are found on stones with inscriptions of names or of epitaphs. They have been found on such items as coins, buckles, bracelets, rings, and horns.

The runic alphabet is named futhorc, after the first six letters,

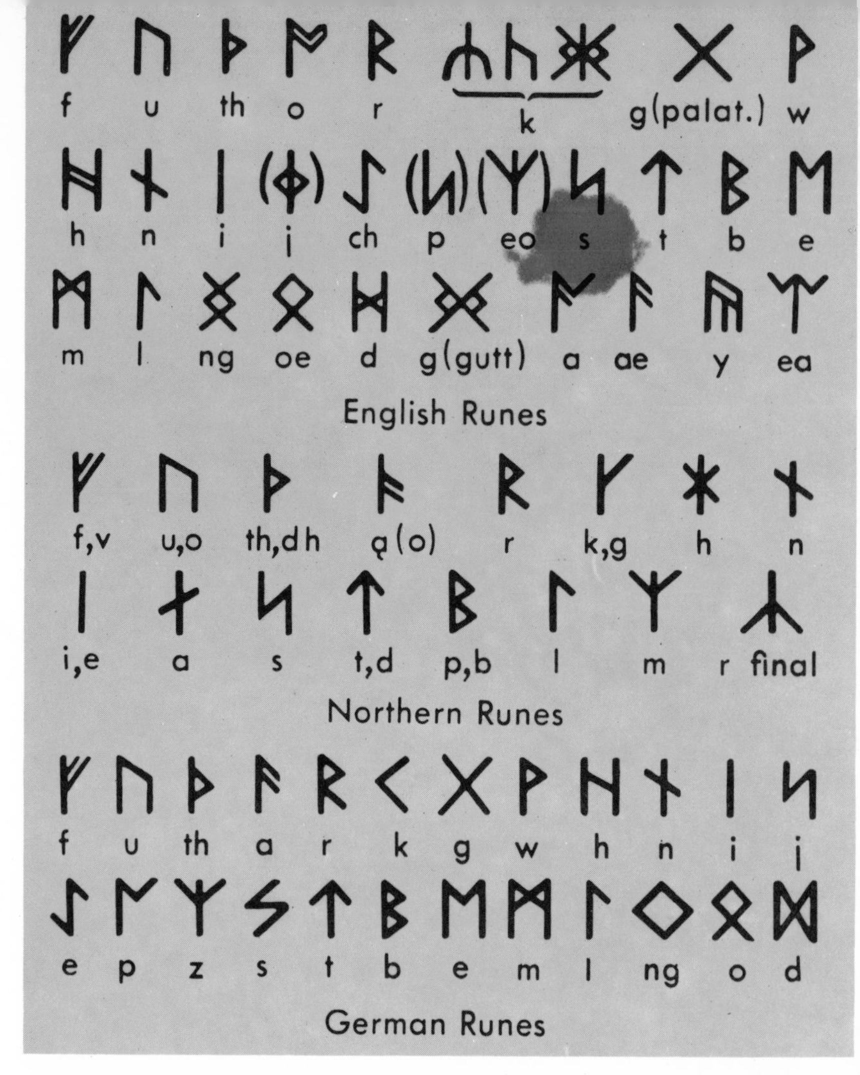

f, u, th, o, r, and *c* (*k*). The German runic alphabet has 24 letters. English and Northern (Scandinavian) variants of the original futhorc have different numbers of letters.

The runic inscriptions seem to be found wherever the Scandinavians are believed to have migrated, including the valley of the Danube River, the United States, and the Isle of Man. The runes have been replaced by the Latin alphabet.

RURAL ELECTRIFICATION. More than a third of the 20th century passed before U.S. farmers began to make productive use of electricity. In 1935 only 740,000 farms (less than 11 percent) had electricity. In May, 1935, the Rural Electrification Administration, a government lending agency, was set up. In 1936 Congress made REA permanent, and in 1939 REA became an agency of the Department of Agriculture. By making long-term, low-interest loans REA has greatly increased the use of electricity on farms and in the rural home. By 1960 more than 3,570,000 U.S. farms (almost 97 percent) had electricity. REA lends money to local organizations, mostly cooperatives, created and operated by local people. REA also finances construction of generation and transmission facilities and provides loan funds for use by members of cooperatives in buying electrical, wiring, and plumbing equipment.

With more than 400 uses of farm power known and more being discovered, electricity has taken the drudgery out of farmwork. Electricity helps the farmer milk his cows, brood his pigs, grind his feed, and do many other chores. REA has brought lights, radio, TV, modern plumbing, and other comforts to the farm home. In October, 1949, when only 38 percent of the U.S. farms had telephones, Congress authorized REA to make loans to improve and extend rural telephone service. By the early 1960's about 65 percent of the U.S. farms had telephone service.

Japan, which is blessed with good hydroelectric-power resources, was the first Asian country to extend extensive electric power into rural areas. In 1926 the Central Electricity Board was established in Great Britain. This board was designed to create a national system of main transmission lines, which was known as the grid. Local and rural distribution undertakings could be linked to power stations that had a high efficiency and low cost of operation. In Australia rural electrification is organized by the states. New South Wales, for example, established in 1946 the Electricity Authority, which has developed a plan of subsidizing the cost of rural electrification. After World War II rural electrification made steady progress in Canada. By 1955 about 75 percent of Canadian farms enjoyed the benefits of powerline service. Other farms generated their own electricity by windmills or engines. Not only did the number of farm customers increase, but the amount of electricity each customer consumed increased even more rapidly. The Union of South Africa established in 1922 the Electricity Supply Commission. In 1949 the commission was empowered to supply electricity on a profitless basis to certain undeveloped rural areas.

In the Soviet Union a small percentage of collective farms had electricity available to them up to the end of World War II. From 1946 to 1949 small rural electric stations brought electric power to an increasing number of farms. Several oblasts, such as Moscow and Leningrad, were almost completely electrified by 1950.

RUSH-BAGOT AGREEMENT, an exchange of diplomatic notes in 1817 that led to practical naval disarmament by the United States and Great Britain on the Great Lakes. The notes were written by British minister to the United States Charles Bagot (Apr. 28, 1817) and acting Secretary of State Richard Rush (Apr. 29, 1817). The notes formalized a proposal initiated by James Madison and James Monroe. Also involved in the agreement were John Quincy Adams, minister to Great Britain, and Viscount Castlereagh, the British foreign minister. In the notes the United States and Great Britain agreed to limit their forces on the Great Lakes to one vessel each of not more than 100 tons, with one 18-pound cannon, on Lake Ontario; two similar ships each for the other four lakes; and one each on Lake Champlain. The agreement was later presented to the Senate, which approved it unanimously on Apr. 16, 1818.

RUSKIN, JOHN (1819-1900), an English art and social critic, was born in London, the son of a successful wine merchant. His early education was conducted by his family, and while he was young, he traveled extensively. He was graduated from Oxford and at the age of 24 published the first volume of his *Modern Painters*. This work, begun as a defense of the English landscape painter Joseph Turner, was (when completed in five volumes in 1860) an exposition of Ruskin's views on art. In 1849 appeared Ruskin's *The Seven Lamps of Architecture* and between 1851 and 1853 the three volumes that compose *The Stones of Venice*. These two works are complementary in that the first venerates medieval, or Gothic, art, and the second attacks the art of the Renaissance. Both contributed to the Gothic revival of the 19th century in England.

Ruskin now turned his attention to social and economic problems, and his remedies for contemporary problems began to appear in various magazines. *Unto This Last* and *Munera Pulveris* were both expositions of Ruskin's views on how society should be run. *Sesame and Lilies* was a work on education. *Time and Tide, by Weare and Tyne* and *Fors Clavigera* were both collections of letters on social questions. These embodied the views more actively propagated in Ruskin's Guild of St. George, an attempt to establish a medieval community. Other works by Ruskin include *The Crown of Wild Olive, The Ethics of the Dust, A Joy Forever, The Two Paths, The Elements of Drawing, The Queen of the Air, Prosperina, Love's Meinie,* and his unfinished autobiography, *Praeterita*.

RUSSELL, BERTRAND (1872-), English philosopher, mathematician, educator, and writer. He is one of the most important thinkers of the 20th century, especially in his contributions to mathematical philosophy and logic. His writings, which are clear, lucid, and frequently witty, cover a wide range of subjects and fill over 40 volumes. On receiving the Nobel prize for literature in 1950, he was praised as "one of our time's most brilliant spokesmen of rationality and humanity." Russell is a pleasant and witty conversationalist. His favorite recreations are reading detective stories and playing chess.

Bertrand Russell was born at Ravenscroft, near Trelleck, in Monmouthshire. The family had been significant in English history—it was Russell's grandfather who had introduced the important Reform Bill of 1832. Bertrand Russell's parents died while he was a child, and he and a brother were raised by their grandmother. Russell began to show an aptitude for mathematics by the time he was 11 years old, and at 18 years of age he entered Trinity College, Cambridge, where he studied mathematics and philosophy. He became a fellow of his college in 1895.

Russell considers 1900 his most important intellectual year, for in that year he discarded Hegelianism for G. E. Moore's metaphysical realism. *The Principles of Mathematics* made Russell known in the academic world. He collaborated with the mathematician-philosopher Alfred North Whitehead in writing the important *Principia Mathematica*. In this work he and Whitehead developed the idea that mathematics is reducible to a few axioms and logical principles.

Russell and his first wife belonged for a time to the Fabian Society, and Russell was active in campaigning for women's rights. His pacifism during World War I earned him a fine and a period in prison, where he wrote the *Introduction to Mathematical Philosophy*. After the war he visited the U.S.S.R., of whose leaders he became critical. He lectured at the National University at Peking in 1920 and 1921. On his return to England he supported himself by journalism, popularizations of scientific principles, and lecture tours in the United States. His interest in education led him to write several books on the subject and to open an experimental school for children in 1927.

In 1931, on the death of his older brother, Russell became the 3d earl Russell of Kingston Russell. His books in the 1930's were concerned with world affairs and cautioned against steps that might lead to war. However, he supported the Allies in their declaration of war against Germany. After 1938 Russell taught at the University of Chicago, the University of California, and Harvard University. His free thinking created a protest that cost him a teaching post at the College of the City of New York. A series of lectures at the Barnes Foundation in Pennsylvania, which he was not able to complete, were compiled into *A History of Western Philosophy*. Russell returned to England on a fellowship at Trinity College in 1944.

In 1950 Russell was awarded the Nobel prize for literature. He continued his literary and philosophical output with such books as *Unpopular Essays, The Impact of Science upon Society, Nightmares of Eminent Persons, My Philosophical Development, New Hopes for a Changing World,* and *Wisdom of the West.*

RUSSIA. See UNION OF SOVIET SOCIALIST REPUBLICS.

RUSSIAN, the language of the Russian people. Together with the Ukrainian and Byelorussian languages it constitutes the East Slavic group of languages. The East Slavic group, together with the South Slavic and West Slavic groups, forms the broader group of Slavonic languages. See SLAVIC LANGUAGES.

The Russian language is spoken throughout an immense territory that embraces two continents, Europe and Asia, from the Baltic Sea to Sakhalin and the Kurile Islands in the Pacific Ocean. As a native tongue it is spoken by more than 100 million people. The Russian language is also a basic means of intercourse between many different language groups of the Soviet Union. It is one of the official languages of the United Nations.

By its grammatical structure Russian is an inflectional language. Distinctions in the number, tense, case, and gender of words are expressed by changes in their roots and endings. There are six cases.

The verb in Russian has only three tenses—past, present, and future. Most verbs have two aspects; the perfective and the imperfective. The perfective indicates action that is or will be completed. The imperfective indicates action that is continuous or not completed. Russian has no articles.

The Russian alphabet, called Cyrillic, contains ten vowels, twenty consonants, a semivowel, and two symbols that harden or soften consonants. Cyrillic is also used for the written Bulgarian and Serbian languages. It was created in the 9th century to translate church literature into Old Slavic, from which modern Russian is derived. It was formed mostly from Greek letters, but later, in the 17th century, it was considerably Latinized.

Russian is a phonetic language. The sounds represented by the letters are regular. However, there is no definite rule for accenting syllables. For this reason good beginning texts should have the accent indicated.

RUSSIAN LITERATURE in its written form is considered to have begun at the end of the 10th century, when Eastern Orthodox Christianity was introduced in Russia. Prior to that time an oral literature had existed in the form of folk tales and songs. All writing of the 11th century was done in the language of the church, a descendant of Old Bulgarian called Church Slavic, and it was almost entirely of a religious nature: biblical translations, lives of the saints, accounts of religious pilgrimages, and sermons. The oldest known manuscript in Church Slavic is a translation of the Gospels, made about 1056. The outstanding secular work of the 12th century was a lyrical epic *The Tale of the Band of Igor.*

Russia was overrun in the 13th century by the Tatars; the result was a cultural decline. Little of literary value was produced during the 14th and 15th centuries. After the Tatars were driven out of the country at the end of the 15th century, Moscow became the center for a new period of literary activity that lasted until the removal of the Russian capital to the new city of St. Petersburg (now Leningrad) in 1703.

The most noteworthy literary pieces of the 16th century were the letters exchanged by Czar Ivan the Terrible and his traitorous courtier Prince Kurbski. In the 17th century Archpriest Avvakum used colloquial Russian for literary purposes for the first time. Religious works, none of any particular literary value, continued to appear in quantity.

Prior to the reign of Czar Peter the Great, Russia had little contact with the countries of Europe. Its literature had developed independently of European literature. Peter, realizing that Russia was militarily, politically, economically, and culturally behind Europe, introduced Western (especially French) manners and thought into his country. Interest in French classical literature was strong and resulted in considerable literary activity during the 18th century.

Much of this writing was feeble imitation of French models, but several authors produced works of high quality. Mikhail Lomonosov is considered the founder of modern Russian literature because he established certain linguistic standards for literature, including a new prosody for Russian poetry. The greatest lyric poet of the 18th century was Gavriil Derzhavin, whose verses were distinctly Russian.

Alexander Pushkin, Russian poet and dramatist

Other important figures were the dramatist Denis Fonvizin, who wrote the first great Russian comedies, *The Brigadier* and *The Minor;* the playwright and critic Alexander Sumarokov; and the essayists Nikolai Novikov and Alexander Radishchev.

The most important and influential novelist of the early 19th century was Nikolai Karamzin; his reforms of Russia's literary language had great effect on his contemporaries. Vasili Zhukovski, the father of modern Russian poetry, was another important innovator of the period. Ivan Krylov was an outstanding fabulist.

The golden age of Russian literature, which extended from about 1820 to about 1880, was dominated by six writers of genius: Alexander Pushkin, Mikhail Lermontov, Nikolai Gogol, Ivan Turgenev, Fëdor Dostoevski, and Leo Tolstoi.

The first great figure of Russian literature was the poet Alexander Pushkin. A superb lyric poet, Pushkin also wrote plays, the best of which was the historical tragedy *Boris Godunov,* and fiction, the best of which were *The Captain's Daughter* and *The Queen of Spades.* His greatest work was *Eugene Onegin,* a novel in verse.

Pushkin's younger contemporary Lermontov was greatly influenced by Byron, Shelley, and Schiller. His poetry is that of a young man in revolt against the shallowness and emptiness of everyday life. Lermontov wrote one novel, *A Hero of Our Times,* in which he exposed many of the vices and follies of his generation.

In the 1820's and 1830's poetry was the principal literary form in Russia. Fedor Tyutchev, Alexei Koltsov, Anton Delvig, Eugeni Baratynski, and Nikolai Yazykov were all notable poets of the period.

Shortly after 1840 the emphasis shifted to prose fiction. The first of the great Russian realists was Nikolai Gogol. He is best remembered for three works: a short story, "The Overcoat," an unfinished novel, *Dead Souls*, and a play, *The Inspector General*, considered the greatest play in the Russian language.

Ivan Turgenev was the first Russian novelist to gain widespread recognition outside Russia. He first attracted attention with his *Sportsman's Sketches*, a series of sympathetic portrayals of Russian peasants that criticized serfdom. The greatest of his many novels was *Fathers and Sons*.

Fëdor Dostoevski is unquestionably one of the greatest novelists who ever lived—many consider him the greatest. His work is characterized by profound insight into the depths of the human mind. The four great novels of his maturity are *Crime and Punishment*, *The Idiot*, *The Possessed* (also translated as *The Devils*), and his masterpiece, *The Brothers Karamazov*. Dostoevski's concern with the irrational in man, with the unconscious and the pathological, foreshadowed and greatly influenced the work of the greatest European and American novelists of the 20th century.

Leo Tolstoi was the last of the literary giants of the golden age. He possessed above all a power of characterization that has never been surpassed by any writer in any language. A voluminous author, his two masterpieces are *War and Peace* and *Anna Karenina*. Among his other works are *Two Pilgrims*, *Childhood*, *Boyhood*, *Youth*, *A Commentary on the Gospel*, *My Confession*, and *My Religion*.

The golden age came to an end in the 1880's with the announced withdrawal of Tolstoi from literature, the death of Dostoevski in 1881, and the death of Turgenev in 1883. Other less important figures of the 19th century were Ivan Goncharov, whose novel *Oblomov* is a classic portrayal of the decline of the Russian nobility, Sergei Aksakov, Alexei Pisemsky, Nikolai Leskov, and Mikhail Saltykov-Shchedrin. The most important dramatist was Alexander Ostrovski. Nikolai Nekrasov, Afanasi Fet, and Alexei Tolstoi were significant minor poets.

At the turn of the century Anton Chekhov was the leading Russian dramatist. His major theme—the inability and unwillingness of human beings to communicate successfully with one another—found expression in the many excellent

Ivan Turgenev, author of *Fathers and Sons*

short stories and the four plays on which his fame rests: *The Seagull*, *Uncle Vanya*, *The Three Sisters*, and *The Cherry Orchard*.

Another literary figure who was at the height of his popularity during the first decade of the 20th century was Maxim Gorky. Most of his works deal with the suffering of the oppressed lower classes; his best known works include *The Lower Depths* (a play) and *The Mother* (a novel). Important authors influenced to some extent by Gorky are Alexander Kuprin and Ivan Bunin.

A number of Russian poets and novelists abandoned the tradition of realism for French symbolism. The finest poet of the group was Alexander Blok; others included Konstantin Balmont, Valeri Bryusov, Vyacheslav Ivanov, and Andrei Bely. Important symbolist novels were Dmitri Merezhkovski's *Julian the Apostate* and *Leonardo da Vinci*, and Bely's *The Silver Dove* and *Petersburg*.

After 1910 first the acmeists and then the futurists reacted against the symbolists; representative acmeists were Nikolai Gumilyov and Anna Akhmatova, and representative futurists were Vladimir Mayakovski and Boris Pasternak.

The Russian Revolution of 1917 greatly affected Russian literature. Early in the Soviet regime writers were encouraged—but were not forced—to write in support of the revolution, and several poets, including Sergei Esenin and Vladimir Mayakovski, who had been ardent revolutionists, wrote some remarkable poetry. Important fiction of the 1920's included Evgeni Zamyatin's "Cave" and *We* and Isaak Babel's *Red Cavalry*.

In 1932 the goal of Soviet literature was officially defined as socialist realism, a doctrine that required all writing to conform to the Communist view of history, society, and human relationships and at the same time to depict some aspect of what the Communists considered to be progress. The result of the enforcement of this doctrine on Russian literature has been a shallow sort of writing that seldom rises above the level of propaganda. Notable exceptions have been Alexei Tolstoi's historical novels *Road to Calvary* and *Peter the First* and Mikhail Sholokhov's epic of the Cossacks *And Quiet Flows the Don*. For the most part, Soviet writing is of greater importance historically as a reflection of communism than as imaginative literature.

From this virtual literary wasteland there emerged in 1957 Boris Pasternak's novel *Doctor Zhivago*, probably the greatest work of Russian fiction since the masterpieces of Tolstoi and Dostoevski. In this novel Pasternak upheld man's right to live life for its own sake rather than for the sake of a political party and its doctrines.

This encyclopedia contains separate entries on many of the important authors mentioned here.

Leo Tolstoi, author of *War and Peace*

Maxim Gorky, 20th-century Russian author

RUSSIAN REVOLT OF 1905, a period of violent opposition to the autocratic and repressive government of Czar Nicholas II, resulting in the calling of Russia's first representative assembly, the Duma. Stirred by Russian defeats in the Russo-Japanese War, smoldering revolutionary sentiment broke out during 1904 and the early months of 1905. Demands were heard for a liberal constitution, the calling of a representative assembly, parliamentary government, the granting of civil liberties, and the institution of universal suffrage. Intellectuals and professional groups sent petitions to the czar. Unrest among the workers led to strikes and the massacre of Bloody Sunday.

The imperial government, fearing the possibility of revolution, issued an order on Aug. 19, 1905, for a Duma that would have discussion privileges but no authority to pass laws. This satisfied no one, and a great general strike swept across Russia. Electricity and water were cut off in the cities; trains came to a stop; and industrial plants were shut down. The strike paralyzed the country, and the government was forced to yield.

On Oct. 30, 1905, the czar issued a manifesto in which he granted a constitution. Voting rights were extended to millions; civil liberties were granted; and no law was to be passed without the approval of the Duma. When the first elected Duma met in May, 1906, a majority of the members were liberal opponents of the regime. Before the meeting, however, the government had issued a set of laws that so restricted the power of the assembly that nothing of importance could be done without the czar's consent. When the Duma protested, it was dissolved. Three subsequent Dumas (1907-1916) were similarly coerced by the government. The czar's autocratic policy continued, and the revolt of 1905 became merely a prelude to the greater revolution of 1917.

RUSSIAN REVOLUTION, one of the greatest social upheavals in modern times. The long-range causes—unsatisfied demands for liberal parliamentary government, civil liberties, and distribution of land—had been growing for centuries and had earlier emerged in the unsuccessful Decembrist Uprising of 1825 and the Revolt of 1905. But the immediate cause of the revolution was the crisis of World War I, in which Russia, on the side of the Allies since 1914, suffered staggering defeats. Its losses in killed, wounded, and captured were estimated as high as nine million men in the first ten months of the war. At home there was widespread demoralization and a serious shortage of food and fuel for civilians. Popular resentment focused on the inept government of Czar Nicholas II, himself the tool of the ambitious Czarina Alexandra and her friend, Rasputin. The repeated warnings of the Duma (the Russian parliament) of impending disaster went unheeded.

Finally, on Mar. 8, 1917, a series of food riots and strikes in the capital, Petrograd (now Leningrad), precipitated the revolution. The mobs, joined by mutinous soldiers, battled the police. When the czar ordered the Duma to dissolve, it refused. Instead, on March 12, it established a provisional government under the leadership of a liberal aristocrat, Prince Georgi Lvov. On the same day the Soviet (council) of Workers' and Soldiers' Deputies was organized by the Socialists in the capital. It was represented in the provisional government by Alexander Kerensky, the minister of justice. On March 15 the last czar of Russia was forced to abdicate, and a popularly elected assembly was scheduled for a future date to provide Russia with a new constitution.

An army band marches in Petrograd (now Leningrad) during the Russian Revolution.

Wide World Photo

At the outset the provisional government proclaimed a program of broad social and political reforms. But it postponed the final decision on the distribution of land, thus displeasing the peasants. It also alienated the war-weary troops by pledging Russia to continue fighting on the side of the Allies. These dissatisfied groups rallied around the Petrograd Soviet and its sister soviets throughout the country, which now began systematically to oppose the provisional government. On March 14 the Soviet had already issued its famous Order No. I to the army, transferring authority from the officers to committees elected by the troops. Opposition increased radically after April with the arrival in Russia of several exiled Bolshevik leaders, among them Lenin and Trotsky. Lenin demanded that the Soviets immediately wrest power from the bourgeois provisional government, stop the war, seize the land and the factories, and turn them over to the peasants and workers. His program, however, did not win over a majority of the Socialists in the Petrograd Soviet until October.

Meanwhile, the provisional government had mounted a new military offensive in July under Kerensky, now minister of war. When it failed, the Bolsheviks attempted to capitalize on the popular disillusionment and to seize power in Petrograd. This premature coup was suppressed; and many of its leaders, including Lenin and Trotsky, either fled or were imprisoned. Kerensky, raised to prime minister, now came under fire, not only from the Socialists, who sought revenge for their defeat, but also from various conservative groups that felt he had been too lenient with the Socialists. In September these conservatives tried to seize the government with an armed attack on the capital, led by General Kornilov. Kerensky managed to defeat them only by enlisting the aid of his other enemies, the Socialists (including the Bolsheviks). Thus released, the Bolsheviks steadily increased their power until by October they had full control of the Petrograd Soviet and by November felt strong enough to try another coup. This time they were successful. On November 7 Bolshevik-led troops stormed the Winter Palace, arrested the members of the provisional government, and took control of the country. Kerensky managed to escape, disguised as a sailor, and went into exile abroad.

The new Bolshevik government,

the Council of People's Commissars, was headed by Lenin and included Trotsky as commissar for foreign affairs and Joseph Stalin as commissar for national minorities. It took immediate steps to reorganize Russian society along collectivist lines, nationalizing all land, industry, and businesses and turning them over to be run by the peasants and workers. In March, 1918, the new government also signed a treaty of peace with the Central Powers (Treaty of Brest-Litovsk), thus ending Russian participation in World War I. The capital was moved from Petrograd to Moscow.

The Bolsheviks themselves were now faced with a new coalition of enemies, including Russian monarchists, liberals, moderate socialists, Cossacks, and other national minorities, as well as the remaining Allies. In the Ukraine and the Caucasus the White Russian forces attacked under Generals Denikin and Wrangel; in the Baltic region, under General Yudenich; and in Siberia, under Admiral Kolchak. British, French, and U.S. troops occupied Archangel and Murmansk in northern Russia, and the Japanese took the Pacific port of Vladivostok. For two years, from 1918 to 1920, a civil war raged throughout the Russian Empire. Gradually, however, the hastily improvised Red Army, under the leadership of Trotsky, pushed back its uncoordinated enemies. By the end of 1920 most of them had been defeated and forced to leave Russian soil. Though Russia itself had been terribly devastated, the Russian Revolution had succeeded.

RUSSO-JAPANESE WAR, the struggle between Russia and Japan in 1904-1905 for control of Korea and Manchuria. Rivalry started with the construction of the Trans-Siberian Railway, begun by Russia in 1891. In 1895 Russia, together with France and Germany, forced Japan to restore the Liaotung Peninsula to China. Three years later Russia obtained a 25-year lease of the same peninsula, including Port Arthur. Russian penetration of Manchuria was furthered by the delayed withdrawal of Russian troops from the area after the end of the Boxer Rebellion (1900-1901). At the same time Russian interference in northern Korea increased. The Japanese, whose protests and attempts to obtain an agreement on exclusive spheres of interest in the two areas were rejected by the Russians, finally decided on war.

Hostilities began on Feb. 9, 1904, without a declaration of war. The Japanese navy attacked the Russian ships in the harbor of Port Arthur. From the outset the Russian forces were handicapped. Supplies trickled along the unfinished Trans-Siberian Railway. The unpopular war lacked the support of the Russian people, and the army was led by inferior commanders. The war became a series of Japanese victories. Korea was quickly brought under Japanese control, and in Manchuria Russian forces were defeated at Liaoyang in September, 1904. After an eight-months' siege Port Arthur fell in January, 1905, to be followed two months later by Mukden. Finally in May, 1905, occurred the famous sea battle of Tsushima Strait. The Russian fleet, which had sailed all the way from the Baltic Sea to the Sea of Japan, was annihilated by the Japanese navy under Admiral Togo.

Through the mediation of President Theodore Roosevelt delegates of the two warring nations assembled in Portsmouth, N.H., to negotiate peace. In the Treaty of Portsmouth, signed Sept. 5, 1905, Russia was compelled to cede its lease of the Liaotung Peninsula and the southern half of the island of Sakhalin to Japan. The special interests of Japan in Korea were also recognized. Manchuria was to be evacuated by both powers and restored to China. Japan also requested (but failed to obtain) a large monetary indemnity. Japan's victory, the first defeat in modern times of a white nation by a yellow nation, raised Japan to the status of a world power. The Russian government, discredited by the humiliating defeat, was faced at home with a wave of criticism that culminated in the Revolt of 1905.

RUST, the iron compound resulting from the oxidation of iron in the presence of water. A tonnage of iron equal to one-sixth of the annual production is lost yearly as the soft, red-brown hydrated iron oxide that is rust. Rusting is a corrosion common in metals. It is an electrochemical reaction initiated by hydrogen ions supplied by either water or an acid. In the rusting process, iron combines with oxygen and hydrogen after the initial reaction with hydrogen. The reaction is as follows: Iron plus water plus oxygen equals hydrated iron oxide.

Rust does not form at humidities of less than 40 percent or in water that contains no dissolved air or oxygen. In cities, smoke deposits of sulfur dioxide and carbon dioxide form dilute acids on metals that are wet from dew or rain. These acids furnish hydrogen ions that react with the iron. Rusting is increased in such buried objects as water pipes when they are near power lines. The induced electrical current in the soil hastens the reaction.

Local areas of surface rust or pitted areas are usually caused by a difference in electrical potential between two points on the rusted object. Where iron contacts another metal, the two points are formed by the iron and the other metal. Two such points also may be formed by the oxygen-rich water film on the object's surface and the oxygen-poor water in a scratch or under loose paint. In both cases, a weak current is created that increases the rate of reaction.

Rust may be prevented by using a metal-pigmented paint, by forming a protective zinc coating (galvanizing), or by making an alloy of iron and chromium. See STAINLESS STEEL.

Dead and dying Russian soldiers lie on this bloody battlefield of the Russo-Japanese War.
The Bettmann Archive

RUST, one of several related parasitic fungi that obtain their nourishment from seed plants and often injure them. Rusts frequently injure or kill their hosts by penetrating host tissues and deriving nourishment from them. Rusts are so named because of the rusty, reddish-brown color of the patches formed by many of their spores upon the leaves and stems of their hosts.

Each species of rust usually attacks only one specific host. Wheat rust attacks wheat plants. During summer it produces orange blisters on the stems and leaves. During some years wheat rust extensively damages the wheat crop in various regions of North America and other continents.

Other rusts infect and injure red cedar, apple trees, white pines, corn, oats, pear trees, peach trees, asparagus, carnations, and numerous wild plants.

RUTH, GEORGE HERMAN (1895-1948), commonly called "Babe" Ruth or "the Bambino," American baseball player, was born in Baltimore, Md., where he attended St. Mary's Industrial School, a Catholic school for boys. Shortly after entering St. Mary's Ruth developed an ardent interest in baseball. In 1914 he began his professional career with the Baltimore Orioles (International League). Although Ruth is remembered as a hitter and especially as a home-run hitter, it was as a pitcher that he first attracted attention. He entered the major leagues with the Boston Red Sox (American League) in 1914 and while with them pitched and won three World Series games. He established a series record by pitching 29 consecutive scoreless innings. He also won the longest World Series game (14 innings) against Brooklyn in 1916.

While he was still serving as a pitcher Ruth began to attract attention as a home-run hitter. In 1919 he led the league with 29. This led to a turning point in his career. He was bought by the New York Yankees and became an outfielder. From 1919 to 1931, with the exception of one year, he led the American League in home runs, reaching a climax in 1927 with 60. His lifetime total was 714. Ruth left the Yankees in 1934, played briefly with the Boston Braves (National League), and ended his baseball career as a coach for the Brooklyn Dodgers in 1938. Ruth held 54 major-league records, and was one of the first players to be elected to Baseball's Hall of Fame.

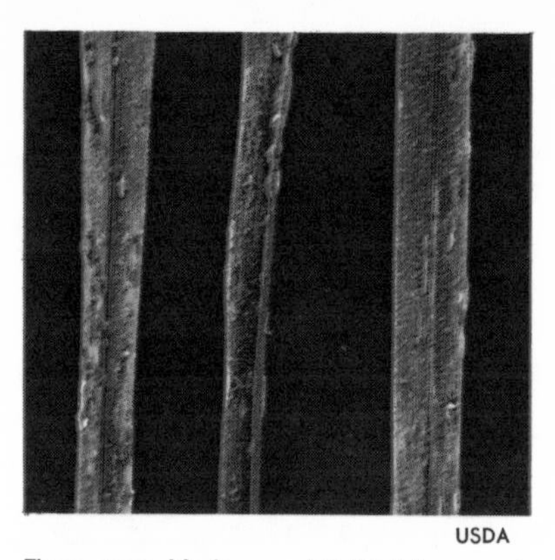

USDA

These grass blades are blighted by a rust.

RUTHERFORD, ERNEST (1871-1937), a British physicist who discovered that atoms consist of positively charged particles of electricity called protons and of negatively charged particles of electricity called electrons. He was born in Nelson, New Zealand. He obtained his B.S. in physics from the University of New Zealand in 1894, and after continuing to study physics at Cambridge, in England, he served as professor of physics at McGill University in Canada from 1898 to 1907 and at the University of Manchester, in England, from 1907 to 1919. In 1919 he became Cavendish professor of experimental physics at Cambridge.

Research into the artificial disintegration of chemical elements and into the phenomena associated with radioactive elements led Rutherford to theorize that an atom is not an indivisible particle but, instead, is composed of positively and negatively charged particles of electricity. The one or more positively charged particles, called protons, are concentrated in a central nucleus. The one or more negatively charged particles, called electrons, revolve in separate orbits around this nucleus. This conception of the atom, in whose development the Danish physicist Niels Bohr participated, became known as the Rutherford-Bohr atom.

In 1904 Rutherford discovered the alpha particle, which he conceived as the positively charged nucleus of a hydrogen atom whose electron has been taken away. In 1908 he was awarded the Nobel prize in chemistry for his investigation of the disintegration of elements and of the chemistry of radioactive substances. In 1919 he artificially disintegrated atoms of the element nitrogen and thereby became one of the first scientists to accomplish atomic fission.

RYE, a cultivated grain that for many centuries has been a staple food of many European peoples. Rye has not been cultivated for as long a time as wheat or barley. It probably originated in the Russian steppes. Although various species of wild rye grow there and elsewhere, botanists cannot determine for certain whether one of them is the true ancestor of cultivated rye.

The rye plant, a member of the grass family, has long, slim, blue-green leaves and ranges in height from 3 to 5 or 6 feet. It is taller than wheat. The fruits of the rye plant are its small brown grains. Each grain is a seed with its adherent pericarp. Rye is usually sowi during autumn, like winter wheat, and is harvested and threshed the following summer. It will flourish in soils that are too poor or too sandy for wheat. It is very hardy and will grow farther north than wheat.

Until recently rye was the principal bread grain of the U.S.S.R., Poland, Czechoslovakia, Germany, and other countries of northeastern Europe. A coarse, heavy, dark-brown or black bread is made from it. This bread is still a major item in the diet of many people of these countries. The chief rye-growing states of the United States are North Dakota and South Dakota. American rye is made into bread, biscuits, and alcohol for whiskey, and is fed to livestock. It is also used to prevent erosion and as a winter cover crop in crop rotation.

Rye belongs to the same family as wheat, oats, barley, and other grains.

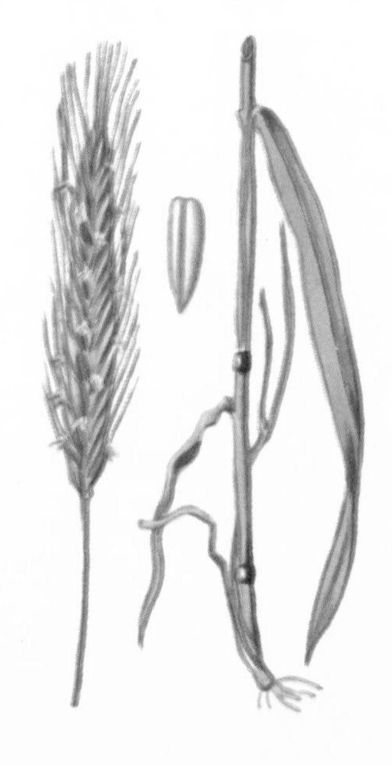

S is the 19th letter of the English alphabet. S is the symbol in chemistry for the element sulfur. The capital of sigma (Σ), the corresponding Greek letter, is the symbol in mathematics for *sum*. According to one study of early manuscripts the dollar sign ($) evolved from the old Mexican sign for pesos (Ps) when the S gradually lowered onto the P.

SABER-TOOTHED CAT, a member of a group of extinct cats that had long, saber-like, upper canine teeth and distinctively hinged jaws. Saber-toothed cats existed from middle Cenozoic times until the beginning of the Pleistocene in Europe. *Smilodon*, one genus of saber-toothed cat, existed in North America until the end of the Pleistocene, or the retreat of the last continental glaciers.

Saber-toothed cats used the long, dagger-like upper canine teeth for stabbing or slashing their prey to death. The lower canine teeth were small. The lower jaw could open until it was at a right angle to the upper jaw. The lower jaw had to be kept out of the way while a cat used the upper canine teeth. Some saber-toothed cats had bony extensions of the lower jaw that helped protect the upper canine teeth when the jaws were closed.

Saber-toothed cats probably preyed on large animals, such as mastodons, giant ground sloths, and elephants.

Smilodon, the last of the saber tooths, was a massive animal, more heavily built than a modern lion. *Smilodon* probably lay in wait for his victims, for he was not built for fast running.

SACAGAWEA (1787?-1812?), American Indian heroine, who was a member of the Shoshone tribe. She was captured by the Hidatsa Indians when her tribe was on a hunting expedition in the Rocky Mountains and was then traded to Toussaint Charbonneau, a French trader, who later became her husband. She accompanied the Lewis and Clark Expedition over the Rocky Mountains and gained for the explorers the friendliness of the Shoshone Indians. Lewis and Clark in their *Journal* tell of Sacagawea's help and resourcefulness. The legends surrounding her later life have been greatly disputed, and the time and place of her death never have been definitely established.

The Indian woman Sacagawea was an invaluable aid to the Lewis and Clark Expedition.

SACCO-VANZETTI CASE, a celebrated case involving the trial of two Italian-born anarchists, Nicola Sacco and Bartolomeo Vanzetti, for the alleged murder of a paymaster of a shoe factory in South Braintree, Mass. Sacco and Vanzetti were tried, found guilty, and sentenced to death in 1921. During and after the trial liberals and radicals in the United States, Latin America, and Europe protested the proceedings and claimed the men were convicted for their extreme political views rather than for murder. Defense committees were formed that succeeded in having the execution delayed for six years. In July, 1927, under pressure of widespread protests that the defendants had not received a fair trial, Governor Alvan T. Fuller of Massachusetts appointed a commission of leading citizens to investigate the case. President Abbott Lawrence Lowell of Harvard University was the chairman. At the conclusion of the study the commission upheld the conviction, and Sacco and Vanzetti were put to death in the electric chair Aug. 23, 1927.

A saber-toothed cat, below, attacks a large ground sloth. These cats probably became extinct in both Europe and North America when the large animals they ate became extinct.

SACRAMENTO, the capital of California, is located on the Sacramento River at its confluence with the American River, in the central part of California. It is a shipping, trade, and distribution center for the extensive agricultural, mining, milling, and recreational area of the Sacramento Valley. It is one of California's leading processing centers. Food processing and the manufacture of metal products are major industries. Large air force bases are nearby. The city had a population of 191,667 in 1960.

Places of interest include the Capitol, the Crocker Art Gallery, and Sutter's Fort, an old trading post erected in 1839 and later rebuilt. Sacramento was settled in 1841 by John Sutter, who had obtained a tract of land from the Mexican government. He and his party developed the settlement, called New Helvetia, into a "baronial establishment." It soon became popular with other settlers. The discovery of gold near Sutter's Mill in 1848 resulted in the great gold rush of 1849 and the 1850's. Present-day Sacramento, which was laid out on Sutter's farm, had a great boom. It became the capital of California in 1854.

SACRED BOOKS, writings that are the scriptures of a religion. Religious writings frequently contain the best literature in the language. For example, the King James Version of the Bible, prepared in Shakespeare's time, is a model of English prose writing.

The sacred books of Hinduism are the Vedas, or Books of Knowledge. The Rig Veda, the oldest document among the world's living religions, dating from at least 1000 B.C., is a collection of lyrics that were probably handed down originally from father to son. Sometime between 800 and 600 B.C. the Upanishads were written. When these books of philosophical speculation were first translated into European tongues, they had a profound effect on Western philosophy. One of the sacred books of Hinduism most esteemed by non-Hindus is the Bhagavad Gita, a dramatic poem of devotional Hinduism.

The Buddhist scriptures are the Tripitaka, which means "Three Baskets (of Wisdom)." The Tripitaka contains rules for the higher classes of Buddhists, explanations of doctrine, and psychology. It was written in Pali, the language of the common people of northwest India, where Buddha taught. The Buddhist scripture is about four times as long as the Bible in English, and it contains many very remarkable passages.

Confucius is one of the few founders of a religion who is supposed to have written one of its sacred books. This one is the history of the state of Lu, which is one of the Five Classics of Confucianism. Written about Confucius by his followers were the Four Books, one of the best known of which is the Analects, or sayings of Confucius. Lao-tzu was said to have written the Tao Tê Ching, or The Canon of Reason and Virtue, the sacred text of the Taoists.

The book Christians call the Old Testament contains the sacred writings of Judaism. It is divided into the Law, the Prophets, and the Writings. Among the other religious books of the Jews is the Apocrypha. Parts of the Apocrypha are also used in some branches of Christianity. The Jewish scriptures were written in Hebrew, with the exception of passages in Daniel, Ezra, and Jeremiah, which are in Aramaic.

Moslems regard the Koran as the direct revelation of Allah to Mohammed. The present text of the Koran was probably put together by Caliph Othman about 12 years after Mohammed's death. The Koran has had a great influence, socially and politically, on the Arab peoples. Only a few decades ago it was still the main textbook at El Gameh El Azhar, the modern Moslem university at Cairo.

Most of the sacred books of Asia were published in English in the 19th century. This immense task was undertaken by scholars working under the supervision of Max Müller. The result was the 51-volume, indexed *Sacred Books of the East*. See BIBLE.

This sagebrush grows on semiarid plateaus.

SAGEBRUSH, one of several species of sagelike bushy plants that belong to a single genus. The sagebrushes grow naturally in semiarid regions of North America, South America, Europe, and Asia. They are members of the composite family, which includes daisies, chrysanthemums, and zinnias.

Several species of sagebrush grow abundantly on the semiarid plains of Colorado, Wyoming, western Nebraska, Utah, Nevada, Montana, and British Columbia. They are commonest in northern deserts of high altitude.

The North American species known as common sagebrush resembles a shrub and may attain a height of 10 feet. From its main stem arise many branch stems that spread widely. The stems, which are covered with silvery-gray hairs, are fragrant when broken. The roots penetrate deeply into the arid soil in order to obtain water. The wedge-shaped, toothed leaves, which are broadest at their outer ends, are about 1 inch long and ½ inch wide. The flowers, which are borne in small heads, bloom from July to September.

The common sagebrush survives unusually severe droughts by shedding most of its leaves so that it will need less water. A bitter tea made from sagebrush leaves was formerly used to treat colds.

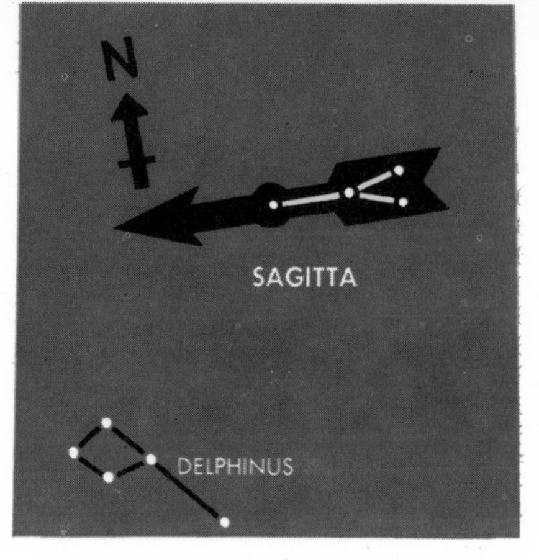

According to legend, Sagitta is the arrow used by the god Apollo to kill one of the Cyclops, or one-eyed giants. In another legend it is called the arrow of Cupid.

SAGITTA, or the Arrow, is a small constellation in the Milky Way. It lies between Cygnus and Aquila next to another small constellation, Delphinus. None of its stars is brighter than fourth magnitude. They form a pattern that really looks like an arrow, unlike many constellations that bear no resemblance to the figure for which they are named. Sagitta is visible in the evening sky from midnorthern latitudes between June and November.

SAGITTARIUS, or the Archer, is a constellation of the zodiac lying between Capricornus and Scorpius. It is visible in the evening sky from midnorthern latitudes between July and September.

Sagittarius' bow is pointed directly at the star Antares in Scorpius. The stars behind the bow form a little dipper called the Milk Dipper because they are in the Milky Way. The Milky Way is very bright in the region of Sagittarius because this is the direction of the center of our galaxy, which lies far behind the stars of the constellation.

Sagittarius, in legend, represents Chiron, a son of Saturn. He changed into a centaur and was wounded by a poisoned arrow. Though immortal, he was let die rather than suffer forever and was set among the stars.

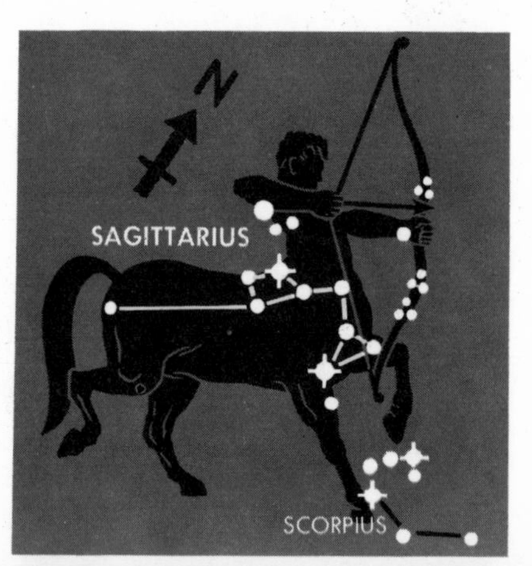

SAGO PALM, a cultivated tropical plant of the cycad family. Although the sago resembles a palm tree or a fern, it and the other cycads are actually primitive gymnosperms.

The trunk of the sago palm is from 6 to 10 feet tall. The glossy, dark-green leaves, which are from 2 to 7 feet long, arise in a cluster from the top of the trunk and arch gracefully upward and outward. Each leaf consists of many narrow, stiff, pointed segments, which extend sideways from the midrib.

Native to Japan or Java, the sago palm is cultivated in conservatories in temperate regions of Europe, North America, and South America. It is grown outdoors in tropical and subtropical regions.

Herbert Lanks—Shostal

Camels, often called ships of the desert, are well suited for travel across the Sahara. People of Arab stock live in the western and northern Sahara; nomadic Tuareg tribes of Berber blood roam the central part.

SAHARA, the world's largest desert. Occupying a belt about 1,200 miles wide, it stretches 3,000 miles across northern Africa, from the Atlantic Ocean to the Red Sea. On the north it is generally separated from the Mediterranean Sea by a narrow fertile coastal strip. On the south, as rainfall increases, it fades into an east-west belt of grassland called the Sudan. The Sahara is the western portion of the great desert belt that continues eastward through Arabia and the rest of Asia. Covering 3,500,000 square miles, it occupies one-fourth of Africa and is about as large as the United States.

The sand dunes that so many people associate with the Sahara cover only about one-eighth of its area. Most of the desert consists of rock and gravel surfaces, which form a series of plateaus. Above them rise the volcanic Ahaggar Mountains and the Tibesti Massif, reaching heights of about 10,000 feet. Although rainfall is scanty everywhere, tufts of coarse grass and stunted bushes grow over most of the Sahara except in the sand-dune areas.

Daytime temperatures may reach over 130° F., and night temperatures may fall below freezing in the north. This great temperature range and violent winds cause constant erosion and breaking up of rock. During the sudden heavy showers that occur occasionally, the dry streambeds, known as wadies, fill up temporarily and flow violently. There is a network of underground rivers; where these come near the surface, oases occur. Petroleum, iron ore, and copper have been discovered in the Sahara.

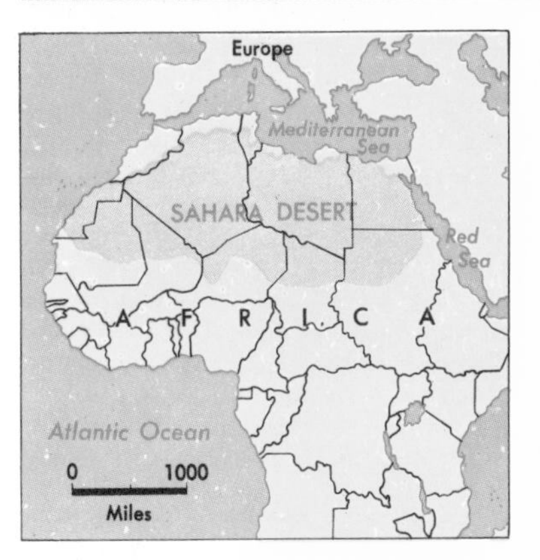

The great Sahara in northern Africa is part of an enormous arid belt extending into Asia.

This oasis in the Sahara is bordered by huge sand dunes that were formed by the violent winds that blow over the desert.

Barnheim Conant, AMNH—FLO

SAILING, the sport of operating a boat powered by the wind. Such boats range in size from the schooner, more than 100 feet long, to the dinghy, which is sometimes under 12 feet in length. The larger craft, with decks, are usually referred to as yachts. For many years the sport was mainly for wealthy people who could afford to build large and expensive yachts operated by professional crews. This is no longer true. Today several classes of small sailboats are built, especially in the popular Star class, and are owned by people of ordinary means. Every summer the lakes, rivers, and coastal waters of many countries are dotted with sailboats of all sizes.

Sailing for sport probably developed first in Holland in the early 17th century. It was introduced into England by King Charles II in 1660 on his return from exile in France. The first yacht club was the Water Club of Cork, Ireland, founded in 1720. The oldest yacht club still operating in the United States is the New York Yacht Club, founded in 1844.

International sailing races began in 1851, when a group of members of the New York Yacht Club built a 101-foot schooner, the *America*, and sailed her to England. Here she won a trophy, called the Hundred-Guinea Cup, in a race around the Isle of Wight. The cup was given by the Royal Yacht Squadron and in 1857 was presented for perpetual challenge to the New York Yacht Club and has been known ever since as the America's Cup. The English challenges for the cup led to the most famous series of international sailing races. British and Canadian yachtsmen have attempted many times to recapture the America's Cup but have always failed.

Ocean racing started in the winter of 1866, when three schooners raced from New York to England. Since then transatlantic races have been held on many occasions. The United States-to-Bermuda race, which had its origin in 1906, has been held annually or biennially ever since and attracts wide interest. Other important distance sailing races are the California-Honolulu, Chicago-Mackinac, Miami-Nassau, and St. Petersburg–Havana races.

While sailing races attract publicity, most boat owners use their craft for noncompetitive sport and recreation. One of the favorite forms of sailing is a weekend or vacation cruise for the family along a coast or down a river.

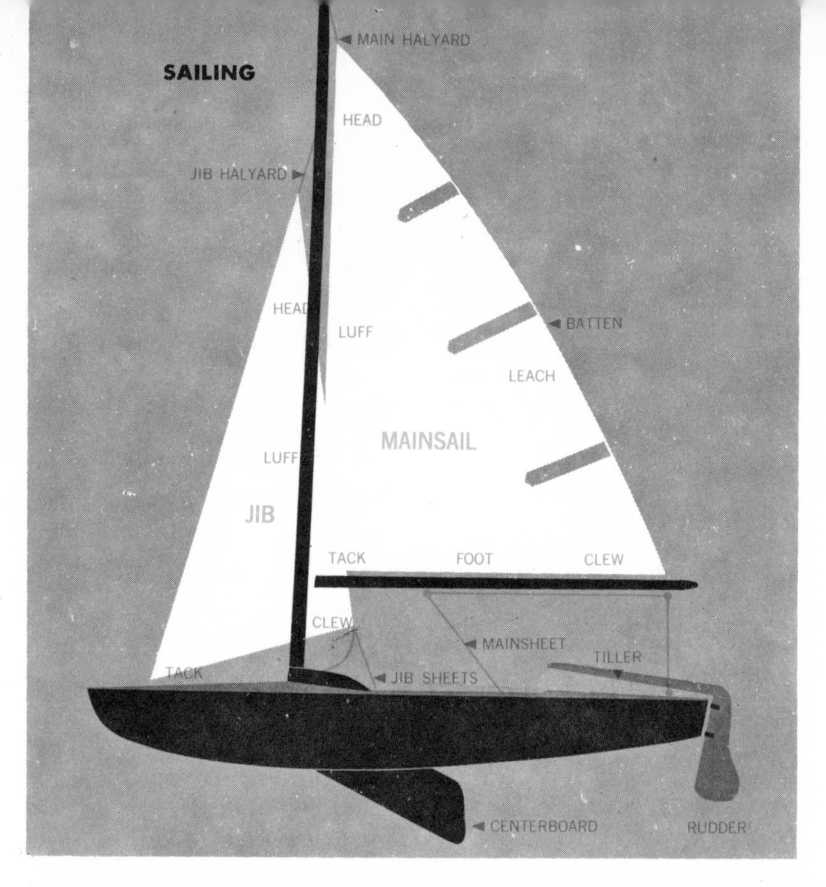

The various parts of a typical sailboat and its rigging are shown in the drawing above.

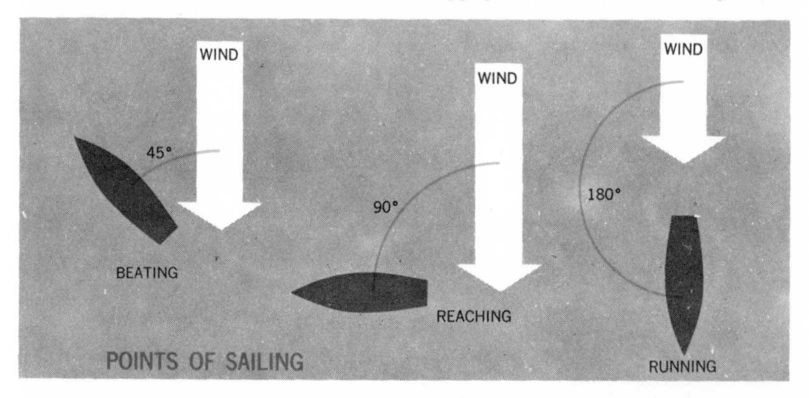

The terms above are applied to the movement of the sailboat at different angles to the wind.

The hull above has a V-bottom and a pivoted centerboard. Its shape is ideal for a small sailboat.

A planing hull, shown above, is a flat-bottomed hull with a center board that slides through a slot in the bottom.

The round-bottomed hull shown above has a full keel and no centerboard. It is most suitable for a large sailing vessel.

This type of hull, used mainly for cruising, has both a shallow keel and a centerboard which slides through it.

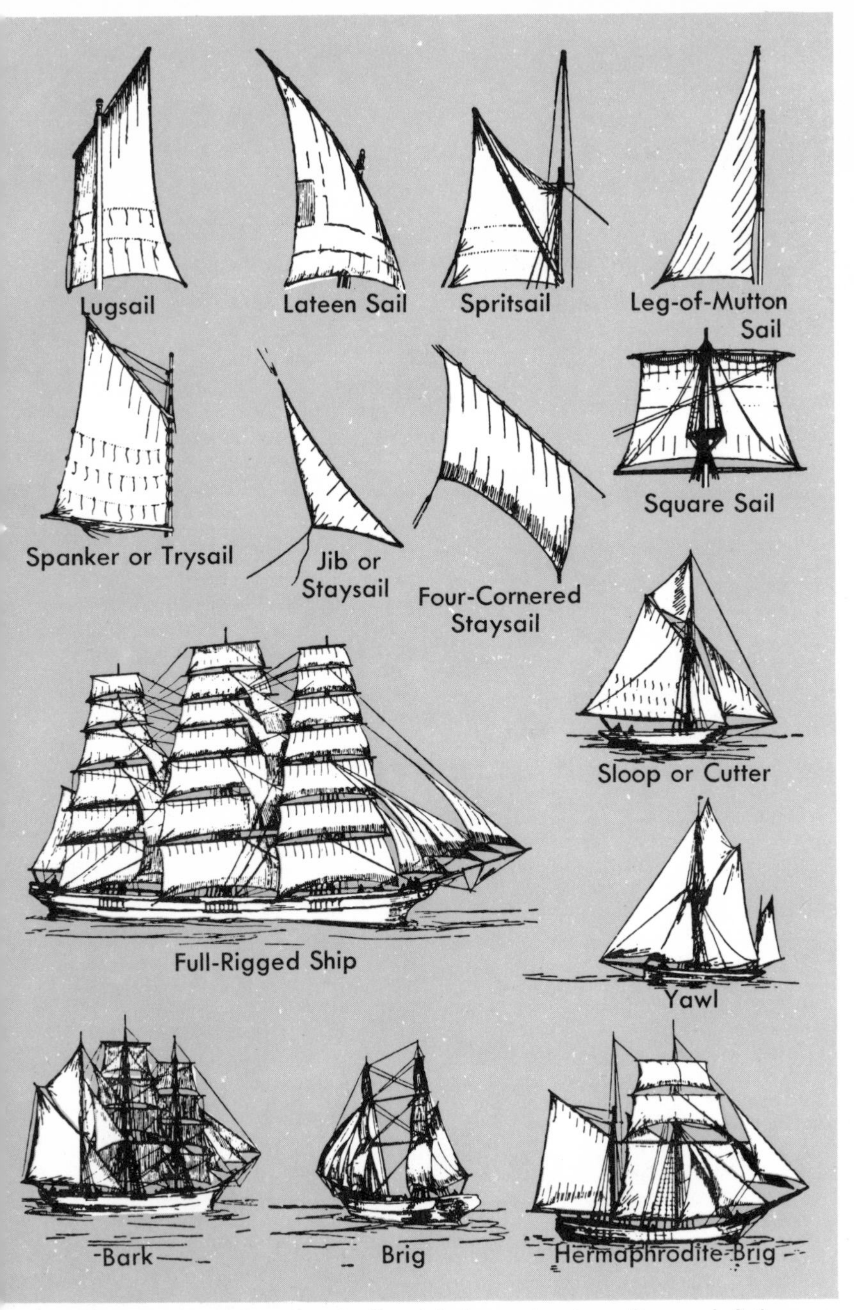

Shown above are various types of sails and rigging employed on sailing vessels. Both square-rigged and fore-and-aft-rigged ships are shown. The rigging determines the type of vessel.

SAILING SHIP, a large oceangoing vessel propelled by sails. Sailing ships are generally classified as either square-rigged or fore-and-aft-rigged craft. In the square-rigged vessel the principal sails are rectangular in shape and are hung before the masts from horizontal spars called yards. Sails are set at an angle to the line of the keel. During the 19th century the term *ship* acquired a specific meaning, namely, a square-rigged vessel fitted with a bowsprit and three masts (foremast, mainmast, and mizzenmast). Each mast consisted of at least three sections. Other types of square-rigged sailing ships include the brig and brigantine.

On the fore-and-aft-rigged ship the principal sails may be either triangular or rectangular and are not supported by horizontal yards but are set behind the masts along the midship line of the vessel. Typically, the triangular fore-and-aft-rigged sail is spread at the bottom by a boom and at the top by a shorter spar called a gaff. The gaff generally extends aft from the mast at an angle of about 45 degrees above the horizontal. Such a sail is raised and lowered by means of the gaff. Other types of fore-and-aft-rigged sails include jib, the foresail, and the staysail, all of which are attached to stays, lines also used to support the masts. Fore-and-aft-rigged vessels include the schooner, yawl, ketch, and sloop. Most small vessels, including most pleasure and sporting craft, are fore-and-aft rigged. The lateen sail is a fore-and-aft-rigged sail generally associated with vessels of the East. Triangular in shape, it is supported by a single long yard reaching nearly to the deck at one end and rising well above the masthead on the other. The lateen sail has been used not only as a mainsail on small one-masted boats but also on the aft masts of two-masted and three-masted sailing ships. Most of the large square-rigged sailing ships of the past were rigged with a number of auxiliary fore-and-aft-rigged sails. The clipper ship, for example, had several jibs, a number of staysails, and a spanker (a large four-cornered sail hung from the mizzenmast). The hermaphrodite brig was a sailing ship that had as many fore-and-aft-rigged sails as square-rigged sails. Its foremast was square rigged, and its aft mast was fore-and-aft rigged.

The earliest ships and boats were propelled by oars and paddles. By the time of classical Greece and Rome, however, ships existed that were propelled entirely by means of sails. These were generally merchant vessels. Until the beginning of the Christian Era ships were fitted with only one mast and one sail. The foresail, hung from a second mast projected over the bow of the vessel, gradually evolved. A triangular topsail was the next sail to be developed. While the sailors of northern Europe continued to use the rectangular square-rigged sail, those of the eastern Mediterranean Sea and areas farther east developed the lateen sail, which is still prevalent in that part of the world. With the coming of the Renaissance and the increased interest in world exploration and navigation also came significant developments in naval architecture. During this period the merchant vessel and the warship became distinct and separate. Sail capacity was gradually increased. The ship of Columbus' time usually had three masts and five sails. One of these,

FSNB

This house in St. Augustine, thought to have been built in the late 1500's, is considered to be the oldest house in the United States.

A plan of St. Augustine (below) shows some of the important historic places of interest in this old Spanish city.

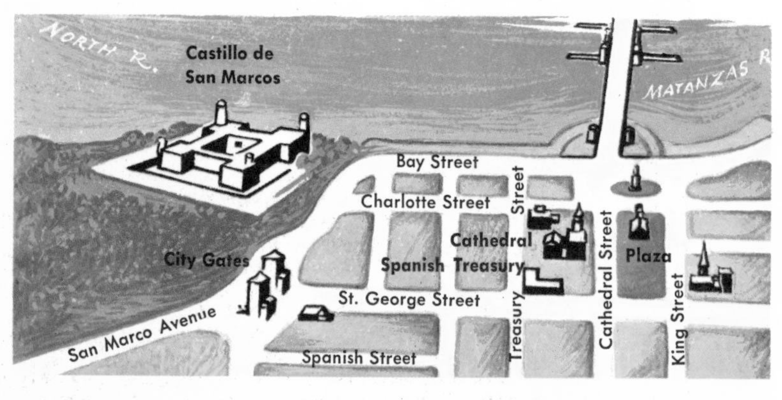

the spritsail, fitted under the bow, was the forerunner of the jib, developed during the 17th century. Also during the 17th century the lateen sail carried on the mizzenmast evolved into the fore-and-aft-rigged sail that came to be called the spanker. The gradual streamlining of the hull and the trend toward more and larger sails reached a climax in the clipper ship by the mid-19th century. However, even the speedy clipper could not compete commercially with the steamboat. The opening of the Suez Canal and later of the Panama Canal was disastrous to the merchant sailing ship. The distances between coaling stations were cut down, thus enabling the steamship to devote more of its hold to cargo rather than to coal. Sail-fitted warships became obsolete before the end of the 19th century, and soon commercial sailing ships were retired from service. Nevertheless, as late as the 1940's square-rigged sailing ships operated in the Australian wool and grain trade. Today only a few of the large square riggers remain. Several of them are utilized as naval training vessels. Fore-and-aft-rigged vessels are used extensively as racing and pleasure craft and, to a limited extent, for commercial enterprises.

SAINT AUGUSTINE, Fla., is the oldest city in the United States. It is situated on the northeastern Florida coast, partly sheltered by Anastasia Island. St. Augustine is an important year-round resort as well as a shipping and shrimping center. Its population in 1960 was 14,734.

Points of interest include the site of the old cathedral and the old slave market. The oldest masonry fort in the United States, the Castillo de San Marcos, is located in the city. This fortification was built between 1672 and 1756. It is now a national monument. Another building of interest to tourists is the old schoolhouse that is said to be the oldest house in the United States. It is believed that it was built in the 16th century.

St. Augustine was founded by Pedro Menéndez de Avilés in 1565. The site remained in Spanish control until 1763, when the English assumed command. In 1783, it was returned to the Spanish, which in turn ceded it to the United States in 1821. Since 1937 a vast historic restoration program has been undertaken.

SAINT BARTHOLOMEW'S DAY MASSACRE. See HUGUENOTS; RELIGIOUS WARS, FRENCH.

ST. DENIS, RUTH (1880-), American dancer, choreographer, and teacher of dancing, was born in Newark, N.J. After attending local grammar and high schools and Dwight L. Moody Seminary, in Northfield, Mass., she acted in a number of plays, including David Belasco's production of *Madame Du Barry*. In 1906 she made her professional debut as a dancer in *Radha*, a ballet she created herself. This and later works, which included *Egypta, Incense, Cobra, Yogi*, and *O-Mika*, were based on themes drawn from oriental and Near Eastern art forms. During the next three years she toured Europe. She and her troupe were especially well received in Germany. In 1909 she returned to the United States and commenced a nationwide tour. In 1914 she married Ted Shawn, also a dancer, and together they established the Denishawn School, in Los Angeles. For a short time after her separation from Shawn in 1930, Ruth St. Denis continued to operate the school from Denishawn House in New York, its headquarters after 1920. In 1940 she, with dancer La Meri, founded the Authentic School of Oriental Dancing, in New York. In addition to numerous articles on the dance she has written *Ruth St. Denis—An Unfinished Life* and a volume of poetry entitled *Lotus Lights*.

SAINT ELMO'S FIRE, a glowing exchange of electricity between the atmosphere and the earth. The crackling discharge of electricity is generally seen as a tip of light on the masts of ships, church towers, and the fingers of an outstretched hand. The phenomenon can be most fre-

St. Elmo's fire is seen below as an electrical glow atop the two masts of a ship.

quently seen during and following winter snowstorms.

According to Pliny the Elder in his *Natural History*, the Greeks invoked the lights of St. Elmo's fire as manifestations of the gods. However, the name comes from St. Erasmus, a bishop of Formiae, in Italy, who suffered martyrdom in the reign of Domitian (about A.D. 303). St. Erasmus became the patron saint of Mediterranean sailors, who called him Sant' Ermo. This name eventually became St. Elmo. The electrical glow was believed to be the sign of St. Elmo's guardianship. English sailors called the phenomenon the corposant. St. Elmo's fire is mentioned in Coleridge's "Rime of the Ancient Mariner." The sailors of the *Pequod* in Melville's *Moby Dick* also observed St. Elmo's fire.

Wide World Photo

Canadian statesman Louis Saint Laurent

SAINT LAURENT, LOUIS STEPHEN (1882-), second French Canadian prime minister of Canada, was born in Compton, Quebec, and was a well-known corporation lawyer before entering politics in 1941. At that time Prime Minister William Lyon Mackenzie King appointed him minister of justice to succeed Ernest Lapointe, who had died. King had depended upon the much-respected Lapointe to hold the loyalty of the French Canadians to the administration; Saint Laurent would have the same task. This he carried out in 1944, when a crisis threatened over military conscription. This issue had nearly split the country during World War I. During World War II French Canadians, while willing to volunteer for overseas fighting, opposed a draft. King had pledged that there would be no conscription for overseas service, but by 1944 he had decided that the draft would be necessary. Saint Laurent, who had told his constituents that he would not oppose a draft if opposition meant splitting Canadian unity, rallied most of the cabinet members from Quebec to King's support.

Saint Laurent was to become King's handpicked successor as head of the Liberal party and of the government. The first step on this course was King's appointment of Saint Laurent as secretary of state for external affairs in 1946. In August, 1948, Saint Laurent was elected as leader of the Liberal party, and in November he became prime minister. In this office he actively supported Canadian participation in the United Nations and in NATO. Saint Laurent's term as prime minister ended in 1957, when the Conservatives defeated the Liberals in national elections. He resigned as leader of the Liberal party in 1958.

SAINT LAWRENCE SEAWAY, jointly controlled by the United States and Canada, is a navigation channel that provides a transportation route for large oceangoing ships traveling approximately 2,300 miles between the Atlantic Ocean and western Lake Superior. Hydroelectric-power projects serve neighboring areas. The seaway, actually part of the St. Lawrence Waterway, extends from Montreal to Lake Ontario. It was opened to commerce on Apr. 25, 1959.

Major features of the seaway are the 27-foot navigation course, 7 new locks (the United States built 2, Canada 5), and 4 canals, which replaced 22 outmoded locks and 6 lateral canals in the previous 14-foot canal system above Montreal. Other projects include a deepened Welland Ship Canal, four new dams in the 46-mile International Rapids section, and the removal of rock shoals in the Thousand Islands region. Total cost of the seaway construction was approximately 600 million dollars for Canada and 400 million dollars for the United States. Government agencies—the St. Lawrence Seaway Development Corporation of the United States and the St. Lawrence Seaway Authority of Canada—were created to construct, operate, and maintain the seaway.

A ship traveling from the Atlantic Ocean to Duluth, Minn., through the seaway rises a total of 602 feet. The Welland Ship Canal (eight locks), which bypasses Niagara Falls and the Niagara River, makes the greatest lift, 326 feet. The seaway is able to accommodate ships with a maximum length of 730 feet and a maximum width of 75 feet and can handle cargoes up to 25,000 tons. The navigation season extends from April through December.

For more than 100 years Canada has been operating a series of canals and locks in the St. Lawrence River in order to bypass rapids between Montreal and Lake Ontario. For the past 50 years the navigable depth has been 14 feet. Canadian proposals and treaties dating from the early 1920's were rejected by the U.S. Congress until 1953. Actual work started in 1954. On June 26, 1959, President Dwight D. Eisenhower and Queen Elizabeth II officially dedicated the St. Lawrence Seaway. The main purpose of this improved course is to provide more commerce, at lower transportation rates, to inland ports, which ship mainly industrial products, grain, and iron ore and which handle imported goods.

Ships wait for the water level to be lowered in one of the locks of the St. Lawrence Seaway.

Brown Brothers

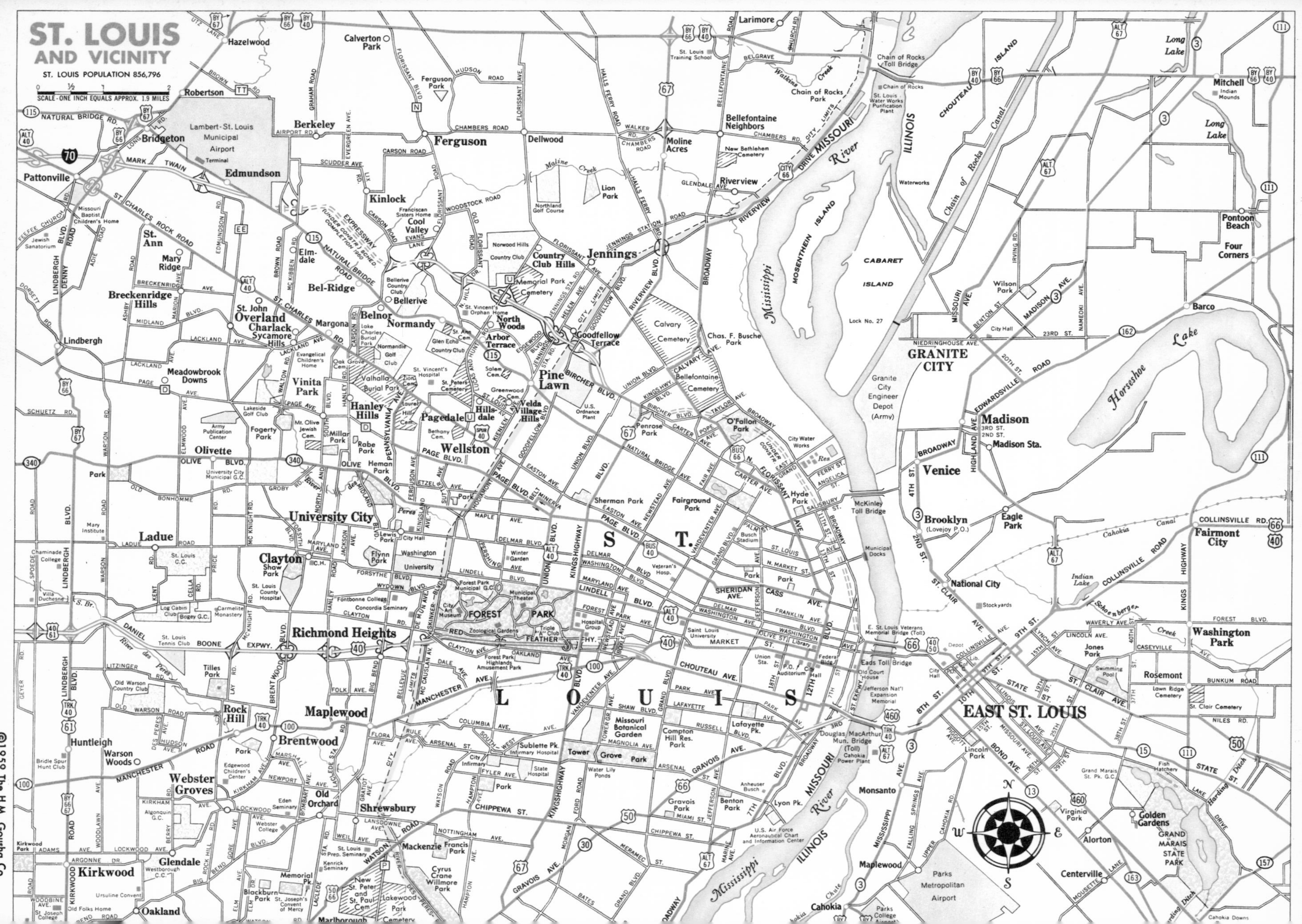
ST. LOUIS
AND VICINITY
ST. LOUIS POPULATION 856,796
SCALE-ONE INCH EQUALS APPROX. 1.9 MILES
©1959 The H.M. Gousha Co.

UPI

Bridges span the Mississippi River and connect St. Louis with Illinois towns.

SAINT LOUIS is the principal city in Missouri and one of the largest U.S. cities. Located on the Mississippi River at the crossroads of north-south and transcontinental routes, it is one of the foremost transportation centers in the United States. St. Louis is also the financial, commercial, and industrial hub of a vast region. It had a population of 750,026 in 1960.

The city is a major raw-fur market and has great livestock, wool, grain, and lumber interests. Next to trade in these commodities, the principal industries are meatpacking and other types of food processing, distilleries, breweries, and the manufacture of shoes, chemicals, airplanes, drugs, machinery, and a great variety of other products.

There are many points of interest in St. Louis. The Missouri Botanical Garden has one of the largest plant collections in the Western Hemisphere. The Municipal Open-Air Theater in Forest Park is the scene of annual summer opera performances. The St. Louis Art Museum has extensive collections of many types of art and is one of the finest in the country. There are also a number of old homes in the city, among them the birthplace of Eugene Field. St. Louis is the seat of Washington and St. Louis universities. It has a well-known symphony orchestra.

In 1764 Pierre Laclède Liguest established a fur-trading post on the site of St. Louis. Though in Spanish possession for a time, the city retained its French characteristics until it was transferred to U.S. possession with the Louisiana Purchase in 1803.

The city developed rapidly with the advent of the steamboat. St. Louis had an advantageous position on the Mississippi River and on overland travel routes. It was a major river port and in the first part of the 19th century served as an outfitting point for westward-bound pioneers. After 1850 a great influx of Germans settled in St. Louis and integrated their culture with that of the French and Americans. Following the Civil War St. Louis' industries greatly expanded with the coming of the railroads and the construction of Eads Bridge across the Mississippi.

SAINT PATRICK'S DAY, March 17, the national holiday of Ireland, dedicated to St. Patrick, patron saint of Ireland, who lived in the 5th century. Wherever Irishmen live, the day is celebrated with parades, speeches, and dinners. The celebrations in Dublin, New York, Boston, San Francisco, and Chicago are especially notable. Green, the color of the day, is worn and displayed everywhere, especially in the form of the shamrock, which legend says the saint used as a symbol of the Trinity.

SAINT PETERSBURG. See LENINGRAD.

SAINT-SAENS, CAMILLE (1835-1921), French composer, pianist, organist, and critic, was born in Paris. His musical education, which was begun privately at the age of seven, was completed at the Paris Conservatory. He served as organist at the Church of St. Merri (Paris) from 1853 to 1857 and at the Church of the Madeleine (Paris) from 1858 to 1877. He taught piano at Ecole Niedermeyer, in Paris, from 1861 to 1865. By the mid-1870's Saint-Saëns was recognized not only as a composer of note and as a virtuoso of the piano and organ but also as a critic of influence. In this last capacity he was prominent in promoting the revival of French music that occurred during his lifetime and to which he contributed as a composer. His best known works include the symphonic poems *The Youth of Hercules*, *Danse Macabre*, *Phaéton*, and *Omphale's Spinning Wheel;* the suite *Carnival of the Animals;* three piano concertos, three violin concertos, and one cello concerto; and three symphonies. He also composed choral music, chamber music, organ music, and several operas, including *Samson and Delilah*.

SALADIN (about 1138-1193), sultan of Egypt and Syria, born at Tikrit, in what is now Iraq. He grew up in Syria and in 1164 accompanied his uncle on a military campaign to Egypt. About 1169 he became vizier of Egypt. Two years later he deposed the Fatimid Dynasty and about 1174 was proclaimed sultan.

From his earliest years it was his great ambition to drive the Christians out of Syria and Palestine. In 1174 he invaded Syria and defeated the army of the Moslem ruler at the Battle of Qurūn Hamāh and proclaimed himself sultan. He totally defeated the Christians in 1187 at the Battle of Hittin and captured Jerusalem shortly afterward. After his capture of the Holy City he behaved with great generosity to the captives.

In 1189 Richard I of England and his ally Philip II of France, leaders of the Third Crusade, laid siege to Acre, which, after a two-year struggle fell to them. After the Crusaders took Caesarea and Jaffa, they marched to Jerusalem and forced upon Saladin a three year's truce (Nov. 2, 1192). Saladin died of a fever at Damascus.

More than a great warrior, Saladin built schools, mosques, and canals and was a great patron of learning.

Flint Civic Opera

At right is a dramatic scene from the opera *Samson and Delilah* by Saint-Saëns. Based on the biblical story of Samson, the opera was first sung at Weimar, Germany, in 1877.

Mud puppies, unlike most other salamanders, retain their gills throughout life.

SALAMANDER, an amphibian that has a long, rounded body, generally four short, weak legs, and a long, tapered tail. It is a relative of the frogs and toads. Although some salamanders resemble lizards, the salamanders and lizards are not related. Lizards are reptiles rather than amphibians. Amphibians have smooth or occasionally warty skins, while lizards have scaly skins. Unlike the frogs and toads, which croak or peep, salamanders are voiceless. Most salamanders are more active at night than during the day.

There are both land-dwelling and water-dwelling salamanders, but all salamanders lay their eggs in a pond, lake, or stream. In many species the young salamander hatches from the egg and lives for a period of months as a larva or tadpole; in some the larval stage is spent within the egg. The larvae resemble the adults but have a pair of bushy or feathery gills attached to the back of the head above the front legs. When the larva undergoes metamorphosis, it loses its gills and develops lungs. However, in one family, which includes many species, most of the members have neither gills nor lungs.

Newts are salamanders that closely resemble lizards. Some newts spend most of their time on land; others, in water. The land dwellers are found under rocks, logs, or dead leaves; they eat small live animals, especially insects and worms.

The aquatic salamanders differ in various ways from the land dwellers. The mudpuppy, or waterdog, measures from 12 to 24 inches long and is somewhat flat from top side to bottom side; it has four feet and has feathery gills throughout life. It is sometimes accidentally caught by fishermen. The siren, 8 to 36 inches long, has an eel-shaped body, feathery gills, and forelegs, but it lacks hindlegs. The congo snake, up to 40 inches long, is found in the southeastern United States. It also is eel shaped, has four tiny legs, and lacks gills. The giant salamander, or hellbender, up to 27 inches long, is four legged and resembles the mudpuppy in shape, but it has wrinkled skin and lacks gills. Aquatic salamanders eat crayfish and other live animals. All are harmless, though some are hideous.

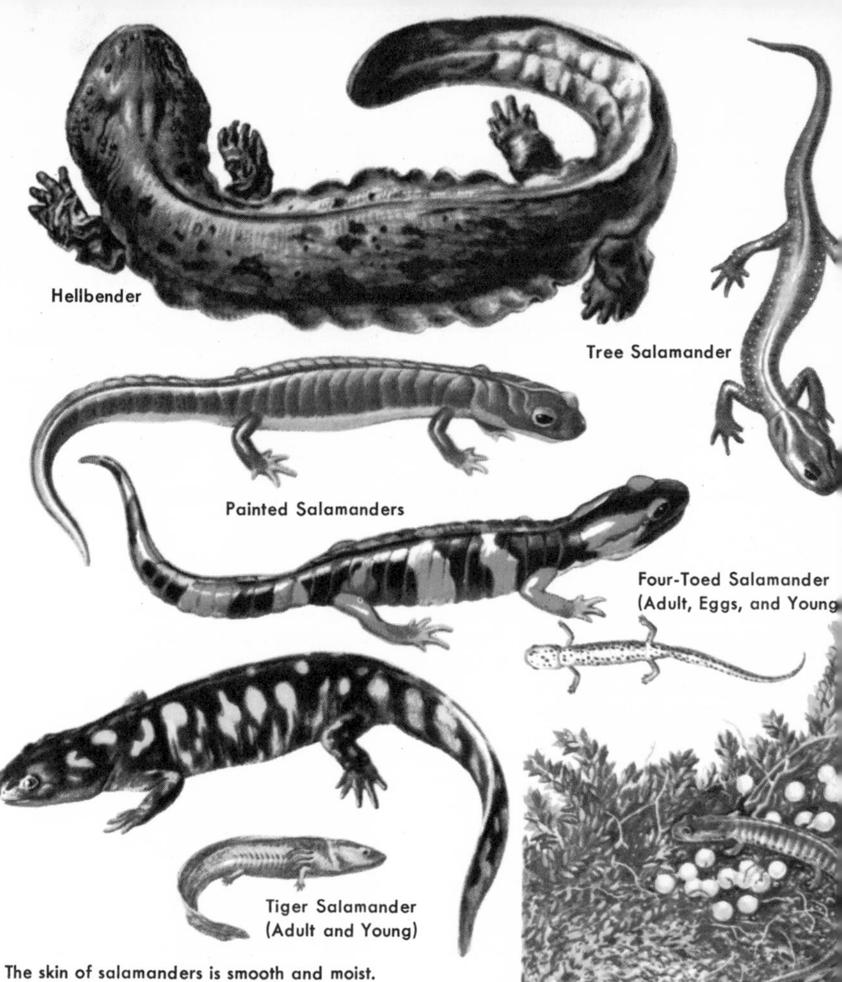

The skin of salamanders is smooth and moist. Terrestrial salamanders inhabit woodland floors, caves, the banks of streams and lakes, and other cool, moist places.

Red and purple salamanders (below)

Slimy and red-backed salamanders (above)

Red efts (terrestrial newts), right

SALEM, the capital of the state of Oregon, on the Willamette River, 50 miles south-southwest of Portland. It is the third largest city in the state, with a population (1960) of 49,142.

The principal industries of Salem are lumber, paper, and pulp milling, textile milling, and food processing. Among the state institutions located here are schools for the blind and deaf and the state penitentiary. Salem is the seat of Willamette University. The Capitol is in the modern style and was built in 1939 to replace the building destroyed by fire in 1935.

Salem was founded by Jason Lee, a Methodist missionary from New England, who built an Indian mission here in 1840. The town was laid out in 1848 and in 1851 became the territorial capital. When Oregon was admitted to the Union in 1859, Salem remained as the capital of the new state.

SALEM WITCH TRIALS, a series of witchcraft accusations and trials at Salem, in Massachusetts, in 1691 and 1692. The trials at Salem were a part of the witchcraft delusion that swept Europe about the same time. New England had already witnessed several witch trials. In 1680 Bridget Bishop had been acquitted of an accusation of witchcraft at Salem. Boston had executed a "witch" in 1688. But the trials at Salem were the largest outbreak of the witch delusion in America.

During the winter of 1691-1692 a group of Salem women and girls whiled away the long winter days by listening to Tituba tell frightening tales. Tituba was an old Negro slave from the West Indies, and she was owned by the Reverend Samuel Parris of Salem. Filled with the lurid products of Tituba's imagination, the girls began to have fits and delusions. They accused witches of sticking pins in them. Nowadays doctors would diagnose the cases as hysteria. The local physician, to be sure, found nothing wrong with the victims. Reverend Parris conferred with ministers from other New England towns. In the meantime a visiting minister preached a fiery sermon on the terrible doings of the devil. People began to suspect others of witchcraft.

This painting by Douglas Volk shows the fear and fervor of the Salem witch delusion.

The governor appointed a special tribunal, and several hundred people were arrested as a result of the town's growing excitement. People were terror stricken, for no one knew who would be accused next by the girls. Between June and September, 20 people were found guilty of witchcraft; 19 of them were hanged and the other was pressed to death. Yet there were some who did not believe in the witchcraft craze, and some of them were brave enough to speak out against it at the risk of being accused of witchcraft themselves. The cooler minds prevailed by October, 1692, and by the beginning of the next year the prisoners held as witches were released.

In 1697 Samuel Sewall, the judge who had presided over the trials, and 12 of the jurors who had passed judgment on the accused admitted their guilt and error in the affair. The Salem trials ended the witchcraft craze in New England. See MATHER, COTTON.

SALES CHECK, in retail selling, a record kept by a salesperson at the time of each individual sale. For the store it serves as a sales invoice, and for the customer it is a purchase invoice. The sales check is the record of the passage of merchandise from the store to the customer.

Sales checks may be made out in two, three, or four copies, depending on the type of merchandise sold. One copy, or a part of one copy, goes to the customer. The salesperson retains one copy for the use of the store records, and additional copies may be sent to the delivery department or may be used for statistical records. There are many kinds of sales checks, but they all carry the following information: the name of the store, the date of the sale, the name or number of the department, the name of the salesperson, the type of sale (cash or charge and so forth), and the name and price of the goods sold. If the goods are bought on credit, the name and address of the customer is necessary.

Together with the sales check, the salesperson may keep a record of the day's sales on a tally envelope. The tally envelope gives a record of each sales-check number and the amount of the sale. At the end of the day sales checks are placed in the tally envelope and are turned in.

SALES TAX, a tax levied on the selling price of goods in one or in several of the steps in the process of distribution. Producers may be taxed when they sell completed products. The goods may be taxed when they pass from wholesaler to retailer. The sales tax may be levied when the retailer sells the goods to the consumer.

The sales tax is an easy way to levy and collect tax money. Its use began in the depression of the 1930's when other taxes could not meet the needs of government. By 1960 about half of the states had a sales tax ranging from about 0.5 percent to 5 percent of the total sales. Selective sales taxes are also applied to such items as gasoline. This tax is commonly regarded not as a general revenue source but as a means of providing funds specifically for highways. The general sales tax is applied to both wholesale and retail sales. Sometimes the tax is levied only on certain goods, such as luxuries, while other goods may be exempt from the sales tax.

The main complaint about the sales tax is that it affects the poor more heavily than the rich, for a larger proportion of a poor man's income is absorbed by the tax than is that of a rich man. Because the sales tax is not based on the ability to pay, some states use it only as an emergency money raiser. See TAXATION.

SALIVA is a digestive juice secreted into the mouth cavity from any of three pairs of glands located in the head. Saliva contains an enzyme called ptyalin. It acts on complex starch molecules (carbohydrates) and begins the breakdown process. The parotid glands are the largest of the glands secreting saliva and are located in the cheek, below and in front of the ears. From the parotids two ducts open into the mouth just opposite the crowns of the second upper molar teeth. The submaxillary glands are located near the angle of the jaw. Two ducts convey saliva into the mouth, opening below and back of the tip of the tongue. The sublingual glands, the smallest of the group, form an elongated mass in the floor of the mouth under the tongue. Numerous ducts of these glands open into the mouth along the base of the tongue; one large pair opens anteriorly beside the submaxillary ducts below the tongue. Salaviary secretion is under the control of the nervous system and is stimulated reflexly by the sight, smell, and taste of food.

SALMON, a fish that belongs to the same order as the herring and the trout. Six species of salmon are found in the North Pacific; all are found on both Asiatic and North American shores except one, which has been found only in the oceans surrounding Japan. Another species, the Atlantic salmon, is found only in the North Atlantic. More salmon are canned than any other fish. More than 500 million pounds of Pacific salmon, most of which are caught in Alaska, are canned each year. The Chinook, the largest salmon, averages 22 pounds, although much larger ones (up to 100 pounds) have been caught. The other Pacific salmon average 3 to 10 pounds. The Atlantic salmon is large like the Chinook.

When the salmon is ready to spawn, it returns to the fresh-water stream where it was hatched. The Chinook migrates up the larger rivers as much as 2,000 miles. The chum and pink salmon spawn in small streams, sometimes only a mile or two from the ocean. Spawning runs occur at different times in different streams from spring to early winter. Species that travel the greatest distances are the first to begin their runs. The eggs are laid in a gravelly streambed in rapid water; they settle down into the crevices between the rocks and remain there until the young fish have hatched. In all species of Pacific salmon the parent fish dies after spawning; the Atlantic salmon, however, returns to the ocean and later returns to the stream to spawn again.

Big dams on the spawning streams in the United States interfere with the normal upstream migration of adult fish and the downstream migration of the young. Fish ladders help the adult fish over the dams, but in some instances the fish cannot be made to use the ladders. The ladders are a long succession of shallow tanks, one built just above the other like steps; they allow the adult fish to leap from tank to tank until they reach the top. Getting the young fish down over the dams without great losses is also a problem. The once-abundant Atlantic salmon has become scarce as a consequence of dams and serious pollution on most of the streams where spawning runs formerly occurred.

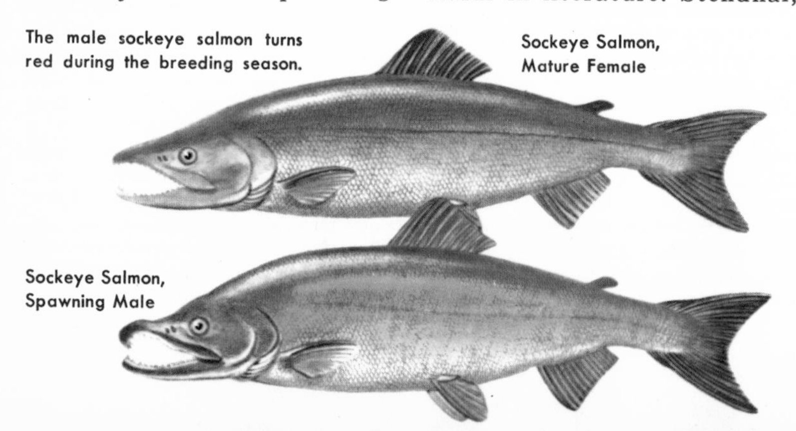

The male sockeye salmon turns red during the breeding season.

Sockeye Salmon, Mature Female

Sockeye Salmon, Spawning Male

SALON, an assembly that gathers, usually on a fixed day or days of the week, at a private home for the purpose of conversation. The lady of the house generally presides over the salon, which draws the same group of people week after week. The salons reached the zenith of their brilliance as a social institution in 18th-century France, but they continued into the 20th century. Some of the most important people of their day were members of particular salons that were famous for the high caliber of their conversation about politics, literature, philosophy, and art. It was considered a great honor to be admitted to such salons.

Some salons of the 18th century were devoted to high society. The intellectual salons were probably more interesting, however. The hostess set the tenor and level of conversation, and by means of salons women of intelligence were able to participate in and influence events. Prior to the French Revolution the salons were gathering places where intellectuals first began to realize their political strength. The American Benjamin Franklin was a welcome figure at these philosophical and artistic salons during his diplomatic tour in France. The French Revolution ended most of the old salons and the society that had frequented them, but new salons arose, presided over by women like Madame Roland, the Marquise de Condorcet, and Madame de Staël.

Although the great days of the salon and its influence ended with the 18th century, there were still salons of note in the 19th century. During the French Restoration period salons fostered a new enthusiasm in literature. Stendhal, Mérimée, the painter Delacroix, and the naturalist Jacquemont frequently were guests of the naturalist Georges Cuvier, whose stepdaughter was the inspiration of a salon. Poets, historians, and social thinkers also visited the salon of Madame Ancelot, where the fine actress Mlle. Rachel entertained by giving recitations. During the July Monarchy literary figures, politicians, and journalists had a choice, if they were invited, of several salons founded by foreigners, English or Russian. During the Second Empire a Bohemian atmosphere was maintained in the salon of Madame Sabatier and a more weighty atmosphere was offered at the salon of Madame d'Agoult, where the statesman Louis Thiers discoursed on any political question put to him. Marcel Proust, who attended the salon of Madame Arman de Caillavet, which featured conversation by such figures as the writer Anatole France, gave many fine descriptions of these social institutions.

SALT is a mineral substance. Its chemical name is sodium chloride, NaCl. Salt is a common food seasoning and is a necessary part of a person's diet. Salt has many industrial and commercial uses and is extremely important as a chemical raw material. Salt is found in extensive deposits of rock salt (halite). Surface deposits of salt are found in some arid regions. Huge amounts of salt are discovered in ocean water and in the water of inland salt lakes and seas. Salt is one of the commonest and most widely distributed of minerals.

Pure, solid sodium chloride occurs as colorless transparent or translucent cubes. It is a soft mineral about as hard as a person's fingernail. Its two most noticeable properties are its taste and its ready solubility in water. Rock-salt crystals may be colored by impurities.

Rock salt is found in many parts of the world and occurs in layers and beds like other sedimentary rocks or in salt domes. Layered deposits of rock salt are commonly associated with gypsum and anhydrite. Nearby rocks may be shale or limestone. Two main regions of layered salt deposits exist in the United States. One region includes parts of Michigan, New York, Pennsylvania, and Ohio. The other region includes parts of Kansas, Oklahoma, Texas, Colorado, and New Mexico. A region of salt domes exists in Louisiana, Alabama, and Texas in the Gulf coast area. Layered salt

Industrial salt is being harvested from an evaporation pond connected to a salt lake in Colombia, South America. The water of lake brine evaporates in the pond, and salt forms.

Annan Photo Features

formations were formed by the evaporation of successive bodies of salt water in a natural basin. The layers of salt formed were buried under younger rocks. Some accumulations of salt layers are several hundred feet thick. Salt domes are large, pluglike bodies of rock salt apparently squeezed upward through overlying sedimentary rocks from their original position in buried rock-salt formations. Salt is lighter than the associated rocks and flows upward when buried under the weight of other rocks.

Surface deposits of salt form in arid and semiarid climates where shallow lakes and marshes evaporate during periods of no rainfall.

Ocean water is almost 3 percent dissolved salt. If ocean water is trapped and allowed to evaporate, the salt is precipitated. Salt lakes, such as the Dead Sea and the Great Salt Lake of Utah, contain salt in solution. The water of the Dead Sea is about 9 percent salt. Salt brines permeate some layers of buried rock. Brines are concentrated ocean or sea water trapped in the rock when it was buried under younger rocks.

Salt may be obtained from layered rock salt deposits by mining operations similar to those used in coal mining. Another method of obtaining salt is to drill wells to a rock-salt layer. Water is allowed to flow down the wells. The rock salt dissolves in the water to form a brine, and the brine is pumped up the wells to the surface. Much of the rock salt that is mined does not need purification and can be sold after it is broken into pieces of suitable size. Salt brines obtained from rock salt require processing and refining.

Some of the impurities common in salt brine are removed by treatment with chemicals. Then the brine is evaporated until salt crystals form. One method is to pour the brine into tanks containing steam-heated coils. The heat from the coils makes the water of the brine evaporate. Salt crystals form and sink to the bottom of the tank, from which they are removed by a rake. Salt formed by this method is called grainer salt. Another commonly used method is to evaporate salt brine in steel or concrete pans under a vacuum. The brine is heated by being circulated through tubes warmed on the outside by steam or hot vapor. When salt crystals precipitate from the concentrated brine, they settle to the bottom of the vacuum pan and fall into long tubes, called salt catchers. Salt produced in vacuum pans is called granulated salt or vacuum salt. Natural brines are refined in the same ways as are artificial brines of dissolved rock salt.

Crystalline salt is obtained from ocean water and inland salt sea water by solar evaporation. Sea water is introduced into shallow ponds, either by flooding at high tide or by pumping. Evaporation causes concentration of the brine.

Salt has thousands of uses. Most salt is used by various chemical industries to make chemicals. The largest single use of salt is in the manufacture of soda ash (sodium carbonate), which is used to make many other products. Salt is used in the manufacture of sodium metal, chlorine, bleaches, hydrochloric acid, chlorates, and other sodium and chlorine chemicals. It is also used in making soaps and dyes and in textile and leather processing. Salt is used in meatpacking and fish curing and in making butter, cheese, and other dairy products. Salt is extensively used in commercial refrigeration. It is used on roads to remove ice and snow and to stabilize the soil in shoulders and in gravel roads. Salt is a component of livestock feed. Salt has many other important uses. Of all the salt obtained, only a small percentage is used as table salt.

SALT LAKE, a body of water from which water loss is primarily by evaporation rather than by outflow, so that the salts are left behind to accumulate.

Most of the lakes that are cut off from inflow from the sea contain little salt and are called fresh-water lakes. However, if the climate in the area of fresh-water lakes should become arid, they might in time become salt lakes. Richard Halliburton tells of the ease of swimming in the Dead Sea in his *Royal Road to Romance*. The salt, of course, acts as a buoyant, making the water heavier.

Salt is a common mineral on the earth. It is found in rocks, in brine beneath the surface of the earth, and as thick beds of rock salt. However, most of the world's salt is contained in the oceans. There is probably enough salt in the seas to build a continent about 15 times the size of Europe.

Most of the salt in the earth was once dissolved in sea water. Seas once covered large areas of the world that are now land. As the earth rose out of the sea, parts of the sea were trapped. When the sea water evaporated, the salt was left behind.

Rainwater leaches the soil and carries the salt into rivers or lakes. If these lakes have no outlet, then they accumulate quantities of salt and become salt lakes. This is the case with the Dead Sea in Israel. The Jordan flows into the Dead Sea, but no river flows out. Water is lost by evaporation. The salt, however, remains behind. So much salt has accumulated in the Dead Sea that it crystallizes out at the bottom as rock salt.

In the United States the most famous salt lake is the Great Salt Lake in Utah. In glacial times a huge, prehistoric, fresh-water lake, of which the Great Salt Lake was once a part, spilled northward into the Snake River. Geologists call this ancient body of water Lake Bonneville. The water supply from the glaciers soon ceased, however. The lake began to evaporate. And since the lake had no outlet, the salt content of the water began to increase. The present Great Salt Lake contains about six billion tons of salt and has left extensive salt flats behind as it has evaporated. Other salt lakes are Sevier Lake, Utah; Mono Lake, California; Lake Van, Turkey; Lake Poopó, Bolivia; Lake Eyre, Australia; and the Aral and Caspian seas. See DEAD SEA; GREAT SALT LAKE.

SALT LAKE CITY is the capital and the largest city of Utah. It is the industrial and commercial center for a vast area. The city is also the world headquarters of the Mormon Church. Located in northern Utah in the foothills of the Wasatch Range, the city processes silver, copper, lead, zinc, and iron from that region. It handles the produce from a rich, irrigated agricultural area that surrounds the city. Industries here include iron and steel mills, an oil refinery, smelters, salt refineries, stockyards, and food-processing plants. The city's population in 1960 was 189,454.

Salt Lake City is attractively laid out, with wide, tree-lined streets. Points of interest include the Capitol, built of native Utah granite and marble; the Lion House, former home of Brigham Young; and the University of Utah.

Salt Lake City was founded by Brigham Young and his Mormon followers in 1847. It was the principal city in the region from its establishment. In 1896 it became the state capital. The city developed as a supply center and stopping point for miners and pioneers bound for California and the Pacific. Growth was further stimulated with the arrival of the railroad in the 1870's. Today the city is an important transcontinental communications center.

SALVADOR, EL. See El Salvador.

SALVAGE, MARITIME, the refloating of stranded ships, the raising of sunken ships, or the recovery of sunken or floating goods. The work of the divers and crews of salvage vessels is difficult and dangerous and is rewarded under maritime law by the payment of compensation based on the value of the recovered vessel and cargo and the risks involved in the salvage operation. Special courts handle cases of disputes arising over salvage claims.

With the aid of modern diving equipment, grappling hooks, pontoons, and machinery many more wrecked or stranded ships are salvaged now than in earlier times.

A stranded vessel is usually pulled into deep water by tugs, and temporary repairs are made. The ship is then towed to a shipyard for permanent repairs.

One method of raising sunken ships is to send down divers to place heavy steel cables under the vessel. The ends of these cables are attached at low tide to two salvage vessels, one on each side of the sunken ship. As the rising tide in turn lifts the surface ships, they lift the wreck on its wire cradle. The wreck may then be taken to shallow water for temporary repairs. Under certain conditions metal pontoons filled with water are submerged on each side of the sunken ship and attached to its sides. The water is then pumped out, causing the pontoons to rise to the surface and to lift the ship with them.

One of the most interesting developments in salvage techniques is the use of compressed air to raise sunken vessels. The air is pumped into the ship either in collapsible containers or into the sealed spaces of the ship itself.

SALVATION ARMY, a Christian social and evangelical organization. The Salvation Army was founded by William Booth in 1865. Booth began to preach in that year in the streets and music halls of London. His words were heard by hundreds of people who had never been in a place of worship. Meanwhile, Booth's capable wife, Catherine, obtained aid for the movement from London's upper classes. The title "The Salvation Army" was chosen in 1880.

The Salvation Army was organized along military lines. General Booth directed all local "corps," which were under evangelists called field officers. The religious teaching of the Salvation Army is much like that of other evangelical groups. Sin, the punishment of the wicked, and redemption are proclaimed. Self-denial for the sake of saving others is the first duty of the members of the Salvation Army.

The International Headquarters is situated in London. The Salvation Army is especially strong in the United States. Booth's son, William Bramwell Booth, succeeded his father in 1912. After 1931 the general was elected by the commanders and officers of the High Council. Unquestioning obedience is expected of all members. The Salvation Army's funds are gathered at open-air collections, from charitable friends, and from its various publications.

The Salvation Army was brought to the United States in 1880 by George S. Railton and a pioneer band of seven lassies, who landed in New York. They were at first received with ridicule and criticism. But some people were inspired by their vigorous methods. The poet Vachel Lindsay saw the genuine accomplishments of the Salvation Army, and on Booth's death he wrote his well-known poem "General William Booth Enters into Heaven." A few lines of the poem will show how well Lindsay captured the feeling of the Salvation Army's street-corner meetings (one can almost hear the bass drum): "Every slum had sent its half-a-score/The round world over. (Booth had groaned for more.)/Every banner that the wide world flies/Bloomed with glory and transcendent dyes."

SAMOA is a group of ten principal inhabited islands and several uninhabited islets in the South Pacific. It lies approximately 2,570 nautical miles northeast of Sydney, Australia, and extends for some 350 miles in an island chain. The islands are volcanic and mountainous.

There are no industries on the Samoan islands. The soil is rich and fertile in the valleys and plains, and the vegetation is plentiful. Fruit (especially bananas and coconuts), taro, and cacao are grown. Copra is the only export. The rainfall is heavy, and the islands lie in the hurricane belt. The majority of the people are Polynesian.

Samoa, formerly ruled by native kings, was divided in 1899 by the United States and Germany. The United States received eastern Samoa; Germany, western Samoa. which was mandated to New Zealand in 1920 and put under UN trusteeship after World War II. The islands were formerly called the Navigators' Islands.

The Territory of Western Samoa consists of Savaii and Upolu and the smaller Manono, Apolima, and several tiny islets. Under the trusteeship of New Zealand Western Samoa took steps toward local government that included the establishment of a popular assembly. Apia, on Upolu, is the administrative center and port. Robert Louis Stevenson is buried near Apia. The territory has a population of about 93,000.

This is the waterfront at Apia, Samoa.
Monkmeyer

American Samoa consists of Tutuila, Aunuu, Swains Island, Rose Island, and the Manua group. Administration, long under the Navy Department, was transferred to the Department of the Interior in 1951 and is carried on by natives under an appointed governor. The Navy maintains a base, an airfield, and a radio station at Pago Pago on Tutuila. Pago Pago, the administrative center, was ceded to the United States in 1878 as a naval and coaling station. American Samoa's population in 1960 was 20,040.

SAMOSET (flourished early 17th century) was an Algonquin Indian who befriended the Pilgrims during their first winter at Plymouth. One day in March, 1621, he suddenly appeared in the middle of Plymouth's main street and astonished the settlers by speaking two words in English: "Welcome, Englishmen!" English fishermen working off the New England coast had taught him a few words of their language. It was largely through Samoset's efforts that a treaty was signed between the Pilgrims and Massasoit, chief of the Wampanoags, on whose land Plymouth was located. In 1625 Samoset, with Unongoit, negotiated the first land sale between the Indians and the English, transferring 12,000 acres of Pemaquid territory to John Brown of New Harbor. Samoset probably died soon after 1653 and was buried with his people at his ancestral home near Round Pond in the town of Bristol, in Maine.

SAMPLER, an embroidered piece of canvas, usually rectangular, which is made to exemplify different kinds of stitches and to show the maker's skill in needlework. Girls in England and colonial America learned to make samplers as a regular part of their household duties. The patterns they used had conventional floral and geometric motifs along the borders and sometimes included figures as well. The name and age of the embroiderer was usually stitched as part of the design, as were also letters of the alphabet, mottoes, verses from the Bible, or poems.

Among the Pennsylvania Dutch the sampler was regarded as a valuable exercise in developing feminine domestic skills. It was hung in the home, much as a piece of tapestry was hung in an earlier age, to decorate a wall. Though modest in scope and intention the sampler was a colorful and attractive piece of work. See EMBROIDERY.

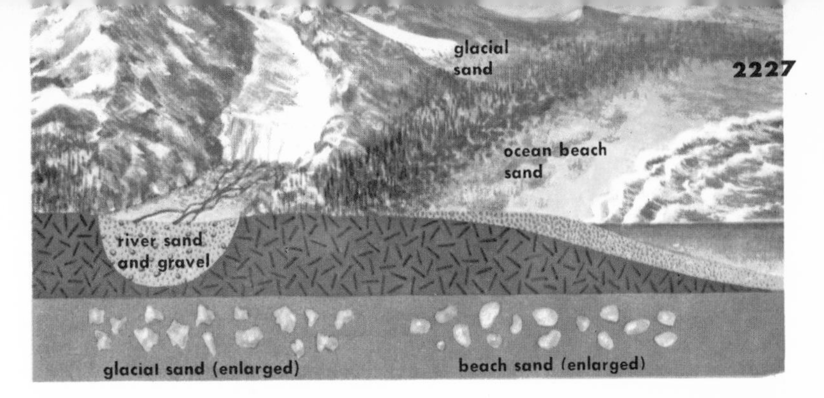

Sands that accumulate in different environments have varied shapes and degrees of roundness.

SAMURAI, a class of warrior-administrators that arose in Japan during the great struggle between the noble families of Taira and Minamoto in the 12th century. At the beginning of the 17th century the Tokugawa shogun, or overlord, of Japan established the samurai as a permanent aristocracy with special privileges. With the restoration of rule by the emperor and the end of feudalism in the middle of the 19th century these privileges were withdrawn. This led to the samurai revolt of 1877, which was easily put down. Thereafter the samurai entered the professions, business, and government service and became the leaders of the new Japan.

SAN ANTONIO, Tex., is one of the largest cities in the state and a distribution and industrial center in southern Texas. It had a population of 587,718 in 1960. San Antonio is the shipping point for cattle, mohair, wool, cotton, fruit, truck-farm produce, and pecans from the surrounding agricultural region. The city's industries include oil refining, food processing, pecan shelling, and the manufacture of wood products, chemicals, and apparel.

San Antonio was founded in 1718, when the mission of San Antonio de Valero (the Alamo) was established here. Within a few years four other missions were founded in the vicinity. From its start San Antonio was the most important Spanish settlement in Texas. It was taken in 1835 by Texas rebels under Ben Milam, during the Texas Revolution. But in the next year an army under Santa Anna took the Alamo fortress and killed all defenders.

After Texas joined the United States, San Antonio was a booming "cow town" during trail-driving days. It later became a shipping center.

The most famous historic attraction in San Antonio is the Alamo. In 1836 a group of Texans heroically defended this old mission against a Mexican army.

SAND, loose mineral or rock particles $\frac{1}{16}$ to 2 millimeters in diameter. The particles may be of any composition. Sand is derived from disintegrated rocks.

Residual sand deposits accumulate where the rocks they were derived from disintegrated. Residual sand deposits are unstratified and have particles of many sizes. They may contain considerable amounts of gravel (particles larger than sand) and silt (particles smaller than sand). Stream sands, accumulations of sand particles transported from their original location by rivers, commonly have a moderate range of particle size. The particles are more or less rounded; degree of roundness in general depends on the physical properties of the mineral particles and the distance they have been transported. One layer of stream sand may be separated from another by lenses of silt or gravel. Beach sands commonly have particles of uniform size that are well rounded. Wave and current action carry away smaller particles and break up larger particles until all the remaining particles are about the same size. Deposits of sand in glaciated areas contain particles of many different sizes. The particles commonly have many sharp edges and may consist of a variety of materials. Windblown sands, such as desert and dune sands, contain particles of uniform minute size that are almost spherical. The particles may have frosted surfaces like ground glass.

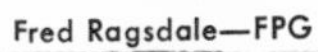

Fred Ragsdale—FPG

The mineral content of a sand depends on the material from which the sand was derived and on how far the particles have been transported. Only the toughest minerals survive long transportation. Most sands consist chiefly of quartz grains because quartz is a very tough mineral. Some sands have unusual mineral contents. For example, islands in the Pacific that are made up of lava flows and volcanic ash may have beach sands composed of olivine, a mineral found in some dark lavas. Some sands contain valuable or rare minerals. Certain beach sands in Florida contain concentrations of monazite, zircon, ilmenite, and rutile and are important sources of the metals thorium, zirconium, and titanium. Monazite-rich beach sands are also found in southern India and in Brazil. Stream and beach sands derived from gold-bearing rocks may contain placer deposits of gold.

Sand is an important natural resource. Large amounts of sand are used to make mortar, plaster, and so on for building purposes. Even larger amounts of sand are used in road and pavement construction. Sands that are nearly pure quartz are used as molding sands in foundries, as material to be made into glass, as abrasives, as filter sands, and for many other purposes. Sands consisting of rounded quartz grains are used to increase the production of oil and gas wells. Ground sand is used as a filler in paint, asphalt, plastic, rubber, and other materials.

SANDBLASTING, the cutting or cleaning of hard materials by a stream of compressed air loaded with graded dry sand or other abrasive material. When the sand is wet, the process is known as mudblasting. Sandblasting is commonly used to clean brick and stone surfaces of buildings and to scour and clean metal castings for further finishing. The sandblast is also used to etch glass. For delicate glassware, the sandblast pressure is applied at about 10 pounds per square inch; for stonework, about 60 pounds per square inch; and for metal work, about 90 pounds per square inch. The area not to be cut is protected with a film of wax or rubber. A variation of the sandblast technique is the spraying of a sandblast into a slowly rotating barrel. By this method about 100 pounds of small castings can be cleaned in 15 minutes. In garages, little automatic sandblast machines are used to clean fouled spark plugs.

Photo, William A. Smith

Carl Sandburg was one of the leading figures of the famous group of gifted Chicago writers associated with that city from 1912 to 1925.

SANDBURG, CARL (1878-   ), American poet, biographer, historian, lecturer, and folk-song recitalist, was born at Galesburg, Ill. His education was haphazard and was mixed with chores on outlying farms and work in Galesburg, where Abraham Lincoln once debated with Stephen A. Douglas. After working as a barbershop porter, milk-wagon driver, scene shifter in a theater, and at other jobs, he hiked west at the age of 17, working in hotel kitchens and wheatfields. During the Spanish-American War he served with the Sixth Illinois Infantry in Puerto Rico. From 1898 to 1902 he attended Lombard College (now Knox College). After college he began a newspaper career in Milwaukee, Wis., and he eventually became secretary to that city's Socialist mayor. From Milwaukee, he moved to Chicago, where he joined the staff of the *Daily News*. He first achieved literary recognition with poems in *Poetry: A Magazine of Verse*. Before the publication of his first book of poetry he had begun his biography of Lincoln, had written stories for children, and had begun collecting American folk songs and stories. While he lived on a farm in Michigan, he wrote poetry and completed the final volume of his monumental biography of Lincoln, for which he received the Pulitzer prize for history in 1940. He was again awarded the Pulitzer prize in 1951; that time the prize was given to him for his *Complete Poems*. His many works included *Chicago Poems, Abraham Lincoln: the Prairie Years, Abraham Lincoln: the War Years*, and *Abraham Lincoln*.

SAND DUNE, an accumulation of wind-driven sand that may be either stationary or migrating downwind. Dunes form where a supply of sand is in the path of winds and where the cover of vegetation is too sparse to keep sand from being moved by winds. Dunes often form in deserts and in semiarid regions along sand-choked streams. They may even form in areas of humid climate inland from sandy beaches. Most dunes consist of quartz sand, but some contain other sand-sized material. Dunes of gypsum particles occur in the White Sands National Monument, in New Mexico.

Sand grains move with the wind by saltation and by surface creep. During saltation individual sand grains are forced by the pressure of moving air to make short, low jumps downwind. The jumps may be several feet long but are never more than a few feet high. As a sand grain hits the surface, it displaces other grains, which then bound downwind. Some displaced grains are only shoved forward and moved downwind by creep.

Windblown sand tends to accumulate wherever vegetation, man-made obstructions, or small sand patches check the wind velocity near the earth's surface. When velocity is lowered, the wind cannot move away as many sand grains as it brought to the area. If moderate-to-strong winds are common, and if sand is available, sand dunes form.

Several types of sand dunes exist. One of the commonest is the barkhan dune, which forms where wind direction is nearly uniform all year. A barkhan dune has a crescent shape; the convex side of the crescent faces upwind and has a gentle slope. The concave side is a slip face—a steep slope, down which sand slides. Traveling sand progresses up the windward, or convex, side in a series of short jumps and finally falls over the top of the dune and slides down the slip face.

In great deserts seif dunes often form. Seifs are long ridges of irregular shape. Each ridge is some distance, usually five or six times its height, from the next ridge. Seif ridges may be continuous for many miles, and some are several hundred feet high.

Longitudinal dunes are long, narrow ridges parallel to the chief wind direction. They tend to form when a relatively small supply of sand is available and the wind direction is constant.

Transverse dunes are ridges at right angles to the predominant wind direction. They tend to form in places that have some vegetation and an abundant supply of sand. Plants grow in the hollows of transverse dunes and stabilize the sand in its ridge shape.

Parabolic dunes are long, scoop-shaped ridges with the points facing upwind. (The points of a barkhan face downwind.) A parabolic dune may form downwind from some local sand source or where vegetation grows on the flanks of a sand ridge. The sand in the flanks of the dune becomes stable, but that in the center migrates downwind.

SAN DIEGO is a year-round resort city, industrial center, and port of entry in southern California. It is situated on San Diego Bay near the Mexican border and about 110 miles southeast of Los Angeles. It possesses one of the finest natural harbors in the United States and is the site of a large naval station and air base. The city has had an enormous population growth in recent years. It had a population of 573,224 in 1960.

Noted for its mild climate, San Diego has long been a residential and resort community. The summers are cool (July average, 67° F.), and the winters are temperate (January average, 55° F.). Numerous outlying resort and residential communities within the city limits include Pacific Beach, Mission Beach, Point Loma, and La Jolla, where the Scripps Institution of Oceanography of the University of California is located.

Balboa Park is one of San Diego's main attractions. Museums, art galleries, a fine zoo, botanical gardens, an open-air pavilion, and buildings erected for two expositions are of special interest. Other notable attractions in the city include a restored mission, Serra Museum, and Old Town. San Diego State College is here.

World War II caused the city to expand rapidly as a defense and manufacturing center. Important industries include aircraft, food processing (fish, meat, fruit, vegetables, and dairy products), brewing, boatbuilding, and sugar refining. San Diego is United States's leading tuna port.

San Diego was the first permanent Spanish settlement in California. The mission of San Diego de Alcalá (now restored) was built here in 1769 and was organized as a pueblo in 1834. In 1850, after acquisition by the United States, San Diego was chartered as a city.

Betty O'Connor

Among the Navahos sand paintings are stylized representations of sacred subjects.

SAND PAINTING, or dry painting, is a ceremonial design made of colored grains of sand arranged on an earth floor. These paintings are of ancient origin among the Navahos, Pueblos, and Apaches; they are used primarily in ceremonies of healing. The designs are made according to exact traditional patterns, which have been handed down for generations. The ceremonies themselves usually take place after the first frost of autumn and last from two to nine days. They are led by medicine men, who have learned all the details of this ritual and who take on assistants to do the sand painting.

In ceremonies lasting over a week, the first four days are devoted to purifying the body. The medicine man chants prayers to awaken the gods and to animate images in the painting, while the sick members of the tribe prepare themselves to receive the revitalizing powers thus magically released. Mental illnesses are also treated in this way. Sometimes the medicine man picks up grains of sand from the painting and sprinkles them on the patient's body. After each ceremonial treatment the painting is removed; then the grains of sand are taken outside and scattered in the four directions.

It is probable that the art of sand painting will soon be lost, for boys who would ordinarily learn all the details of the ceremony from the medicine man now attend public schools.

SANDPAPER, a sheet, disk, belt, or roll of paper, cloth, or vulcanized fiber, on one side of which are particles of crushed flint, emery, or garnet (natural abrasives) or crushed silicon carbide or aluminum oxide (furnaced abrasives). These abrasives are used in all kinds of metallic and nonmetallic work to produce smooth surfaces and finishes.

The grit size of sandpaper is based on diameters of particles that will pass through standardized mesh screens: 400 to 220, superfine; 180 to 120, fine; 100 to 80, medium fine; 60, medium coarse; 50 to 36, coarse; and 30 to 16, extra-coarse. Size 50 and coarser are used for heavy stock removal; 100 to 60, for medium work; and 120 and finer, for finishing. Before varnishing a piece of wood, use only fine or very fine sandpaper, because scratches in the surface will show through the final coat of varnish. In hand-sanding operations a sandpaper block should be used whenever possible to get a true flat surface. All sanding should, if possible, be done with the grain of the wood.

Conventional sandpapers were made by sprinkling abrasive particles onto the warm, glued surface of the backing; but most modern coated abrasives are made by the upward electrostatic principle. The positively charged particles seek out a grounded metal plate but become embedded in the adhesive layer in a vertical position. Since the heavier end is buried and the sharper, pointed end protrudes, the modern product is far more efficient, either for hand-sanding operations or for the tremendous variety of modern mechanical applications of such products. Portable and stationary electric and pneumatic tools and machines are now used widely. See ABRASIVE.

SANDPIPER. On a sandy shore almost anywhere in the world (and sometimes on the rocky coasts as well) may be found the small, active birds known as sandpipers. This family consists of 77 species, more than half of which are found at least occasionally in North America. Many of them breed in the North American arctic areas and migrate through the continent to spend the winter in the southern states or in South America.

Sandpipers are generally slender birds with long legs and slim toes, sometimes partially webbed. They usually feed on insects, worms, and small crustaceans found along the shore or in the water. The nest is likely to be a small depression in the ground, scantily lined and containing four eggs, which are incubated by both parents. The young birds are usually able to walk soon after hatching. Customarily sandpipers have colorful, or at least brownish, plumage in the spring. They change to a duller, somewhat grayish plumage in the fall. Bird watchers in the central part of the continent see many of the sandpipers only on migration and must learn to recognize two very different aspects of the same birds. Sandpipers are more confusingly alike in the fall; but that season is, in one way, the better time to study them, for their southward journey is usually made somewhat more leisurely than the northward trip.

But generalizations regarding this large family have many exceptions. Although most sandpipers are small, the Madagascar curlew, the largest of the sandpipers, is 24 inches long and has a wingspread of 42 inches. Although most sandpipers lay their eggs on the ground, three species (including the North American solitary sandpiper) use abandoned nests of tree-nesting birds. A few species have exceptional feeding habits; some eat berries, and some capture small fish. The hardy little purple sandpiper feeds on wave-washed rocks on northern coasts and rarely migrates farther south than the northern United States. The upland plover is another interesting exception. (It is a sandpiper even though called a plover.) This nondescript but sweet-voiced bird is distinguished by its habitat—grassy fields instead of sandy shores. It is often seen perching on a fencepost or a pole. Its food consists largely of grasshoppers, weevils, and other pests.

The woodcock, another strange bird of this family, lives in damp, swampy places and feeds principally on worms. Its long, pointed bill is inserted straight down in the mud, and the flexible outer end is then opened to clasp a worm and pull it from the mud. The woodcock's eyes are placed high on the head. The male woodcock is famous for its evening and early-morning courtship flights, in which its wing quills make whistling sounds as the bird mounts high in the air. Other notes accompany the downward plunge. This exhibition is made to impress the female woodcock on the ground.

The common snipe, also of this family, has a long bill for probing in the mud and inhabits grassy

The spotted sandpiper teeters as it walks.

COMMON SANDPIPERS OF NORTH AMERICA

Common name (alternate names in parentheses)	Approximate overall length	Approximate length of bill	Distinguishing characteristics in spring
Baird's sandpiper*	7½	⅞	Buffy head, black legs
Buff-breasted sandpiper	8	⅝	Buffy under parts, yellow legs
Common snipe (Wilson's snipe)	11¼	2⅝	Long slender bill, short orange tail, pointed wings, striped head
Dunlin (red-backed sandpiper)	8½	1½	Rusty back, black belly
Greater yellowlegs	14	2⅛	Very long bill, yellow legs
Hudsonian godwit	15	3	Upturned bill, rusty breast
Knot	10½	1⅜	Short bill, rusty breast, white rump
Least sandpiper*	6	¾	Slim bill, yellow-green legs
Lesser yellowlegs	10½	1⅜	Yellow legs, slim bill, whitish rump
Long-billed curlew	23	6	Very long decurved bill, buffy body, bright cinnamon wing linings
Long-billed dowitcher	12	2⅝	Dark above, salmon-colored below
Ma bled godwit	18	4½	Buff-brown body, long upturned bill
Pectoral sandpiper	9	1⅛	Brown markings of breast ending sharply against white belly
Purple sandpiper	9	1¼	Slaty plumage, yellow legs; found on rocky coasts
Rock sandpiper	9	1⅛	Dark rusty back, yellow legs, dark spot on breast
Sanderling	8	1	Rusty color, white wing stripe
Semipalmated sandpiper*	6¼	¾	Black legs, bill stouter than bill of least sandpiper
Short-billed dowitcher	12	2½	Rusty breast, lower back and tail white; feeds by perpendicular jabbing of bill
Solitary sandpiper	8½	1¼	Dark back and legs, eye ring
Spotted sandpiper	7½	⅞	Spotted breast, teetering walk
Stilt sandpiper	8½	1⅜	Transverse bars on breast, rusty ear patch, greenish legs
Upland plover	12	1⅛	Small head, short bill, thin neck, brown coloring; found in fields
Wandering tattler	11	1½	Long heavy bill, brown-gray above, gray-barred under parts
Western sandpiper*	6½	1	Tip of long bill slightly drooped, black legs, rusty on back and crown
Whimbrel (Hudsonian curlew)	17	3½	Decurved bill, striped crown, brownish color
White-rumped sandpiper*	7½	1	White rump, striped back, buffy crown and scapulars
Willet	15	2⅛	Gray, bill stocky, legs bluish, flashy black-and-white wing pattern in flight
Woodcock	11	2¾	Long bill, short rounded wings, dead-leaf color, neckless appearance

*These five species collectively nicknamed "peep"

swamps and bogs. It is considered a good game bird because of its sudden, zigzag flight.

North American sandpipers bear a great variety of other names, being known as curlews, whimbrels, willets, yellowlegs, tattlers, knots, dunlins, dowitchers, godwits, and sanderlings, besides the great number of names that include the word *sandpiper*, as the spotted sandpiper, the least sandpiper, the solitary, the purple, the pectoral, the white-rumped, the buff-breasted, semipalmated, stilt, western, curlew, Baird's, and so forth. Elsewhere in the world sandpipers have still other interesting names, as greenshanks, redshanks, spoon-billed sandpipers, and ruffs.

Typical sandpipers that inhabit the beaches and mudflats are often associated with plovers, which are somewhat stockier, shorter-billed shore birds. See PLOVERS AND TURNSTONES.

Two specimens of sandstone are shown here.

SANDSTONE is a rock composed of sand grains held together by cement. By definition sand grains are $\frac{1}{16}$ to 2 millimeters in diameter. Most sandstones are made up chiefly of quartz grains, but some sandstones also contain orthoclase and microcline feldspar, mica, garnet, magnetite, or other minerals that are resistant to chemical and physical breakdown. Sandstone is a detrital, or clastic, sedimentary rock. It is mainly composed of particles that were mechanically dislodged and carried to their present location. Sandstone is the second most abundant sedimentary rock (shale is more abundant) and is found in many places on the earth's surface.

Sandstones have a granular texture—a surface something like that of a cube of sugar. They are rough to the touch. Most sandstones are white, buff, red, brown, or yellow. The quartz grains are colorless, and the color of the sandstone depends on the cement that holds the grains together. Sandstone cemented with clay or a carbonate mineral, such as calcite, is commonly light gray or buff. Sandstone cemented with silica is white. Red and red-brown sandstones contain hematite, an iron oxide, in their cement. Yellow and yellow-brown sandstones contain limonite, a hydrous iron oxide. Green sandstones that contain glauconite are called greensands. A few green sandstones contain chlorite. Some sandstones have a uniform texture and occur in thick beds. Others are thinly laminated. Many sandstones show cross-bedding and ripple marks.

Most sandstones are porous and permeable. They contain many small empty spaces and many of the spaces are connected. In many parts of the world sandstones are important aquifers—rocks that can rapidly supply large amounts of water to wells. The reservoir rocks of most oilfields, the rocks through which oil and gas flow to an oil well, are sandstones.

Thick-bedded, firmly cemented sandstone of uniform texture was much used in the past as a building stone. The brownstone houses in the eastern United States are built of sandstone. Many of the buildings of Edinburgh, Scotland, are constructed of sandstone.

SANDSTORM, a windstorm on the desert. Sandstorms often carry along such quantities of sand that visibility is nil. The duststorms so common in U.S. plains states during the 1930's were a variation of the sandstorm. For winds to pick up large amounts of sand they must exceed 30 miles per hour. A sandstorm originating in the Sahara once dumped an estimated 1,800,000 tons of dust over Europe and as much more over the Mediterranean Sea. Travelers in the desert must halt as best they can during sandstorms, else they will lose their way. Camels, which are most suited for travel in the desert, have slitlike nostrils that can be closed at will as a protection against sand. So well adapted is the camel that groups of wild camels that were found in Turkestan were believed to be the descendants of camels from caravans caught in the terrible sandstorms in the Taklamakan Desert over 200 years ago. The human beings among these caravans must have perished, but their hardy beasts of burden were able to survive.

SAN FRANCISCO, the second largest city in California, is a great seaport and cosmopolitan center. It is located in western California on a hilly and narrow peninsula, bounded by the Pacific Ocean on the west and by San Francisco Bay on the east. The city's population in 1960 was 742,855.

San Francisco has a fine port. It has one of the best landlocked harbors in the world. It imports such commodities as coffee, tea, cacao, copra, sugar, tropical fruit, spices, lumber, cotton, tung oil, and burlap. Exports include iron and steel products, canned fruit, and fish, rice, and hops.

The city is the commercial and distribution center for a large area of inland California and the Pacific coast. Industries include meatpacking, oil refining, canning, shipbuilding, and steel milling. San Francisco is the financial center of the West. A U.S. mint is located here.

San Francisco has certain characteristics for which it is known. These include the even, cool climate, the fogs, the many hills, the picturesque cable cars, the many fine restaurants and smart shops, and the foreign communities. The interest taken by its residents in art, music, and theater make it one of the foremost cultural centers in the United States. The Opera House is the home of the city's symphony orchestra. Golden Gate Park in the city covers more than 1,000 acres. It is one of the largest and most beautiful parks in the United States.

The discovery of gold in 1848, almost simultaneous with the U.S. acquisition of California, caused San

Wide World Photo

This view of San Francisco was taken from Nob Hill, once the site of many elaborate mansions. The city has many interesting areas, including Chinatown, the Latin Quarter, and Fisherman's Wharf.

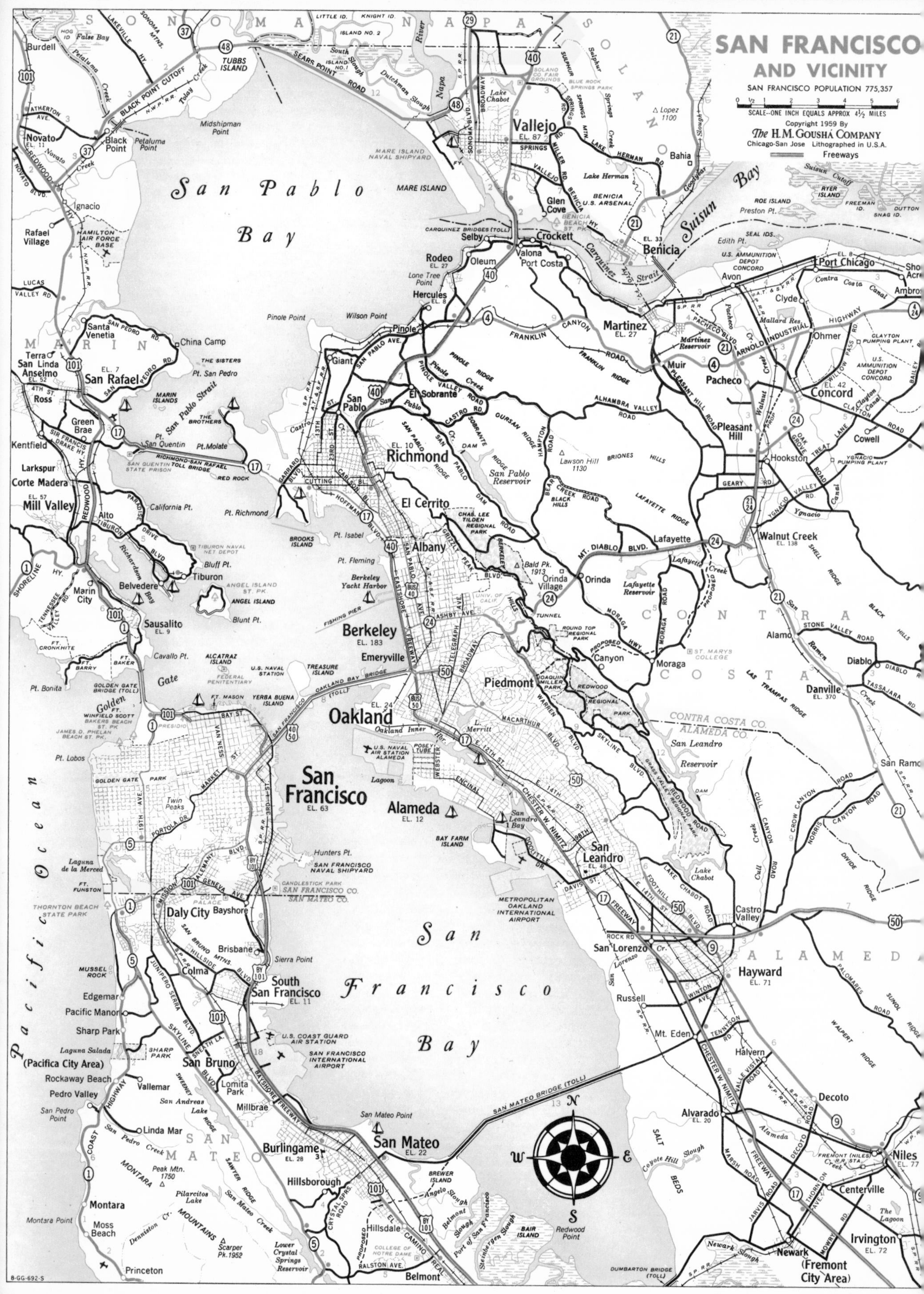
SAN FRANCISCO
AND VICINITY
SAN FRANCISCO POPULATION 775,357
SCALE--ONE INCH EQUALS APPROX 4½ MILES
Copyright 1959 By
The H.M. Gousha Company
Chicago-San Jose Lithographed in U.S.A.
Freeways
San Pablo Bay
San Francisco Bay
Pacific Ocean
Suisun Bay
Carquinez Strait
Golden Gate
San Francisco
EL. 63
Oakland
EL. 24
Berkeley
EL. 183
Richmond
EL. 10
Alameda
EL. 12
Vallejo
EL. 87
San Rafael
EL. 7
Novato
Mill Valley
Sausalito
Tiburon
Belvedere
Daly City
South San Francisco
San Bruno
Burlingame
San Mateo
Hillsborough
Belmont
San Leandro
Hayward
EL. 71
San Lorenzo
Castro Valley
Alvarado
Niles
Centerville
Irvington
Newark
(Fremont City Area)
Walnut Creek
Concord
Martinez
Benicia
Crockett
Pinole
El Cerrito
Albany
Emeryville
Piedmont
Orinda
Lafayette
Moraga
Danville
Alamo
Pleasant Hill
(Pacifica City Area)
Montara
Princeton
Alcatraz Island
Angel Island
Treasure Island
Yerba Buena Island
San Francisco International Airport
Metropolitan Oakland International Airport
San Mateo Bridge (Toll)
Dumbarton Bridge (Toll)
Golden Gate Bridge (Toll)
Richmond-San Rafael Toll Bridge
8-GG-692-S

Francisco to boom as a port and commercial center. A period of lawlessness arose, and the notorious Barbary Coast caused the city to form organizations of Vigilantes, who fought crime and corruption.

In 1915 the city was the site of the Panama-Pacific Exposition, celebrating the opening of the Panama Canal. The city's Civic Center was presented by the Exposition. In 1936 the gigantic San Francisco–Oakland Bay Bridge was opened, and in 1937 the Golden Gate Bridge was completed. The Golden Gate International Exposition (1939-1940) was held in San Francisco on manmade Treasure Island. In 1945 San Francisco was the site of the conference that drew up the charter of the United Nations.

SANITATION. In medieval cities garbage was thrown into the streets. Occasionally, an unwary passerby was deluged with garbage thrown from an upper window. In Scotland the housewife would shout "gardy-loo" as a warning to the pedestrian in the street below. Garbage disposal was left to the hogs that roamed the streets. Fresh air and sunlight were rare in these crowded cities, which were surrounded by walls for protection. All in all, the medieval city was an unhealthy place in which to live. Epidemics were frequent, and now and then a terrible plague, such as the Black Death, would sweep over Europe. The average city dweller did not live very long under these conditions. The modern city has allowed its inhabitants a longer life through the use of sanitation.

Sanitation methods are not a modern invention. Sewers of a sort were found in Babylon and Nineveh. The Romans constructed drains to carry off surface water. However, underground sewers were first built on a large scale in Paris in the early 19th century. The Paris sewers were made famous by Victor Hugo's *Les Misérables*. A cholera epidemic in London in 1848 caused the city's sanitation system to be placed under a single commission. This was a great step forward, for it made planning and sanitation standardization easier. United States cities profited by London's example. In 1890 Worcester, Mass., began to filter sewage before it poured into rivers and streams. A chemical process prepared the sewage for use as fertilizer.

A city's sewers are usually the responsibility of an engineer and his assistants. Crews are maintained to inspect and clean the system.

UPI

While crowds still line the street, trucks of the city sanitation department clean up after a parade down Broadway in New York.

Progressive cities also maintain office staffs to devise scientific improvements for the sewers.

Ashes and garbage are collected by city crews or private companies. Most cities incinerate this waste rather than dump it into lakes and rivers, as was once done. Again, science has devised methods of preparing grease, fertilizer, and food for hogs from the waste of a big city.

Machines have been invented to wash and sweep streets. Crews are also maintained for the necessary hand sweeping. In Paris the streets are flushed from jets in the curb. Women with brooms follow this washing with a vigorous sweeping up. This system is quite effective. The tidy streets of old Holland were cleaned by the housewives, each responsible for the area in front of her house.

The discovery, by such men as Louis Pasteur, of the effects of bacteria allowed sanitation departments to battle a recognizable enemy. The first sand filter for a city water supply in the United States was introduced in Poughkeepsie, N.Y., in 1885. Other cities let their water supply stand so that debris settled out, a method used long ago by the Romans. After great numbers of bacteria were removed by these methods, chlorine could control the remaining germs.

Not all problems of sanitation have been solved, of course. But the modern city is already a much healthier place to live in than it was 100 years ago. See CITY PLANNING; SLUM; SMOG.

SAN MARINO is a small independent republic in Europe. It is situated within Italy near the Adriatic coast, southwest of Rimini. The people are Roman Catholics, speak Italian, and use Italian currency. The principal sources of revenue are agriculture, stock raising, and the sale of postage stamps. The republic's approximate population is 13,500.

San Marino's legislature, the Grand Council, has 60 members, elected every five years. Two regents are selected from the council every six months and act as heads of the government.

The republic was founded in the 4th century and has been an independent state, with few interruptions, since that date. In 1960 women received the right to vote.

SAN MARTÍN, JOSÉ DE (1778-1850), Argentine general and revolutionary leader, was born in Argentina in 1778. He was educated in Spain and entered the army at the age of 21 but resigned in 1811 and sailed for Buenos Aires to offer his services to the South American countries who were fighting with Spain for their independence. In January, 1813, he defeated the Spanish at San Lorenzo. The next year he was appointed commander in chief of the forces of upper Peru and prepared to attack the Spanish by an approach through Chile. An army was drilled for two years at Mendoza, Argentina, and San Martín began, on Jan. 17, 1817, his famous march over the Andes, meeting and routing the Spaniards at Chacabuco on February 12.

This victory led to the occupation of the capital and to the formation of the new republic of Chile, of which San Martín was offered the headship but refused. After freeing Chile from Spanish power he entered the capital of Peru with an army of 4,500 men, proclaimed the country independent, and was chosen protector.

In order to avoid a struggle for leadership San Martín left the task of completing the conquest of Peru to Simón Bolivar, who in 1822 came to the aid of the Peruvians. San Martín resigned his command in 1822, sailed for Europe, and, since he believed that his being in Argentina would make establishment of a stable government more difficult, spent the remainder of his life in France in comparative poverty.

SAN SALVADOR ISLAND. See BAHAMA ISLANDS.

Brown Brothers

Antonio López de Santa Anna

SANSKRIT, the language of ancient and medieval Indian religious, philosophical, artistic, and scientific literature. In the broadest sense Sanskrit includes the Vedic language, epic Sanskrit, and classical Sanskrit. In the narrow sense classical Sanskrit is preeminent. The term *samskrta* (cultivated) was introduced by the Indians themselves to distinguish the classical language. Sanskrit resulted from the development of the language of previous Vedic literature, but it is substantially different from the language of surviving Vedic hymns. The elaboration of the Sanskrit language from late Vedic prose literature occurred in the 4th century B.C. and brought together the literary norms of the language of the Brahmins, of scholarship, and of court poetry. The basis of Sanskrit was the dialect of the region adjacent to the modern cities of Delhi and Agra, the economic, political, and cultural center of ancient India. The vocabulary of Sanskrit is basically Indo-European, but as the result of thousands of years of cultural relations with neighboring people there appeared many elements of Dravidic and eastern-Asian languages. Sanskrit also contains a small number of Greek and Arabic words. On the other hand the existence of Sanskrit as the language of the ancient national culture has had a strong influence upon newer Indian languages, such as Hindi and Bengali.

Two national epics of the Indian peoples, the *Mahabharata* and the *Ramayana,* were written in Sanskrit at a time when it was linked directly to the spoken language. Also, a large part of Sanskrit literature is composed of scientific works on such subjects as astronomy and medicine. The classical period of Sanskrit literature embraced the 4th to the 9th century A.D. and included drama, love poetry, and adventure stories. Sanskrit prose literature continued into the 19th century.

SANTA ANNA, ANTONIO LÓPEZ DE (1795-1876), Mexican dictator and revolutionary, was born in Jalapa. A man without principles, his unscrupulous opportunism enabled him to exert a power in Mexican affairs out of all proportion to his abilities. He led armed revolts against the native emperor Agustín I (Agustín de Iturbide) in 1822, and against Presidents Guerrero (1828) and Bustamante (1832) before he became president himself in 1833. When the Texans proclaimed their independence in 1836, Santa Anna gathered an army of Indian conscripts and marched northward, where he attacked about 150 Texas militiamen in the Franciscan mission of the Alamo. Two weeks later he shocked even his own officers by ordering the slaughter of more than 300 prisoners held by the Mexicans at Goliad. He then attacked a Texan force under Sam Houston and was defeated and captured. He was soon released and returned to Mexico in disgrace. In 1838 he restored his prestige by losing a leg while opposing the occupation of Vera Cruz by the French. In 1841 he overthrew Bustamante, who had again become president, and ruled with dictatorial powers until 1844. Santa Anna was deposed in the latter year and was sent into exile in 1845. After the outbreak of war with the United States (1846) he returned and again seized power. His defeat by General Winfield Scott led to another exile, from which he was recalled in 1853 to assume power again. In 1855, with another revolt brewing, Santa Anna fled to Colombia and later went to Venezuela and finally to the United States. This was the end of his stormy political career. He did not return to Mexico until 1874 and then lived in poverty until his death.

SANTA CLAUS. Many legends survive concerning St. Nicholas, the man who has come down to us as Santa Claus. He was born in Patras, a city of Lycia, in Asia Minor nearly 300 years after the birth of Christ. Stories are told of the miraculous powers of Nicholas even in his infancy. As a boy he devoted his time to the study of the Scriptures. He is the patron saint of children.

As archbishop of Myra, a city of Lycia, additional miracles are told of Nicholas. He is remembered especially for his courageous defense of his faith against the Roman emperor Diocletian.

It was Vladimir I of Russia who brought the tales of St. Nicholas to the north. Nicholas was made patron saint of Russia, and his fame spread among the Lapps and Samoyeds. The Lapland image of St. Nicholas as a heavy man dressed in red and riding in a sled pulled by reindeer was brought to the United States by early Dutch settlers. In Europe December 6, the traditional date of the saint's death, is the day when gifts are exchanged. But in the United States December 25, Christ's birthday, is the day used.

SANTA FE, the capital of New Mexico and the oldest seat of government within the United States. It is located in the north-central part of the state in the Sangre de Cristo Mountains. It is a health resort, an art center, and a shipping point for livestock, grain, minerals, and Indian handicraft items. It has been a trade center since its founding. According to the 1960 census Santa Fe had a population of 34,676.

Santa Fe was founded in 1609 by Don Pedro de Peralta, governor of New Spain. Indian pueblos stood on the site in prehistoric times. It was always exposed to Navaho and Comanche Indian raids. Northern Pueblo Indians revolted in 1680 and occupied Santa Fe until 1692.

In 1821 the first American traders arrived at Santa Fe from the plains. From 1821 to 1880 the famous Santa Fe Trail brought many travelers from Missouri to New Mexico and the terminus, Santa Fe. Wagon caravans could travel over the route since it avoided rivers. The Santa Fe Trail helped the United States obtain much-needed silver and to gain control of New Mexico in 1846 during the Mexican War.

When Mexico freed itself from Spain in 1821, Santa Fe remained the northern capital under the Mexican regime. In 1850, when New Mexico was organized into a U.S. territory, Santa Fe continued as the capital, as it did in 1912, when New Mexico became a state.

The modern New Mexico Capitol at Santa Fe

Esther Witt

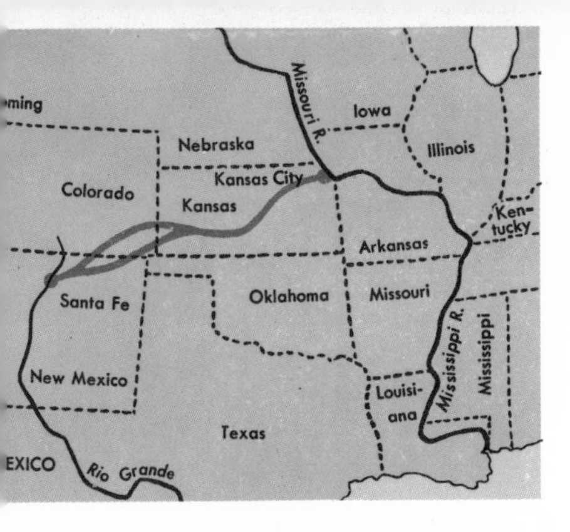

The Santa Fe Trail was a historic route.

SANTA FE TRAIL, a trail for wagon trains in the western United States leading to Santa Fe from Missouri —first from Franklin, then Independence, and finally Westport (now Kansas City). Before Mexico obtained freedom from Spain in 1821, trade with people of the United States was forbidden. Thereafter the number of wagon trains that used the trail increased yearly. A stagecoach line, established in 1849, made a trip between the cities every month. The trail fell into disuse after the establishment of the Atchison, Topeka, and Santa Fe Railroad, which reached Santa Fe in 1880 and which for some distance was built parallel to the trail.

SANTIAGO, the capital of Chile, is beautifully situated on a wide plain at the foot of the Andes in central Chile. It is on the Mapocho River, about 60 miles from Valparaiso, its port on the Pacific Ocean. One of the largest cities in South America, it has a population of about 1,850,000.

Santiago is essentially a modern city with the usual skyscrapers and lavish residential areas, yet some of the architecture of the colonial period remains. Points of interest include the historic Plaza de Armas, the National Archives, the Museum of Natural History, the Civic Center, the National Capitol, and the University of Chile. Many fine plazas and parks enhance the city. Cerro Cristóbal Park, reached by a funicular railway, gives a splendid view of the city.

The capital is the leading industrial and commercial center of Chile. More than half of the country's industries are here. They concentrate mainly on textiles, food, chemicals, and leather.

The city was founded in 1541. Indian raids, earthquakes, and floods were an early menace to Santiago's development. It became the capital of the Chilean Republic in 1818.

SÃO PAULO, the largest city in Brazil, is the leading industrial city of South America. It is also the financial and commercial center and a leading cultural center of the country. São Paulo lies on a plateau about 2,700 feet above sea level in southeastern Brazil. It is located 33 miles northwest of Santos, the city's seaport on the Atlantic Ocean. It is one of the fastest growing cities in the world. In the last 50 years it has developed from a provincial city of over 200,000 inhabitants to the second largest city in South America. It has a population of about 3,500,000.

São Paulo is irregular in outline, with the avenues radiating in no set pattern from the Triângulo, the heart of the city. Modern skyscrapers abound here. The city has many cultural, educational, and recreational facilities. The ancient University of São Paulo, the Butantan Institute, or "snake farm" (scientific research), the Ipiranga Museum, the Museum of Modern Art, and numerous parks, theaters, and recreational areas are some of the major points of interest.

The concentration of industry in and around the city is the chief reason for its spectacular growth. The nearby port of Santos, the great hydroelectric potential, and the mineral wealth in the area have been some of the factors that have aided this industrialization. Textiles, furniture, processed food, drugs and chemicals, apparel, footwear, and metallurgical products are among the chief manufactures. In addition, São Paulo is becoming the center of heavy industries. The city handles much of the interior's huge agricultural output. More coffee flows through São Paulo than through any other city in the world.

Founded in 1554, the city prospered because of its important geographical position and the enterprising spirit of its Paulista population. The city experienced a tremendous growth in the second half of the 19th century, when coffee became the outstanding crop of the area. Heavy foreign immigration began near the end of the 19th century.

At the left is an uncut star sapphire. At the right is a fancy-cut sapphire.

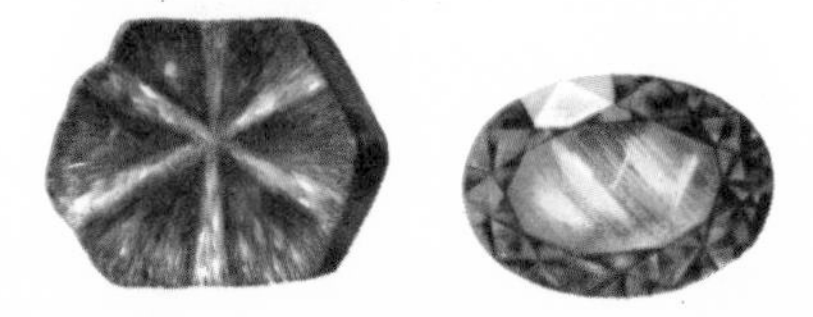

Dana Brown—FPG

The prosperous and modern city of São Paulo

SAPPHIRE, a transparent gem variety of the mineral corundum, Al_2O_3. Corundum is found in a variety of colors. When red and of gem quality, it is the ruby. (See RUBY.) All other colors of gem-quality corundum are called sapphire. True sapphire is blue in color, because of the presence of a small amount of titanium oxide. Colorless stones are almost pure aluminum oxide and are called white sapphire. Gem-quality corundum may also contain small quantities of other substances that color the mineral. It is a common practice to name these colored stones after other gems, with the prefix *oriental;* for example, oriental topaz is yellow, oriental amethyst is violet, and oriental emerald is green. When gem corundum is cut rounded, or *en cabochon*, it occasionally shows a six-rayed star, the rays of which are white. Such a gem is called star sapphire or, if red, star ruby. The cornflower-blue stones are the most valuable, especially those from Kashmir. Sapphires are also found in Thailand, Ceylon, Burma, Australia, China, and in the United States in Montana and North Carolina.

Sapphires and rubies are manufactured artificially on a large scale, and even the star varieties are so made. These artificial stones resemble natural stones, and it is exceedingly difficult or impossible for an untrained person to tell the difference. Artificial corundum is used in making gems, watch jewels, and instrument bearings.

SAPROPHYTE, a living plant that obtains its nourishment from the dead bodies or waste products of plants or animals or from other nonliving organic substances. A saprophyte differs from a parasite, which obtains its nourishment from the bodies of living plants and animals. Saprophytes include many fungi, many bacteria, and a few flowering plants.

Most mushrooms and toadstools are saprophytic fungi that may grow in the soil or on decaying logs or tree stumps. They obtain their nourishment from dead vegetation in the soil or from the dead, decaying wood. Some molds are saprophytic fungi that grow on, and obtain their nourishment from, bread, stored citrus fruits, and leather, paper, or wood stored in warm, moist, dark places. Some mildews also are saprophytic fungi that grow on, and are nourished by, leather, cloth, and other organic substances.

Some saprophytic bacteria live in and obtain their nourishment from animal excrement and the dead bodies of animals and plants. These bacteria cause the decomposition, or decay, of excrement and dead bodies. Saprophytic bacteria also cause the souring of milk, the putrefaction of unrefrigerated, uncured meat, and the decay of unpreserved vegetables and fruits.

Indian pipe is a saprophytic angiosperm, or flowering plant, that grows in close proximity to decaying wood in the soil and obtains its nourishment from the wood.

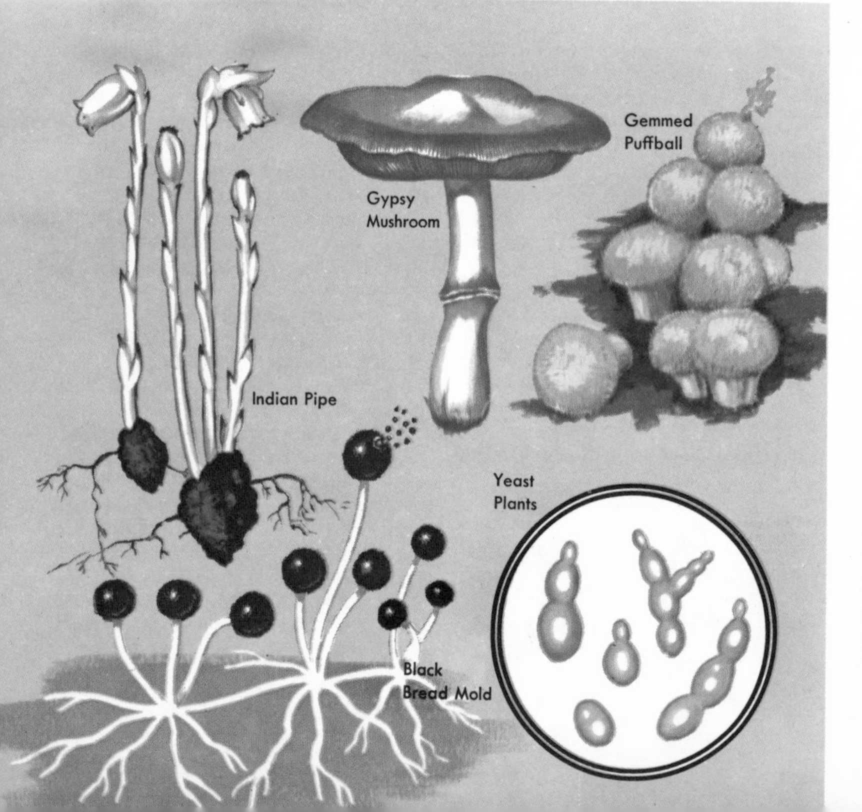

These saprophytes lack chlorophyll and cannot photosynthesize their food. They obtain food from nonliving organic substances.

SARACEN, a term of uncertain origin applied by the Christians of the Middle Ages to the Moslems who invaded and occupied parts of the Christian world during the 7th and 8th centuries. The Saracens included the people of Palestine and Syria, the Moors who conquered Spain, and the Seljuk Turks, against whom the Crusaders fought.

SARDINE, small, silver-sided fish, a member of the herring family; there are several species. Sardines are distributed throughout the world in temperate oceans. The common sardine in European waters is the pilchard sardine, known in England simply as the pilchard. Sardines are schooling fish; schools are often tremendously large, and catches are also often large.

In terms of weight caught annually, they are among the world's most important commercial fish. As canned fish they are a cheap source of animal protein for human use. They are converted into fishmeal and oil used in livestock feeds and are used as bait for catching mackerel and tuna.

The sardines caught off the coast of California spawn in the open sea at an age of two or three years, when they are 8 or 9 inches long. They are caught in commercial nets when about that size or larger. The record length is 16 inches.

Arthur H. Hearn Fund, 1916
The Metropolitan Museum of Art,
John Singer Sargent's "Madame X"

SARGENT, JOHN SINGER (1856-1925), American painter, was born in Florence, Italy, the son of a Massachusetts couple of means. His early education was in Europe, and he studied at the Academy of Fine Arts in Florence, where he won a prize. Sargent visited the United States when he was 20 years old and thereafter was a constant traveler in the United States and Europe. A pupil of Carolus Duran, the French teacher of painting, Sargent first attracted attention in 1878 with his painting "En Route pour la Pêche," and his painting of Madame Gautreau aroused considerable controversy when it was exhibited in 1880.

In 1890 Sargent visited the United States and there painted his famous portrait of Carmencita, the Spanish dancer. Throughout the following years Sargent painted the many works that were responsible for his election to the Royal Academy in 1897.

Sargent is noted for his many fine portraits, which include those of Ada Rehan the actress, Woodrow Wilson, and Edwin Booth. Equally famous is his mural depicting the history of religion that hangs in the Boston Public Library.

Sargent declined the knighthood offered him in 1907, saying that he was an American citizen. Asked to run for the presidency of the Royal Academy in 1918, he refused. On his death, memorial services were held in Westminster Abbey.

SASKATCHEWAN is commonly called the "Breadbasket of Canada." This western Prairie Province grows more than one-half of Canada's wheat. Chief cities in the province include Regina (the capital), Saskatoon, Moose Jaw, and Prince Albert. Its area of about 251,700 square miles supports approximately 900,000 people.

The southern portion of the province is chiefly a high and fertile prairie, with sufficient moisture for rapid growth. It is regarded as one of the greatest wheat-producing areas in the world. Great mineral wealth and forests containing a vast supply of timber and pulpwood are found in northern Saskatchewan.

There are many lakes and rivers in the province. Athabaska (the larger part of which is within the province), Reindeer, Wollaston, and Churchill are a few of the numerous lakes. The province is drained by the Saskatchewan, Beaver, Churchill, Qu'Appelle, and Assiniboine rivers.

Saskatchewan has considerable natural resources, although the province is mainly agricultural. In addition to the southern wheatfields the province has large grazing areas.

Sask. Govt. Photo

Many oil refineries, like this one, are located in southern Saskatchewan.

Cattle raising and dairying are carried on in the south. Mixed farming is also important. Mining and lumbering are making substantial gains.

Saskatchewan was first visited by white men in the last of the 17th century. In the following century fur-trading posts were established. Saskatchewan was part of the Northwest Territories before it became a province in 1905.

Fort Battleford National Historic Park in Saskatchewan was established in 1876 as district headquarters for the North West Mounted Police in Cree Indian territory.

Canadian Government Travel Bureau

SASKATCHEWAN

Shield: British lion above three sheaves of wheat
Flag: Shield on Canada's red ensign
Flower: Prairie lily
Capital: Regina
Largest city: Regina
Area: 251,700 sq. mi. (including 31,518 sq. mi. inland waters)
Rank in area: 6th (including territories)
Population: 900,000
Chief university: University of Saskatchewan
Chief rivers: Saskatchewan, Beaver, Churchill, Qu'Appelle Assiniboine
Chief lakes: Part of Athabaska, Reindeer, La Ronge
Average temperature: Regina, 2° F. (Jan.), 67° F. (July)
Average annual rainfall: 10 to 26 inches in east, 7 to 20 inches in west
Chief economic activity: Agriculture (including cattle raising)
Chief crop: Wheat
Chief minerals: Petroleum, natural gas, potash, uranium, copper, zinc
Notable attraction: Prince Albert National Park
Important historical dates:
- 1670 Area under charter of Hudson's Bay Company
- 1691 Henry Kelsey first white man to reach Saskatchewan
- 1774 Post on North Saskatchewan River established by Hudson's Bay Company
- 1870 Sovereignty in Northwest Territories (including Saskatchewan) transferred to Dominion
- 1885 Riel Rebellion
- 1905 Province of Saskatchewan a part of Confederation

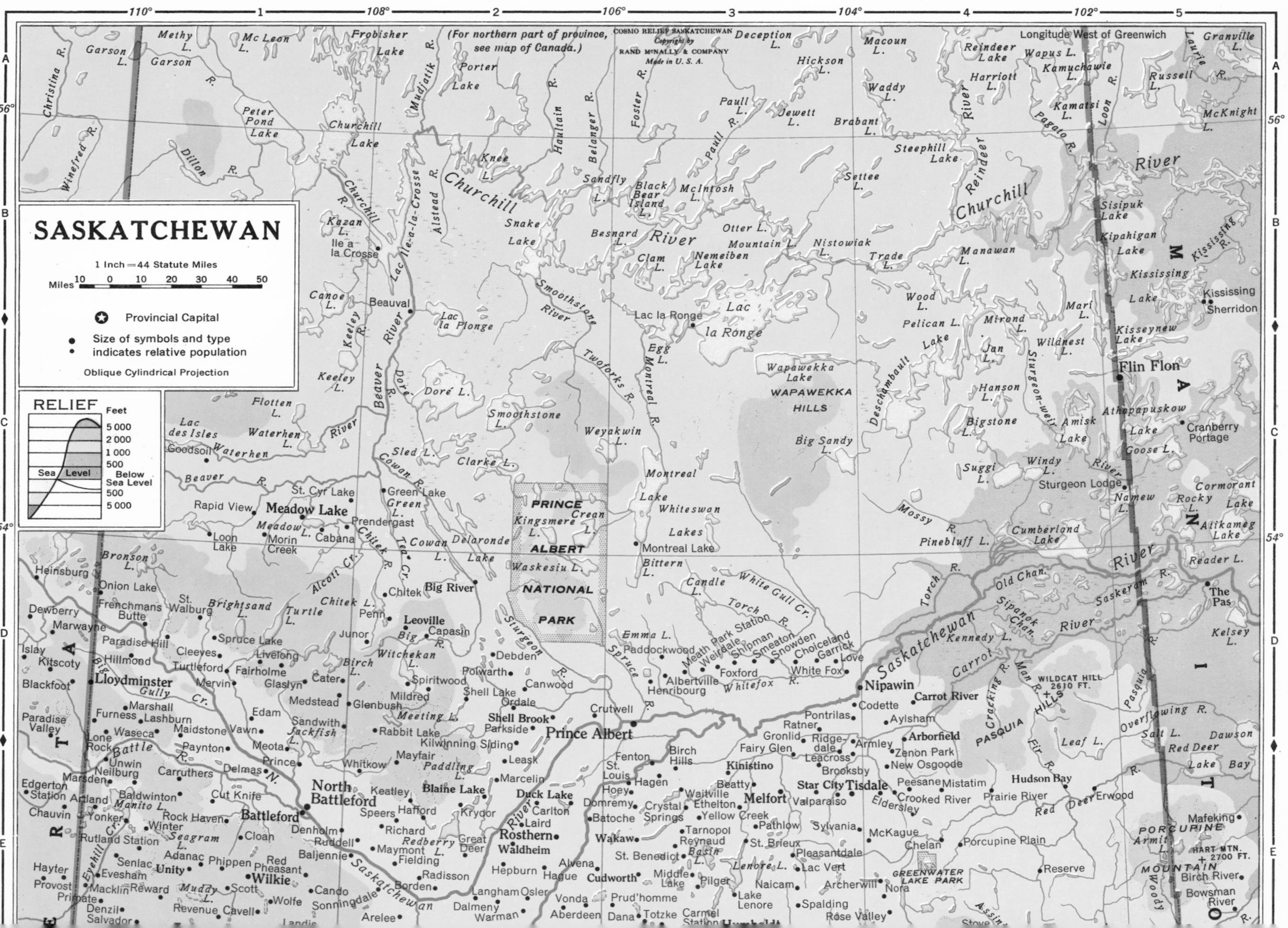
SASKATCHEWAN
1 Inch = 44 Statute Miles
Miles 10 0 10 20 30 40 50
Provincial Capital
Size of symbols and type indicates relative population
Oblique Cylindrical Projection
RELIEF
Feet
5 000
2 000
1 000
500
Sea Level
Below Sea Level
500
5 000
(For northern part of province, see map of Canada.)
COSMO RELIEF SASKATCHEWAN Copyright by RAND McNALLY & COMPANY Made in U. S. A.
Longitude West of Greenwich
110°
108°
106°
104°
102°
56°
54°
Churchill River
Lac la Ronge
Lac la Ronge
Flin Flon
The Pas
Cranberry Portage
Kississing
Sherridon
Sturgeon Lodge
Cumberland Lake
Saskatchewan River
Nipawin
Carrot River
Prince Albert
PRINCE ALBERT NATIONAL PARK
Kingsmere L.
Waskesiu L.
Montreal Lake
Meadow Lake
Big River
Ile a la Crosse
Beauval
Green Lake
St. Cyr Lake
Lloydminster
North Battleford
Battleford
Unity
Wilkie
Rosthern
Waldheim
Duck Lake
Shell Brook
Melfort
Tisdale
Star City
Kinistino
Hudson Bay
Cudworth
Wakaw
WAPAWEKKA HILLS
Wapawekka Lake
Big Sandy L.
Deschambault Lake
Reindeer Lake
Wapus L.
Kamuchawie L.
Peter Pond Lake
Churchill Lake
Frobisher Lake
Garson L.
Methy L.
Mc Leon L.
Porter Lake
Snake Lake
Knee L.
Lac la Plonge
Doré L.
Smoothstone L.
Smoothstone River
Twoforks R.
Weyakwin L.
Montreal R.
Whiteswan Lakes
Candle L.
White Gull Cr.
Torch R.
Sturgeon R.
Spruce R.
Beaver River
Waterhen L.
Lac des Isles
Flotten L.
Cowan L.
Delaronde Lake
Witchekan L.
Meeting L.
Jackfish L.
Battle R.
Eyehill Cr.
Manito L.
Red Deer R.
Dawson Bay
Red Deer Lake
PASQUIA HILLS
WILDCAT HILL 2610 FT.
HART MTN. 2700 FT.
PORCUPINE MOUNTAIN
Porcupine Plain
GREENWATER LAKE PARK
Athapapuskow Lake
Amisk Lake
Namew L.
Cormorant Lake
Kisseynew Lake
Sisipuk Lake
Kipahigan Lake
Mafeking
Bowsman River
Birch River

The region that is now Saskatchewan was first explored in 1731 by Pierre de La Vérendrye, who discovered the Saskatchewan River. The river became a trade route of the Hudson's Bay Company, which established fur-trading posts in the area. The company's rights were taken over by the Dominion in 1870, and the region was added to the Northwest Territories. It became a province in 1905.

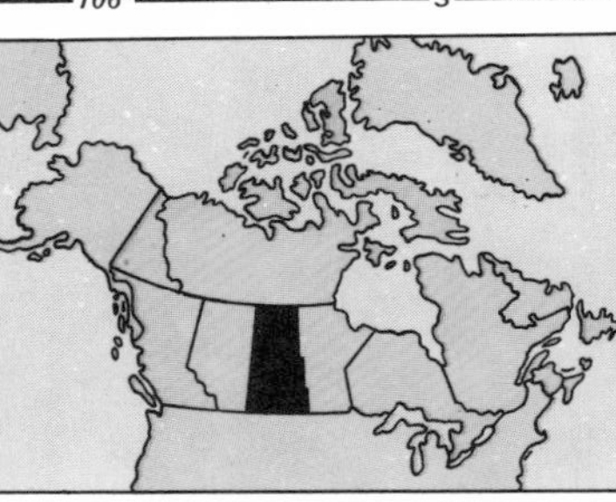

Location map

Saskatchewan was the scene in 1885 of an uprising of the métis, or halfbreeds, led by Louis Riel, who had led a similar uprising in Manitoba in 1870. An expedition sent from the east defeated Riel and captured his forces. He was tried at Regina in August, 1885, and was executed on Nov. 16, 1885. Both uprisings were the resistance of hunters and trappers to the new society of farmers.

For map index, see Volume 20.

SATAN, the name given to the chief among the fallen angels mentioned in the Bible. Satan is the prince of the forces of evil against the Kingdom of God. The concept has been highly developed in Judaism, Christianity, and Islam, but it is found in many other religions as well.

In animism, phenomena are personified. A character is ascribed to good and evil, or pleasure and pain. The phenomena of good may be regarded as gods; those of evil, as demons. If the source of good is regarded as one god, the demonic powers may be thought of as united in one devil, or Satan. In the myths of Babylonia the serpent goddess Nina came to stand for all the forces hostile to the heavenly powers. Apapet was believed by the ancient Egyptians to try each day with an army of monsters to stay the sun in its course. Hel and Loki led the forces of evil in Norse mythology. In Zoroastrianism the concept was carried to its extreme conclusion: Ormazd, the source of all good, was opposed by Ahriman, the originator of all evil.

The word *satan* means "adversary" in Hebrew, and it is often used in the Old Testament to refer to human adversaries. Satan, the fallen angel, appears in the Book of Job, where he doubts the possibility of unselfish virtue; in the Book of Zechariah, where he opposes the high priest Joshua; and in First Chronicles, where he provokes David to take a census of Israel. In the New Testament Satan is definitely personal. He is called tempter, evil one, Beelzebub, prince of this world, dragon, and serpent.

The scholastics of the Middle Ages pondered much about Satan. Aquinas believed that Satan's sin was pride and envy. In his present state he possesses natural knowledge, but he can never attain the knowledge of ultimate truth. He dwells in pits of darkness with condemned sinners and emerges with other fallen angels to tempt men to sin. This concept passed also into Protestantism. Martin Luther, for example, was ever conscious of the opposition of Satan. Religious people in 17th-century Scotland were particularly impressed with the idea of Satan's constant presence. Christians regard the power of evil as broken by Christ's life. Some believe that the power of Satan will not be annihilated until the Last Judgment. Some theologians, such as Friedrich Schleiermacher, opposed the belief in Satan and stressed introspection in the process of dealing with evil. Other theologians regard the existence of Satan as impossible to establish, but they point to the community of sinners as a kingdom of darkness. Still other theologians regard the concept of Satan as the best explanation for the existence of evil.

Satan is sometimes mentioned in literature. John Milton's *Paradise Lost* describes the great battle in heaven between the hosts of Lucifer (Satan's name before the fall) and the angels of God. The immense pride of Satan is well depicted. In Goethe's *Faust* the hero wants to fulfill his insatiable desire for knowledge. Mephistopheles (Satan) promises to fulfill this desire in return for the soul of Faust.

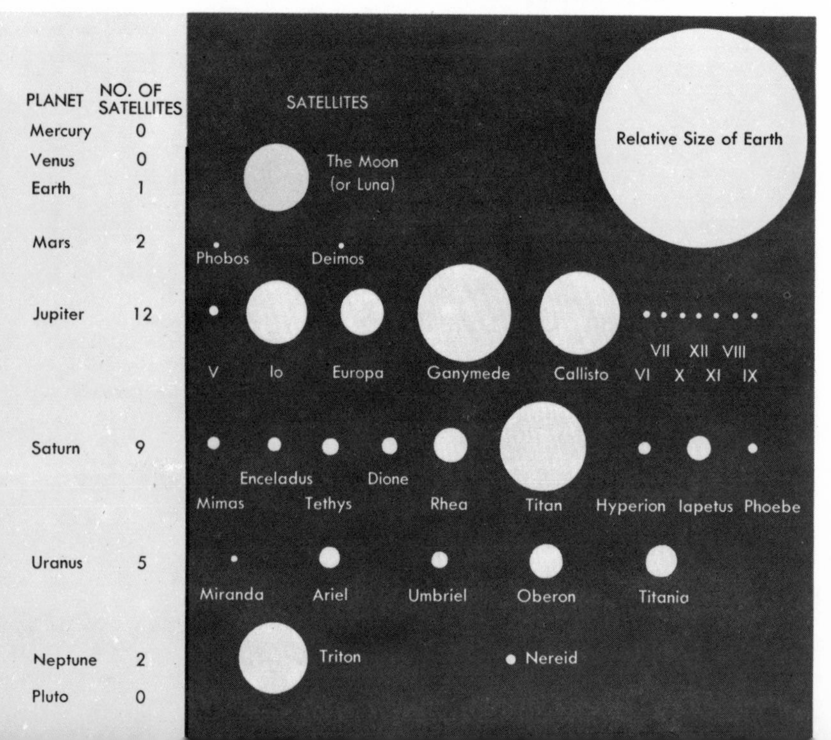

SATELLITE, any object in space whose orbit is a closed curve around another body of greater mass, known as the satellite's primary. A satellite is held in its orbit by gravitational attraction between it and its primary. It has sufficient speed to escape falling into the primary, but it lacks the speed necessary to break free of the gravitational attraction. (See ORBIT.) According to this definition all the planets of our solar system are satellites of the sun. The term is sometimes applied to clusters of stars under the gravitational influence of a galaxy. However, the term normally is taken to mean any of the 31 bodies in satellite orbits around the principal planets of our solar system and more often referred to as moons.

Objects placed in orbit around a planet by man are called artificial satellites. Manmade objects placed in orbit around the sun are called artificial planets. Space probes traveling from one planet to another are also artificial planets while in unpowered trajectory. See SATELLITE, ARTIFICIAL.

Three planets of our solar system have no known satellites—Mercury, Venus, and Pluto. Pluto, in fact, may be an escaped satellite of Neptune that has entered a planetary orbit. The 31 natural satellites are distributed among the planets as follows: Earth has 1; Mars, 2; Jupiter, 12; Saturn, 9; Uranus, 5; and Neptune, 2. These vary in size from Mars's tiny Deimos—only 5 miles in diameter—to Jupiter's Ganymede, 3,100 miles in diameter and somewhat larger than the planet Mercury. The other large satellites include: Saturn's Titan, 2,850 miles in diameter; Jupiter's Callisto, 2,800 miles; Neptune's Triton, 2,350 miles; Earth's moon, known as Luna, 2,160 miles; and Jupiter's Io, 2,000 miles, and Europa, 1,800 miles.

The only satellite known to have an atmosphere is Saturn's Titan. The satellite closest to its primary is Phobos, only 5,800 miles from Mars and orbiting so rapidly that it overtakes the rotating surface of Mars.

The satellites that are farthest from their primaries belong to the two largest planets, Jupiter and Saturn. Phoebe is over 8 million miles from Saturn, and some of Jupiter's satellites are 14 million miles or more from that planet. The earth's moon is uniquely massive in relation to its primary. Its mass is $\frac{1}{81}$ that of the earth, while all the other satellites are less than $\frac{1}{1,000}$ the mass of their primaries.

Shown above are the first eight artificial satellites to go into orbit. They are **1**, Sputnik I, launched Oct. 4, 1957; **2**, Sputnik II, launched Nov. 3, 1957; **3**, Explorer I, launched Jan. 31, 1958; **4**, Vanguard, launched Mar. 17, 1958; **5**, Explorer III, launched Mar. 26, 1958; **6**, Sputnik III, launched May 15, 1958; **7**, Explorer IV, launched July 26, 1958; and **8**, Atlas, launched Dec. 18, 1958. The smallest one, 3¼-pound Vanguard, is expected to remain in orbit for 200 to 1,000 years. The majority of these early satellites were small instrument packages that remained in orbit for only a few months, broadcasting information on outer space to scientists. Sputnik II carried a live dog. Recording devices attached to the dog relayed valuable information on the effects of space travel on a living organism. Atlas was an instrument package in a complete rocket airframe. Its total weight was 8,750 pounds.

SATELLITE, ARTIFICIAL, a manmade object in space, traveling in orbit around a natural body, such as the sun, a planet, or a planet's natural satellite (moon). A satellite is actually falling freely around a planet or other body while under its gravitational influence. However, the satellite's velocity is so high that its own centrifugal force takes it outward from the planet as fast as the planet's gravitational attraction pulls it toward the planet. When these forces are in balance, the shape of the satellite's path is circular or elliptical. See ORBIT.

In the case of the planet earth an artificial satellite must have a velocity of about 17,000 miles per hour to maintain an orbit 300 miles above the surface. At velocities less than this it will spiral inward until it contacts the earth's surface. However, farther away from the earth, where the gravitational force is less, a satellite requires less velocity to maintain its orbit. For example, in the moon's orbit the necessary velocity is only about 2,250 miles per hour.

If a satellite's velocity is so high that its centrifugal force exceeds the gravitational force restraining it, it will escape from a planet or other body permanently. The escape velocity for an object leaving the earth's surface is about 25,000 miles per hour.

The power necessary to place a satellite in orbit around the earth is presently supplied by rocket-propulsion systems. (See ROCKET; SPACE TRAVEL.) Satellites ranging in weight from a few pounds to several tons have been successfully orbited.

Because present rocket power is limited, the primary problem in constructing an artificial satellite is to minimize weight. This is accomplished by using special design and lightweight materials and by miniaturizing the instruments carried aboard the satellite. Very thin walls can be kept under tension, by means of gas pressure, to prevent their collapse, or they can be strengthened by means of a waffle or honeycomb design. Aluminum and titanium are among the most efficient construction materials for performance out of the high-temperature range.

If the satellite is designed for recovery after reentering the earth's atmosphere, its materials must be able to resist the high temperatures resulting from atmospheric friction. Among the best high-temperature metals are nickel, chromium, molybdenum, and iron alloys. Ceramics are also useful, being strong and heat resistant though brittle.

Temperature control while the satellite is operating in space subject to solar radiation can be achieved by means of surface color and smoothness of finish. These factors affect the amount of absorption, reflection, and reradiation of solar heat. Movable flaps are sometimes used to change the amount of surface area of black that is exposed, black having the highest heat-absorbing qualities.

Electronic instruments carried aboard a satellite are miniaturized to save weight and space. For the same reasons they are often designed to function for more than one purpose. The smallness of the instruments is indicated by the $1\frac{1}{2}$-pound transmitter of the minilock tracking system. Two specialized communications developments are the ultrasensitive receiver and the directional antenna, which reduce power requirements several hundred times. Lunik II's television signals carrying pictures of the moon were received though they were 100 million times weaker than normal; Pioneer V's 150-watt radio transmitter was heard at a distance of 22 million miles. Radio tracking of a satellite is accomplished by telemetry (measurement of the angles formed by the satellite's broadcasting at different points along its path) and by the Doppler effect (an apparent change in frequency as the satellite's transmitter moves).

Infrared detectors and radar, two other of the satellite's instruments, are sensing aids used to locate various types of objects. Infrared detectors, because of their sensitivity to the heat emitted by all things, have been of particular value in determining the different heat masses in clouds and storm centers (Tiros satellites). These detectors also are useful in differentiating between planetary and stellar bodies for space navigation. Other instruments used are the photoelectric eye (Pioneer IV) for taking location fixes and the Geiger counter for determining radiation areas.

The most readily available power for operating instruments is the battery, such as the mercury and hydrogen-oxygen types that give high watt-hours per pound of weight. The disadvantages of using batteries as power sources are that batteries are heavy, provide low voltages, and may be damaged by vacuum or radiation. Silicon solar cells that cause direct conversion of solar radiation to electricity were used in Pioneer V as battery chargers. Their efficiency is not high, but they last several years.

The satellite was originally a simple collector of information. It is now evolving into several categories of space vehicles, each category having its own function. The various types are in the following list, with the launching dates of the first of each series.

Several series are designed as data collectors on space radiation, temperature, meteors, magnetic fields, and gases. These series are Sputniks, Oct. 4, 1957; Explorers, Jan. 31, 1958; and Vanguards, Mar. 17, 1958.

The interplanetary class also is of the above type. This class includes Luniks, Jan. 2, 1959; and Pioneers, Mar. 3, 1959.

A series of satellites designed to relay messages includes Project Score, Dec. 18, 1958; Echo (the balloon type), Aug. 12, 1960; Courier, Oct. 4, 1960; and Advent, a planned series of three satellites giving worldwide 24-hour coverage. These radio satellites have relayed messages from point to point on earth by reflection of radio waves (Echo). They also have received, recorded, and rebroadcast messages (Score and Courier). Courier also has 20 teletype channels in addition to its voice facilities.

The navigational-aid satellites (Transit, Apr. 13, 1960) transmit at a certain frequency, thereby permitting ships to locate themselves by using the Doppler effect.

The weather series (Tiros, Apr. 1, 1960) records atmospheric conditions (by television and infrared instruments) to assist in weather forecasting.

The manned-satellite program consists of several projects. The Discoverer series (Feb. 28, 1959) is designed to explore the possibility of life in space and to make satellite-recovery trials. Mercury and Apollo are projects for carrying man himself. Apollo is a maneuverable satellite. See SPACE RESEARCH.

A system of national-defense satellites is designed to warn of an enemy's preparation and of an imminent attack. Samos (Jan. 31, 1961) photographs areas from which attacks may be launched. Midas satellites, by infrared detection, will be able to give warning of enemy rocket firings.

Sputnik I, above, was the first artificial satellite, sent into space by the Soviet Union in 1957. Sputnik I remained in orbit for three months, then fell back into the atmosphere, where it was burned up by air friction. Vanguard, right, was launched by the United States in 1958. Vanguard will remain in orbit for several hundred years. Both satellites were filled with battery-powered measuring devices and radio transmitters to relay information back to the earth's surface.

SATIRE, a literary composition in verse or prose in which someone or something of public interest is held up to ridicule, often with the intention of reform. The poetic form of satire was invented by the Roman Gaius Lucilius; it is considered by many scholars to be the only original literary form produced by the Romans. The satire was a highly concentrated and epigrammatic lyric characterized by serious moral purpose and often extremely violent and cruel invective.

During the Renaissance European writers of satire were greatly influenced by Roman models. This influence reached its peak in the 17th and 18th centuries in the works of such poets as John Dryden (*Absalom and Achitophel* and *Mac Flecknoe*), Nicolas Boileau-Despréaux, and Alexander Pope (*The Rape of the Lock*). Satire gradually moved away from the formal and poetic manner of the Romans, and writers employed a greater variety of literary forms and techniques to express their criticism of social evils, politics, religion, philosophical systems, and important individuals. Satire came to designate less a specific form than a critical spirit, in which wit, sarcasm, irony, and ridicule played important parts.

The satirical spirit has been one of the dominant qualities in French literature; important French satirists include Francois Rabelais (*Gargantua and Pantagruel*), Agrippa d'Aubigné, Boileau, Jean de La Bruyère, Voltaire (*Candide*), Victor Hugo, and Anatole France.

Outstanding English satirists include Jonathan Swift (*Gulliver's Travels*), Henry Fielding, Joseph Addison, Richard Steele, Lord Byron, and George Orwell (*Animal Farm*). American satirists include Mark Twain, Sinclair Lewis, James Russell Lowell (*Biglow Papers*), Washington Irving (*Knickerbocker Papers*), and James Thurber.

Saturn and its ring system are shown above, compared in size with the earth and with Saturn's largest moon, Titan. Saturn itself is nine times larger in diameter than earth, and its volume would contain over 700 earths. Each of Saturn's rings is wider than the earth's diameter. Titan's diameter is about one-third the earth's diameter.

SATURN, the sixth principal planet of our solar system. Its mean distance from the sun, 886,200,000 miles, is nearly twice that of the next nearer planet, Jupiter, and nearly ten times that of Earth. Saturn revolves once around the sun in about 29½ years.

With a diameter of 71,500 miles Saturn is second in size only to Jupiter and, like that planet, rotates rapidly on its axis, completing a full rotation in only 10 hours 2 minutes. Saturn's mass is 95 times that of Earth, but its density is the lowest of any planet in the solar system, actually less than the density of water. Saturn probably consists mainly of hydrogen, strongly concentrated toward the center of the planet. Its cloud-level temperature is about −150° C.

Nine satellites, or moons, orbit around Saturn—more than around any other planet except Jupiter. Several are closer to Saturn than is our own moon to Earth, while the outermost satellite revolves more than 8,000,000 miles from Saturn. Titan, the sixth moon, is by far the largest and brightest, being not only larger than our own moon but nearly as large as the planet Mercury. Titan is also the only satellite in the solar system known to possess an atmosphere.

Saturn's rings are perhaps its most fascinating feature. These consist of countless small particles, possibly consisting of ice. Each particle revolves in its own circular orbit around Saturn in the planet's equatorial plane. Together the particles appear as a wide, flat, reflective ring system extending to a diameter of 171,000 miles. An outer ring about 10,000 miles wide is separated by a 3,000-mile gap from the middle, or bright, ring 16,000 miles wide. From its inner edge the dark, or crape, ring extends to within 9,000 miles of the planet's surface. The rings exist because within a critical distance the planet's tidal forces are so strong they break up larger bodies or prevent them from forming.

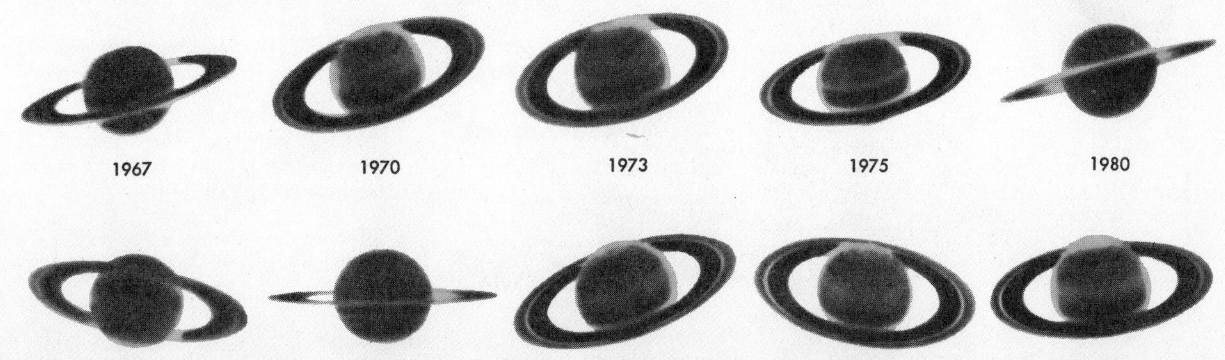

Our view of Saturn's tilted rings changes as Saturn slowly moves around the sun.

Courtesy of TWA—Trans World Airlines

American employees of a large oil company live in the above community at Dhahran. Oil is the most important industry in Saudi Arabia, which is in a large part an expanse of desert land. More than half of the population is composed of Bedouin nomads.

SAUDI ARABIA is a kingdom occupying most of the Arabian Peninsula. In 1932 Ibn-Saud, king of Hejaz and Nejd and its dependencies, changed the name of his dominions to the kingdom of Saudi Arabia. Saudi Arabia is estimated to cover between 600,000 and 900,000 square miles. The people, mainly pastoral nomads, probably number about 6,500,000. See ARABIAN PENINSULA.

SAUERKRAUT. See CABBAGE.

SAULT SAINTE MARIE CANALS, two parallel canals in Michigan and the Canadian province of Ontario. Bypassing the falls of the St. Marys River connecting Lake Superior and Lake Huron, they are an important part of the St. Lawrence Seaway. The Michigan canal, which is 1.6 miles long, has two channels, each with two locks. The canal in Ontario has one lock and is 1.4 miles long. The annual cargo volume through the canals is among the world's greatest.

The first canal and lock, built on the Canadian side in 1797, were destroyed during the War of 1812. The United States started construction on the canals, popularly known as the Soo Canals, in 1853. They were subsequently enlarged.

Oscar Meyer & Co.

SAUSAGE, a general term for a wide variety of spiced pork products combined with other meats and flour and meal. Sausages are mentioned by Homer in the *Odyssey*, and they were known in China in the time of Confucius. The great variety available today is due to the fact that each nation has made sausages to suit its particular taste and according to the limitations of climate and of available seasonings. In southern Europe dry sausages with extra keeping qualities were demanded. The northern peoples developed smoked and cooked sausages that kept well in a cool climate.

The origin of many types of sausages is revealed in their names: bologna sausage from Italy, Berliner from Germany, and wienerwurst from Austria.

The manufacture of sausage is important to the packing industry because perfectly edible cuts of meat that would normally be difficult to market are fully utilized. Pork, alone or combined with beef, is made into a great variety of sausages. Among these varieties are fresh pork sausage, smoked sausage, dry sausage, and cooked specialties. In all sausages the meat is ground two or three times, spiced, and smoked, cooked, or otherwise treated according to the kind.

Fresh pork sausage should be thoroughly cooked. Smoked, cooked sausage requires reheating only, although bologna is often eaten without cooking. Dry sausage is sold ready to serve. See FRANKFURTER AND WIENER.

After sausage ingredients are ground and mixed, they are forced under pressure into long casings of animal membrane or plastic.

SAVANNAH, the oldest and second largest city in Georgia. It is located on the Savannah River, 17 miles upstream from the Atlantic Ocean. In addition to its important industries Savannah is also a popular winter resort. The city's population in 1960 was 149,245.

Savannah is a historic city. During the American Revolution it was taken by the British in 1778. In trying to recover it, Count Casimir Pulaski of the Continental army was killed. Savannah served as the state capital from 1782 to 1785. In 1819 the first steamship to cross the Atlantic, the *Savannah*, sailed from the city for which it had been named to Liverpool, England.

During the Civil War Savannah was held by the Confederates until it was taken by General William T. Sherman in 1864. Savannah was the goal of Sherman's famous march to the sea from Atlanta.

SAVING, in economics, putting aside present income for future needs. In order to save, individuals, companies, or nations must earn a surplus over what they must use in the present. Savings are indispensable for the security of individuals and the economic progress of nations. The art of saving is to steer a moderate course between extravagance and miserliness. Well-planned saving allows the maximum enjoyment of both the present and the future. The practice of saving, in nations as well as individuals, is best nurtured by habit.

Individuals may save to accumulate money for a costly purchase, such as a house; for emergencies, such as sickness; for the purpose of sending children to college; or for security in old age. Nations must save in order to expand old industries and to develop new ones. They must also meet the cost of replacing worn-out equipment, including machines, harbor facilities, and roads. Some nations save just enough to replace their depreciated equipment. However, to make economic progress a nation must produce a surplus of wealth that allows it to develop new industries. The great problem of underdeveloped nations is the inability to save. Progress cannot begin until present industries begin to produce more than is immediately necessary and people can put aside a little of their income in order to invest it.

There are two major forms of saving. The first, conservation, consists in obtaining the greatest possible use out of what a person or a nation has. The individual saves if he takes good care of his car so that it lasts a long time. A nation saves when it seeks to conserve its forests, minerals, and farmlands. The United States was very prodigal with its forests in the 19th century, which explains in part the high cost of wood products in the 20th century. In an important way, the cook who uses food carefully and wastes little of it is saving the nation's food supply. The second method of saving is accumulation, or the postponement of consumption. Some people postpone consumption indefinitely by investing their money and living off the interest. The individual may save by placing his income in the bank, which invests it in safe securities and loans; by investing in government or corporation bonds; by putting his money into savings-and-loan associations; by buying insurance; and by investing in real estate. (See INSURANCE; STOCKS AND BONDS.) Corporations save by retaining a part of their net income instead of distributing it among their stockholders. Businesses use these savings, rather than money obtained by issuing new common stock or bonds, to expand their operations.

SAVONAROLA (1452-1498) was an austere Dominican monk who tried to reform the Italian city of Florence by means of a popular revolution against the all-pervading patterns of licentiousness. He temporarily converted the people to his own ascetic morality and aroused them to expel the ruling Medici family. But he was finally destroyed by the rulers of Italy and by the disillusioned people of Florence.

Savonarola was born into a well-to-do intellectual family. At 22 years of age, after a disastrous love affair, he underwent a religious conversion and joined the Dominican order. In 1482 he went to Florence and became prior of St. Mark's in 1491.

He preached his gospel of contempt of the world in Bologna, Ferrara, Brescia, and, chiefly, Florence, where he tried to convert the great popular tyrant Lorenzo the Magnificent. Lorenzo had richly endowed Savonarola's cloister and had shown him kindness and respect. But Savonarola would not be bought. He denounced the sinful life of Lorenzo with "a terrible sermon" that aroused the entire city to intense fear and then to a temporary repudiation of its pagan way of life.

After Lorenzo's death in 1492 Savonarola assumed political and moral leadership in Florence. He bolstered his power by an alliance with King Charles VIII of France, to whose army he opened the gates of the city. With the enthusiastic cooperation of the people Savonarola ruled Florence as severely as Lorenzo had ever done. In an orgy of self-abasement men and women burned in public their gay party clothes and openly confessed to having lived sinful lives.

When Savonarola denounced the rulers of Italy for what he considered to be their wicked ways, they tried to reason with him and offered him ecclesiastical advancement. Finally the church excommunicated Savonarola. The people of Florence, tired of being "good," rose in rebellion. Savonarola and his two most faithful followers were tortured for 40 days and were killed. Their bodies were burned on a cross in the Piazza della Signoria.

Above are side and edge views of crosscut saw teeth (left); teeth of ripsaw (right).

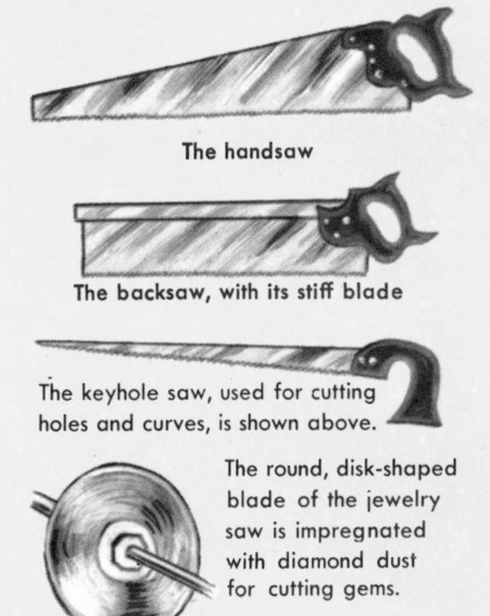

The handsaw

The backsaw, with its stiff blade

The keyhole saw, used for cutting holes and curves, is shown above.

The round, disk-shaped blade of the jewelry saw is impregnated with diamond dust for cutting gems.

SAW, a tool consisting essentially of a steel blade with a toothed edge, used for cutting wood or metal. There are two main classes of saws—reciprocating (handsaws that cut with a push-and-pull motion) and continuous action (circular saws and bandsaws). Continuous-action saws are a modern invention, the first circular saw being made by Samuel Miller, an Englishman, in 1777.

The crosscut saw is used for cutting wood across the grain; the ripsaw, for cutting along the grain. The two types differ in the size and shape of the teeth. On the crosscut saw the forward edge of each tooth is 15 degrees from the perpendicular and is beveled to a sharp edge. On the ripsaw the forward edge of the tooth is only 8 degrees from the perpendicular and is square. The ripsaw usually has 5½ teeth to the inch, and the crosscut saw has 8 to 12. The hacksaw, used in sawing metal, has very small teeth, with up to 32 of them for each inch of blade length. Saw blades differ in thickness, size, and shape, depending on the kind of cutting to be done.

Handsaws are among the most ancient of human tools. Saws of flint, used by men of the Stone Age about 130,000 years ago, have been found in caves in France and have been dug out of ancient stone heaps in Denmark, Sweden, and Switzerland. The ancient Egyptians used saws of bronze, some of which had inserted jeweled teeth for cutting stone. The oldest iron saw blade was discovered at Nimrud, near Nineveh in Mesopotamia, and dates from about 4000 B.C.

SAXOPHONE, a brass wind instrument with a single-reed mouthpiece resembling that of the clarinet. The saxophone's sonorous tone is a compromise between the characteristic sounds of the brass and woodwind groups.

The saxophone was invented in 1840 by Adolphe Sax, a Belgian maker of musical instruments. Although the saxophone has never become fully established as a member of the symphony orchestra, it has become a mainstay of marching, concert, and dance bands and is often prominent in jazz "combos." Of the seven recognized types of saxophones the alto, tenor, and baritone are the most widely played today.

The saxophone is one of the most recently developed of all musical instruments.

The scales and plates of lizards and snakes

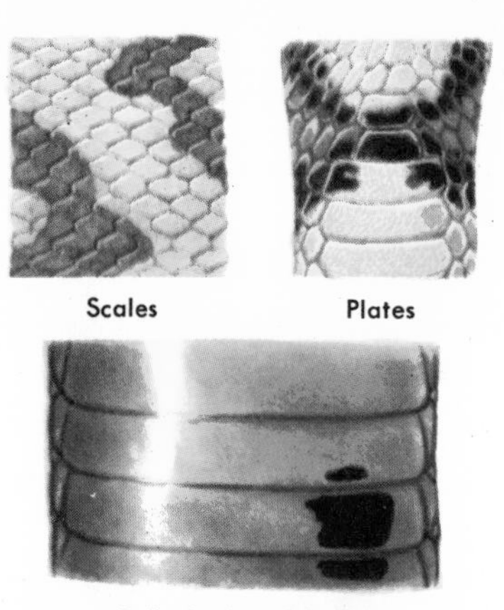

Belly Scales of Snakes

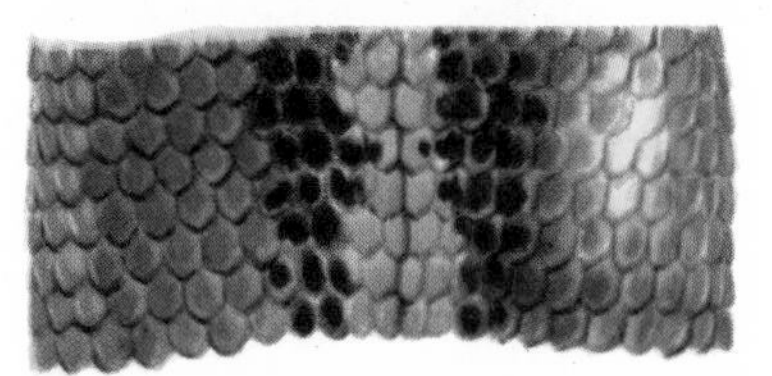

Belly Scales of Lizards

SCALE. Like hair of mammals and feathers of birds, scales of fishes develop from cells in the skin. A few kinds of fish have no scales—ordinary catfish, electric eels, spoonbill catfish, and others. Ordinary eels have very minute scales, which lie below the surface of the skin and are not visible. The placoid scales of sharks have enamel-covered spines embedded in the skin. The spines project above the surface of the skin and make it harsh to the touch. Placoid scales do not overlap. Gar pikes are covered with hard, flat, smooth, rhomboidal scales, held together by a mat of tough fibers on their undersides.

The most familiar scales are the cycloid and ctenoid types. These thin, semitransparent, overlapping plates lie within pockets in the skin. They are fibrous in texture, about as hard as fingernails, and neatly arranged in rows. They differ in the various kinds of fish; some are round, some oval, some squarish. The ctenoid type has pointed teeth along the back edge. The teeth project slightly above the skin surface. Because of these teeth, or spines, many fish are more easily stroked from head to tail than in the reverse direction. Cycloid scales have no spines. The cycloid and ctenoid scales appear when the fish are a few weeks old. The outer surface of a cycloid or a ctenoid scale is covered with closely spaced ridges approximately parallel with the scale margin. A slight change in the direction of growth and spacing of the ridges occurs when the fish begins its annual growth in spring or summer, and this change usually results in marks—the annual ring. These rings can sometimes be seen by holding the scale to a bright light and may be counted with a magnifier to find the age of the fish. However, false rings are sometimes formed on the scale, and they are often indistinguishable from true annual rings. Cycloid and ctenoid scales are often lost, because of attacks of other fish or for other reasons. These lost scales are replaced in a few weeks' time, but the new scales do not show the age rings.

Scales of lizards and snakes are formed by folds and creases in the skin. The horny scales of the pangolin, or scaly anteater, a mammal that lives in Africa and southeastern Asia, are outgrowths from the skin.

Ganoid scales, which are thin, flat, and rectangular, lie in rows on the body of the primitive garfish.

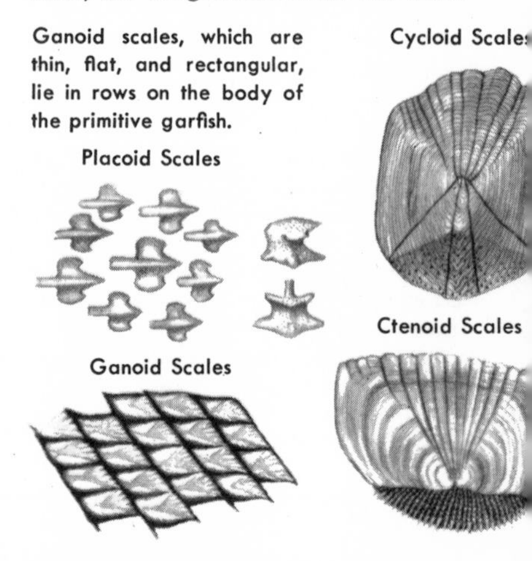

SCALE, an instrument or device for weighing. The balance, used in ancient Egypt, was the first device of this sort. It consisted of a fulcrum placed in the exact center of an arm. It is still used as the most accurate method of determining weight. The steelyard is a later device; in it the fulcrum is placed relatively near one end of the crossbar, and the weighing is done by means of leverage. Platform scales, invented in 1831 by Thaddeus Fairbanks, are usually a variation of the steelyard principle. Spring scales, because of the varying pulls of gravity in various parts of the world, and because the springs stretch with use, are less accurate. Most governments require periodic examinations of all scales used in buying and selling.

SCALES, THE (constellation). See LIBRA.